PRAISE FOR DOROTHY WICKENDEN AND *THE AGITATORS*

"An original portrait of three original women who muscled aside expectations, obligations, and neighborhood gossip for the sake of their consciences. Dorothy Wickenden not only resurrects these unlikely agitators but plunges us deep into their volatile world, with a supporting cast that includes Julia Ward Howe, Elizabeth Cady Stanton, and Abraham Lincoln. This is rich and rousing history, crisply and intimately rendered, its moral collisions vivid and vital on the page."

—STACY SCHIFF, AUTHOR OF *CLEOPATRA* AND *THE WITCHES*

"This is an extraordinary peek into the lives of three women who courageously pushed past the tight worlds that confined them to create the bones and muscle of the freedom movements that we now know. That they walked in a land of giants—Lincoln, Lee, John Brown—is no surprise. That they knew one another, were giants themselves, and were accorded second-class status is no surprise either. The treat is the refreshing decency, skillful ease, and extraordinary skill with which their stories are intertwined, showing how each pressed against the seams of imprisonment with such force and resilience that their collective song continues to resonate today. That is why Dorothy Wickenden is one of the deans of our game."

—JAMES McBRIDE, AUTHOR OF *DEACON KING KONG*

"When writing about the Civil War era, focus is everything: how it is seen depends entirely on who is seeing it. In *The Agitators*, Dorothy Wickenden has fortunately chosen three brilliantly engaging characters. The result is unexpected, original, and profoundly illuminating."

—S. C. GWYNNE, AUTHOR OF *HYMNS OF THE REPUBLIC* AND *REBEL YELL*

"Inspiring and important—and a rousing good read—*The Agitators* reminds us how, even in the darkest of times, there is light. And when a few fierce women join forces against that darkness, they can win."

—JEANNETTE WALLS, AUTHOR OF *THE GLASS CASTLE*

"This is a unique, lyrically written, exhaustively researched, triple biography of epic proportions about three women, mothers and organizers all, woven into a single narrative about their activist struggles before and during the Civil War. Their lives burst from these pages, as do the crusades that began the liberation of African Americans and women across the nineteenth century. Wickenden possesses a novelist's eye for detail and a historian's passion for story, in a book about women with no formal political rights who changed their world."

—**DAVID W. BLIGHT**, AUTHOR OF ***FREDERICK DOUGLASS: PROPHET OF FREEDOM***

"Dorothy Wickenden seamlessly weaves together the lives of her protagonists with the times that influenced them, and that they in turn profoundly affected. Vivid, enlightening, and engrossing, here is the story of three women who are fixtures of history but whose relevance to the present could scarcely be more apparent."

—**JELANI COBB**, AUTHOR OF ***THE SUBSTANCE OF HOPE: BARACK OBAMA AND THE PARADOX OF PROGRESS***

PRAISE FOR *THE AGITATORS*

"An epic and intimate history . . . *The Agitators* is a masterpiece, not least, of structure. . . . Entwining these three asymmetrical lives as deftly as Wickenden does proves illuminating."

—Jane Kamensky, *The New York Times Book Review*

"An original portrait of three original women who muscled aside expectations, obligations, and neighborhood gossip for the sake of their consciences. Dorothy Wickenden not only resurrects these unlikely agitators but plunges us deep into their volatile world, with a supporting cast that includes Julia Ward Howe, Elizabeth Cady Stanton, and Abraham Lincoln. This is rich and rousing history, crisply and intimately rendered, its moral collisions vivid and vital on the page."

—Stacy Schiff, author of *Cleopatra* and *The Witches*

"Absorbing and richly rewarding . . . [Wickenden] traces the Auburn women's lives with intelligence, compassion, and verve . . . [and her] assessment of the era leading up to the Civil War will resonate with readers in our own fractious era."

—Melanie Kirkpatrick, *The Wall Street Journal*

"*The Agitators* tells the story of America before the Civil War through the lives of three women who advocated for the abolition of slavery and women's rights as the country split apart. Harriet Tubman, Martha Coffin Wright, and Frances A. Seward are the examples we need right now—another time of divisiveness and dissension over our nation's purpose 'to form a more perfect union.'"

—Hillary Clinton

"Riveting . . . [Wickenden] weaves [these] stories together with gravity and humor in a narrative so tightly knit it reads like accomplished literary fiction. . . . *The Agitators* will move you, and it will make you sad. So much of what convulsed the country in the nineteenth century remains with us: mob violence, virulent racism, and an appalling disregard for human dignity. But there's another message: People of fierce and heartfelt principles can bend history to their will. If you're an agitator, even a quiet one, read this book."

—Mary Ann Gwinn, *Minneapolis Star Tribune*

"This is an extraordinary peek into the lives of three women who courageously pushed past the tight worlds that confined them to create the bones and muscle of the freedom movements that we now know. That they walked in a land of giants—Lincoln, Lee, John Brown—is no surprise. That they knew one another, were giants themselves, and accorded second-class status is no surprise either. The treat is the refreshing decency, skillful ease, and extraordinary skill with which their stories are intertwined, showing how each pressed against the seams of imprisonment with such force and resilience that their collective song continues to resonate today. That is why Dorothy Wickenden is one of the deans of our game."

—James McBride, author of *The Good Lord Bird*

"Abraham Lincoln had his team of rivals, but they were all white men with high opinions of themselves. Female alliances also worked to end slavery and perfect the union in nineteenth-century America. In *The Agitators* Dorothy Wickenden of *The New Yorker* profiles three neighbors who sought women's rights and freedom for African Americans. They banded together at a time when society mistrusted female activists."

—*The Economist*

"This is a unique, lyrically written, exhaustively researched, triple biography of epic proportions about three women, mothers and organizers all, woven into a single narrative about their activist struggles before and during the Civil War. Their lives burst from these pages, as do the crusades that began the liberation of Blacks and women across the nineteenth century. Wickenden possesses a novelist's eye for detail and a historian's passion for story, in a book about women with no formal political rights who changed their world."

—David W. Blight, author of *Frederick Douglass: Prophet of Freedom*

"When writing about the Civil War era, focus is everything: *how* it is seen depends entirely on *who* is seeing it. In *The Agitators*, Dorothy Wickenden has fortunately chosen three brilliantly engaging characters. The result is unexpected, original, and profoundly illuminating."

—S. C. Gwynne, author of *Hymns of the Republic* and *Rebel Yell*

"Wickenden does a brilliant job of weaving all the complicated threads together, telling a compelling story that we thought we knew well. This is history at its best: personal, powerful, and inspiring."

—Marissa Moss, *New York Journal of Books*

"Dorothy Wickenden seamlessly weaves together the lives of her protagonists with the times that influenced them, and that they in turn profoundly affected. Vivid, enlightening, and engrossing, here is the story of three women who are fixtures of history but whose relevance to the present could scarcely be more apparent."

—Jelani Cobb, author of *The Substance of Hope: Barack Obama and the Paradox of Progress*

"Inspiring and important—and a rousing good read—*The Agitators* reminds us how, even in the darkest of times, there is light. And when a few fierce women join forces against that darkness, they can win."

—Jeannette Walls, author of *The Glass Castle*

"Told with literary flair, Dorothy Wickenden's *The Agitators* sheds some much-needed light on the lives and passions of a small circle of abolitionists: Harriet Tubman, Martha Wright, and Frances Seward."

—*Bustle*

"*New Yorker* executive editor Wickenden (*Nothing Daunted*) expertly weaves together the biographies of 'co-conspirators and intimate friends' Harriet Tubman, Martha Wright, and Frances Seward in this novelistic history. . . . Through extensive research and fluid writing, Wickenden rescues Wright and Seward from obscurity and provides a new perspective on Tubman's life and work. This is an essential addition to the history of American progressivism."

—*Publishers Weekly* (starred review)

"*New Yorker* executive editor Wickenden brings three fascinating women to life in rich, humanizing detail. . . . Wickenden pulls this history out of the dry dustiness of fact and adds color and warmth to its retelling. The women of our shared past deserve more treatments like this."

—*Booklist*

"In the strength of the bonds forged among Wright, Seward, and Tubman, Wickenden offers hope for a healing of old wounds and a future where 'the dignity and equality of all Americans' is an authentic reality."

—*Kirkus Reviews*

"Wickenden (*Nothing Daunted*) follows the lives of three friends and heroes of the women's rights and abolitionist movements, and describes the ways they impacted both causes. . . . Filling a gap in the telling of women's and abolitionist history, this highly readable book gives these women their due."

—*Library Journal*

"She brings a reporter's eye for detail to this complex history . . . [and] invites readers to take a closer look at the path of American progress and the women who guided it."

—*BookPage*

ALSO BY DOROTHY WICKENDEN

Nothing Daunted: The Unexpected Education of Two Society Girls in the West

The New Republic Reader: Eighty Years of Opinion and Debate (editor)

grave ten years ago—
Compromises based
on the idea that the
preservation of the Union
is more important than
the Liberty of nearly
4,000,000 human beings
cannot be right.—
The alteration of the
Constitution to perpetuate
slavery—the enforcement
of a law to recapture
a poor, suffering fugitive,
—giving half of the
Territories of a free Country
to the curse of Slavery
—these compromises cannot
be approved by God

"Compromises based on the idea that the preservation of the Union is more important than the Liberty of nearly 4,000,000 human beings cannot be right."
Frances A. Seward to William H. Seward, January 19, 1861

The Agitators

THREE FRIENDS WHO FOUGHT FOR ABOLITION AND WOMEN'S RIGHTS

DOROTHY WICKENDEN

SCRIBNER

New York London Toronto Sydney New Delhi

Scribner
An Imprint of Simon & Schuster, Inc.
1230 Avenue of the Americas
New York, NY 10020

First Scribner trade paperback edition February 2022

Manufactured in the United States of America

1 3 5 7 9 10 8 6 4 2

Library of Congress Control Number: 2020951905

ISBN 978-1-4767-6073-5
ISBN 978-1-4767-6074-2 (pbk)
ISBN 978-1-4767-6076-6 (ebook)

For Sarah and Rebecca

"God's ahead of master Lincoln. God won't let master Lincoln beat the South 'til he does *the right thing*. Master Lincoln, he's a great man, and I'm a poor Negro, but this Negro can tell master Lincoln how to save the money and the young men. He can do it by setting the Negroes free."

—*Harriet Tubman, January 1862*

Contents

PART THREE
WAR (1861–1864)

PART FOUR
RIGHTS (1864–1875)

Prologue

Fort Hill Cemetery, high above the city of Auburn in Central New York State, is not one of those cramped, fenced-in graveyards often found behind old churches, with weather-scoured slabs tipping into the earth. On grounds once occupied by a fortress built by the Cayuga Nation, it meanders up and around eighty-three acres of grass and old-growth forest. Fort Hill retains some of the wildness the region had when the first white settlers arrived after the Revolutionary War, so sprawling that many of the gravestones, obelisks, and crypts, as various as the people they commemorate, are almost hidden in the landscape. Buried there are three women whose joint story of insubordination against slavery and the oppression of women has never been told: Harriet Tubman, Martha Coffin Wright, and Frances A. Seward.

Much of American history is made by little-known people living far from Washington. Over the course of a decade in the 1850s, when Auburn was a thriving commercial center and well-off white men seemed destined always to rule the country unchallenged, Harriet Tubman was a nameless freedom seeker who repeatedly risked her life returning to the Eastern Shore, to guide some seventy enslaved people out of Maryland, through Delaware and Pennsylvania, across New York, and into Canada. Soon after Tubman liberated herself, she met Martha Wright and Frances Seward, who lived in Auburn, midway on what became one of her most well-traveled underground railroad routes. Wright, a middle-class Quaker mother of six, helped to organize the 1848 Seneca Falls Convention, the first women's rights meeting in America. Seward was the wealthy wife of the anti-slavery politician William H. Seward, who, esteemed by some and despised by others, rose from governor of New York to United States senator to secretary of state under Abraham Lincoln. When Martha Wright and Frances Seward got to know Tubman, they were in the process of transforming themselves from conventional homemakers into insurgents who fought to overturn slavery and to demand the dignity and equality of all Americans.

Tubman saw Wright and Seward as two of her most trusted associates, and they drew strength and inspiration from her. In the coming decades, these women, with no evident power to change anything, became co-conspirators and intimate friends—protagonists in an inside-out story about the second American revolution.

PART ONE

Provocations

(1821–1852)

The Miller-Seward family, ca. 1846

1

A Nantucket Inheritance

1833–1843

Martha Coffin Wright, 1820s

Martha Coffin Wright's mutinous mind had its origins in a place she never lived: a jagged fourteen-mile-long fishhook of an island thirty miles off the coast of Massachusetts. She rarely encountered an institution she didn't question, and although convention dictated most of the circumstances of her life, she liked breaking rules, and then explaining why she had no choice. Her parents, Anna Folger Coffin and Thomas Coffin, were Quaker descendants of two of the first English settlers who had fled the Massachusetts Bay Colony rather than submit to the fines, floggings, and prison terms the Puritan clergy imposed on anyone who bucked church dogma. The women of Nantucket took for granted their equality with men. Mary Coffin Starbuck, Martha's great-great-grandaunt, ran the island's first general store, out of her house on Fair Street, and traded with the Wampanoag Indians: tools, cloth, shoes, and kettles in exchange for fish and feathers. In 1708, Starbuck organized the island's first meeting of the Society of Friends, and she became a minister, a position closed to women of other denominations. The Nantucket Quakers opposed slavery, which was legal in all thirteen colonies, holding early meetings to advocate abolition. As financiers of the whaling business, they were at once frugal and profit-minded.

The Coffin family was a matriarchy, headed by Martha's mother, Anna, and Martha's tiny but indomitable sister, Lucretia Coffin Mott, who was fourteen years older than she was. Anna kept her own small store and taught her children to oppose slavery and to practice "the Nantucket way," the egalitarian social and business relations followed on the island. Martha's father, Thomas, had been a whaling captain like his ancestors, one of the most dangerous professions in the world. A harpooned whale could eliminate a boatload of harpooners with a single thrash of its tail. In 1800, Thomas switched to the somewhat safer business of trading—buying sealskins in South American ports, and exchanging them in China for soft nankeen cloth and silk, tea, and porcelain. But he was still gone for years at a time, and he and Anna finally moved the family to Boston, where Thomas started an import business. Martha, the last of their five living children, was born there on Christmas Day in 1806. Three years later, the Coffins moved to Philadelphia, and Thomas bought a factory that produced cut nails.

Quakers in Philadelphia had their own anti-slavery tradition, but a fractious one. Many Friends owned slaves until 1775, when the city's Quaker meeting called upon all members who hadn't freed them to do so. That year, Quakers led the founding of the first abolition group in America: the Society for the Relief of Free Negroes Unlawfully Held in Bondage. By 1789, the elderly Benjamin Franklin—a former owner of two slaves—was president of the organization, renamed the Pennsylvania Abolition Society, which worked with the Free African Society to create Black schools and to help Black residents find jobs. Anna Coffin proudly informed her children that Franklin was a first cousin of her great-grandfather Nathan Folger. In 1827, when Quakers split into two groups—the egalitarian

Hicksites and the hierarchical, Scripture-following Orthodox—Anna and her family strongly allied themselves with the most liberal of the Hicksites, whom other Philadelphians deplored.

Thomas died from typhus when Martha was eight, leaving her mother in debt. Anna, drawing on her experience as a shopkeeper and her husband's as a trader, opened a store selling goods from East India. In 1821, at the age of twenty-six, Lucretia followed the example of Mary Coffin Starbuck, becoming a Quaker minister. She and her husband, the wool merchant James Mott, were abolitionists, but it was Lucretia whose work often took her out of town, and James who cared for their five children when she was away, with help from Anna. In Philadelphia, Lucretia and James made themselves unwelcome in polite society by socializing with anti-slavery friends, including members of the Black middle class.

As a young woman, Martha had a mischievous elfin look. Her curls escaping her bonnet, her eyes flashing, she was funny, willful, and outspoken. She had resented the strict regulations and prim teachers at her Quaker girls' school, later commenting to Lucretia that she never saw "the little urchins creeping like snails unwillingly to school without rejoicing that I am not one of them." Anna supplemented her income by turning the family home into a boardinghouse, and Martha, at sixteen, fell in love with one of the boarders, Peter Pelham. A thirty-seven-year-old army captain who had fought the British in the War of 1812, Pelham had lingering ailments from a bullet wound in his upper thigh. Martha found him worldly and romantic, and soon he was wooing her with poetry books by the popular British writer Oliver Goldsmith, slipping love letters between the pages.

Anna disapproved, and so did Lucretia, who was a second mother to her: Martha was too young, and Pelham was a non-Quaker, a military man, and the son of Kentucky slaveholders. Refusing to give him up, Martha married Pelham in 1826, shortly before she turned eighteen, and they moved to Fort Brooke, in the Florida territory. She described her exhilaration at living "far from the conventionalities that interfered with one's freedom of action." Upon receiving a letter of expulsion from Philadelphia's Society of Friends for "marrying outside the meeting," she tartly replied that she found the rule regrettable, and she continued to call herself a Quaker. According to the teachings of Friends, men and women were equal in the eyes of God, and everyone contained a divine spark—an "inner light." Martha interpreted those beliefs as permission to follow her principles.

When she got pregnant, she returned to Philadelphia, and realized how much she had missed the commotion and culture of urban life—the markets, libraries and bookstores, theaters, and the lively discussions in her own family. In 1826, not long after Martha's daughter, Marianna, was born, Peter died from complications of his war wound, leaving her a widow and a mother at nineteen. She expected to live in Philadelphia, but Anna was moving to a remote village in western New York to help a cousin run the Quaker Brier Cliff boarding school, and she insisted that Martha go with her, to earn her living by teaching writing and art. It was a joyless prospect, but Martha saw no alternative, and she and one-year-old Marianna accompanied Anna to Aurora, a village of five hundred people.

Martha's only hope of avoiding a career as a schoolteacher was to marry again, and in 1829, she had an appealing suitor. David Wright, the son of a farmer in Bucks County, Pennsylvania, and a Quaker mother who had died when he was young, was not a dashing figure like Peter Pelham, but he had a quiet sense of purpose and an open mind. Seeking professional opportunities, David found work in a law office in Aurora, while studying for the New York bar. Martha, won over by David's solicitude, his intelligence, and his drive, married him five months later. With Martha's savings from Pelham's bequest and a contribution from Anna, they bought a small house and an acre of land on Cayuga Lake. David established a law practice and Martha had two more children, Eliza, in 1830, and Tallman, in 1832.

From the start, Martha found motherhood constricting. David travelled for work, a freedom that she yearned for. In a letter to him after Tallman was born, she wrote, "You complain of feeling lonely, in a crowd, surrounded by the gaieties of a city, how then do you suppose I now feel, the children all asleep, mother gone to meeting." In the long winter months of upstate New York, one storm followed another, layering snow up to the windowsills. As it melted, the mud and slush pulled at Martha's long skirts just as the children did, willing her back home. After going out for tea with friends, she atoned by kneeling over her washtub, scrubbing the stains from her dress and petticoats. She was only twenty-five, and could not bear the thought of being trapped in that narrow existence. In 1833, Anna moved back to Philadelphia, and Martha became listless and gloomy. David had never seen her like that, and he asked his sister to stay with him and the younger children while Martha took Marianna to Philadelphia for a few months.

They stayed with Lucretia and James, who were preparing for the first national anti-slavery convention, to be held in Philadelphia in early December. In the vibrant household of adults, the pall on Martha lifted. Lucretia was fully in her element, putting out anti-slavery pamphlets in the parlor and talking authoritatively with her white and Black visitors about the weekend of meetings and lectures. Martha helped Lucretia prepare a tea for fifty people in honor of the convention's sharp-tongued leader, William Lloyd Garrison.

At twenty-seven, Garrison was already a figure of notoriety. He singlehandedly ran *The Liberator*, an abolitionist newspaper in Boston. Three years earlier, he had been convicted of libel after publicly accusing a merchant from Massachusetts of being "a highway robber and murderer," for using his ships to transport slaves. Garrison was released after serving forty-nine days of his six-month sentence, and Lucretia and James arranged for him to speak in Philadelphia. In Garrison's talk, he attacked slavers as "man-stealers," and argued for immediate rather than gradual emancipation—"not tomorrow or next year but today!" Lucretia was impressed with his speech, but not with his wooden speaking style. She advised him: "William, if thee expects to set forth thy cause by word of mouth, thee must lay aside thy paper and trust to the leading of the spirit." Garrison credited Lucretia and James with inspiring him to burst "every sectarian trammel."

Garrison regarded slaveholding as a heinous sin, and the political system as innately corrupt—starting with the Constitution, which euphemistically referred to enslaved people as "those bound to Service," and counted each one as three fifths of a person. Insisting that Black Americans had every right to live as equals, Garrison opposed the American Colonization Society, which subsidized their resettlement in West Africa. Influenced by Quakerism and imbued with the evangelism of the Second Great Awakening, Garrison thought that God's will, latent in each person's conscience, needed only to be lit to spread and reform the public mind. He was a "non-resistant"—a pacifist—who called upon Americans to save their souls by finding the inner strength to renounce slavery, through the practice of "moral suasion."

Martha met Garrison at Lucretia's tea. Balding, pinch-faced, and bespectacled, he looked more like a censorious young parson than a dangerous dissident. Describing him to David as "the great man, the lion in the emancipation cause," she admitted, "I had always supposed he was a coloured brother but he isn't." She was also surprised to learn, after Lucretia's years of working alongside men in the abolitionist movement, that women were not invited to attend the anti-slavery convention. As an afterthought on the second day, someone was dispatched to the Motts' house to rectify the slight. Lucretia, Anna, and the Motts' oldest daughter rushed to the meeting.

During a discussion of the society's manifesto, its Declaration of Sentiments, Lucretia stood up and proposed a change in one of the resolutions. "Friends, I suggest—," she began as if she were at a Quaker meeting, but stopped when heads turned and a man gasped at her temerity. "Promiscuous" political meetings of both sexes were taboo among non-Quakers, and some delegates saw Mrs. Mott's disruption as proof that women should have been kept from the room. The chairman, though, asked her to continue, and she suggested stronger wording, invoking the founders: "With entire confidence in the over-ruling justice of God, we plant ourselves upon the Declaration of Independence and the truths of Divine Revelation as upon the everlasting rock." The change was made. To Martha, the sentence perfectly captured Lucretia's sense of her own mission.

On December 5 and 6, Martha attended a few of the public talks, and she was captivated by the words of a Unitarian minister, Rev. Samuel J. May, one of the society's co-founders. Unitarians had much in common with Quakers. They rejected the belief in a holy trinity and the doctrine of eternal damnation, preached the inherent goodness of all people and salvation through social action, and they took part in temperance, abolition, women's rights, and other reforms. May had a kindly face and wavy whiskers that cradled a dimpled chin, but he spoke sharply about immediate, unconditional emancipation. Martha rapturously told David the speech was the most beautiful discourse she had ever heard.

Delegates at the convention resolved to organize anti-slavery societies, "if possible, in every town, city, and village in our land." Lucretia and a dozen or so other women, white and Black, prevented from working with Garrison's group, quickly created the Philadelphia Female Anti-Slavery Society. Following the lead of organizations recently formed by

African American women in Salem and a group of interracial women in Boston, they invited speakers, initiated educational programs for women, and collected money for schools for Black children, disseminated petitions for immediate abolition, and held annual fairs to raise money for the abolitionist cause. The society was another revelation to Martha: women organizing across racial lines to do the same work as their male counterparts. Reverend May converted Martha to abolition; Lucretia and her friends opened her to the idea of white and Black women working together as reformers on their own.

Back at home with Marianna, Eliza, and Tallman, Martha soon saw how dangerous that kind of organizing could be. In October 1835, as members of the Boston Female Anti-Slavery Society made their way to a meeting they had called at their office on Washington Street, they had to push through a crowd of jeering men, who jostled them threateningly, forcing some to turn back. Inside, men lined the corridors, pelting them with insults and orange peels as they made their way into the meeting room. The women told a reporter that they had every right to advance "the holy cause of human rights." When the mayor arrived, ordering them to go home before anyone was hurt, they reluctantly voted to reconvene at the home of one of their leaders. White men had little compunction about attacking Black women, and as the group left the building, they all linked arms, walking into a mob of several thousand men. The crowd shouted for Garrison, whom the women had invited to speak. He calmly wrote up the scene for *The Liberator* before escaping through an upstairs window onto a roof and into a carpenter's shop. Discovered in the loft of the store, he was tied up and yanked toward Boston Common for a tar and feathering. His wife, Helen, saw such threats as inevitable, saying, "I think my husband will not deny his principles; *I am sure* my husband will never deny his principles." The mayor and a phalanx of constables intervened, getting Garrison safely to a jail in West Boston.

Such scenes only helped to draw more women. By 1837, from Boston to Canton, Ohio, 139 female anti-slavery societies were holding local meetings and circulating petitions for abolition. That May, in New York City, Lucretia chaired the first national Anti-Slavery Convention of American Women, attended by 173 women from ten states. The delegates resolved that every Christian woman in the country must do all she could, "by her voice, and her pen, and her purse," to "overthrow the horrible system of

American slavery." Martha, who had once been aggrieved by Lucretia's unasked-for guidance about how to live her life, now fully understood why she was considered an invincible leader. Two other women stood out: Angelina and Sarah Grimké, who had witnessed slavery firsthand. Raised by patrician parents in Charleston, South Carolina, among nine siblings and more than a dozen slaves, the Grimké sisters had renounced their heritage, moving in the 1820s to Philadelphia, where they became Quakers, abolitionists, and early women's rights advocates.

In Angelina's speech at the meeting, she summarily rejected the so-called separate spheres for the two sexes—an artificial set of constraints imposed by white men on middle- and upper-class white women. Men went out into the world to pursue money and influence; women cooked, cleaned, produced babies, and cultivated the attributes of piety, purity, and submissiveness. Women who voiced strong opinions or who showed any indelicate emotion, such as anger, were called vixens or shrews—or worse. Certain words were not spoken in the presence of ladies: a leg was a "limb," hidden beneath voluminous layers of petticoats. In some households, even the "limbs" of chairs and pianos were covered in skirts, to avoid unseemly male fantasies. Women were men's moral guardians; men were women's overseers. At the convention, Angelina announced that every woman must refuse to accept "the circumscribed limits with which corrupt custom and a perverted application of Scripture have encircled her." Henceforth, women would plead "the cause of the oppressed in our land" by using the one legal tool available to them—the right of the people, enunciated in the First Amendment, *to petition the Government for a redress of grievances.*

The following year, Sarah Grimké wrote a book, *Letters on the Equality of the Sexes and the Condition of Woman*, in which she said, "All I ask of our brethren is, that they will take their feet from off our necks." Lucretia regarded the book as just as important as the British writer Mary Wollstonecraft's 1792 *A Vindication of the Rights of Woman*, a treatise that American women saw as a declaration of independence for their sex. Wollstonecraft wrote, "I wish to persuade women to endeavor to acquire strength, both of mind and body, and to convince them that the soft phrases, susceptibility of heart, delicacy of sentiment, and refinement of taste are almost synonymous with epithets of weakness."

Predictably, newspapers treated the New York convention as farce. One anti-slavery journalist, disapproving of women assuming the roles of men, wrote, "The spinster has thrown aside her distaff—the blooming beauty her guitar—the matron her darning-needle—the sweet novelist her crow-quill—the kitchen maid her pots and frying pans—to discuss the weighty matters of state—to decide upon intricate questions of international polity—and weigh, with avoirdupois exactness, the balances of power." The female anti-slavery societies, goaded by the derision, printed thousands of petition forms, organizing petitioners by county, then divided them up by town, and circulated the forms house by house. They would then send the petitions to Congress for debate, as Garrison's society did with its petitions.

In May 1838, the women chose the grand opening of Pennsylvania Hall as the ideal occasion for their second Anti-Slavery Convention of American Women. Lucretia and other members of the Pennsylvania Abolition Society, who had trouble finding landlords willing to rent to them, had raised the money for the construction of the resplendent building. The ground floor contained lecture and committee rooms, a bookstore for abolitionist literature, and a store selling products made without slave labor. The two-story lecture hall seated three thousand people, its ceiling hung with a mirrored chandelier lit by gas. Most Philadelphians were scandalized by Pennsylvania Hall, where men and women would meet together, and whites would conspire with Blacks to overturn the social pecking order. In the days leading up to the meetings, pro-slavery activists passed out racist leaflets and tacked up posters advising citizens "to interfere, *forcibly* if they *must*." Reaction to the hall came from as far away as Georgia, where the *Augusta Chronicle and Sentinel* published a letter describing it as "this tabernacle of mischief and fanaticism."

On the first day, protesters gathered outside to harass convention-goers. A New Orleans paper raged, "Men were seen gallanting black women to and from the Hall." The numbers grew exponentially and by the third evening, the hordes had become a mob, hurling rocks and other projectiles, shattering the hall's windows, and pounding on the doors of the locked meeting room. Lucretia, speaking to the women of the female anti-slavery societies, shouted over the din not to be unnerved by "a little *appearance* of danger." After the meeting concluded, the white and Black sisterhood linked arms, as the women in Boston had in 1835. They pushed past thousands of rioters shouting obscenities about Quakers and African Americans. Lucretia wrote in her report of the meeting, "I believe

I was strengthened by God. I felt at that moment that I was willing to suffer whatever the cause required."

Moving into the lecture hall, protesters turned on the gas jets, and set it on fire. Firemen saved the houses in the vicinity, but left Pennsylvania Hall to burn. The next day, some of the women reconvened at a school, and pledged to continue their work. Lucretia, unfazed by all of it, told an abolitionist son-in-law about the "rich feast" of events during the week, "which was not seriously interrupted even by the burning of the Hall."

In the fall of 1839, Martha and David moved to Auburn, fifteen miles northeast of Aurora. David's law practice was growing, and so was the town. But if Martha imagined a place like Philadelphia, with its free-thinking minority, she was disappointed. Her new neighbors found her perplexing if not alarming. Although she dressed plainly and kept her house impeccable, she didn't take her family to church on Sunday, or spank her children, who were regarded as rude and wild. Provoked by disapproval, Martha, like Lucretia, placed *A Vindication of the Rights of Woman* on her parlor table, where, she said, "it was sure to shock guests."

Martha instantly claimed as her friend the only other known outlier in Auburn: Frances A. Seward, the wife of William H. Seward, the young governor of New York. Their husbands had gotten to know each other when both were lawyers, arguing their cases at the Cayuga County Courthouse on Genesee Street. Seward had been elected first to the state senate, and, that January, he had won the governorship, but you would hardly know that the self-effacing Mrs. Seward was the First Lady of the state. She would rather hear about Martha's exotic family history and Lucretia's revolts than discuss her new life. Frances saw nothing appealing about being mistress of the palatial Kane Mansion in Albany, where her husband entertained legislators, the "best" families, and visiting dignitaries. Martha and Frances had much in common: Quaker roots, older sisters who resisted social norms, small children, a passion for reading, an antipathy to pretentiousness, and a burgeoning interest in social reform. Frances's sister, Lazette Worden, often visited, and Martha became close to her, too.

In 1840, Martha had a fourth child, Ellen, and the following year, the Wrights spent their savings on a seven-bedroom house on Genesee Street near David's office and the courthouse. Martha had grown up amid the friendly bedlam of a large family, and she had not foreseen how wearing it would be to run such a household. She envied Frances her cook, gardener, and housemaids. Except for an Irish girl who helped in the kitchen, Martha did her own housework. She was a good cook, and she knew how to drive a nail. She took care of the children, sewed the family's clothes by hand, changed soiled hay in the mattresses for fragrant oat straw, washed the windows, shook out the carpets and darned them when they grew threadbare. Each fall, she made soap, rendered tallow for her candle making, and canned berries, peaches, and tomatoes for the winter.

Martha compensated for her abbreviated education by borrowing books from Frances's library, and after supper, as she sewed, she asked Eliza or Marianna to read aloud—their favorite form of entertainment. They praised Pope's "Essay on Man" and delighted in Sir Walter Scott's novel *Kenilworth*, about the reign of Queen Elizabeth ("well written," Martha thought, "with a touch of Scott's quiet humor"), and Edward Bulwer-Lytton's *Last of the Barons*, about Edward IV and the House of York. David, too, had become an abolitionist, and when the children were in bed, they read *The Liberator* and *The New-York Tribune*, a newspaper recently founded by Horace Greeley—an enterprising young editor discovered by Seward and his wily political adviser, Thurlow Weed.

The Wrights agreed about almost everything. They opposed slavery and New York State's death penalty, supported temperance, and entrusted themselves with the children's religious education. Martha's expulsion by the Quakers had left her with a strong aversion to organized religion. One of her targets was the venerable Auburn Theological Seminary, which trained Presbyterian ministers according to strict Calvinist doctrine. She kept a stack of American Anti-Slavery Society pamphlets near the front door, handing them out to the seminarians who came to the house to proselytize and to warn her about the fate of children who failed to devote Sunday to God. Martha replied that she didn't believe in forcing her family to read the Bible or go to church, and that she would read the seminarians' tracts only if they would read hers. "These ascetics give religion such a repulsive character," she wrote to Lucretia. "I wonder who was ever made better by the perusal of such nonsense." As such practices became known, the people of Auburn branded her an infidel.

The only ideological source of tension between Martha and David was the issue of women's rights. Spurred by Lucretia and other activists, Martha had concluded that measures to address the wrongs done to women were long overdue. Back in the 1770s, Abigail Adams had futilely warned John Adams not to give husbands undue power, saying, "All men would be tyrants if they could." David did not see any similarity between the demands of abolitionists and those of women, especially those, like his wife, who were comfortably supported by their husbands.

In December 1841, Martha invited Governor and Mrs. Seward and other guests for tea. One of the subjects they discussed was an unusually controversial bill before the state legislature: the Married Women's Property Act. Under American law, when a woman married, she turned over to her husband any money, land, or goods she had inherited. The proposed bill, if passed, would grant married women the right to their own property, and it would have a stunning ramification: women who owned property would pay taxes; if they paid taxes, they deserved the right to representation—and thus to vote. As one legislator said, the measure raised "the whole question of woman's proper place in society, in the family and everywhere."

Martha wholeheartedly supported the bill, as did Governor and Frances Seward. She had borrowed a printed lecture from Frances, by an unusually enlightened judge who made the case succinctly: women were "entitled to the full enjoyment" of unalienable rights. Frances had approvingly marked a passage saying that unqualified submission by the wife to her husband "renders her the slave, rather than his honorable associate." The lecture was a sign of progress: an American magistrate making an argument that Wollstonecraft had made the previous century.

At Martha's tea, she pointed out that the bill would also be a boon to husbands when they encountered business setbacks. To her embarrassment, David tersely contradicted her, saying that since wives shared in their husbands' good fortunes, they also should share in their reversals, and that, in nine cases out of ten, when a man failed in business it was due to a wife's extravagance. That night, in a letter to Lucretia, Martha tried to make light of the remark: "Now, I think it a great shame for David to make so ungallant a speech as that." Governor Seward did his best to get the bill passed, but the legislature voted it down.

Martha couldn't help but see political issues in personal terms. When the Wrights finally had enough money to hire a seamstress to help with the sewing, she told David that it was unjust to pay Miss Soulé half of what they paid the man who helped with the outdoor chores. Surely a woman should have the same opportunity as a man to save up for the time when, suffering from rheumatism and failing eyesight, she could no longer work.

David replied that equal wages would be "a curse to the community, raising the price of labor and setting people by the ears." Besides, a man had a family to support. Martha pointed out that half of working men relied on their wives to take in washing and other work to supplement the family income. David wouldn't hear any more such nonsense, Martha wrote to Lucretia. He went off in a huff "to hoe his corn or cut asparagus."

One evening, Martha told David that her kitchen girl, Susan, had quit, after Martha chastised her for breaking a tumbler—the tenth, by her count, not to mention a dozen cups, plates, bowls, and pitchers. David reminded her that she often complained that the hired girls were as much trouble as the children, and he cavalierly said they could get along without Susan. Martha fumed, thinking how David would respond if his law clerks were to leave at a busy time, and all of the firm's work fell to him. She began each day before dawn, and often didn't finish her chores until after David was fast asleep. She closed that letter saying: "Past 11. Susan nearly done washing, pleasant as a sick monkey. Frank just gone to bed after a bath. Willy gone over to ride on Fred's rocking horse. Ellen coughs pretty bad, but she is able to go to school."

By 1842, Martha had five children—Marianna, Eliza, Tallman, Ellen, and an infant, William. Seeing no end to her drudgery, she complained to Lucretia, "The only way is to grub & work & sweep & dust, & wash & dress children, & make gingerbread, and patch & darn." Unable to afford extra domestic help, she couldn't travel to the women's anti-slavery meetings, but she felt compelled to act. She and David agreed with Garrison that all white and free Black Americans faced a clear choice: they could side with the slavers—the "man-stealers"—or with the enslaved. If the former, they were the foe of God and man. If the latter, he demanded, "What are you prepared to do and dare in their behalf?"

The Motts and their friends in Philadelphia took in fugitive slaves on the underground railroad, as did a small number of families in Auburn, and Martha realized that she could offer her basement kitchen as a haven. She and David talked it over. Would they be jeopardizing the children's safety by letting strangers into their home? That seemed unlikely: no one was more defenseless than a terrorized freedom seeker hoping for a safe place to spend the night. Prying neighbors might discover that they were station masters and report them to the authorities, which would mean a five-hundred-dollar fine, but what was that worry compared with the fiendish punishment meted out to freedom seekers who were caught? Slavers were known to brand the cheeks of returned "runaways," sever their Achilles tendons, or lock spiked iron "punishment collars" onto their necks.

The underground railroad, a loose network that had been running for four decades with no central office or command structure, was staffed by free and enslaved African Americans, white businessmen and housewives, ministers and farmers, sailors and captains. Although the majority of freedom seekers came from the upper South—North Carolina, Tennessee, Kentucky, Virginia, Washington, D.C., Delaware, and Maryland—others found their way from Louisiana, Mississippi, and Alabama. They disguised themselves by dressing as members of the opposite sex or by passing as white. They hid in cramped root cellars and rat-infested holds of boats or traveled on trains with forged papers.

People arrived on moonless nights and left before the cows were milked. One route took them from Albany straight across New York State, through hamlets and open stretches of unpopulated countryside to Syracuse, Auburn, Rochester, and Buffalo. Many settled in those towns. Others continued on to Canada, a province of the United Kingdom, which had abolished slavery in its colonies in 1833. From Rochester, they took the train across the Niagara River to Ontario.

As Martha and David made their home a station on the underground railroad, they knew that they had the full support of the only neighbor who really mattered. Governor Seward had already proved his anti-slavery credentials in a much-publicized extradition case in the summer of 1839: a fugitive slave from Norfolk, Virginia, was discovered amid a load of oak timber on a ship in New York Harbor, and sent back to his owner, as required by the Fugitive Slave Clause of the Constitution and the Fugitive Slave Act of 1793. In Virginia, the three Black seamen who had smuggled the man aboard were charged with "property theft," and Seward received an official request to extradite them. He refused, arguing that in his state, no man was regarded as the property of another, and no man could be stolen from another. In retaliation, the Virginia legislature passed a bill requiring that ships to New York be searched for fugitives, which would complicate trade with Virginia, but Seward stood his ground. In 1840, he worked with the legislature to pass a "personal liberty law" affording every fugitive slave in New York a jury trial, with attorneys provided for the defense. He also signed a second law, which empowered agents to travel south to reclaim freeborn New Yorkers of color unlawfully sold into slavery.

The Wrights' first passenger knocked on the back door one January night in 1843, as Martha was putting the children to bed. A man presented her with a slip of paper addressed to "the spiritually minded," which entrusted "a runaway slave to the care of whom it may concern." He said that Gerrit Smith had sent him. Smith, whom Martha knew through Lucretia, was the president of the New York Anti-Slavery Society and one of the most radical abolitionists in the country. Smith lived in rural Peterboro, a village founded by his family about sixty miles east of Auburn. A large, emotional man with a lock of brown hair falling over his brow, Smith had inherited a fortune from his father, a partner of the fur trader John Jacob Astor, and he managed his investments from his estate. He and his wife, Ann, advocated temperance, land reform, nonsectarianism, and equal rights for women. They hid underground railroad passengers in their barn, and were said to donate more money to the anti-slavery cause than anyone else. One Black guest said after visiting the Smiths, "There are yet two places where slaveholders cannot come, Heaven and Peterboro."

Martha nervously took the man downstairs, gave him a warm supper, and left him to read by the fire. When David got home, he learned from their visitor that he had offered his "master" in Baltimore three hundred dollars to buy his freedom, but he was told the price had increased to eight hundred—a common ploy. After hearing that he was to be sold to the Deep South, he escaped and made his way to Pittsburgh. He was heading to Massachusetts, to join some of his family there. Martha loaned him one of David's cloaks to use as a blanket, and invited him to sleep on her settee. Recalling her aimless days in Aurora, she said in a letter to Lucretia, "How little I imagined to what use it was to be applied."

Eliza, who was thirteen, had trouble getting to sleep, and told her mother she wasn't sure she would dare stay in the house if they were visited by another fugitive slave. Ten-year-old Tallman saw escapes from slavery as adventure stories, and hoped to talk to the man "about the land of chains," but David had supplied him with some money, shirts, and bread and butter, and he'd left before sunrise. The visit left Martha with a sense of satisfaction unlike any she'd ever experienced. She was violating a law she could not tolerate, transforming her kitchen—the symbolic heart of woman's sphere, where she stored her washboards and made her mother's Nantucket corn pudding—into a place of political asylum.

2

A Young Lady of Means

1824–1837

Frances A. Seward, 1844

In the autumn of 1824, the future governor's wife was a nineteen-year-old girl getting ready for her wedding day. Frances Adeline Miller lived a quiet, pampered life in the house on South Street in Auburn where she had grown up. The household included her beloved sister, Lazette; her irascible father, Elijah, a county judge; her maiden aunt, her grandmother, a retinue of servants, and an array of pets that ranged, over the years, from dogs to doves. She was planning a brief ceremony in a simple gown at St. Peter's Episcopal Church, followed by a small reception. There would be no languorous honeymoon abroad, or anywhere, for that matter. The bridal tours of Europe popular among wealthy British couples had not yet caught on in America, and even if they had, Frances would have considered that kind of trip an indulgence. Accompanied by her family and a few of her father's friends, she was to spend the night at Rust's Hotel outside Syracuse, then return to Auburn with her husband, who would move in with the Millers.

Frances's mother had died when she was only five years old, so there was no one to tell her what to expect from marriage. Serious and deeply read, Frances scorned the propaganda of the time. One poem portrayed the ideal wife as "a bright sunbeam, in high or lowly home"—the lucky recipient of the greatest right of all: "to comfort man on earth and smooth his path to heaven." No one would have called Frances a bright sunbeam, but she excitedly cleared some space in her bedroom for Henry, as she called her groom, and for his books and cigars in her father's library, expecting that they would live there companionably with their children and grandchildren for the rest of their lives.

The Miller house was an imposing Federal brick mansion on four acres between the countryside and the village's business district. Evergreens and spreading shade trees softened its angular lines, and the lawn gave way to a peach orchard and meadows where the cows and horses grazed, and the hay was cut. Miller, though taciturn, was a good host, known for the barrel of strong peach whiskey he kept on hand in the cellar. Frances oversaw the care of the gardens in back: a grape arbor, a plot for vegetables, a labyrinth of red pole bean plants, and a wealth of perennials—lilacs, daffodils, narcissus, oleanders, hyacinths, syringas, and cupid's arrow. Behind the barn was an expanse of virgin forest.

The trappings and rhythms of the house were as familiar to Frances as the beating of her heart: the family portraits lining the walls, the tall windows letting in shafts of light until the sun set and the candles were lit, the clockwork regularity of mealtimes. All ran according to her father's dictates. Six-foot-six at a time when most people didn't grow very tall, Judge Miller was growing corpulent, and the floors creaked under his heavy step. He was fussy about the crimp in his ruffled shirtfronts, and it made him nervous to be in the presence of a man with a beard, citing George Washington, who, he said, found an unshaven face to be an insult to decency.

Frances and Lazette had never rebelled against their elders—what was there to rebel against? But Lazette, who was two years older and far more assertive, encouraged Frances to disobey some of their father's rules. The kitchen was the friendliest room in the house, and when they were little they often crept down the steep back stairs to visit with the cook, chattering as she bent over the wide hearth, a black kettle on a pothook containing a fragrant soup or pudding, a chicken roasting in a tin oven in front of the fire.

Auburn was a few miles from Owasco Lake, one of the Finger Lakes of Central New York, where the winters were long and bone-chilling. Frances always joyfully greeted the first signs of spring, touring the garden each day, taking note of new shoots and buds and the plants that hadn't survived. In the autumn, when the sugar maples turned gold and red, she and Lazette rode their horses to Owasco Lake, where the hills sloped down to the water and the sky opened up and they could watch the Canada geese, the pied-billed grebes, and the shivery-voiced loons begin their long migrations south.

Frances and Lazette loved their father's and grandmother's stories about the pioneer days. Their father was born in 1772, four years before American independence. The eldest of ten children, he thought of his Quaker parents, Josiah and Frances's grandmother Paulina, as "neat as a bandbox in their persons and dress." Josiah suspended his Quaker pacifism to serve as a captain in the Continental Army while Paulina ran their farm in Bedford, New York. The pickets of the warring armies were posted near the house, and Paulina looked out for marauders as she tended the crops and the livestock. Each night, she hid her butter and sugar, but sometimes a forager removed loose bricks from the back of the oven and made off with a loaf of baking bread. Frances was daunted by her grandmother's bravery. A friend of Judge Miller's said that Paulina had performed "a great woman's part in a great emergency." Frances never had been called upon to sacrifice anything.

Elijah went to a Quaker school in Bedford, and then to a small academy in Williamstown, which in 1793 became Williams College. There he met Hannah Foote, whom he married on the first day of the nineteenth century. A contemporary saw her as "a tall, bright, handsome, stately, and highly accomplished lady"—just the sort of wife he wanted to take west, which in those days meant the farthest reaches of New York State.

Miller became an attorney who specialized in real estate law. With property he inherited from his father's military dispensation, he began to buy and sell lots, earning a fortune from land speculation. Lazette was born in November 1803 and Frances in September 1805 in their parents' wooden house on Cayuga Lake, a remote spot raked by damp winds from mid-fall until late spring. In 1808, the Millers moved to Auburn. Hannah was frequently sick, and during the summer of 1809, hoping to restore her health, Miller took her and the girls to Williamstown, to stay with Hannah's parents for a few months.

Frances and Lazette assumed that the doctor would cure their mother with the pills and syrups he pulled from his large black medical bag, but they came to dread his visits—his demand for silence as he put his ear to her lungs, the snap of the bag, his solemn face as he spoke with their grandparents. The diagnosis was pulmonary consumption, words that never lost their power to terrify them. Hannah died in February 1811 at the age of twenty-seven, leaving Frances with a melancholy temperament and a preoccupation with invalidism. Miller nearly lost his mind with grief, a response that was almost as disturbing as the disappearance of the girls' mother into a pine box in the frozen earth far from home. Their father asked his youngest sister, Clarinda—Aunt Clara to Frances and Lazette—to move to Auburn and oversee their upbringing.

The house on South Street was completed in 1817, the year Miller was appointed to his judgeship. After Elijah's father died, his mother moved in with them. Miller's worshipful biographer wrote that he was "a giant in mind and body"—a model citizen leader. Judge Miller initiated the fund-raising drive for Auburn's first church, the Episcopal St. Peter's, and for its first school, the Auburn Academy for boys; he started the town's first major manufacturing business, a cotton mill along Owasco Falls; and he was president of the board of inspectors at Auburn Prison, a forbidding new state corrections facility outside town. The board originated a penal philosophy known as the Auburn System, which designed distinctive gray-and-black striped uniforms for inmates, making it easier to catch escapees, and featured a strict code of silence, religious instruction, communal labor, and solitary cells—all thought to encourage self-study and penitence. The convicts marched in lockstep to workshops, where they produced furniture, rope, tools, carpets, and steam engines, ensuring Auburn's rapid rise as an industrial center. Disruptive prisoners were flogged with a cat-o'-nine-tails or beaten with a wooden paddle, but the Auburn

System was seen as a progressive example for prisons around the world, promising rehabilitation through hard work and discipline.

When Frances and Lazette were young, they didn't question their father's inconsistencies. Although he spoke of equity, he enslaved two young men, Jack and Peter. In the winters, Jack pulled the girls to school on a sled, then Miller allowed him to attend class. Other parents were affronted by his permissiveness, and Frances, parroting her classmates, once called Peter a "nigger." She confessed to Henry soon after they were married, "I shall always remember the first and last time that I ever used this term. Pa reproved me very severely and I honour him for it." Under pressure from Quakers, a series of laws gradually repealed slavery in the state. Judge Miller appears to have given Jack and Peter their freedom sometime before July 4, 1827, when New York fully abolished the institution.

There were no colleges in America for women, but Judge Miller provided Frances and Lazette with the best education available. They first attended Brier Cliff, in Aurora, the Quaker boarding school where Martha Coffin Wright later taught, then went on to Emma Willard's Troy Female Seminary, north of Albany. Miss Willard gave "young ladies of means" a rigorous grounding in mathematics, science, history, literature, and foreign languages, while preparing them to be the wives of upstanding citizens. Trained to think critically and act independently, Frances and Lazette nonetheless knew that they would soon marry, and that their father would determine the merits of their suitors.

The Miller girls, Auburn's young aristocrats, were known for their quick minds, their good looks, and their father's wealth. Frances, the quiet one, was tall and slender with a patrician nose and brown, sorrowful eyes that appeared almost black. Lazette had the confidence of a man. A contemporary recalled her as "a young lady of very independent character": in church one hot summer day, she removed her large Leghorn hat, adjusted her chestnut curls "despite the remonstrances of her very stately Aunt Clara," and then replaced the hat "as if she had done nothing outré or indecorous." Frances willingly deferred to Lazette, enjoying the reaction as she sparred with their father and his guests. A friend later said that Lazette was charming "even as she demolished sophistries," her wit as "keen as a Damascus blade."

In the spring of 1821, when Frances was sixteen, Cornelia Seward, a friend from Miss Willard's, had invited her to her parents' home in

Florida, New York. William Henry, Cornelia's voluble twenty-year-old brother, was there, and Frances found him spellbinding—a quick-witted conversationalist who drew her out and put her at ease. Cornelia and Henry had a background much like Frances's: their father was a doctor, judge, land speculator, and a member of the state legislature. At seventeen, Henry had taken some time off from Union College, in Schenectady, and went to Georgia, where he taught school for eight weeks and traveled around the state, witnessing slaveholders' casual cruelties and talking to enslaved people who wanted to know about the "big North."

As one of three student commencement speakers in 1820, Henry had given an oration titled "The Integrity of the American Union." Congress had recently passed the Missouri Compromise, which prohibited slavery west of the Mississippi River, except in Missouri. Henry, filled with youthful idealism, argued that the country could amicably settle the matter of slavery if everyone would agree to a plan of gradual emancipation, like the one that New York and other northern states had followed. Neither Frances nor Henry could have foreseen that, three decades later, southerners would blame him for inciting civil war, and that Frances would reproach him for not being radical enough.

Henry moved to Auburn in December 1822, attracted by the town's growing class of bankers, lawyers, merchants, and entrepreneurs—and by Frances. She, too, was interested in history, literature, and current affairs, and, not incidentally, she was due to inherit a small fortune. Elijah Miller approved of young Seward, and he helped the relationship along by asking Henry to join his law practice. At five feet six inches, Henry was a foot shorter than Miller, and a bit shorter than Frances. Slight and hawk-nosed, he had unkempt rusty-red hair, blue eyes overhung with bushy eyebrows, and sloping shoulders that never quite filled his jackets. But his imperturbable optimism was a welcome counterpart to Frances's brooding tendencies. One observer noticed that he had a deceptively sleepy look when he was gathering his thoughts, but then "the eyes grew bright, and we felt the fascination of his voice, look, manner, and brilliant conversation."

Frances and Henry fell in love, but that was almost incidental: marriage was a contractual matter overseen by parents. Henry assured his father that Frances would have a comfortable inheritance, and that she would be "a wife with a strong mind together with a proper respect for me." Judge Miller made his acquiescence contingent on one condition:

Frances and Henry must live with him until his death. In return for overseeing the household and keeping him company, Frances would inherit the house, and split the rest of his fortune with Lazette. Frances saw nothing unreasonable about the demand; it was an opportunity to repay her father for his years of generosity. Henry regarded the domestic arrangement as "in every way pleasant and desirable." He had a wife who seemed close to flawless, and although they wouldn't have much privacy, he would be free to pursue his business interests outside town, knowing that Frances had her doting family to keep her company.

The course of Frances's life with Henry was forever changed by a chance encounter the summer before they were married. Returning from a prenuptial excursion to Niagara Falls with Frances's father and Henry's parents, they were passing through Rochester when a linchpin came loose from a front wheel of their carriage. It lurched suddenly, throwing everyone except Henry into a ditch. A tall passerby came to their assistance, introducing himself as Thurlow Weed: a twenty-six-year-old aspiring newspaperman and politician with a cleft chin and an arched eyebrow, which gave him an amused and calculating look.

Weed was a quintessential self-made American. His father was in and out of debtors' prisons, leaving Thurlow to support himself and to take care of his own schooling. He went to work for a blacksmith at the age of eight. By eleven, he was a printer's apprentice, and at fifteen, a quartermaster sergeant in the War of 1812. When Henry and Frances met him, he was running for the state assembly. Weed fueled Henry's passion for politics, and they soon reconnected at upstate political meetings.

Frances assumed that Henry, like her father, would run his own law firm, lead the community, and devote himself to his family. But thankfully, he did not have Judge Miller's reserve; he was almost as easy to confide in as Lazette. At first, they were blissfully happy. Henry encouraged her to speak up at the dinner table, convincing her that she had more to say than she thought she did. The conversation that fall of 1824 centered on the coming presidential election. Both of them supported John Quincy Adams, a son of the second president, who advocated a strong federal government and aid for economic development. New York was rapidly becoming the most powerful state in the nation, and Auburn—on the Seneca Turnpike between Albany and Buffalo—had a promising future. A network of regional railroads was under construction, and the Erie Canal, about fifteen miles north, was almost complete. The rapid growth of railways, which eventually connected every town and city in the North, ensured New York's future as a global industrial power. It was already known as the Empire State.

Henry soon made it clear just how wrong Frances was about his aspirations. He told her that he thought politics was the most important business in the country, and that he was not suited to practicing law: "I fear, abhor, detest, despise and loathe litigation." As Frances put it to Lazette, "He would prefer to be in a bustle." He sought out challenging legal cases that required travel and novel lines of attack, but he was happiest at regional political meetings. Four candidates ran for president in 1824, all Democratic-Republicans, the country's only party. Adams came in second, after Andrew Jackson, who won a plurality, but not the majority, of electoral and popular votes. The election was thrown into the House of Representatives, which elected Adams. Jackson, feeling cheated of victory, began to build the Democratic Party, to take down Adams in 1828. Henry and Weed, seeing an opportunity to shape New York politics, began to publicize the rampant corruption in Albany, where the legislature was controlled by U.S. Senator Martin Van Buren, a canny ally of Jackson.

As Henry was building his new career, Frances was preparing for the birth of their first child. The previous fall, Lazette had married Alvah Worden, the former supervisor at Judge Miller's cotton mill, and she, too, was expecting a baby. Childbirth was a frightening ordeal, and the sisters tried to forget the stories they'd heard about breach births, stillborn babies, and new mothers who contracted puerperal fever and died. The physical agony of delivery wasn't discussed in the Miller house. Frances's grandmother, who had ten children, made it sound as though she'd gotten right up out of bed after producing each of them and resumed churning her butter.

Frances safely gave birth to a son, Augustus, at home on October 1, 1826, but for weeks she was tearful and short-tempered. Lazette, who had a daughter two months later, reminded her what experienced mothers said: such symptoms usually receded along with the exhaustion. Women trusted each other more than doctors, who bled new mothers, believing it relieved the buildup of harmful body fluids. One impeccably credentialed authority advised feeding newborns no more than a tablespoonful of milk every four hours. Angelina Grimké, who had conscientiously followed that advice, credited her sister Sarah with saving the life of her first child, whom she had almost starved to death.

Propped up in bed in a cloud of pillows, Frances had her meals delivered on a tray, and the maid whisked away the baby when he was fussy. She had plenty of time to worry; the more she worried, the more irrational her thoughts became. This was supposed to be the most joyous time of a woman's life. What was the matter with her? Some mothers who failed to get over postnatal depression were judged mad and locked up in lunatic asylums.

Frances did recover, and she treasured the summer months, which she and Henry always reserved for themselves. They planned to introduce Augustus to Henry's parents in June of 1828. But Jackson was threatening Adams's reelection, and Henry and Weed were organizing another new party, the Anti-Masonics, which they hoped would help prevent a Jackson victory that fall. The Freemasons, an elitist, secretive order to which Jackson belonged, controlled countless legal and political jobs in New York. Henry told Frances he could not suspend his campaigning for Adams at that critical time, which left her and Augustus to visit Henry's parents without him.

Henry was a loving, entertaining correspondent, but epistolary romance was no substitute for his companionship. When he sent her a lock of his hair, she was surprised to see four white strands mixed in with the red. He was only twenty-eight. She teasingly reproached him, "I think you must have had more than ordinary perplexity with your business to turn your hair white so soon." When he asked her to treat his parents kindly, she reminded him that it was not her nature to be especially amiable, but she would try not to be obstinate, adding with a frown, "My Henry once would not have thought this advice necessary."

Jackson handily won the election, but Henry redoubled his work for the Anti-Masonics, and in early September 1830, a few months after Frances gave birth to their second son, Frederick, Henry was nominated to the state senate. Weed, already adept at working his will on politicians, made sure Henry won the seat, and at the end of December, Henry left for Albany. He wanted Frances and the boys to go with him, but the Miller women and the Judge thought that would be unwise. The trip was a four-day, 175-mile stagecoach ride, often in foul weather, with passengers huddled under buffalo hides. Henry would be living in a boardinghouse, not a suitable place for a mother with a four-year-old and a six-month-old baby.

When Henry was gone, the house felt hollow and Frances's elders more irritating. He was contributing to a dynamic new America; she was stuck inside with her waspish grandmother and her domineering father, who didn't offer any more in the way of comfort than the parlor's horsehair furniture. They were both deaf, relying on her as their interpreter at meals. Henry's letters were a lifeline to the outside world. Addressing "You dearest who are never absent from my mind," she wrote, "Remember that you cannot describe any thing too minutely to interest me, a thousand trifles which might be deemed unimportant to others will have attractions in my eyes from the circumstances of your being the narrator." She shared his fascination with the country's brief history, and he wrote about meeting the former vice president Aaron Burr, who was practicing as a lawyer in Albany decades after the 1804 duel in Weehawken, New Jersey: "Do I actually grasp the hand which directed only too successfully the fatal ball which laid low Alexander Hamilton?"

Henry often mentioned Weed, who founded an Anti-Masonic newspaper, the *Albany Evening Journal*, to further their political agenda. He and Henry spent most evenings together, welcoming politicians who dropped by to smoke cigars and swap stories. Frances could easily imagine the scene Henry conveyed in a letter one night: Weed resting a long leg on Henry's coal scuttle, Henry crossing his own short legs and lighting his cigar, the two talking about theater, the novels of Walter Scott, and politics. Henry saw Weed as one of the great men of the age—a master of the arts of persuasion and patronage, a "magician whose wand controls and directs" the Anti-Masonic Party. As far as Frances was concerned, Weed controlled her husband, too. Increasingly, he seemed to be the partner Henry chose to spend his life with.

Miss Willard had made Frances and Lazette think that a good marriage was a stimulating companionship between equals, but some days, looking out at the cows in the fields, Frances felt almost bovine herself. The drained mother of two young children, she had little more to offer Henry than chronicles from the nursery. She reported one day in February 1831 that Frederick, who had a cold and a stye and a tooth coming in, had been up crying most of the night. Later that month, she mustered some humor at her own expense, writing about an encounter with a born-again Christian. The Second Great Awakening was sweeping across New York, and although Frances agreed with the movement's messages about slavery as the worst of all sins, about the nature of free will, about allowing women to speak freely, and about temperance, she found the evangelists' outpourings excessive. They reciprocated her dislike. A local come-outer persuaded Lazette to accompany her to a camp meeting, but the woman had no interest in Frances, whom she regarded, Frances wrote to Henry, as a starchy Episcopalian "plastered over with self righteousness." When Frances did go out for a few hours, she was punished for it. After returning from a brief visit with a friend, she had to bite back a retort when her grandmother told her that people ought not to have children if they couldn't stay home and take care of them.

Frances's aggravations were negligible compared to Lazette's plight. Lazette and Worden rented a house from Judge Miller on East Genesee Street. Worden had failed at banking, and was now studying law, with no source of income. He squandered whatever extra money he had on drink, and his flashes of temper flared into rages. Frances and Lazette had supported the temperance movement since its start in the 1820s, never thinking that they would one day be victimized by a violent drinker. Worden sometimes hit Lazette, threatening to force her to leave and prevent her from seeing their daughter. He turned on Frances, too. "My own Dear Henry," she wrote in April 1831, "Worden has turned me out of the house and abused me in every possible way." He snatched away the book she was reading and threw it across the room, swearing at her and ordering her to go home. Lazette wept as Worden grabbed their daughter—Frances's namesake—who screamed for her mother. Desperately unhappy, Lazette told Frances that she would do anything to get away from Worden—even cross the ocean if she could take her child with her.

Frances and Lazette had read John Locke and John Stuart Mill, who proclaimed the rights of the individual, and Wollstonecraft's *Vindication of the Rights of Woman*. Wollstonecraft wrote from experience: her father was an alcoholic and her sister, too, had been married to a man who beat her. Arguing for equal education for girls and boys, Wollstonecraft proclaimed, "Strengthen the female mind by enlarging it, and there will be an end to blind obedience." Women were chattel: "They may be convenient slaves, but slavery will have its constant effect, degrading the master and the abject dependent."

Frances, incensed to see her strong sister cowering before "the brute she lives with," feared that Worden was "past all hope." Lazette was Worden's property, trapped in an inescapable web of social practice and law. Convention barred women from attending meetings with men, from eating alone in restaurants, and from driving their own carriages. Women had no legal recourse even when their husbands threatened their lives. They had no access to their inheritances. They could not sit on juries or on their church vestries. They could not make a will, sign a contract, or file a lawsuit. They could not vote. If a woman pursued divorce, she became a social pariah and lost everything: her children, any financial support, and her reputation.

Most men ridiculed the outlandish idea of women's rights, and most women caught in abusive marriages were too cowed or ashamed to speak about it. Frances wrote to Henry, echoing Abigail Adams, "Men have framed laws I believe to uphold themselves in their wickedness." Henry found the inequities between the sexes outmoded and, in cases like Lazette's, indefensible. Frances asked him to intervene, and when he returned, he told Worden to stop drinking and victimizing his blameless family, and to get his law degree. The experience turned Frances from a notional supporter of equality between men and women into an impassioned believer.

Worden's behavior improved dramatically, and Henry persuaded Frances to move with the children to Albany for the winter of 1831–1832. She and Lazette corresponded regularly, and Frances tried to make the most of the spartan rooms Henry had rented, heated by a single coal stove. Henry didn't pay much attention to creature comforts, but even he noticed the wind whistling through the windows.

He introduced Frances to his constituents, taking her with him each day on a dozen or so trips by sleigh, and to evening parties hosted by members of Albany society. Frances admittedly was hard to please: she hated being at home without Henry, but she didn't share his idea of a good time, finding it difficult to talk with people who did not interest her. She wrote disdainfully to Lazette after one interminable affair, "Mrs. T. was dressed with as little taste as usual," wearing "a white figured silk dress and a superabundance of things on her neck lace, handkerchief, ribbon, etc." Her hair was "in the unbecoming style of the day"—cascading ringlets and an elaborate topknot anchored with combs, hair pins, and ribbons.

The menu was similarly ostentatious: calf's foot jelly, plum cake, blancmange, and pyramids of ice cream and sweetmeats, oranges, and coconut. It was enough to make Frances ill, and she retreated to her room with a blinding headache for a few days.

One person whose company Frances enjoyed was Albert Tracy, a state senator eight years older than Henry who had served three terms in the U.S. House of Representatives. Henry had accurately told her that Tracy was beguiling and learned. Frances told Lazette, "I believe Henry tells him everything that passes in his mind. He and Henry appear equally in love with each other." She expected that Tracy would be disappointed in her, as everyone seemed to be who met Henry or Lazette first. Tracy hoped to supplant Weed as Henry's political adviser, but when he realized that Henry had no intention of letting that happen, he began ingratiating himself with Frances—dropping by when Henry was out, playing with Augustus and Frederick, and reading poetry and studying French with her. She was twenty-eight, but had no experience with men outside her family, and didn't see that Tracy, who was married, was trying to seduce her.

He pursued her more aggressively in the summer of 1833, while Henry was traveling in Europe with his father. Many parents of means treated their adult children to a grand tour of the Old World, and Henry told Frances that he could not ignore his filial duties. She found that galling. He treated her and the boys like constituents whom he periodically rewarded with his presence. Frances wrote during one of his early absences, Augustus "says 'Pa gone leave Ma alone—Ma cry—cry—cry.'" The resentment was mutual. Henry didn't like being made to feel guilty for enjoying his work and taking an opportunity to travel, a pleasure she didn't happen to share. Lonely and bored, Frances welcomed Tracy's regular letters, but as the weeks went by, she began to suspect that his intentions were dishonorable.

One afternoon, her father saw one of Tracy's letters on the parlor mantel, where a maid had left it for her. He casually took it down and broke the seal. She snatched it away, saying that she would like to read it herself. Seeing her father's stunned reaction, she realized that it was the first time she had firmly defied him. The awkward exchange was a revelation to Frances: her father could not see her as a grown woman, with a right to privacy. His unthinking control over her was not unlike Henry's habit of taking her for granted—knowing she would always be at home, ready to order his meal and offer advice about his "business" troubles.

Still, Frances was not blameless, and she was mortified at having been lured into a tawdry liaison straight out of Richardson's *Clarissa*. When Henry returned, she presented him with the packet of Tracy's letters, imploring him to read them and tell her if she had done anything wrong. Henry tossed the letters into the fire, put his arms around her, and assured her that he fully trusted her. She tearfully told him that she could never love anyone more than she loved him.

Henry, refreshed by his European sojourn, resumed his political maneuvering. Andrew Jackson had won a second term in 1832, and the Democratic Party was flourishing. By 1834, the Anti-Masonics had run their course, and Henry joined the Whig Party, a new coalition of northerners and southerners led by Senator Henry Clay of Kentucky. The Whigs promised to be a true national rival to the Democrats—ushering in a two-party system. Henry and Weed had developed a mutually satisfactory division of labor. Weed, less interested in elected office than in backroom finagling, twisted arms and distributed political favors while Henry spoke about the issues: restoring a struggling state economy and opposing Jackson's imperial presidency. In September 1834, at the Whig convention in Utica, Weed secured Henry's nomination as governor, and at the end of the month, hundreds of backers traveled the thirty miles from Syracuse to Auburn in carriages, wagons, and on horseback to pay tribute to him. Frances had not realized how respected her husband had become, and she felt a surge of pride as she watched members of the crowd wave their banners and shout their praise.

But the upstart Whigs didn't yet have the power to defeat the Democrats, and in November, Henry lost to the Jacksonian incumbent, William Marcy. Having expected a different outcome, Henry was in Albany. It was his first real setback, and Frances received several fevered early-morning letters from him. Other men drank or cheated on their wives. Henry was in thrall to politics, admitting, "What a demon is this ambition." He apologized for his neglect, begging, "Tell me in your own dear way that I am loved and cherished in your heart as I used to be when I better deserved so happy a lot."

Frances hoped that Henry's defeat would dispel the demon, but he and Weed began to plot their next moves. In one letter, referring to his well-being while thinking of hers, she sighed, "I who love you best of any would once have pointed to a different path as more likely to secure peace of mind—but the time has gone by." Suffering increasingly from headaches, insomnia, and depression, she sensed that they sprang from the strains of her marriage and of raising eight- and four-year-old boys with little help from their father. In 1835, she and Henry concurred with the family doctor's suggestion that they take a summer trip, and stop in Philadelphia to see a specialist. Frances left Augustus with her father and Aunt Clara, but she couldn't bear to part with Frederick, so he accompanied them on a three-month excursion through Pennsylvania, Maryland, Virginia, and Washington. The specialist had no remedy, but Frances's mood improved as she experienced ordinary family pleasures: picnics, long conversations with Henry, gathering wildflowers, and reading under the shade of a tree as he fished for trout with Fred. In southern Pennsylvania and Maryland, strawberries and melons were ripening in the fields.

As they traveled into Virginia, the roads became rougher and the farmhouses, taverns, and shops fewer and farther between. In terms of industrial progress, the state was a hundred years behind New York, and the blight of slavery was pervasive. Virginia enslaved 470,000 people—nearly half its population. The legislature had become even more punitive after Nat Turner's armed revolt in 1831, forbidding slaves to hold religious meetings, leave the property without a written pass, and to read and write.

Stopping one morning in the countryside to rest at an inn, Frances went to speak to a Black woman, elderly and blind, who was laboriously turning the wheel of a farm machine. The woman told Frances that her husband and six children had been sold, and that she had never heard from them again. Frances asked, "Do you not find it hard to bear up under such afflictions?" The woman answered with wrenching resignation, "Why, yes, mistress; but God does what He thinks it best with us."

Another day, as the Sewards pulled up at a tavern north of Richmond, they heard the sounds of weeping and moaning, and saw ten naked boys, between six and twelve years old, tied together by their wrists and fastened to a long rope, being driven forward by a tall white man holding a whip. They watched with horror as he led them to a horse trough to drink, and then to a shed, where they lay down, sobbing themselves to sleep. The slave trader had bought the children from several plantations, and he was taking them to Richmond, where they would be sold at auction—a few of the tens of thousands of people Virginia supplied to the cotton and rice fields of the Deep South every year.

Afterward, their Black coachman, William Johnson, sat silently next to Frederick on the front seat, while Frances and Henry talked quietly in the back of the carriage. Frances couldn't get the two scenes out of her mind. When she closed her eyes at night, she saw the solitary old woman at her endless task and the ragged, sobbing boys, stumbling and falling as they tried to avoid the lash. She wrote in her journal, "Slavery—slavery the evil effects constantly coming before me and marring everything."

Frances returned to Auburn with a heightened sense of injustice and renewed hope about her marriage. She and Henry, remembering how much they had in common, and how they cherished each other's company, pledged to spend more time together. A few months later, Frances was pregnant again, and in August 1836, as they had hoped, they had a daughter, whom they named Cornelia, after Henry's sister. They were enchanted by the baby's red hair and easy disposition. In 1837, Henry took a lucrative job as a land agent in Westfield, two hundred miles west of Auburn, where he rented a large house, expecting Frances and the children to spend the summer with him there. But in early January 1837, Cornelia contracted smallpox, and Frances frantically sent word. By the time he arrived, six-month-old Cornelia was scarred and blind, and she died a few days later. Frances remembered that the doctor, during a social call over the Christmas holidays, had held Cornelia just after leaving his office. When she and her father surmised that he had not washed his hands, bringing the illness into their house, Judge Miller dismissed him.

In an age of rudimentary medicine, every parent feared losing a child. Henry, whose work was a diversion from the tragedy, went back to Westfield, but Frances was inconsolable. Concerned that her mourning was jeopardizing her health, Henry wrote that he could no longer contentedly think of her in her "sanctuary"—imagining her instead "alone, drooping, desponding, and unhappy." He added darkly, "I wish I could be with you, to lure you away to more active pursuits, to varied study, or more cheerful thoughts. I might save you—for yourself, for the children, and for myself."

But there were few active pursuits available to women like Frances, who were conditioned to see idleness as a mark of refinement, and to follow the rituals of mourning. She wrote to a friend: "There is a sort of satisfaction, melancholy it is, in being once more in the room where my darling babe lived and died—in looking over her little wardrobe—in talking with those who missed and loved her." Henry, who might have coaxed her outside and helped her to think "more cheerful thoughts," was not there.

The following November, at the age of thirty-seven, Henry won the governorship of New York. Turnout was high, and his margin of victory was a solid 10,000 votes. In a moment of self-doubt, he wrote to Weed about securing the "fearful post I have coveted," saying he shuddered at his temerity. Frances, pregnant again and unable to contemplate greeting five thousand guests at Henry's public reception, didn't travel to Albany to hear him deliver his inaugural address, on January 1, 1839. Weed managed all of the arrangements, including the choice of the gubernatorial residence, the capacious Kane Mansion, which turned out to cost twice as much to rent, furnish, and staff as Henry's annual salary.

Henry had run as a moderate, and most New Yorkers had no idea how progressive he was. He rectified that in his speech, consulting with Frances as he worked through his argument. Taking positions that remained contentious well into the twenty-first century, he argued that crime was high among the Black population because they were denied access to the schools and jobs available to whites. Immigrants, who were treated abominably, represented the country's future, he said, and barriers to citizenship should come down. He denounced the practice of flogging prisoners at Auburn and Sing Sing, saying that they should be treated with "equality and justice, kindness and gentleness, combined with a firmness of temper." Public schools should be open to all children—white, Black, and immigrant: "Education banishes the distinctions, old as time, of rich and poor, master and slave. It banishes ignorance and lays axe to the root of crime." Weed was Henry's tactician. Frances was his private counselor and his political conscience—a trying position for a woman repelled by an occupation based on expediency and dealmaking.

3

Escape from Maryland

1822–1849

THREE HUNDRED DOLLARS
REWARD.

RANAWAY from the subscriber on Monday the 17th ult., three negroes, named as follows: HARRY, aged about 19 years, has on one side of his neck a wen, just under the ear, he is of a dark chestnut color, about 5 feet 8 or 9 inches hight; BEN, aged aged about 25 years, is very quick to speak when spoken to, he is of a chestnut color, about six feet high; MINTY, aged about 27 years, is of a chestnut color, fine looking, and about 5 feet high. One hundred dollars reward will be given for each of the above named negroes, if taken out of the State, and $50 each if taken in the State. They must be lodged in Baltimore, Easton or Cambridge Jail, in Maryland.

ELIZA ANN BRODESS.
Near Bucktown, Dorchester county, Md.
Oct. 3d, 1849.

☞The Delaware Gazette will please copy the above three weeks, and charge this office.

Runaway advertisement for
Harriet Tubman, October 1849

Harriet Tubman had several stories to tell about her childhood, all with one stark message: this is how it was to be enslaved, and here is what I did about it. She did not know the year of her birth, let alone the month or day—only that she was the fifth of nine children, and that she was born in the early 1820s. Her parents, Ben and Harriet Ross, named her Araminta, and as a child she was called Minty. Almost two centuries later, a scholar unearthed her birthday—March 15, 1822—by piecing together a notation in a slaveholder's ledger, a legal dispute about who owned her, and an October 1849 advertisement in a newspaper on Maryland's Eastern Shore for a twenty-seven-year-old runaway slave. When Tubman was in her eighties, she told a friend in Auburn that her first memory was of lying in a cradle made from the trunk of a sweet gum tree: "You seen these trees that are hollow. Take a big tree, cut it down, put a bode in each end, make a cradle of it and call it a 'gum. I remember lying in that there, when the young ladies in the big house where my mother worked, come down, catch me up in the air before I could walk."

Harriet couldn't remember her oldest sister, who was sold when she was three years old. Two other sisters had been leased away by their enslaver, as her mother, who went by the name of Rit, pleaded for mercy. In a recurring nightmare, Harriet heard the thud of horses' hooves and the shrieks of women as men rode in and tore children out of their mothers' arms. Rit's owner was an impecunious farmer named Edward Brodess. When Rit learned that Brodess intended to sell her son Moses, she hid him in the swamp behind the cabin. Brodess spent a month trying to find him, finally sending over a neighbor with the pretext of needing a light for his cigar. Rit told the neighbor, "You are after my son, but the first man that comes into my house, I will split his head open." Tubman later took Rit's full name, Harriet, as her own—a tribute to the woman who showed her that it was possible for a slave to resist a slaver.

Rit and her children lived on Brodess's two-hundred-acre farm, eighty miles east of Washington, across the Chesapeake Bay, amid the tidewaters and marshes, the fields and forests of Dorchester County, in a hamlet called Bucktown, marked by nothing more than a Methodist church and a dry goods store. Tubman's father, Ben Ross, was owned by Anthony Thompson, a plantation owner ten miles away. Tubman and her siblings belonged to Brodess: by law, if a mother was enslaved, so were her children. Rit worked in Brodess's house, but Harriet was put to work very young in the fields—corn, wheat, and rye.

The landscape of the Eastern Shore was flat and bleak all winter, with little delineation between earth, sky, and water except for the tall trunks and high green canopies of loblolly pines. In the springtime, white visitors exclaimed over the scents of honeysuckle and spicebush and at the pink and white blossoms of the fruit trees. Harriet had an expedient view of the natural world. Rabbits, waterfowl, and fish could be surreptitiously trapped and eaten, and ripe apples plucked from the orchards; the forest, the swamp, and the shore grasses provided lifesaving hiding places; and on a clear night the North Star was a beacon to a better place.

Maryland's population was an unusual mix of free and enslaved people: 418,000 whites, 90,000 slaves, and 75,000 free Blacks. Its planters believed they were more benevolent than the large plantation owners in the Deep South, but they didn't think twice about selling off a child or a parent if they needed money. On Sundays and holidays, they permitted slaves to visit family members on other farms; and they condoned marriages between slaves and free Blacks because it reduced the risk of flight, and because the children of enslaved mothers provided the next generation of unpaid labor. In rural counties, when the fields were fallow, slaveholders generated cash and saved on the cost of food by hiring out their human property, usually allowing them to save a portion of what they earned. Over many years, some enslaved people were thus able to buy their freedom.

Harriet recalled that Brodess first sent her away at the age of six or seven, to work for a planter named James Cook and his wife. It was winter, trapping season for muskrats, and Cook ordered her into the marshes to check his traps. She slept on the floor by the fireplace, crying for her mother. At the age of nine, Harriet found herself working for another family, answering to a vicious woman she called Miss Susan. She had never performed the duties of a maid. Miss Susan ordered her to move the parlor chairs and tables into the middle of the room, sweep the carpet, dust everything, and return the furniture. She did as she was told, dusting until she could see her face in the shining surfaces, then set the table, and went to do her other chores. A little while later, Miss Susan called her back. A whip in one hand, she ran a finger of the other through a film of dust that had settled on the table and piano. She thrashed Harriet on her neck and shoulders, then told her to do the cleaning again. The excruciating sequence of work and punishment was repeated four times until Miss Susan's sister, unable to bear the child's screams, came in, said she'd take care of it, and told Harriet that after sweeping, she must allow some time for the dust to gather, and then do her dusting.

At night, Miss Susan ordered Harriet to watch her sick, fretful baby.

She kept her whip within reach as she slept, and if she woke to the baby's cries and saw that Harriet had dropped off to sleep, she beat her again. The scars, emotional and physical, were permanent. Still, she was luckier than some. In a case in the next county, which caused a stir even among people mostly inured to the savageries of slavery, the mistress of a girl of fifteen or sixteen who fell asleep while tending the woman's baby picked up a heavy stick from the fireplace, beat the girl on her head and breastbone, and left her to die. Criminal laws in such cases were rarely enforced.

Harriet's most grievous injury occurred sometime after working for Miss Susan, when she was hired out to a man named Thomas Barnett and his wife, a prizewinning weaver. While breaking flax in a field outside Bucktown, she was ordered to pick up some supplies at the dry goods store. Before setting off, she put a shawl over her hair, which had never been combed. It "stood out like a bushel basket," she said, "and when I'd get through eating I'd wipe the grease off my fingers on my hair." At the store, Barnett's overseer ordered Harriet to restrain an enslaved man who was there without permission. She refused, and the overseer took a two-pound iron scale weight from the counter, hurling it at the man, but it fell short and hit Harriet instead. She recalled, "The weight broke my skull and cut a piece of that shawl clean off and drove it into my head. And I expect that hair saved my life."

They carried her to the house, bleeding and fainting. "I had no bed, no place to lie down on at all, and they lay me on the seat of the loom, and I stayed there all that day and next." Then she was sent back to the fields, "and there I worked with the blood and sweat rolling down my face til I couldn't see." Weak and injured, she wasn't much use, and she was returned to Brodess. He hired her out to a neighbor who had her clean the house, milk the cows, and take care of the children. That neighbor, too, sent her back to Brodess, complaining, "She don't worth the salt that seasons her grub." Tubman said that Brodess attempted to sell her, but "They wouldn't give a sixpence for me." As an adult, she suffered from agonizing headaches and seizures, dropping off to sleep mid-sentence; her left eye drooped and she had a scar on her temple—all legacies of the iron weight. The trouble in her head, as she called it, prevented her from learning to read and write, and it gave rise to visions that she considered prophetic.

Despite this handicap and a height of barely five feet, Tubman became known for feats of strength. In the late 1830s, a wealthy farmer and shipbuilder named Joseph Stewart hired her out from Brodess. She worked for Stewart for several years, and as an adult she boasted that she did all the work of a man—driving oxen, carting, and plowing. She could cut half a cord of wood a day, lift barrels, and pull boats loaded with goods through a canal in Parsons Creek funded by Stewart, Thompson, and other landowners, and built by slaves and freedmen. Tubman said, "I was getting fitted for the work the Lord was getting ready for me."

Harriet's father, Ben, was freed in 1840, by Anthony Thompson's son, Dr. Anthony C. Thompson. Several years later, the younger Thompson began to acquire a two-thousand-acre timber plantation at Poplar Neck, in Caroline County, twenty-five miles northeast of Bucktown, and he hired Ben as his foreman. Ben was a skilled carpenter who knew all of the local hardwoods—sweet gum, white oak, maple, birch, mahogany, cedar, locust, loblolly pine. He could look at a tree and gauge how many logs it would yield, and see from its curving limbs whether it would be suited for building a ship's hull or keel.

Thompson Jr. sometimes hired Rit and her children to work for him, and Harriet was allowed to keep an allotment of the fifty or sixty dollars that she earned for her labor. People were often illegally enslaved, and Harriet, suspecting that her mother's original owner had made provisions in his will for releasing his slaves after his death, paid a lawyer five dollars to investigate Brodess's claim to Rit. Such inquiries were common enough that one slaveholder complained that slaves employed white lawyers to "pry into every man's title to his negroes." Harriet's hunch was right. Brodess's great-grandfather had stipulated that the women and children he owned be freed once each turned forty-five years old. Rit should have been released around 1830, more than a decade earlier. Instead, she and her sons and daughters had been passed along in turn to three other family members, until Brodess assumed ownership. The Brodess clan was tied up in decades-long litigation, and Harriet's discovery did not result in freedom for her, Rit, or her siblings. It only hardened her hatred of the Brodesses and her determination to break away.

Brodess saw Ben and Rit as hard, loyal workers, but they were agents on the local branch of the underground railroad, hiding slaves and advising them about the best means of escape. Harriet paid close attention to her parents' acts of sabotage. Bewildered slavers of the Eastern Shore knew that abolitionists helped slaves vanish, but they couldn't fathom how. As one said, they concealed people "in a labyrinth that has no clue." Ben and Rit, familiar with the Delmarva Peninsula's many escape routes by land and water, also knew which white families provided shelter, and advised freedom seekers how to evade bounty hunters and bloodhounds. Harriet became familiar with the tides and learned how to find fresh water, and she interrogated free Blacks about the coded body language and personal networks that made escape possible. Men who drove oxen and cut logs knew wharf workers, who knew ship hands, called black jacks, on the boats heading north. By her early twenties, Harriet was starting to assemble a map in her mind, memorizing the safest routes to Delaware and Pennsylvania.

In about 1844, at age twenty-two, Harriet married John Tubman, a free man who worked as a general laborer. Four years later, she started plotting her escape. There were persistent rumors that Brodess, who was again in debt, intended to sell off more slaves. Harriet spoke to God, she said, "as a man talketh with his friend," and she began praying that Brodess would repent: "I groaned and prayed for old master: 'Oh Lord, convert master! Oh Lord, change that man's heart!'" Brodess began to bring around potential buyers, and when Tubman heard that she and her brothers Henry and Ben would be joining a chain gang headed for the cotton and rice fields of the Deep South, she prayed: "Oh Lord, if you ain't never going to change that man's heart, kill him, Lord, and take him out of the way." Six days later, Brodess died at the age of forty-seven, bequeathing Rit and her grown children to his widow, Eliza. Harriet, sure that Eliza would go through with the sale, decided to flee with her brothers.

Bereft at leaving her parents and her other siblings, she assumed that her husband would be with her. But John Tubman was a stolid man with steady work who had no desire to take his chances elsewhere. Free people caught escaping with fugitive slaves were liable to be sold into slavery, shot in the back, or torn apart by bloodhounds. John mocked Harriet for the credence she gave to her dreams and visions. In one of them, she saw a line dividing South from North, "and on the other side of that line were green fields, and lovely flowers, and beautiful white ladies who stretched out their arms to me over the line." Her destination was Philadelphia, a city known to have paying jobs for Black people and schools for their children, where white and Black anti-slavery friends shared meals at each other's homes, attended abolitionist meetings, and helped lost souls start again. Harriet dismissed John's warnings, confident that she would find work and a place to live, and that when she came back for him, he would join her.

On the night of September 17, 1849, Harriet, Henry, and Ben started on their journey from Anthony Thompson Jr.'s property in Poplar Neck, where their parents were living. The plantation was just a mile from an old Quaker settlement, the Marshy Creek Friends of the Northwest Fork Meeting, where two Friends, Jacob Leverton and his wife, Hannah, were trusted contacts of Ben and Rit. The Levertons' home was a busy underground railroad depot for freedom seekers moving through the area. The Levertons fed, clothed, and directed people, some of them bloodied from a recent beating, "onwards toward the North Star." Familiar with Patrick Henry's famous words, Harriet later said, "I started with this idea in my head, 'There's *two* things I've got a *right* to, and these are, Death or Liberty—one or t'other I mean to have. No one will take me back alive; I shall fight for my liberty, and when the time has come for me to go, the Lord will let them kill me.'"

Eliza Brodess placed an advertisement in the local paper, *The Cambridge Democrat*, describing Henry as nineteen, Ben as about twenty-five, and "Minty" as "a chestnut color, fine-looking, and about 5 feet high." She offered a hundred dollars for each if captured out of state; fifty if taken in state. As they got under way, Henry and Ben had second thoughts. More terrified of capture than of their punishment on a voluntary return, they refused to continue. Not sure they could make it safely on their own, Harriet returned with them. The following night, after one of Thompson Jr.'s slaves told her that she was to be sold immediately, she prepared to leave again, this time alone.

Freedom seekers who reached the North and spoke publicly about their escapes emphasized the cruelty and perils they had overcome. Harriet did, too, but she also liked to show how she exploited the obtuseness of slaveholders. As she was getting ready to depart, she told her mother she would do the milking that evening, and sent her back to the cabin. Walking down the dirt lane, away from the plantation house to the gate, she sang a few bars from a familiar spiritual, within range of friends who would understand the message and convey it to Rit: *"I'm sorry I'm going to leave you / Farewell, oh farewell / But I'll meet you in the morning / Farewell, oh farewell."* Thompson's slaves always stopped singing when he appeared, but as he rode by, Tubman bowed to him and continued, *"I'll meet you in the morning / I'm bound for the promised land / On the other side of Jordan / Bound for the promised land."* He turned in his saddle to look at her. She lifted the latch on the gate, waved at him, and walked out of slavery.

She took shelter the first night with a white woman who gave her a slip of paper with two names on it. The woman told her to sweep the yard, to distract any passersby. After dark, the woman's husband had her climb into his wagon, covered her, and drove her to the next house. In the coming week or so, Harriet slept during the day and traveled at night, walking along creeks and other waterways, through high brush and forests, much of the way from Maryland to Pennsylvania, a distance of nearly ninety miles.

An old stone marker indicated the Mason-Dixon line between Maryland and Pennsylvania. When Harriet crossed into freedom, she said, she looked at her hands, to confirm that she was the same person. "There was such a glory over everything. The sun came like gold through the trees, and over the fields, and I felt like I was in heaven." Then she was overcome with homesickness. She missed John, and her siblings and parents "down in the old cabin quarter." She compared herself to a prisoner being released after decades behind bars, who returns to find that his house has been pulled down and replaced with another. "Oh, dear Lord," she prayed. "I haven't got no friend but you. Come to my help, Lord, for I'm in trouble." Shaking off her despair, she resolved to go back for her entire family. "I would make a home for them in the North, and the Lord helping me, I would bring them all here."

Philadelphia was the central hub on the Eastern Seaboard's branch of the underground railroad, and some of the stories Harriet had heard about the city were true. Although racial discrimination was rampant and sometimes violent, the city had the largest population of free Black people in the country. City life was noisy, dirty, and stimulating to someone who had known nothing but rural Maryland, where little had changed since Colonial days. In Philadelphia, carriages clattered on cobblestone streets; dark billows rose from factory smokestacks; foundries hammered steel and iron into locomotives; Black sailors and longshoremen worked on docks crowded with coal barges and tall ships; men and women sold flowers, bread, oysters, and roasted chestnuts on the street. There was also a noticeable Black middle class: caterers, barbers, grocers, and bakers, many of them participants in the underground railroad.

Harriet was directed to the Philadelphia Vigilant Committee, founded in 1837 by a prosperous mixed-race farmer, Robert Purvis, a friend of Lucretia Mott's. Purvis's committee, replicated in other northern cities, provided food, shelter, clothing, money, and medical and legal help to "colored persons in distress." The Vigilant Committee was run by William Still, a dapper, bookish-looking young man with short hair neatly parted just left of center. The youngest of eighteen children born to two former slaves from the Eastern Shore, Still had grown up in New Jersey, taught himself to read and write, and moved to Philadelphia in 1844, working first as a janitor and mail clerk at the Pennsylvania Abolition Society, and then for the Vigilant Committee.

Still coordinated the arrival and dispersal of freedom seekers, taking detailed notes about their places of birth, their owners, the work they did, and their escapes. When possible, he used his meticulous record-keeping to help reunite families, a task complicated by their lack of surnames. Some people adopted the names of men who had enslaved them; others took new ones. Harriet went by her free husband's name. In 1872, Still published a detailed compendium of freedom seekers' experiences, a book titled *The Underground Railroad.*

Harriet got a job as a domestic worker, rented a room in a boardinghouse, and introduced herself to Philadelphia's leading abolitionists. One of the first people she met was fifty-six-year-old Lucretia Mott—the very incarnation of her vision of ladies in white. Mrs. Mott, who had pronounced cheekbones and round hazel eyes, was even shorter than Tubman, and weighed under a hundred pounds. She looked as fragile as bone china, but she preached against slavery and lambasted slavers and clergymen for citing the Bible to justify their sins. Most white abolitionists shared some of the racial prejudices of the time, doubting that Black people could ever live on an equal footing with whites. Mott disproved that theory, socializing and working with African American women and men, raising money for freedom seekers, and holding public meetings to advocate an immediate end to slavery.

Abolitionists still talked about Lucretia's defiance of the mob at Pennsylvania Hall a decade earlier. Robert Purvis described Mrs. Mott as the most belligerent non-resistant he ever saw. She said of that characterization, "I glory in it." Quakerism, she explained, did not mean quietism. She modeled herself on the early Friends, whom she described as "agitators, disturbers of the peace." Tubman and Mott understood each other perfectly. The young fugitive slave from Maryland and the older Quaker woman both believed they were directed by the will of God.

Harriet began to think about traveling back to Maryland for her family, a plan that others saw as suicidal. Very few people ever returned to the place they'd risked their lives fleeing. Those forced to leave behind a spouse, siblings, or children saved their wages and solicited money from abolitionists until they had enough to buy their family's freedom. William Still at first regarded Harriet as "a woman of no pretensions, indeed, a more ordinary specimen of humanity could hardly be found among the most unfortunate-looking farm hands of the South." But in 1850, as she began to exfiltrate relatives from the Eastern Shore, he revised that view. Seeing how she used her unassuming appearance to her advantage, he called her peerless "in point of courage, shrewdness and disinterested exertions to rescue her fellow-men"—a judgment shared by every friend she made in the North.

4

The Freeman Trial

1846

Freeman Stabbing Child, ca. 1847

Frances awoke on the morning of March 13, 1846, to the usual sounds of the household preparing for a new day—the piping voices of her youngest children, two-year-old Fanny and six-year-old Willy, the crackle of the morning fire in the bedroom fireplace, the hurried footsteps of the maids at work. Henry, who ran a law firm in Auburn after two terms as governor, was away on business. The older boys were at school—Augustus at West Point and Frederick at his father's alma mater, Union College. At breakfast with Aunt Clara, her father, and her grandmother, Frances learned that something unfathomable had happened the previous night: four members of the Van Nest family, acquaintances of the Millers and Sewards, had been stabbed to death in their farmhouse in the village of Fleming, just south of Auburn. Details of the attack emerged over the coming days. At about 9:30 p.m., as John Van Nest and his wife, Sarah, got ready for bed, an intruder walked through the front door. The man was described as young, Black, solidly built, and dressed in a blue roundabout coat and cloth hat. He carried a crude knife made from a club and a five-inch blade. Confronting Van Nest in the kitchen, he thrust the knife into his heart, killing him instantly. He then stabbed Sarah, who staggered into the room where a houseguest was staying. Sarah cried out, "John is dead, and I am dead—They have killed me and they will kill you."

Stepping over Van Nest's body, the killer found two-year-old George asleep in his bed, and stabbed the boy with such force that he tore him open from shoulder to abdomen. Then he picked up a candle and went upstairs, where he encountered Van Nest's hired man, who wrested the candlestick away, hit him with it, and chased him outside. Sarah's mother, Phoebe Wyckoff, took a carving knife from the kitchen and ran off for help, but the man overtook her at the front gate, stabbing her, too. She sliced his wrist, then broke away and staggered to a neighbor's house, dying two days later from her wounds. The Van Nests' older son, Peter, and their daughter, Julia, were spared.

Until that day, Frances had felt safe in her own home. More than that—in the past few years, she had been lulled into the contentment she had once imagined for her married life. Henry, who had entertained lavishly at the governor's mansion and landed himself badly in debt, was quickly attracting clients and recouping his losses. He seemed content. He played games with Fanny and Willy, and on the weekends, he relaxed in his arduous way, clearing away old brush, overseeing the transplanting of trees from the woods to the lawns, digging beds for raspberry bushes. On warm evenings, Henry and Frances sat in the garden, admiring his handiwork as he smoked a cigar, and reading aloud to each other.

The Van Nests' killer just as easily could have walked into the Miller house and attacked Frances and her family. She thought about the victims: pregnant Sarah; John, reaching for his rifle as he was stabbed; two-year-old George, torn open by the knife; brave Phoebe Wycoff—and about Peter and Julia, suddenly orphaned. "The occurrence of that fearful murder," she confessed in a letter to Henry, "has made me feel very much alone with the little ones."

The killer had fled on a horse from the Van Nests' stable. Captured the next day, he was identified as twenty-three-year-old William Freeman, who had been released from Auburn Prison six months earlier. Freeman readily admitted to the crime, telling the police that if his knife hadn't broken, he would have murdered everyone in the house. A local lawyer commented that the massacre was "without a parallel in the history of crime, an event that was horrid beyond all description, dreadful in its character and shocking to the community." Most people believed that the color of Freeman's skin predisposed him to depravity. One newspaper referred to him as "the black demon."

Frances, wondering what experiences could have driven Freeman to commit such an act, addressed Henry as if she were his legal associate: "There is still something incomprehensible about it, to my mind," she wrote, noting that Freeman hadn't known any of his victims. "He manifests no remorse or fear of punishment. If it was an act of revenge alone, why so long delayed? I believe he must have been impelled by some motive not yet revealed."

After Freeman's arrest, he was taken to the Van Nest farmhouse, to be identified by the hired man and the houseguest. The *Auburn Daily Advertiser* reported that, confronted with the bloody scene he had left behind, Freeman became uncontrollably agitated. The sheriff and deputies tied him up and loaded him into a wagon. Someone threw a rope over the branch of a tree, and as the wagon made its way along the frozen mud of South Street, followed by vigilantes, Frances heard the cries of "Lynch him!" and "Don't let him live—burn him at the stake!" Another mob, waiting at the jail, knocked down the wooden fence and surged toward Freeman as he was led through a side entrance. "Fortunately, the law triumphed," Frances wrote, "and he is in prison awaiting his trial, condemnation, and execution. I trust in the mercy of God that I shall never again be a witness to such an outburst of the spirit of vengeance as I saw while they were carrying the murderer past our door."

Henry returned about a week later, and after discussing the case with Frances, he took on Freeman's defense. He wrote to Weed, anticipating his objections: "He is deaf, deserted, ignorant, and his conduct is unexplainable on any principle of *sanity*." The case would "raise a storm of prejudice and passion, which will try the fortitude of my friends," but he felt he must do his duty. "I care not whether I am to be ever forgiven for it."

Lazette, Worden, and their daughter had moved to Canandaigua, where Worden practiced law. Frances kept Lazette apprised of developments, writing about Henry's decision: "How much I wish you were here to see how beautifully his character contrasts with those by whom he is surrounded." That included their father, whom Frances and Lazette had once regarded as unimpeachable: "Pa torments Henry exceedingly by endeavouring to make him abandon the 'nigger,' " but he "will not close his eyes and know that a great wrong is perpetrated. I can conceive of no spectacle more sublime than to see a good man thus striving to win others to deeds of mercy and benevolence."

Only three people in town sided with Henry and Frances: Martha and David Wright and the Sewards' friend John Austin. A Universalist minister, Austin shared the Unitarians' opposition to slavery and other liberal social teachings. At Henry's request, the court assigned David to assist him. David opposed the death penalty and he was known for his concise arguments in court, but his practice centered on patent law and contract disputes, and he had reservations about taking on a criminal case that was attracting national attention. Martha assured him that he was fully up to it, and she and Frances scoffed at threats that their husbands would be tarred and feathered.

Both actively involved themselves in the case. Martha dipped into David's law books and offered occasional advice, expressing satisfaction to Lucretia when he took it. She no longer stood on ceremony with "the Governor." When Seward joked that he and David would be paid one day from "the exchequer of heaven" for their pro bono work on Freeman's defense, she commented that she would be happier if David were paid from an earthly one as well, since a clear conscience "does not make pots boil."

Frances helped Henry with his research and discussed all of the details with him. As she had speculated, something terrible had happened to Freeman. When he was sixteen or seventeen, he had been convicted of stealing a horse—a theft that another man later confessed to—and sent to Auburn State Prison for five years. A guard had slammed the side of his head with a wood plank, cracking his skull and causing him to go deaf in one ear. Despite Henry's efforts as governor to make the state prisons more humane, inmates were still subjected to such beatings. Lashings with the cat-o'-nine-tails, known to have caused the death of at least two prisoners, were not banned until that year. Flagellation was replaced by the "shower bath" (an early form of waterboarding), and time in the "dungeon," an unlit space where the confined received only bread and water.

In one of the first uses of the insanity defense, Henry and David decided to argue that Freeman was not sane when he murdered the Van Ness family. Frances became fascinated by the causes of mental illness, reading and noting relevant passages in a new medical textbook, *Principles of Forensic Medicine*. The author cited four sorts of *non compos mentis*: 1. *Idiota*, referring to someone born mentally infirm. 2. "He that by sickness, grief, or other accident wholly loseth his memory and understanding." 3. A "lunatic," or person suffering from dementia, who was periodically lucid. 4. He who "depriveth himself of his memory and understanding, as he that is drunken." Henry and David believed that Freeman fell in the second category—unable to distinguish right from wrong. The argument would not lead to an acquittal, but it might spare his life. If they persuaded the jury that Freeman was insane, he would be sent to the State Lunatic Asylum in Utica rather than going on to stand trial for murder.

The prosecutor was the state attorney general, John Van Buren, chosen by the governor to work alongside the Cayuga County district attorney. Henry abhorred Van Buren, the son of President Martin Van Buren, describing him as a man lacking in decency, who won "golden praise from the vicious and vulgar" by playing to popular prejudice. The patently partisan national press debated whether Freeman's race explained his crime, and whether he should face execution. William Lloyd Garrison's *Liberator* and Horace Greeley's *Tribune* opposed the death penalty; the staunchly conservative *New York Herald* called for a return to the days when a murderer was treated as he should be: a "wretch who should be disposed of as quickly as possible."

The proceeding to determine whether Freeman was competent to stand trial began on June 25, 1846, and ended on the night of July 5. David made the opening statement to the jury, saying that Freeman had been wrongly charged with theft, and beaten on the head in prison to the point of deranging his mind. He argued that Freeman's lack of motive and the brutality of his crime were clear indications of insanity. Judge Bowen

Whiting told the jury to determine only whether Freeman could distinguish between right and wrong. If so, Frances knew, he would be declared legally sane, tried for murder, and doubtless be convicted and hanged.

On the morning of the Fourth of July, it was lightly raining as she rode in the family carriage the brief distance to the Cayuga County Courthouse. She walked up the steps past hundreds of demonstrators shouting for Freeman to be put to death. As she found a seat in the courtroom, she could feel the scrutiny of other spectators. Almost as austere in her dress as Martha, Frances was pale and drawn after a recent illness. Her hair was parted in the middle and combed close to her temples, which were framed by two ringlets—a reluctant concession to fashion. Martha, in her white bonnet and plain attire, her hands demurely folded in her lap, nevertheless was an arresting and rather intimidating figure—tall and dignified with dark, flashing eyes. When someone spoke to her about the case, citing the Scriptural command against murder, she replied that the Bible was equally binding on those who would hang the killer.

Henry had rehearsed his legal argument with Frances, but his eloquence in court brought her to tears. He spoke for nine hours, with an hour's break, creating a portrait of Freeman as a victim of bigotry. There were no schools for Black children in Auburn, and Freeman had been put to menial service at the age of eight. When Freeman was asked what would happen if he was convicted and executed, he replied that he would "go to heaven because he was good." He was barely older than Augustus. Henry, gesturing toward the defendant, said that although he was "in the greenness of youth," he was "withered, decayed, senseless, almost lifeless." He was the descendant of slaves, and his kin were scattered. The jurors must recall the Commandment "Thou shalt not kill."

Concluding his statement by candlelight around 11:00 p.m., Henry urged the jury to think of him "not as the prisoner's lawyer," but as "the lawyer for society, for mankind." Speaking, oddly, not about his client, but about his own legacy, he said, "In due time, gentlemen of the jury, my remains will rest here in your midst. It is very possible they may be unhonored, neglected, spurned! But, perhaps, years hence, when the passion and excitement which now agitate this community shall have passed away, some wandering stranger, some lone exile, some Indian, some negro, may erect over them an humble stone, and thereon this epitaph, '*He was faithful.*'"

At 8:00 the next evening, the jury returned its verdict. Disregarding

Judge Whiting's order to decide whether Freeman was sane or insane, the jurors had come up with a hazy middle ground, finding him "sufficiently sane" to know right from wrong. Nevertheless, the judge accepted the decision, which meant that Freeman was competent to stand trial for murder. Henry futilely objected, telling a friend that Whiting's failure to rule directly on the question of insanity "a contemptible compromise."

At the arraignment, Freeman stood in manacles before the judge as the district attorney shouted at him, to make sure he heard: "Do you plead guilty or not guilty to these indictments?"

"Hah!" Freeman said.

The prosecutor repeated the question, and Freeman replied in a low monotone, "I don't know."

"Are you ready for trial?" the prosecutor asked.

"I don't know."

"Have you any counsel?"

"I don't know."

Although Freeman clearly did not understand the questions, Judge Whiting ordered the clerk to enter a plea of "not guilty." The defendant would go to trial the next week. Henry put his face in his hands, trying to stifle his sobs, the only time Frances had seen him cry. David Wright rose to say he could no longer take part in the proceedings, which he called "a terrible farce." The judge asked, "Will anyone defend this man?" Henry composed himself, and after a long silence, said, "May it please the court, I shall remain counsel for the prisoner until his death." Martha pointedly told David that a refusal to continue might look like a lack of moral courage, and he agreed to stay on.

The high drama of the insanity proceeding continued during the two-week trial. Van Buren said that Freeman was "vicious and intemperate in his habits; of a race socially and politically debased. Seward countered, "There is not a *white* man or *white* woman" who, so brutalized and so confused, would have been forced to endure that prosecution. Recalling New York State's history of slavery, he asked, "What has been done by the white man to lift up the race from the debasement into which he had plunged it?"

On July 24, after two hours' deliberation, the jury found Freeman guilty. Judge Whiting conceded that society was partly to blame for criminality among Blacks, but that Freeman had been judged legally responsible for the murders. He sentenced him to die. Henry appealed, arguing that fall before the state supreme court that Judge Bowen's acceptance of the compromise verdict was improper, and that he had wrongly excluded evidence of insanity from the main trial. A few days before Freeman was scheduled to hang, the court granted a stay of execution, but Freeman contracted tuberculosis, and Judge Whiting declared him too sick to withstand the ordeal of a retrial. Frances, haunted by the thought of all the wrongs done to Freeman, went to see him in his cell. "I pray God," she wrote to Lazette, "that he may be insensible to the inhumanity of his relentless keepers—He stood upon the cold stone floor with bare feet, a cot bedstead with nothing but the sacking underneath, and a small filthy blanket to cover him."

In August 1847, Freeman was found dead in his cell. Henry was in Washington, working on a case, and Frances let him know: "Poor Bill is gone at last. I am glad the suffering of the poor benighted creature is terminated—he has gone to Him who openeth the eyes of the blind and causeth the deaf to hear, one whose benevolence is not chilled by the colour of the skin of his children. The good people of Auburn can now rest quietly in their beds."

Everyone, including the vaunted Weed and Judge Miller, had been wrong about how Henry's defense would affect his future. An autopsy on Freeman showed brain damage, vindicating the arguments of the defense. Henry's entire summation was printed in newspapers, and published in a widely disseminated pamphlet. Legal and medical journals began to reexamine the nature of insanity. Weed's *Evening Journal* called Seward "one of the first men of our country." For Frances, the triumph was shadowed by the recognition that she had encouraged Henry to take a position that would ensure his future in national politics—precisely the life she had spent two decades trying to avoid.

5

Dangerous Women

1848–1849

Elizabeth Cady Stanton and her sons
Daniel and Henry, 1848

On the afternoon of July 9, 1848, as Martha and Lucretia opened the gate of the white picket fence surrounding the large brick home of Jane and Richard Hunt in Waterloo, Martha looked forward to spending a few hours among adults—a rare respite from mothering. It had been a stifling fifteen-mile train ride from Auburn, and she was glad to take off her traveling bonnet and gloves and sit down in the cool parlor. Forty-one years old and six months pregnant with her seventh child, she was impatient for the day she could pity other women for their "prospects"—a family euphemism for pregnancies.

Lucretia was staying with Martha for part of the summer, and Jane Hunt, a Quaker originally from Philadelphia, had invited them to her house for a small reunion of Lucretia's friends. Martha was particularly eager to meet Elizabeth Cady Stanton, whom Lucretia saw as "one belonging to us"—a clear-eyed woman with strong views about social injustice. Elizabeth, the only non-Quaker there, was married to Henry Stanton, a lawyer and anti-slavery orator ten years her senior, whom she had persuaded to omit the word *obey* from their vows. Thirty-two and the mother of three young sons, she had recently moved with her family from Boston to Seneca Falls, near Waterloo.

Stanton's father, Daniel Cady, was a conservative justice of the New York Supreme Court. She'd inherited his steel-trap mind and his love of argument, but she recoiled at his reactionary beliefs. He had told her when she was eleven, regretting that her brilliance would be wasted, "I wish you were a boy." A superb student, Stanton had attended Miss Willard's Female Seminary four years after Frances. Drawn to political philosophy, she fastened on the principle of natural rights: life, liberty, and the consent of the governed. Poring over her father's law books and debating legal theory with him and his clerks, she concluded that men never would willingly cede any power to "the weaker sex," and that women would have to wrest it from them.

Stanton had spent her honeymoon in London, where her husband was a delegate at the 1840 World Anti-Slavery Convention, an event called to coordinate transatlantic efforts on American abolition. Lucretia was a delegate too, but the group in charge, the British and Foreign Anti-Slavery Society, refused to let the women speak or to sit with the men, cordoning them off in the back of the hall. Lucretia had not hesitated to point out the hypocrisy of silencing women at a conference on human rights. Stanton, then twenty-four, was staggered by forty-seven-year-old Mott, a woman, she wrote, who dared "to question the opinions of Popes, Kings, Synods, Parliament, with the same freedom that she would criticize an editorial in the London *Times*." Mott seemed like "a being from some larger planet."

Back home with her children, Stanton later recalled, she had felt rebellious, as her husband went about "where and how he pleases," while she had to hold all her "noblest aspirations in abeyance in order to be a wife, a mother, a nurse, a cook, a household drudge." Still, she had pursued her interest in reform, getting to know Boston's famed transcendentalists and abolitionists—among them, Ralph Waldo Emerson; Lydia Maria Child, the author of the 1835 *The History of the Condition of Women in Various Ages and Nations*; and Margaret Fuller, who had published *Woman in the Nineteenth Century* in 1845 and edited Emerson's journal *The Dial*.

Stanton did not want to leave the city, but her husband had lung congestion, and doctors had advised him to move to a rural area with clean air. Elizabeth's father gave them one of his investment properties, a small farmhouse in Seneca Falls—a community of four thousand people that specialized in producing wheelbarrows. It was a sorry comedown from the literary salons and lyceum talks of Boston. When farmers got together, they spoke about their crops, and Stanton was unsettled, she later wrote, by "the wearied, anxious look" of the wives, particularly those married to drinkers. Children learned to run to her house when their drunken father was pummeling their mother. She wrote about her fury at the conditions that left "terror-stricken women and children" the victims of "strong men frenzied with passion and intoxicating drink." Stanton would confront the assailant, and, "much to his surprise and shame, make him sit down and promise to behave himself."

Usually Lucretia dominated social get-togethers. She projected a calm, wise manner, and others deferred to her authority and wisdom. But Stanton led the discussion in Waterloo. Afflicted with a "mental hunger, which, like an empty stomach, is very depressing," she said that extensive measures must be taken "to remedy the wrongs of society in general and of women in particular." Suddenly that seemed possible. Just a few months earlier, the New York State legislature had passed a landmark bill: the Married Women's Property Act. It was the measure that Martha and David had argued about seven years earlier, but while Martha stewed about David's cavalier dismissal of the bill, Stanton had gone to Albany to lobby for it. Stanton later recalled about the afternoon with the other four women that after years of mounting discontent, she spoke "with such vehemence and indignation that I stirred myself, as well as the rest of the party, to do and dare anything."

As Martha listened to Stanton, she heard a resounding echo of her own resistance to the life that had been assigned to her. In the fall of 1846, annoyed by an article in the Philadelphia *Gazette* that instructed women to fulfill their "conjugal duty" with obedience, "a heartful of kindness," and "a cheerful smile," she'd written her first piece for publication—a lacerating essay she titled "Hints for Wives." While the "liege lord" of the house went off each day to the "every-varying scenes of everyday business," his wife spent all her time tending to others: cooking meals, cleaning dishes, drying tears and stopping fights, sewing the family clothes, doing the laundry, and getting the children off to sleep. Then she was expected to delight her husband with the "little arts of pleasing." If they had sex, they might conceive another child and start the cycle all over again. Martha asked: "Why is it not oftener insisted upon that the husband should always return to his fireside with a smile, and endeavor to soothe the perturbed spirit, that has for hours been subjected to the thousand annoyances of the nursery and the kitchen?" He had a good night's rest, while she calmed the "restless inmates of the trunnel bed and the crib, all of whom are sure to be astir at the earliest dawn, and demanding the immediate care of the mother, who rises weary and unrefreshed, again to go through the same routine—truly, she should smile!" Lucretia was a forceful speaker, but she knew she lacked Martha's verve on the page, and it was likely she who made sure that "Hints for Wives" was printed in the *Gazette*.

Emboldened, Martha soon wrote a short piece for *The Liberator*, under the byline M.C.W, after a minister, in an evangelical journal, vilified Garrisonian abolitionists as "irreligious." Martha dismissed the charge as a form of "pseudo-Christianity," accusing the minister of abandoning the principles of "Justice, Mercy, and Humanity." She didn't have the time or the confidence to seriously pursue her talent as a writer, but when the children napped and late at night, she wrote long letters to Lucretia, known as "family sheets," often in installments over a week. They unfolded as a sardonic serial of life in the Wright household. One day, describing her failure at beating eggs with a quill, as another housewife had suggested, she concluded that the idea "must have been invented by *a goose*—my nice wire egg beater is good enough for me." Lucretia was entertained by the letters, which she passed along to relatives in Philadelphia and Nantucket, but she warned Martha not to "cultivate mirthfulness at the expense of other faculties." It became a running debate between them. Martha wrote, "People love to laugh. If it were not for the blessed organ of Mirthfulness, what would become of us all."

Fired up by Stanton, the women at Jane Hunt's house agreed to call for the country's first women's rights convention, to take place in Seneca

Falls. The planning had to be done quickly, while Lucretia was still in Auburn. They set the convention dates for just ten days hence, July 19 and 20, at the plain, brick Wesleyan Chapel, a short walk from Stanton's house. Their announcement in the *Seneca County Courier* described it as a forum to discuss "the social, civil, and religious condition and rights of woman." Lucretia sent a copy of the notice to Frederick Douglass, to publicize the convention in *The North Star*, the abolitionist newspaper he had recently started in Rochester. Mary Ann M'Clintock, the fifth organizer of the convention, knew Douglass from the Western New York Anti-Slavery Society, and she issued him a personal invitation.

It was an astute decision. Douglass, one of the world's best-known abolitionists, strongly supported women's rights, and his presence would lend weight to the occasion. In 1845, he had published an international bestseller, *Narrative of the Life of Frederick Douglass*, a searing portrayal of his life in slavery on the Eastern Shore, just north of where Harriet Tubman had grown up. Martha had her own indirect tie to Douglass, who credited her distant cousin William C. Coffin with initiating his career. Coffin, a member of the Massachusetts Anti-Slavery Society, had invited Douglass in August 1841 to attend Nantucket's first anti-slavery convention, and pressed him to make some remarks. Douglass, then about twenty-three, never had addressed a white audience. "It was a severe cross," he wrote, "and I took it up reluctantly." Garrison was there, and he leaped up to ask, "Have we been listening to a thing, a piece of property, or to a man?" Everyone shouted, "A man, a man!," and agreed never to send anyone back to slavery from Massachusetts.

Douglass's *Narrative* was a tale, against all odds, of self-actualization. With some initial help from the wife of one of his enslavers, he had taught himself to read and write, and he viscerally evoked the experience of slavery. "My feet have been so cracked with the frost," he wrote in one passage, "that the pen with which I am writing might be laid in the gashes." Douglass's mother, a field hand hired out to other slaveholders, slipped out several times at night and to walk twelve miles to visit her children, returning by sunrise. She died when he was about seven, and he couldn't recall her face. His "owner," a tyrannical sadist, was rumored to be his father. When Douglass was about twenty, Anna Murray, a free woman he was courting, aided him in his escape from Baltimore to Manhattan. She followed him to New York, and they married and moved to the whaling port of New Bedford, Massachusetts, where he found odd jobs sawing wood, shoveling coal, and cleaning chimneys.

Garrison hired Douglass as a lecturer for the Massachusetts Anti-Slavery Society, and paid for his trip to Britain, where he was invited to talk about the book. During a two-year tour through England, Ireland, and Scotland, Douglass raised enough money to buy his freedom. By the time he returned, he was questioning Garrison's belief in nonpolitical resistance, and he was planning to start his own newspaper. Garrison saw the idea as a betrayal, and in November 1847, Douglass moved with his wife and their four children to Rochester, where he joined a circle of upstate abolitionists. Gerrit Smith, who financially supported Douglass's *North Star*, became a lasting friend.

The first issue of the newspaper was published on December 3, 1847, seven months before the Seneca Falls Convention. At the top of the front page, it proclaimed, "RIGHT IS OF NO SEX—TRUTH IS OF NO COLOR—GOD IS THE FATHER OF US ALL—AND ALL WE ARE BRETHREN." Douglass replied to M'Clintock that he would gladly attend the convention, and he brought along some friends, also members of the Western New York Anti-Slavery Society. The out-of-the-way village of Seneca Falls soon came to be known for something more exciting than its wheelbarrows.

Martha and Lucretia returned to Auburn, and Stanton met with M'Clintock and two of her daughters to compose a Declaration of Sentiments for the convention. M'Clintock, a Quaker who had been hardened in the abolitionist struggle, was as radical as Stanton, but less incandescent in her fury, and she didn't have Stanton's determination to put herself at the center of every story. Stanton and M'Clintock consulted the published reports of anti-slavery and temperance conventions, but rejected them as too tame for what Stanton declared would be "the inauguration of a rebellion such as the world had never before seen." Instead, they appropriated the Declaration of Independence, starting with the Preamble: "All men *and women* are created equal." Their Declaration went on to portray women as the age-old victims of male despotism: "The history of mankind is a history of repeated injuries and usurpations on the part of man toward woman, having in direct object the establishment of an absolute tyranny over her."

When Lucretia read the women's Declaration, she approved of all but the most daring plank, demanding the vote: "*Resolved, That it is the duty of the women of this country to secure to themselves their sacred right to the elective franchise.*" A Quaker and a Garrisonian, she wanted no part in a political system that sanctioned slavery and war, and she thought that women would only hurt their cause by pressing for a goal that was widely considered laughable. She told Stanton, "Lizzie, thou wilt make the convention ridiculous." Stanton, though, believed that women would not achieve parity until they achieved the same political and legal rights as men. The plank remained.

At eleven o'clock on July 19, 1848, about three hundred white women from around the region traveled by train and wagon, some accompanied by their children and husbands, to Seneca Falls. Most had long been abolitionists and supporters of women's rights. To encourage an open exchange, the organizers—Lucretia, Martha, Stanton, Jane Hunt, and Mary Ann M'Clintock—had excluded men from the first day's proceedings. Stanton introduced their objectives: to organize and expand the movement by hiring lecturers, circulating tracts, petitioning state legislatures and the U.S. Congress, and holding annual conventions around the country.

She began tentatively, but gathered strength as she read aloud the Declaration of Sentiments. They followed the colonists' objection to unjust governance, replacing the "absolute Tyranny" of King George over the states with that of "mankind" over woman:

> *He has never permitted her to exercise her inalienable right to the elective franchise.*
>
> *He has compelled her to submit to laws, in the formation of which she had no voice.*
>
> *He has withheld from her rights which are given to the most ignorant and degraded men—both natives and foreigners. . . .*
>
> *He has made her, if married, in the eye of the law, civilly dead.*
>
> *He has taken from her all right in property, even to the wages she earns. . . .*

As Stanton continued, she took control of the convention, reciting how women's natural rights had been trampled—in marriage and divorce laws, in church and state governance, in education, and in all the professions.

The demand for the vote caused considerable disagreement, but Stanton won the debate, convincing a majority of the women to pass the resolution.

That morning, Lucretia asked the participants to express themselves without inhibition, a prospect that Martha found impossible. Unusually blunt with her friends and neighbors, and witty and incisive in her writing, she felt unable to speak in public, and she used her pregnancy as an excuse to observe from the back of the room. But Lucretia refused to let Martha go unnoticed, and the next afternoon she read aloud "Hints for Wives." Martha was surprised by the appreciative response, and astounded when Douglass introduced himself, asking if he might republish the essay in *The North Star*. Martha and David had been shaken by Douglass's *Narrative*, and read his newspaper as closely as they did *The Liberator*. Martha had looked forward to meeting him, never imagining that their first conversation would open with Douglass congratulating her for something she had written. She granted his request, and they struck up a friendship.

It was Douglass who convinced Martha that Stanton was right about the vote for women. In his report on the convention in *The North Star*, Douglass said the meeting was "the basis of a grand movement," and asserted, without the slightest caveat, that "all political rights which it is expedient for man to exercise, it is equally so for woman." Douglass wrote that women who accused men of degrading them would be subjected to the "fury of bigotry and the folly of prejudice"—something that wouldn't change anytime soon. Saying that the nation was founded on the consent of "free and equal citizens," he concluded, "There can be no reason in the world for denying women the exercise of the elective franchise."

Lucretia and Martha and sixty-six other women signed the Declaration of Sentiments. After some discussion, the men were invited to add their names, and thirty-two did so. Martha, who fifteen years earlier had left the founding meeting of the American Anti-Slavery Society committed to abolition, left Seneca Falls sworn to full equality for women. When Lucretia reproved her for her refusal to speak, Martha replied, "I plead guilty to being very stupid & dispirited at Seneca Falls." Hoping to disarm her sister with a pun about her pregnancy, she said she had been subdued by "the prospect of having more Wrights than I wanted."

Stanton, seeing how useful Martha could be to the new movement, wrote to her after Seneca Falls, "Keep your pen busy." Douglass printed the committee's report on the convention at *The North Star*'s offices, and

Stanton sent copies to Martha, who distributed them around Auburn. In August, when Martha learned that Douglass would be giving a lecture in Auburn she invited him to her house for a visit—itself a small insurrection.

David was away, and Martha, who thought it was never too early to expose her children to great men and women of the age, took Ellen, her precocious eight-year-old, to hear Douglass speak. He addressed the national crisis over slavery, and its implications for the presidential election that fall. The United States had recently won the Mexican-American War, which resulted in the acquisition of more than 500,000 square miles, from the Rio Grande to the Pacific Ocean. The Democratic Party's nominee, Lewis Cass of Michigan, adapting the doctrine of "popular sovereignty," said that voters in the new territories must be permitted to decide for themselves whether to permit slavery as they entered the Union. The Whig candidate was Zachary Taylor of Louisiana, a slaveholder and Mexican War hero whom the party recruited because of his appeal to its southern faction. Douglass found both Cass and Taylor unacceptable. He had just come from Buffalo, where he'd attended the founding convention of the Free Soil Party, comprised of disaffected Democrats and Whigs. The new party was the first to dedicate itself to prohibiting the expansion of slavery.

Martha knew what her friend Seward was arguing in that polarized year: Taylor was the best candidate one could hope for. Better to elect Taylor, Seward thought, and mold his politics, than stand on principle and lose to Cass. Douglass, more bracingly, called the Whig Party "the grave of all independence, self-respect and decency," whose members allowed themselves to be "whipped into the support of this same 'bloodhound,' Zachary Taylor." During Douglass's talk, Ellen applauded along with her mother, and said she thought that he spoke better than her aunt Lucretia. Douglass escorted Martha and Ellen home, and stayed for an hour or so. Martha, unable to keep Willy and Frank from showing off in front of their visitor, dispatched seventeen-year-old Eliza to put them to bed.

When the next issue of *The North Star* arrived, containing Martha's essay, she was unable to fully conceal her pleasure, writing to Lucretia, "To think of one having that threadbare Hints for Wives in it."

The baby Martha was expecting at Seneca Falls was born in October. She and David named him Charley, and a few weeks later, Martha wrote to Lucretia, "I can't help loving my little brown eyed homely boy, even if I did want him to be a girl." It took her three hours one morning to bathe Ellen, five-year-old Willy, and three-year-old Frank, what with the hauling and heating and dumping of water from the well, the scrubbing and toweling of the children, slick as baby seals. "How tired I was!" Martha confessed. "I wished for a bath tub where I could put them all in and stir them up with a long pole, but they looked nice when I had done."

Seneca Falls, though, had changed Martha's thinking about her future. She decided that when the children were grown, and she and David could enjoy a quiet, orderly house, she would fully join Stanton and Douglass in their crusades. Douglass returned to Auburn in April 1849 to give another lecture, and Martha asked him to stop by the house again. She sympathized with Anna Douglass, who had risked her own freedom by helping Douglass escape and now lived in an unfamiliar city, alone with their children while he traveled. Anna Douglass was illiterate, and so didn't have the pleasure of reading Douglass's lectures or losing herself in a book. Douglass held Charley on his lap while Martha read aloud a letter from Lucretia about a group of enslaved people who had just smuggled themselves out of Richmond.

Martha's friendship with Douglass gave rise to ugly gossip in town. Ellen told her mother that someone had asked her whether he ate at the dinner table with the family. Neighbors who already disapproved of Martha now saw her as a provocateur who promoted social equality between the races. At a party, Martha overheard two guests gossiping. "Who is that fine-looking lady?" asked one. The other replied: "That is Mrs. David Wright. She is a very dangerous woman."

6

Frances Goes to Washington

1848–1850

View, southeast from Pennsylvania Avenue, of the construction of the Capitol extension and dome, 1857

It was John Quincy Adams, the first candidate Frances had supported for president, who persuaded her that it was Henry's duty, even his destiny, to assume Adams's mantle as the leading anti-slavery spokesman in Washington. She and Henry regarded Adams as one of the country's greatest public figures. He had served as an ambassador under presidents George Washington and Adams's father, John Adams; as secretary of state under James Monroe; as a U.S. senator; as president; and, finally, seventeen years in the House of Representatives, where he was ridiculed as a dotard and threatened with assassination for his persistent, vocal opposition to the "gag rule," a measure that prevented any debate on the petitions sent to Congress by the anti-slavery societies.

Henry had cultivated Adams for decades, and Adams considered him his protégé, but Frances had met him only once, on a sweltering August evening in Auburn in 1843. The encounter began like a comedy of manners. Henry, always absentminded about household matters, had failed to tell Frances that they would be entertaining the former president. As she wrote to Lazette, she was relaxing in a light gown and slippers, "and otherwise dishabille owing to the extraordinary heat," when she heard a commotion, and looked outside to see Henry headed toward the house leading the elderly Adams and his family, the fire company, and a torch-lit retinue of fifty townspeople. Frances asked a maid to light the candles in the parlor, and hurriedly changed her clothes. Her aunt Clara, peering out the parlor window, provided a doleful narration as the procession tramped onto the lawn: "There goes a rose bush." "They have broken one of the oleanders." "The gates are down." "The fence is falling." The drama took a somber turn the next morning when another guest asked Adams at breakfast whether he thought slavery would be peacefully abolished. Frances never forgot his reply: "I used to think so, but I do not now. I am satisfied that it will not go down until it goes down in blood."

In April 1847, when Henry visited Adams at his house on F Street, Adams had said as they parted, "I trust, Mr. Seward, you will allow me to say that I hope you will do a great deal for our country: you must, and you will. I am going. I shall be here but a little while." Ten months later, in February 1848, eighty-year-old Adams collapsed at his desk in the House, and he died two days later.

Henry, a prominent Whig with a knack for extemporaneous speaking, campaigned hard for Zachary Taylor that fall, traveling from Massachusetts to Pennsylvania, to New York City, and back to Pennsylvania; then on to Washington, Delaware, and Ohio, giving speeches at each stop. He enjoyed being on the stump and getting himself known to voters outside New York. Frances, who found southern Whigs' tolerance of slavery reprehensible, didn't share Henry's enthusiasm for Taylor.

During Henry's prolonged absence, she supervised a substantial renovation of her father's ten-room house. With four generations under one roof, it was crowded. Her father had retreated to the basement to sleep, where, his biographer wrote, "his chosen bed was a plain but handy bunk." Henry liked to live large. He had collected books, paintings, furniture, and other possessions during his governorship, and as their own family grew, they needed more space. A new wing was being added to the back with a modern kitchen and dining room, a coal furnace, servants' rooms, and a three-story tower containing an office for Henry. Frances was trying to retain some of the character of the original house, and to keep her father at bay. As Frances instructed the workers, Judge Miller padded behind her, complaining about the mess, the noise, the expense, and the paint colors. "The sound of the hammer has ceased for a time in our dwelling," Frances wrote to Henry. "The masons have succeeded the carpenters."

Knowing that Henry would return with a peace offering for being away so long, she said: "Do not on any account get me a velvet dress—I have one now which is nearly useless—neither do I want a hat though I am much obliged." She would have appreciated a tender letter commemorating their anniversary. No letter arrived, and on October 21, she wrote, "This is our 24th wedding day. Though the years that have passed have had alternations of shade and sunshine in the retrospection the sunshine predominates." Her poor health and Henry's inordinate dedication to his career sometimes caused her to overlook her "many blessings."

Frances followed Henry's campaigning and speeches in the newspapers, fearing that he would soften his anti-slavery position. But he didn't. At Tremont Temple in Boston, he said he opposed the expansion of slavery, and in Cleveland, where the Free Soil Party was gaining momentum, he emphasized that the nation was "founded in the natural equality of all men"—meaning "all men of every country, clime, and complexion." Sounding more like an abolitionist than a Whig, he stated, "Slavery can be and must be abolished and you and I can and must do it." He even advised his audience to "extend a cordial welcome to the fugitive who lays his weary limbs at your door, and defend him as you would your paternal gods." Frances thought it was the best address of his tour—and she knew that his enemies would not forget it.

Henry's months of speechmaking helped to clinch Taylor's election—and his own, as a senator from New York. Until 1913, U.S. senators were selected by state legislatures, rather than directly by voters, and with Weed greasing the machinery, Henry was chosen in February 1849 to represent New York, alongside a Democrat. Henry's Whig opponent, John A. Collier, had spread such lies about him that Frances was actually glad about his victory. Disappointed that even some of Henry's supposed political allies had fallen for Collier's dishonesty, she wrote to Lazette, "Disinterested benevolence must be very rare to be so hard to comprehend." Henry hired nineteen-year-old Frederick as his private secretary, and he moved at once to Washington. Fred, who had just graduated from Union College, was smart, hardworking, and steadfast, without Henry's unabating drive. Frances hoped he would not pursue a political career, but she too thought he was an ideal choice for the job.

Nine months later, in November, Frances went to Washington with Willy and Fanny to help Henry and Fred settle into larger quarters: a newly rented brick rowhouse near the Capitol. Invigorated by the change of scene and glad to have the family together, she enjoyed taking charge of the move, and as they waited for the furniture to arrive, she didn't complain even about sleeping on straw-stuffed bags in the parlor.

The city felt almost as unfinished as it had when Frances and Henry had visited with Frederick during their summer excursion nearly fifteen years earlier. The Capitol was being expanded to make room for senators and representatives from new states, and the grounds were strewn with marble columns, lumber, wagons, and workmen's sheds. Two of the nine towers of the Gothic Revival Smithsonian Castle were finished. The Washington Monument, designed to evoke an Egyptian-style obelisk, was just beginning to rise, but due to inadequate funding and political squalls, it wouldn't be completed for thirty-six years. The city had no public schools and no police force. Streetlights were sporadic, private houses were not numbered, and pigs rooted through refuse in the alleys. The Washington City Canal, connecting the Anacostia and Potomac rivers, was filled with the contents of open sewers, and flowed malodorously through town. An official report referred to the canal, a breeding ground for mosquitoes and disease, as "that pestiferous ditch."

Washington was very much a southern city. When riding along the Mall in Henry's carriage, Frances saw people of all ages herded in coffles to one of the slave pens between the Capitol and the White House: Robey's Tavern, the Yellow House, and the St. Charles Hotel—which advertised a fine restaurant and, in the basement, six holding cells for people about to be sold at auction. In 1831, Garrison had damned the capital in the first issue of *The Liberator*: "A fouler spot scarcely exists on earth. In it the worst features of slavery are exhibited; and as a mart for slave-traders, it is unequaled." Free Blacks were under constant threat of kidnapping, and if they were found violating the ten o'clock curfew or not carrying the required papers, they would be arrested and liable to be sold at auction.

In December, Frances attended her first state dinner at the White House, in the required costume of the time: a modern corset girded with light steel rather than traditional whalebone, overlaid with a wide hoop skirt and gown, her hair in a braided chignon. One of four hundred guests, she was seated next to President Taylor—a mark of his respect for Henry. A Kentuckian who had served as a captain in the War of 1812 and a general in the Mexican War, Taylor knew nothing about Washington politics, and he relied heavily on Henry for guidance. He agreed that slavery must not be allowed to expand into the West, and he was unexpectedly winning—sociable and straightforward, a military man who was mystified by the city's elaborate etiquette. Sympathizing with his discomfort, Frances told him, "They should have a book like the Army regulations, and reduce such matters to a system that might be studied." He laughed and agreed. She wrote to Lazette about their banter, "Henry says the President looked at no one but me during dinner."

Frances's pleasure in her new role was short-lived. She found the omnipresence of slavery oppressive, and within weeks, she came to see Washington's strict social hierarchy as more in keeping with a royal court than a democratic republic. There was a protocol, based upon one's husband's position, that determined who must pay the first social call upon whom. Senators' wives had the same status as the wives of Supreme Court justices—second only to the president's family. Frances couldn't see the point of it all, except to make the women feel almost as busy and important as their husbands. She wrote to Lazette that she hadn't done one important thing all week. "Visiting and receiving visits constantly is certainly not the kind of life adapted to my taste, feelings, or constitution either physical or mental."

The women she met did not share her interest in abolition and women's rights. Frances wasn't sure she agreed with Martha that women must achieve the vote and become officeholders, but she believed they should be permitted to be physicians and jurors, and, she wrote to Lazette, "I will say that if there is no other way of elevating them I would rather see them more masculine than to see them what they are now." Every day, she dressed formally, and spent four hours fulfilling her social obligations. The six years of Henry's term loomed uninvitingly. It was, she said morosely, "the life to which I am doomed."

As Frances returned home one afternoon, a white man wandered into the street and was knocked down by one of her carriage horses. He was uninjured, but berated William Johnson, the Black coachman who had worked for her and Henry for decades. William thought that the man would have him arrested, or hunt him down and beat him. If he had, Frances wrote to Lazette, there would be no legal redress. "Is it not disgraceful to a civilized community?"

One of Henry's legislative goals was to end slavery and the slave trade in Washington, an idea most members shunned. When a political friend from New York wrote to say that Henry must be surrounded by flatterers, he responded that, actually, he alone dared to speak out for disenfranchised men. That wasn't quite true. His party was composed of "Cotton Whigs" who condoned slavery and a smaller number of "Conscience Whigs" who opposed it. Henry was the most forthcoming of the latter faction, not the only one. Frances, though, agreed with Henry's self-assessment, telling Lazette, "Whatever my own timid nature might prompt me to do I hope I shall never fail in the generosity which will enable me to encourage the action of nobler spirits." Referring to the refusal of most northern Whigs to frankly oppose slavery, she added, "I only hope the time may come when they may appear as craven to themselves as they do to me." That time never came, but Frances was far less timid than she thought. No longer the introverted girl who had married Henry, she was evolving in ways that she didn't yet recognize. A year later, she found her own way to oppose slavery.

For three decades, the Missouri Compromise of 1820 had held the nation together by maintaining an equal number of free and slave states, and by prohibiting slavery in the northern regions of the country acquired as part of the Louisiana Purchase—about 828,000 square miles stretching north of Missouri and west of the Mississippi to the Rocky Mountains. By the summer of 1850, there were thirty states, still evenly split, but the country was rapidly expanding into the territories acquired in the Mexican War, including the future states of Arizona, New Mexico, and California. Struggling to build a civil society as hundreds of thousands of gold prospectors descended, California was requesting admission to the Union, with a state constitution that banned slavery. President Taylor supported California's entry—but it would upset the precarious symmetry. Southerners threatened to secede, and Congress sought to thrash out another compromise.

Members from the South, knowing of Henry's influence over President Taylor, equated his position on slavery with that of "ultra" abolitionists, like Garrison. Frances sat in one morning on a Senate session. The moment Henry stood up to speak, she wrote to Lazette, he "drew upon him the tornado; not because they cared what he said, but because one who entertained anti-slavery principles should venture to speak at all." She swore that the Freeman trial, four years earlier, had inured her to such venom. "I speak truly when I say that my strongest sentiment was contempt and pity for malice so impotent." Looking at her diminutive husband, and feeling that he was the only one "sufficiently fearless to vindicate human rights," she was very glad that she was there to support him. Henry was preparing his first major speech to the Senate, which addressed California and slavery in all the territories. Frances vetted successive drafts, advising him to be bold, and not to budge from his position.

The aged Great Triumvirate—Henry Clay of Kentucky, John C. Calhoun of South Carolina, and Daniel Webster of Massachusetts—were to speak first. Frances knew Clay a little. Now seventy-two years old, he had fashioned the Missouri Compromise when he was Speaker of the House. Fourteen years later, with the support of Henry and Weed, he had helped found the Whig Party, itself a balancing of southern and northern interests. In the summer of 1839, when Clay was seeking the Whig presidential nomination, Frances had entertained him alone in Auburn. Henry, who was then governor of New York, knew that the slaveholding Kentuckian could not win the state, and, avoiding an awkward conversation, arranged to be away. She had felt then that Clay would do whatever it took to protect slavery.

Frances wanted to hear him speak. On February 5, 1850, the opening day of debates about the future of the territories, she arrived early at the Capitol and made her way to the Senate through the jammed halls and lobbies. In the visitors' galleries, as the crowds closed in, several women fainted. On the floor below, the president of the Senate presided beneath crimson swags and a canopy bearing a gilt eagle and shield. Senators had no offices, and they carried out their work at small lift-top desks, like schoolchildren. The floor was littered with papers, and more. Members, ignoring the spittoons around the room, lazily spat out their chewing tobacco from their seats.

Clay took the floor to deafening applause. As the room settled, he brandished a roll of papers, announcing that he held a series of resolutions that could amicably settle all of the questions about slavery: "I have seen many periods of great anxiety, of peril, and of danger in this country, and I have never before risen to address any assemblage so oppressed, so appalled, and so anxious." His new "Compromise" appealed to Conscience Whigs by admitting California as a free state and by ending the slave trade in the District of Columbia, although it stopped short of freeing any slaves there. It appealed to Cotton Whigs and conservative Democrats by declaring that other territories acquired in the Mexican War would follow the doctrine of popular sovereignty. The bill would overturn the restrictions Clay himself had placed on slavery in 1820—permitting slavery to metastasize across the continent.

The newly draconian Fugitive Slave Act, a central part of the Clay Compromise, would allow slavecatchers to travel into free states to hunt down "runaways," overriding personal liberty laws such as the ones Henry had signed as governor, which provided legal protections to freedom seekers. The act would require citizens and police to deliver suspected "fugitives" to federal commissioners, who would hold a perfunctory hearing before returning them to the South. Citizens who protected them would risk fines of $1,000 and six-month prison terms. Frances found Clay's entire bill utterly repugnant. Still, she conceded to Lazette, "He *is* a charming orator. I have never heard but one more impressive speaker and that is *our* Henry (don't say this to anybody)." *Their* Henry thought of Clay's bill as "magnificent humbug."

Senator Calhoun, who considered slavery as "instead of an evil a good—a positive good," was mortally ill with tuberculosis and unable to read his own speech, so on March 4, a colleague from Virginia read it for him. Calhoun rejected Clay's compromise, recapitulating his core beliefs: the Constitution was pro-slavery, states' rights were paramount, and "the agitation on the subject of slavery" would end in disunion. If California entered as a free state, he warned, the South would interpret it as an act of aggression that would irretrievably destroy the "equilibrium" between North and South.

On March 7, Frances returned to the chamber to hear Daniel Webster of Massachusetts, a conservative Whig intent on safeguarding New England's textile industry, which depended on southern cotton. She found him even more repellent than Clay and Calhoun, whom she partly excused because they had been raised amid slavery. She had nothing but contempt for men in the North who were willing to perpetuate the institution. Webster began: "I wish to speak today not as a Massachusetts man, nor as a Northern man, but as an American." He said, "I speak today for the preservation of the Union. Hear me for my Cause!" Webster said of abolitionists, many of them his own constituents in Boston, Concord, Worcester, and other towns, "Everything that these agitating people have done" only fortified the resolve of slaveholders.

Frances thought Webster was less engaging than Clay "because his heart is decidedly colder—people must have feeling themselves to touch others." He had been in office for thirty-seven years without once speaking for the oppressed. He "would not be very likely to do it now when all of the country were seeking of him a *compromise*—the word is becoming hateful to me." Henry's political friends feared that he would falter under the pressure. Frances commented: "How little they know his nature. Every concession of Mr Webster to Southern principles only makes Henry advocate more strongly the cause he thinks just."

Henry spoke on March 11. Frances was fully satisfied with the speech, which invoked the founders and cogently argued for gradual emancipation. Still, she stayed home when he left for the Capitol. Ever since his days as a state senator, she had been unable to listen to him deliver a major address, finding it more nerve-racking than he did, and the rebukes of his opponents unbearable. Henry wasn't given to grand gestures or booming oratory, and, as others described it afterward, he started off in his low, husky voice, twirling his eyeglasses in his left hand. His unassuming delivery had its own effect, forcing his audience to sit forward, straining to hear him. He said that secession would end trade and travel between North and South, and turn families into enemies. Civil war would ensue. He conceded that the Constitution left it to individual states to resolve their position on slavery, and emphasized that emancipation must be pursued only through "lawful, constitutional, and peaceful means." He spoke enthusiastically about the advantages of the westward migration to a nation that aspired to be the most powerful in the world.

Then he came down hard on the Clay Compromise. Slavery must be abolished in Washington, and it would not be permitted in the new states. He accused Clay and Calhoun of disregarding the Preamble to the Constitution, in which the framers, in pursuit of "a more perfect Union," swore to "secure the Blessings of Liberty to ourselves and our Posterity." Slavery was "radically wrong and essentially vicious." As for the new Fugitive Slave Act, which required northern states to participate in a system that they had abolished, citizens would not stand for it.

In his most provocative passage, and Frances's favorite, Henry said that God, not the laws that men wrote, should guide the country. "There is a higher law than the Constitution, which regulates our authority over the domain, and devotes it to the same noble purposes." The western territories were "part of the common heritage of mankind, bestowed upon them by the Creator of the universe." He titled his address "Freedom in the Territories," but it instantly became known as the "Higher Law" speech.

Southern Fire-Eaters, the most extreme pro-slavery faction, saw it as proof of their suspicions about Henry's malevolent intent. The *Richmond Enquirer* called him "a wretch whom it would be a degradation to name." The Washington *Republic* accused him of defaming the Constitution by attempting to legislate in the name of God Almighty. On the floor, Clay made the same argument, and—referring to Henry's speech in Cleveland two years earlier—said, not inaccurately, that Seward would encourage a man to give fugitive slaves "assistance, and succor, and hospitality."

Frances reported to Lazette that the week after the speech felt like an entire season of darkness, and that the reaction "would have sunken a spirit less buoyant than Henry's." But as people read it, the mood shifted. The American and Foreign Anti-Slavery Society, a group that had split off from Garrison's because it found his ideas too radical, printed ten thousand copies, and Horace Greeley's *Tribune* and other newspapers published supplements that reproduced the ten-column speech in full. In early April, Frances wrote ebulliently, "I never shall cease regretting dear sis, that you are not here to read with us the letters and papers about Henry's speech—They are coming now from Ohio and Michigan—I shall keep them for you—They amply atone for the abuse from other quarters." Greeley wrote that Seward's words would "exert a more potential and pervading influence on the national mind and character than any other speech of the session."

When Weed weighed in disapprovingly from Albany, saying that Henry had threatened the tenuous unity of the Whigs and nakedly exposed his ambition, Frances countered that he had to do what was right, and disregard how it might affect his party and his political fate. She found

Weed's argument specious: an attempt to hold the country together by accommodating the very institution that was annihilating it.

In May, Frances returned to Auburn with Fanny. Judge Miller had been asking for her. He was losing his eyesight, and looked old and vulnerable as he bent over his books and papers with a magnifying glass, painstakingly making out each line.

Henry wrote every day after breakfast, consulting Frances on sensitive matters of state, knowing that she would not discuss them with anyone but Lazette, whose discretion he fully trusted. His birthday was May 16, and, as he entered his fiftieth year, he indulged in a sentimental moment, asking for Frances's wishes that what remained of his life be spent "serenely and more wisely." Serenity was not a quality she associated with Henry, but he seemed to mean it when he said that he was looking forward to retirement.

In early July, President Taylor contracted a violent stomach ailment variously attributed to gastroenteritis, cholera, and typhoid fever. He died several days later. Frances, who had grown fond of the president and his wife, wrote to Henry, "To say that I am inexpressibly grieved but faintly expresses my feelings—I grieve for his family, for the loss of one I felt to be a personal friend but above all for the irredeemable loss" to the country. "You can imagine how my heart yearns to be with you." She knew he would read between her lines. The Clay Compromise was now sure to pass. Vice President Millard Fillmore, a conservative Whig who had served three years in the New York State Assembly and disliked Henry, was president. Fillmore supported Clay's bill, and he appointed Daniel Webster as secretary of state. Henry was so overwrought by the sudden turn of events that Frances feared for his health, reminding him, "It is your nature when well to find hope everywhere." He said with glum vanity that his own character traits—fidelity, constancy, justice, humanity—had become unfashionable in Washington. "Why, John Jay and Franklin would be mocked in the streets, if they were to revisit Washington!"

On July 22, Clay gave the last major speech of his career, saying of his omnibus bill, "It is equal; it is fair; it is a compromise." A week later, the Senate voted it down, but the bill was rescued by thirty-seven-year-old Senator Stephen A. Douglas. A Democrat from Illinois, Douglas was a small, pot-bellied man with hooded eyes and big ambitions who had an ability to crash through legislative logjams. Douglas split the measure into separate acts, enabling members to oppose or accept individual measures. In the fall, the bills were voted on: California was granted entry as a free state and the slave trade in Washington was abolished. Slavery, though, would remain untouched in the capital, and the New Mexico and Utah territories were opened to slaveholders—a major victory for Douglas, the country's most influential champion of popular sovereignty.

The Senate passed the Fugitive Slave Act by a vote of 27 to 12. On September 12, as the measure was rushed through the House, Frederick Seward was in the Congressional Library, where a number of northern representatives were milling about—"dodgers" unwilling to vote either for or against the measure. He hurried over to the House gallery in time to see Thaddeus Stevens, a no-holds-barred Conscience Whig from Pennsylvania, on his feet, moving that the Speaker "send one of his pages to inform the members that they can return with safety, as the slavery question has been disposed of!" The bill had just passed the House, 109 to 76. Ralph Waldo Emerson captured the effect of the Fugitive Slave Act among citizens in the North, calling it "a sheet of lightning at midnight." In the months that followed, arrests mounted. One man who had been living in Auburn for two years was returned to slavery, leaving behind his wife and child. Free Blacks, too, were caught in the dragnets and sent south to be sold. The transaction was so abhorrent, Frances wrote, it had roused even "the most phlegmatic." Hundreds of people who lived in Syracuse, Rochester, and Buffalo fled to Canada.

As Henry had warned, many northerners refused to abide by the new law. Abolitionist groups and entire jurisdictions fought back. Vigilance committees sprang up in cities that didn't already have them, protecting Black people from arrest and organizing rescue operations when necessary. Black citizens bought guns to protect themselves and their families. In Auburn, Frances took on a new role, as Henry's go-between, keeping him fully apprised of the political mood in New York. She wrote to Augustus, "The public opinion against Slavery is daily growing warmer—It is impossible to see when it will all end."

Harriet Tubman showed just how mistaken Henry Clay was about the pacifying effects of his compromise. The Fugitive Slave Act turned her into a guerrilla operative, marking the beginning of her years on the underground railroad. As she told Sarah Bradford, who wrote Tubman's first biography, "I wouldn't trust Uncle Sam with my people no longer; I brought them all clear off to Canada." A few months after the bill was enacted, Harriet was in Philadelphia when she learned that Eliza Brodess intended to auction off her niece Kessiah and Kessiah's two children. She got word to Kessiah's husband, John Bowley, a free shipbuilder in Cambridge, Maryland. Through a series of coded letters, they devised a plan to thwart the sale, and get the Bowley family to Baltimore, where Harriet would meet them.

The auction took place just before noon one winter day in front of the Dorchester County Courthouse in Cambridge. As a free man, Bowley was entitled to bid for members of his own family, and he made the highest offer for his wife, son, and daughter. The auctioneer brought down the gavel and left for his midday meal. When he returned, he called for payment, but Bowley had made off with his family, hiding them in the house of an anti-slavery white woman who lived just steps from the wharf. After the search parties had given up, Kessiah and the children set off at night with Bowley up the rough, frigid waters of the Choptank River. Bowley, familiar with the winds and the tides, sailed his family on a small boat into the Chesapeake Bay and on to Baltimore Harbor, finding protection among the Black watermen of the Chesapeake.

Harriet was waiting for them in Baltimore, where she was staying with her brother-in-law Tom Tubman, a free man who worked on the docks and ships of the harbor. She took the Bowleys to Philadelphia, where she helped them find living quarters and work. Some months later, she arranged for Kessiah, John, and their younger child, Araminta, to travel to Chatham, Ontario, a village that welcomed freedom seekers. They could live in Canada without fear, as Harriet said, referring to the symbol of Britain's greatness, "under the Lion's paw." She persuaded Kessiah and John to leave seven-year-old James with her, so that he could attend one of Philadelphia's Black schools, foreseeing a future for him as an educated man. He did not disappoint her. Nineteen years later, James Bowley was elected to the General Assembly in South Carolina, during Reconstruction, when freed men briefly served on juries, worked on county and state commissions, and held state and national office.

Harriet soon returned to Baltimore, and formed a second escape plan, for her brother Moses and two other men from Dorchester County.

She would have agreed with Senator Calhoun on only one thing: fugitive slaves, Calhoun said, posed "the gravest and most vital of all questions," to southerners and to "the whole Union." Harriet knew that no law could stop enslaved Americans from seeking liberty. Slavery apologists, like so many other men in power faced with insurgencies, underestimated the will and the sophistication of the people they set out to subdue.

7

Martha Speaks

1850–1852

DELEGATES TO THE WHIG STATE CONVENTION.—Suffolk Co.: 1. Henry P. Hedges.

Lewis: Alanson H. Barnes, who is instructed for Washington Hunt, for Governor.

Rockland: Edward Pye, Haverstraw.

Fulton: William G. Wait.

Greene: W. D. Gunn, Wm. Greene.

The Whigs of Brooklyn held a very large and enthusiastic meeting on Friday evening. Gen. LESLIE COOMBS, of Kentucky, delivered one of his masterly speeches of about an hour in length.

The Louisville Courier says that Col. Benton is authoritatively announced as a candidate for the Senate of the United States in 1854, and sooner if Geyer can be forced to resigned by instructions from a Loco Foco Legislature.

There were fourteen deaths from cholera reported to the Board of Health of Rochester, during the forty eight hours ending at 5 P. M. Friday.

The region about Lake Superior has been dry and hot this summer. Very little rain has fallen, and the Lake settled very perceptibly. Immense fires have ranged through the woods.

One hundred thousand quarts of milk are used in New York daily, for which $5,000 is paid. This would amount to $1,825,000 per year.

Seventeen deaths by cholera were reported by the City Inspector of New York, for the week ending September 5,—and six in Brooklyn.

Mrs. Forrest, it is said, is about to marry an "English soldier of fortune!" *A Soldier of Fortune!*—what profession is that!

The Tobacco crop will be largely deficient in Kentucky, but is good in Maryland and Virginia.

The Loco Focos of the Twenty-First District have nominated Hon. ELISHA B. SMITH, of Chenango, for Congress.

The Rochester University opened on Thursday. The attendance is large.

Localities.

THE NATIONAL WOMAN'S RIGHTS CONVENTION.

After a duration of three mortal days, this august convocation came to a "happy and peaceful end" Friday evening. We have furnished our readers with a pretty full and, carefully prepared sketch of its doings, and those of them who did not attend the Convention, have consequently had a fair opportunity of ascertaining its character from our columns. That our readers have found entertainment, and no small amount of information, in these reports, we feel confidence in presuming. As reporter, we were present during the entire settings of the body, and we enjoyed no inferior opportunity to judge of the character of the proceedings, and—so far as was possible in such a place—of the participants in these proceedings.

All who attended any portion of the Convention, or the whole, will unite with us in pronouncing it the most dignified, orderly and interesting deliberative body, ever convened in this City.—The officers—and, most especially, the distinguished woman who occupied the President's Chair—evinced a thorough acquaintance with the duties of their stations, and performed them in admirable manner. The speakers, who were mostly of the number who have devoted themselves in a considerable degree to the advocacy of the objects for the promotion of which the Convention was held, were women of decided ability, and they appeared in the capacity of public speakers to equal advantage with any who have ever participated in meetings of like nature in this "City of Conventions."

No person acquainted with the doings of the assemblage, and competent to pass judgment in the matter, will deny that there was a greater amount of talent in the recent Woman's Rights Convention, than has characterized any political gathering in this State during ten years past, and probably a longer period, if ever. It was a peculiar kind of talent, it is true. The possessors of it are women who have "made their marks" in the republic of letters. Several have been acknowledged, for years, as foremost among the literati of the country, and have not seen their best days of usefulness. For compact logic, elegant and correct expression, and the making of

"All who attended any portion of the convention . . . will unite with us in pronouncing it the most dignified, orderly, and interesting deliberative body, ever convened in this City."

Martha was just as disparaging as Frances about feckless politicians. Even Stanton's husband, once one of the finest abolitionist speakers, had succumbed to the lure of public office, and was now serving as a Democrat in the New York State Senate. Martha wrote to Lucretia, "What a pity that he was not willing to remain great. I feared Mr. Seward would be like the rest, but so far he has done well." Still, she was honest enough with herself to acknowledge how difficult it was to act even on one's profoundest beliefs.

She wanted to work with Stanton, but force of habit and heart-shattering sorrow kept her at home. A few days after Charley's first birthday, in November 1849, he died of a sudden illness. Lucretia, who years earlier had lost a young son, commiserated with Martha and gave her time to mourn. Then, assuming her ministerial role, she said Martha must regard Charley's death as part of the "operation of the natural laws," and move on. Not yet ready to do so, for the time being, Martha settled on acting within her family to reorder relations between the sexes. She thought of equality not as an ideal to strive for, but as a belief system to instill in one's children. She sent five-year-old Frank and eight-year-old Willy to the Auburn Female Seminary, deaf to any teasing they would endure, and she was teaching the boys how to knit. Willy made a bag for his marbles. Martha commented to Mary Ann M'Clintock that it was not bad for a beginner—and "quite marvelous considering the *slow perceptions* of the sterner sex."

Martha mocked herself for her own lapses, and David for his professed inability to do even the simplest domestic tasks. "His equanimity sometimes forsakes him at the want of a button," she wrote to Lucretia. If he found a button missing on a shirt, "he comes to me with a most dejected air as if he had just heard of the failure of his principal creditor and assures me that it is the little things that make the sum of happiness, as if my fingers were not constantly flying with my needle, and as if he never forgot either little or great things, when there are so many hundred little things that want attending to that he makes a point of forgetting on purpose." Martha consulted with Lazette, who confirmed that "there never was a man whose good temper was proof against a missing button."

Lucretia was accustomed to Martha's excuses, and in the autumn of 1850, two years after Seneca Falls, she pressed her to attend the First National Woman's Rights Convention, a milestone for the movement. It was to take place in Worcester, Massachusetts, a town that a radical local pastor happily characterized as a "seething center of all the reforms." Lucretia was elected president, and the chief organizer was a protégé of hers, thirty-two-year-old Lucy Stone. In 1847, Stone had graduated with honors from Oberlin College, the first woman in Massachusetts to earn a college degree, and she was currently a paid lecturer for the American Anti-Slavery Society. A rousing speaker, Stone always drew large audiences of supporters and hecklers. Lucretia warned Martha that she was in danger of "rusting out," arguing that the convention was an opportunity to escape her grief, meet other stimulating women, and make herself useful to the cause. Martha conceded, "That catastrophe occurred long ago. I feel very rusty."

Still grieving for Charley, Martha didn't attend, and then she wished she had. She was sorry to miss Douglass, Garrison, and Rev. Samuel J. May, whose speech in 1833 at the American Anti-Slavery Convention had made her an abolitionist. May now lived in Syracuse, where he presided at the Unitarian Church of the Messiah, and operated the city's underground railroad with another cleric, a freedom seeker from Tennessee named Jermain Loguen. May had long supported women's rights, demanding to know in one of his first sermons in Syracuse why "half of the people have a right to govern the whole." Martha also would have enjoyed meeting Lucy Stone and other emerging young activists, along with two renowned speakers: Sojourner Truth, who in 1826 had escaped from slavery in Ulster County, New York, and Wendell Phillips, an associate of Garrison's known as abolition's "golden trumpet." Phillips supported women's rights as emphatically as Garrison.

The convention attracted more than a thousand women and men from eleven states, as far away as Iowa and California, to discuss the goals expressed at Seneca Falls: women's rights to own property, to be granted equal education and access to every profession, and to vote. Other items on the agenda included medical education for women and dress reform, a movement in itself, for less restrictive clothing. The organizers expressly supported "equality before the law, without distinction of sex or color." In Lucretia's remarks, she spoke about the difficulties ahead: they would have to "take an antagonistic position and to meet the prejudices and opposition of the world with directness and an earnest expression of the truth."

Stanton, pregnant with her fourth child, could not be there, but she sent a spirited letter, which was read aloud. Anticipating skeptical questions about how much women might demand, Stanton rhetorically asked, "Would you have her hold office?" And answered: "Most certainly." Many women, free from domestic encumbrances, would grace a Senate chamber, "for whose services the country might gladly forgo all the noise, bluster, and folly of one-half the male dolts who now flourish there and pocket their eight dollars a day." (It was sixty-six years before the first woman—Jeannette Rankin of Montana—was elected to Congress. Rankin's opponent, one newspaper reported, killed himself because of shame over his defeat and voters' chants, "Beaten by a woman!")

Lucy Stone's words rang out even in a long column of gray newsprint: "We want to be something more than the appendages of Society. We want that woman should be the coequal . . . of man in all the interest and perils and enjoyments of human life." And, "We want that when she dies, it may not be written on her gravestone that she was the 'relict' of somebody." It was painful to think of millions of women, remembered, if at all, for the menial services they'd performed for husbands and children. The convention, responding to Sojourner Truth's speech detailing the far more egregious state of enslaved women, resolved to make the same demands for "the trampled women of the plantation." Thirty-nine-year-old Abigail Kelley Foster, a Quaker native of Worcester and an "ultra" associate of Garrison, coolly stated that women had the same right to rebel as the Founding Fathers—"the right to rise up and cut the tyrants' throats."

At Seneca Falls, Douglass had said that women were men's equal. Now Garrison and other abolitionists celebrated them as partners in reform. Garrison wrote that the Worcester convention "was really the noblest series of meetings that we ever attended," praising the speakers for "a clearness, an earnestness, a directness, an eloquence, that inspired us with a fresh hope of humanity." Greeley's *New-York Tribune* favorably covered the proceedings, citing Ernestine Rose, the atheist daughter of a Polish rabbi who had spent more than a decade petitioning for New York's Married Women's Property Act long before most women had begun circulating petitions. The bombastic *New York Herald*, horrified by the proceedings, caricatured fifty-seven-year-old Lucretia as a "Caesar": "all bone, gristle, and resolution," and the participants as "fantastical mongrels, of old grannies, male and female," who spoke "the most horrible trash." That "piebald assemblage" dared to claim that a woman was as qualified to be president as a man. The convention injected "terror into the heart of the stoutest of man." Phillips and Garrison helped Foster and Stone create a central committee to organize annual women's rights meetings and publish their proceedings; enlist sympathetic clergy and press; and write tracts about women's right to serve on juries, to work in law, medicine, and other fields, and to vote.

Martha, galvanized by the triumph at Worcester and tired of being a bystander, finally threw herself into the movement. With Ellen, Frank, and Willy at school, she took the train to Seneca Falls, and walked to Stanton's small white farmhouse, which Stanton called "the center of the rebellion." Martha wrote to M'Clintock that she loved Stanton for her ardor, and that she wished she had the same ability to "clothe her thoughts in words that burn!" Stanton appreciated Martha's smart ideas and her sense of humor, noting that "her pungent wit and satire, without a ripple on the surface, burst forth at unexpected moments to the surprise and delight of us all." Martha helped Stanton organize petition drives and plan future conventions. As they set agendas and considered upcoming speakers, Stanton distractedly watched her children and dashed off letters to followers, insisting they keep up a drumbeat for reform—at home, in their churches, and in their legislatures.

In September 1852, at the Third National Woman's Rights Convention, in Syracuse, Martha held an officer's position for the first time. She had come a long way since Seneca Falls, where, pregnant and unable to foresee a life outside her home, she had tried to disappear. Two thousand people attended the convention, where the leaders called their movement "a great moral civil war, upon the subject of women's true sphere."

Martha made two new alliances there, with Lucy Stone and Susan B. Anthony. Anthony was a thirty-two-year-old temperance and anti-slavery advocate from Rochester who had met Stanton on a street corner in Seneca Falls the previous year, and begun a professional partnership with her that would last fifty years. Anthony had quit her job as a schoolteacher rather than accept a salary of $2.50 a week when men were paid $10. Unmarried and lacking an inheritance, she lived with her parents and siblings. Martha praised Anthony's work ethic and her organizational talents, but privately commented to Lucretia, referring to Charles Dickens's dour educator in *Hard Times*, "I hope it isn't wicked to say that people of the Gradgrind stamp do not attract me so much as some others do." She felt more temperamentally akin to Stone, who dodged Bibles thrown at her during her lectures, for "violating God's word." Stone, who had been excommunicated from the Congregational Church, objected to a proposal to turn the women's movement into a formal national group, saying that she'd had enough of "thumb screws and soul screws ever to wish to be placed under them again."

As an officer, Martha was expected to serve on an executive committee, draft resolutions, and maintain order during sessions. None of that fazed her, but she had been dreading the idea of speaking on a dais along with her proficient colleagues. When the time came, it was far easier than expected. Conservative clerics always made an appearance at women's rights conventions. Ministers held considerable power in their towns, and they would spring up from the audience uninvited to volunteer their misogynistic views. At Syracuse, one man advised the women to stick to the domestic sphere, lest they become masculine. Another cited such biblical passages as "Thy desire shall be to thy husband, and he shall rule over thee." Martha—her heart thudding with vexation and fear—rose and said that it was ridiculous to dredge up such hoary injunctions in an attempt to attack the rights of modern women. She found it satisfying to tell a man in front of thousands of people that he didn't know what he was talking about.

The next day, a Rev. Junius Hatch tried to win over the convention with a metaphor about female loveliness. Women should show a "shrinking delicacy, which, like the modest violet, hid itself until sought"—the same quality that led them to wear long skirts, instead of imitating the sunflower, which lifted its head, "seeming to say, 'come and admire me.'" He was alluding to Stone, whose straight brown hair was daringly cropped above the chin, and who had taken to wearing bloomers, promoted by Amelia Bloomer in her newspaper, *The Lily*. The outfit allowed women more freedom of movement: a mannish short jacket with baggy trousers under a skirt that came just below the knee. The audience shouted at Hatch, "Sit down! Sit down! Shut up!" Lucretia called the meeting to order, and told him that he had outraged the audience. When Stanton, at home awaiting the birth of her fifth child, heard about the exchange, she congratulated Lucretia and Martha on "the utter annihilation of the Rev. Hatch."

A Whig newspaper in Syracuse praised the officers, calling the meeting "the most dignified, orderly, and interesting deliberative body, ever convened in this City." Martha was grateful to Lucretia and Stanton for spotting in her a quality that she hadn't seen, and for pushing her to join them. The movement was winning important backers in Britain and France. Harriet Taylor Mill, a philosopher who was married to John Stuart Mill, stated in the British *Westminster Review* that "the example of America will be followed on this side of the Atlantic."

As Garrison had once said about abolitionists, "Are we enough to make a revolution? No, sir. But we are enough to begin one, and, once begun, it never can be turned back." Although the women's rights cohort was small and reviled, Martha saw it as an explosive force, capable of blasting open narrow hearts, minds, and laws.

PART TWO

UPRISINGS

(1851–1860)

Harriet Tubman, ca. 1908

8

Frances Joins the Railroad

1851–1852

The Seward House, 1853

A quieter rebel than Martha, Frances worked covertly, through Henry, and she focused more on slavery than on women's rights. After the passage of the Fugitive Slave Act, she began to regularly report to him what the citizens of Auburn and nearby towns were saying and doing. Everyone faced new questions about what it meant to be a good citizen. New York State had abolished slavery twenty-five years earlier. Did you now capitulate to the new federal statute, which required you to report neighbors who had once been enslaved below the Mason-Dixon line? In Washington, although Henry read the newspapers and discussed the matter at length with other members of Congress, it was hard for him to fully comprehend the fraught mood in his own state. Some acquaintances, knowing that Frances's letters had Henry's undivided attention, asked her to enclose their notes to him, to be sure that he read them. In Frances's mind, the question was not whether she would oppose the Fugitive Slave Act, but how she should go about it.

She was not surprised by the grim gusto with which Daniel Webster, President Fillmore's secretary of state, talked about the government's intention to enforce the new law. In May 1851, Webster traveled to Syracuse, a city he denounced as a "laboratory of abolitionism, libel, and treason." Gripping the iron railing of a narrow balcony overlooking the yard in front of City Hall, Webster called out: "Those who dare to oppose the law are traitors! traitors! traitors!" As he recalled the response, listeners below shouted, "Yes, yes!"

Rev. Samuel J. May, who was in that crowd, described the scene differently. "Indignation," he wrote, "flashed from many eyes in that assembly." Frances knew about May from Martha, from his activism on abolition and women's rights, and from his correspondence with Henry, whom May saw as a key ally in Congress. A member of the Syracuse Vigilance Committee, May punctuated his sermons with reminders that his home was a station on the underground railroad and requests for clothing and money. Speaking to his congregation about the Fugitive Slave Act, he said, "We must trample this infamous law underfoot, be the consequences what they may. It is not for you to choose whether you will or not obey such a law as this. You are as much under obligation not to obey it, as you are not to lie, steal, or commit murder."

On October 1, the government fulfilled Webster's threat. A fugitive slave from Missouri known as Jerry who had lived in Syracuse for a few years was at his place of work in a barrel-making shop when a slave catcher arrived with a posse of deputy U.S. marshals. The marshals shackled Jerry and took him to the office of the U.S. commissioner, Joseph Sabine, who had issued the arrest warrant and was required to oversee a hearing on the case. But the anti-slavery community was far better prepared than Webster expected. Learning of Jerry's arrest, Charles A. Wheaton, a hardware store owner and member of the Vigilance Committee, alerted Gerrit Smith, who was holding a political meeting at the Congregational Church. The ring of the church bell set off a cascading call in the city's places of worship to alert protesters to the abduction.

Smith entered Sabine's office with Rev. Jermain Loguen, who'd once been enslaved in Tennessee and had recently declared of the Fugitive

Slave Act, “I won’t obey it! It outlaws me, and I outlaw it.” Others pushed into the crowded room, shouting and causing so much confusion that Jerry, his wrists in handcuffs, managed to escape, only to be captured a few blocks away. He was taken to the police station, where his feet were shackled and he was put under heavy guard.

Wheaton set out axes, iron rods, and clubs in front of his hardware store, which protesters picked up and hid under their coats in preparation for an assault on the police station. At a hastily organized Vigilance Committee meeting, May advised a peaceful protest, but Loguen argued that they were fighting a war against federal tyranny. If white men wouldn’t take part, “Let fugitives and black men smite down marshals and commissioners.” May offered a prayer: “If anyone is to be injured, let it be against us, and not by us.”

By about 8:00 p.m., only several hours after Jerry’s arrest, the crowd numbered in the thousands. Armed with Wheaton’s axes and clubs, the protesters charged into the building, broke down two doors, and, overwhelming the petrified marshals, took Jerry to the apartment of a Black family in town, where two sisters broke his shackles with a hammer and flatiron and called on a blacksmith to file off the handcuffs. They gave Jerry a dress, shawl, and hood to wear, and directions to an unlikely protector: a pro-slavery butcher who reviled May, but objected even more to the federal government kidnapping an innocent man in his city. The butcher hid Jerry for four days, and, on the night of October 5, armed him with a pistol and drove him out of town in his meat wagon.

Over the next few weeks, Jerry moved through several rural stations on the underground railroad between Syracuse and Lake Ontario, and finally sailed across the lake to Kingston, Canada, on a British schooner. The story was covered nationally, and a newspaper in Savannah, Georgia, warned that if such conspiracies continued, “northerners alone will be responsible for all the ills that may betide this government.”

“The Jerry Rescue” became a point of immense pride in the state, and a rallying cry for abolitionists everywhere. May wrote to Henry, saying that he hoped to be put on trial for planning the rescue, so he could explain to the public that they had been “resisting the execution of a Law so extremely wicked.” Henry welcomed such letters, maintaining a correspondence with Smith and Douglass, too, reasoning that he could not get federal laws changed until abolitionists, speaking from the pulpit, the lyceum, the press, and the street won over more citizens.

Frances noticed that while May was boasting about his role in the Jerry Rescue, his friend Rev. Loguen—a freedom seeker who had made Syracuse his home and was charged with assault with intent to kill—had to flee to Canada. Eventually, twenty-six participants, May among them, were indicted for violating the Fugitive Slave Law. After learning that eight were to be arraigned at the Cayuga County Courthouse, Frances wrote to Henry, "These are all respected men," adding that two local fugitive slaves, fearing a wave of arrests, had left for Canada. Henry returned home for the arraignment, and signed a bail bond for the first Black defendant—an example others followed for the rest. Then he invited the group to the house for refreshments. Henry wrote to Horace Greeley, "The reaction in this state against slavery is signal, and yet I do not see who is to shape or in what way the course of events. We are at sea without rudder or compass." In the end, only a single Black participant was put on trial, and he was acquitted. The other twenty-five defendants were not convicted. May called the Jerry Rescue "the greatest event in the history of Syracuse."

Frances and Lazette watched over their father that fall as his health declined. Bedridden and blind, Judge Miller bore little resemblance to the man who had so lovingly and imperiously ruled over them. He died on November 13, 1851, at the age of seventy-nine. As promised, he left Frances the house and much of the property he'd bought up around town; the rest of the inheritance went to Lazette. The Miller House became the Seward House, but, thanks to the Married Women's Property Act of 1848, it was Frances who retained ownership of the estate. Henry was in Auburn for the funeral, and in December, Frances took Fanny and Will to Washington to spend the winter and early spring with him there, a pattern that she followed in years to come.

Frances had trouble adjusting to her duties as the hostess of a senator, a taxing job for which she had no affinity. Henry saw his formal entertaining—several times a week during the social season, from December through March—as indispensable to his political success, and invitations to his soirées were as prized as those to the White House. Frances planned the elaborate dinners and receptions for members of the diplomatic corps and visitors from abroad, Supreme Court justices, prominent journalists, and politicians from every region. She glided through the rooms, counting the minutes until the end of the evening, smiling politely as women flicked their fans at the men and appraised one another's silks. She wrote in her scrapbook, "The moral & intellectual degradation of woman increases in proportion to the homage paid by men to external charms." By her estimate, dressing and socializing consumed two thirds of the time of upper-class women—making them as vapid as they were presumed to be.

Henry was an impresario of dinner diplomacy, loosening up allies and opponents under the influence of rich meals and good wine, followed by after-dinner brandy, cigars, and often a game of whist. Two regular guests were Senator Jefferson Davis of Mississippi and his wife, Varina, who had been educated in Philadelphia—one of the few women in Washington whose company Frances enjoyed. Henry thought nothing of Davis's attacks on him in the Senate, thinking that if political foes got along outside Congress, they were more likely to overcome their differences. Frances loved Henry's optimism, but Davis seemed to her an intractable southern ideologue. She was proved right a decade later, when Davis was elected president of the Confederate States of America, and Henry served as Abraham Lincoln's secretary of state—each determined to destroy the other side in the Civil War.

In the months after Judge Miller's death, Frances felt homesick in a way that she hadn't since her years at boarding school. She wrote from Washington to Lazette, "Our old home standing alone & deserted in this cold, dreary winter time is continually before me." A few months later, thinking about how she had cared for their father for three decades, she said, "I feel as if my occupation were gone." She added longingly, "We will furnish Grandpa's room, for your room and I cannot but hope that you will be there much of the time to make us all more cheerful."

In Auburn, Frances had Lazette and Martha as confidants. In Washington, she had little time alone with Henry and no close female companions. Her only regular caller that winter was Henry's friend Charles Sumner, the recently elected forty-year-old Free Soil Party senator from Massachusetts. Sumner was a six-foot-two, barrel-chested bachelor with blue eyes and wavy brown hair that resisted the taming influence of a brush. He antagonized enemies, and sometimes friends, with his vanity and sanctimony, but Frances thought he was candid, bold, and sincere.

She also liked the clarity of his politics. Unlike the Whigs, whose southern faction usually held sway, the Free Soilers were single-mindedly opposed to the expansion of slavery. Sumner was candidly contemptuous of politicians who opposed his views, and he defended unpopular causes that Frances cared most about: abolition, women's rights, and universal public education. In 1849, Sumner and Robert Morris, one of the first Black attorneys in the country, argued before the Massachusetts Supreme Court that segregated schools were unconstitutional. The court ruled against them, but six years later, in a historic vote, the state legislature banned racial segregation in public schools. Frances's high regard for Sumner endeared her to him as a woman of unusual discernment. Before long, he became closer to Frances than to Henry, whom he found insufficiently radical.

Sumner often stopped to see Frances on his way home from the Capitol to his rented rooms. Married woman didn't often meet privately with single men, but Frances saw no reason why she shouldn't discuss books and politics with him just as she would with Martha and Lazette. She wrote to Lazette that she was reading a collection of Sumner's speeches about slavery, and that she saw in him "a natural truthfulness of character with a quick perception of right & wrong." He confided to Frances that his colleagues constantly found fault with him: "Sometimes I suffer from Democrats, sometimes from Whigs. Very well. In the consciousness of a life sincerely devoted to truth, I can abide even this. Let me say, that I am unwilling to be regarded as a politician." The statement was calibrated to appeal to Frances. She believed him when he claimed that he would prefer a literary life, and told Lazette she doubted that he would remain in politics for long.

Frances returned to Auburn in May 1852. As she helped Aunt Clara organize her father's papers and dispose of his belongings, she realized that at age forty-seven, she finally had the freedom to run the house as she liked. In Auburn, she'd meekly obeyed her father. In Washington, she had to follow Henry's rules—thus becoming complicit in his accommodations with southerners. He was a public figure and, by extension, so was she. The nation's laws and prejudices had once seemed solid and immutable, but over time she had realized how hidebound the framers were—perpetuating the enslavement of Black Americans and denying women any true autonomy.

Frances had many Black acquaintances in town, and she made sure that Fanny, who was seven, played with children of both races, noting with satisfaction to Lazette that Fanny did not seem to notice her playmates' skin color. Frances was close to Harriet Bogart and her husband, Nicholas. Once enslaved, the Bogarts had long worked for Judge Miller—Harriet as a maid and Nicholas as a coachman—and now Frances and Henry employed them. Harriet Bogart had delivered Frances's children and Lazette's daughter. The couple were agents on the underground railroad, and their trust in Frances helped her to expand her connections. Luke Freeman, a barber who owned two properties in town, one of them across the street from Frances, was the local conductor. Frances knew how the system worked. Lazette and Martha had been part of the railroad for more than a decade. When Lazette lived on East Genesee Street, she had hired a fugitive slave named Jacob as a cook for her family. He told her only that he had "run away from slavery," and he'd left after a few months, saying that he wanted "to go on still further."

In Henry's 1848 speech in Cleveland, he had issued his infamous command, "Extend a cordial welcome to the fugitive who lays his weary limbs at your door." Now Frances did exactly that. Finding at last a "meaningful activity" of the kind Henry had suggested after Cornelia's death, she decided to use the old basement kitchen and dining room to house fugitive slaves. Henry approved the idea, rather enjoying the subterfuge. Who would suspect the very proper Mrs. Seward of being a subversive?

On cold nights, Frances kept a fire going in the hearth downstairs, and when Harriet Bogart let her know that travelers were expected, she had bedding and a hot meal prepared. In the spring and summer, Frances turned the woodshed behind the house into a shelter that she referred to as her dormitory. The Sewards' Universalist friend John Austin wrote in one of his diary entries that at Henry's urging, he collected some money for a man taking refuge in the Sewards' house, and went over to deliver it. Frances was too discreet to put anything in writing about her activities, but on one occasion when Henry was at home and she was away, visiting a friend, he could not resist mentioning the arrival of a pair of unexpected guests: "The 'underground railroad' works wonderfully," he wrote to her. "Two passengers came here last night." Their bulldog, Watch, mistaking them for intruders, growled at one of the men. Henry remarked, "I am against extending suffrage to dogs. They are just like other classes of parvenues."

Since the early 1800s, about two hundred former slaves had settled in

Auburn, first in the segregated neighborhood of New Guinea, along the Owasco Outlet. As they prospered, they spread out into white and immigrant neighborhoods. Frances and Henry helped speed along the process of integration by building frame houses on the lots they owned, and selling them inexpensively to immigrant and Black families. The Bogarts had bought a house from them on Miller Street, half a mile away. Because New York law prevented Black men from voting unless they owned at least $250 worth of property, the acquisition of a house or land was a necessary step toward full citizenship.

The railroad tightly guarded its secrets, and no one recorded how Harriet Tubman got to know Martha and Frances, but they came together around this time, almost certainly through Lucretia. Abolitionists, closely knit but geographically scattered, depended on reliable personal contacts across the country. Women, underrated as a matter of course, were less likely to fall under suspicion. Harriet was living in Philadelphia, and Auburn was a convenient stop in Central New York. During one of Martha's visits to Philadelphia, Lucretia likely introduced her to Harriet. Martha, in turn, must have introduced Harriet to Frances. In short order, Martha and Frances became Harriet's collaborators and two of her most devoted friends.

Like others who knew Harriet, Martha and Frances were transfixed by her personal story. The sale of three of her sisters. The scars on her neck from Miss Susan's lash. The dent in her skull and the blackouts from the hurled iron weight. The futile discovery that she, her mother, and her siblings were illegally enslaved. Her husband's refusal to accompany her, and the solitary walk to Philadelphia. Her plea to God not to abandon her. Others subjected to such adversities would be embittered or broken. Harriet, who said she was just following God's instructions, finished one extraction in Maryland only to plan the next one.

Although Harriet could not read, she had memorized long passages of the Bible and literally applied its teachings to her life. To Frances, Harriet brought to mind Isaiah: "Forget the former things; do not dwell in the past. I am making a way in the wilderness and streams in the wasteland"; and Corinthians: "God hath chosen the weak things of the world to confound the things which are mighty." This small, unstoppable woman, eighteen years younger than Frances, unafraid of the slave power of the

South and the lawmakers in Washington, embodied the urgency and the potential of abolition.

Members of Auburn's Black community routinely sent people who needed money or jobs to Frances. In May 1852, she took in a young freedom seeker named John, tutored him, and paid for his books and room and board at a private school in McGrawville. The school was part of an integrated, coeducational college that had opened three years earlier, with support from Smith and Douglass. To be sure that John got there safely, Frances sent thirteen-year-old Will to accompany him. In July, Frances wrote to Henry that a man named William, who was heading to Washington, was trying to buy his daughter's freedom. She had given him some money, and, telling him to pay a call on the senator, promised that Henry would give him more: "He is very desirous that I should employ his daughter when he gets her which I have engaged to do conditionally if you approve."

Frances had far less faith than Henry did in the Whigs. In 1852, Henry and Weed supported the party's candidate for president, General Winfield Scott, a war hero, like Zachary Taylor in 1848, who had no strong political views. Henry said that Scott would appeal to moderates in the North and the South, but the two sections increasingly seemed like separate countries, and it wasn't clear what the Whigs could do about it. Frances asked Henry to give Sumner a message that was directed just as much to him: she found the party "not so singularly ingenious" as she once had. In a second letter that night, she instructed Henry to tell Scott to stop his public endorsements of the Clay Compromise. Referring to the Whigs' fretful attempts to soothe their southern members, she asked, "Why can we not have a candidate about whose Anti Slavery principles we have no doubt."

At the same time, she faulted Douglass and other abolitionists for a harsh new militancy, which she thought could backfire. Writing about the Fugitive Slave Law, Douglass said, "The land will be filled with violence and blood till this law is repealed." In August 1852, he declared at the Free Soil convention, "The only way to make the Fugitive Slave Law a dead letter is to make half a dozen or more dead kidnappers." Frances wrote to Henry, "I wish Fred Douglass would not make such violent speeches, which only disgust moderate people and encourage the advocates of Slavery."

In the summer of 1852, Frances wrote regularly to Sumner, who made his first speech in the Senate in August. Introducing a bill he had written to repeal the Fugitive Slave Law, he said what no Whig—not even Henry—would say just then: the framers never meant slavery to be a national institution, and they saw it for the evil it was. Frances told Sumner, "It is a noble plea for a righteous cause." To her disappointment, Henry abstained from voting for the bill, reasoning that it had no chance of passing, and that before the election, he must not do anything to upset the Cotton Whigs.

The gesture was meaningless. Winfield Scott, brought down by the Whigs' divide over slavery, badly lost the presidential election to Franklin Pierce of New Hampshire, a Democrat who had campaigned against the "agitation" over slavery. Pierce won twenty-seven states; Scott just four. Weed called the results a "Waterloo defeat." Henry J. Raymond, the editor of the recently founded *New-York Daily Times*, which became *The New York Times* in 1857, privately predicted the death of the Whig Party. Sumner impatiently wrote to Henry, "Now is the time for a new organization. Out of the chaos the party of freedom must arise."

Henry, though, persisted in saying that the Whigs could be resurrected. In Washington over Christmas, Frances learned that he was contemplating a last-ditch effort: an alliance between the Whigs and the Free Soil Party. On December 29, he invited the Senate's entire Free Soil delegation to dinner: John Hale of New Hampshire, Sumner of Massachusetts, and Salmon Chase of Ohio, who had been elected in 1849. Frances could not understand why Henry refused to see what was obvious to his abolitionist friends: the North would only accept a future in which slavery did not exist.

9

Reading *Uncle Tom's Cabin*

1852–1853

Eliza crossing the Ohio River, from *Uncle Tom's Cabin; or, Negro Life in the Slave States of America*, Clarke and Co., London, 1852

Harriet Beecher Stowe's *Uncle Tom's Cabin* was a pious melodrama by a forty-year-old mother of seven who described herself as "about as thin and dry as a pinch of snuff." The novel was not distinguished by subtlety or fine writing, but it was a powerful polemic at a moment of national reckoning. Second only to the Bible, it became the bestselling book of the nineteenth century. Three hundred thousand copies sold in the United States the first year, and in the United Kingdom, 1.5 million copies. In Sumner's Senate speech demanding the repeal of the Fugitive Slave Law, he cast Stowe as a heroine: "A woman inspired by Christian genius enters the lists, like another Joan of Arc, and with marvelous powers sweeps the chords of the popular heart." Garrison wrote appreciatively in *The Liberator*, "If the shrewdest abolitionist among us had prepared a drama with a view to make the strongest anti-slavery impression, he could scarcely have done the work better." Douglass wrote that the book had reached "the universal soul of humanity," and he compared Stowe to Shakespeare—one of "the favored ones of earth."

Frances recognized one of Stowe's characters: "honest old John Van Trompe," a lightly fictionalized depiction of a poor farmer, John Van Zandt, who had been caught a decade earlier assisting a group of fugitive slaves near his home in Ohio. Salmon Chase, then a lawyer in Cincinnati, represented Van Zandt. Admiring Henry's defense in the Freeman case, Chase had asked him to help argue an appeal before the Supreme Court. Chase wrote that he considered Seward to be one of the first statesmen of the country: "His course in the Van Zandt case has been generous and noble; but his action in the Freeman case, considering his own personal position and circumstances, was magnanimous in the highest degree."

John Van Zandt lived outside Cincinnati, along an underground railroad route from Kentucky to Canada. One night in April 1842, armed slave catchers stopped him while he was ferrying nine freedom seekers in his wagon. Two escaped; the others were returned to slavery. Eight years before the Fugitive Slave Act of 1850, the slaveholder, Wharton Jones, sued Van Zandt for violating the original Fugitive Slave Act, of 1793. Henry, addressing the Supreme Court, asked the justices to reconsider the constitutional protection of slavery in light of the Declaration of Independence, which, he argued, denied "a right of property in man." The Court ruled against Van Zandt, who died later that year. Chase called *Uncle Tom's Cabin* "Van Zandt's best monument."

Stowe's message was simple: it was every Christian's duty to demand an end to slavery. She dramatized this lesson through her two protagonists. Eliza flees slavery from a farm in Kentucky with her young son in her arms. She scrambles down the bank of the Ohio River, pursued by a slave trader, leaping from one ice floe to another, stumbling and slipping. "She saw nothing, felt nothing," Stowe wrote, "till dimly, as in a dream, she saw the Ohio side and a man helping her up the bank." The man, large, warmhearted Van Trompe, takes her to his farmhouse, where, he promises, "I've got seven sons, each six foot high," and if anyone comes, "they'll be ready for 'em." Eliza eventually reunites with her husband, and they reach Canada. In the second plotline, Uncle Tom heads south from Kentucky, and he is sold and bought several times. The final buyer, Simon Legree, tortures and kills him, but fails to destroy his faith in God. As Frances wrote to Henry, quoting the Unitarian minister William Ellery Channing, "'To look unmoved on the degradation and wrongs of a fellow creature, because burned by a fiercer sun, proves us strangers to justice and love.'"

In Britain, the book kindled an even more tremendous response. The Earl of Shaftesbury wrote in his diary that he was "touched to the heart's core" by *Uncle Tom's Cabin*, and that he wanted to write "An Address from the Women of England to the Women of America," hoping to "stir their souls and sympathies." He did so, and women across England, Scotland, and Ireland started a petition campaign to accompany the address, which urged their "sisters" across the ocean to work in a concerted way "for the removal of this affliction from the Christian world." The address was published in *The Liberator*, *The New York Times*, and *The National Era*, an abolitionist newspaper in Washington.

The women of Britain knew how persuasive such a campaign could be. In 1833, culminating a nine-year campaign to end slavery in the British colonies, the female anti-slavery societies alone had presented Parliament with petitions containing 298,785 signatures, nearly a quarter of the total number of names, and Parliament abolished the system later that year. In early 1853, during Stowe's lecture tour in Britain, the Earl of Shaftesbury held a reception for her at Stafford House, the sumptuous London residence of the Duchess of Sutherland, who led the "Stafford House" campaign. Women in the United Kingdom who had no experience in anti-slavery activism gathered more than half a million signatures, which were bound in twenty-six volumes and shipped to Stowe's home.

Frances wrote to Lazette, "The Abolitionists & women's rights women will act for us," but "are we sure that we can join them & is it right for us to be silent?" The question expressed the conundrum of her life: how to follow her conscience without damaging Henry's career, or her own sense of what was seemly. As if divining Frances's dilemma, Sumner stopped to see her at Henry's house in Washington in mid-January 1853, showing her a letter from a Congregationalist minister in New Haven. The minister suggested that American women select highly placed figures in every large city to organize the kind of petition campaign that had been so successful in Britain. Sumner suggested that Frances lead a group in Washington. Startled by the proposal, which went well beyond putting her name on paper, she refused him: Henry was certain to object, and she didn't want to do anything that would be seen as "extravagant or unwomanly."

After Sumner left, Frances changed her mind. Flooded with thoughts about the treatment of enslaved people just steps from her door, she decided there was little danger of doing too much. That evening, she told Henry that if she was asked to sign the women's petition, she would feel bound to do so. He strongly advised against it. Still hoping to salvage the Whig Party, he counted on her to be discreet in her political activities. Frances complained to Lazette, "He seemed to think that duty would depend upon circumstances—& that I, or you and I alone, joining the abolitionists would do the cause more harm than good. Here we differ." Henry prevailed. She neither headed up the undertaking, as Sumner had hoped, nor signed the petition. Frustrated by her own ambivalence and by the restrictions on her as a political wife, Frances told Henry, "I cannot be idle," and she took on an issue that he supported: Black education.

An acquaintance of theirs, Myrtilla Miner, had recently founded the Normal School for Colored Girls in Washington, and she needed help. Miner, an evangelical Christian from Rochester, New York, had gone to teach in Mississippi in 1846. The practice of slavery had so disturbed her that she became seriously ill, and, convinced she was dying, she returned to New York. When she recovered, she decided that God had sent her a message. She knew Henry from his gubernatorial days in 1841, when she'd pressed him about literacy for girls. Writing to him in 1850, she said that she felt it was her "mission on Earth" to help "the oppressed and the afflicted, the castdown & downtrodden colored race in our own free country." Miner, like Frances and Henry, saw education as the best way to prepare the next generation for emancipation.

When Miner was planning her school, she went to see Douglass at his newspaper office in Rochester, expecting his congratulations and advice.

Instead, he said her project would "bring only persecution and death." It was hard enough to provide a decent education for Black children in the North, where their schools were poorly funded and overcrowded: Douglass had been trying, without success, to convince Rochester's white teachers and school board to integrate their classrooms. Undeterred, Miner found allies among Black abolitionists in Washington. John F. Cook Sr., once enslaved and now an influential member of the city's African American educational and religious community, enrolled his daughter as one of Miner's first students. Frances and Henry provided financial assistance and moral support for the school, as did Lucretia and James Mott, the Reverend May, Wendell Phillips, and other reformers.

By early 1852, Miner, who was thirty-seven, was teaching forty-one free Black students, between seven and sixteen years old. She was a taskmistress, drilling the girls in arithmetic, reading, and history; giving lessons in domestic science, diet, and hygiene; and teaching them religion. They learned about abolition and women's rights by reading Douglass's autobiography and *The North Star*, Garrison's *Liberator*, and Greeley's *Tribune*.

Frances did not warm to Miner, who talked about redeeming her students from a state of degradation—"bringing out & developing these rubbish-hidden treasures." Nevertheless, it took a certain type of personality to do the work Miner did, and Frances respected her "courage and firmness." Frances took Fanny with her when she visited the school, with gifts of books and mittens, and she asked William Johnson to park the Seward carriage outside the building so that the senator's support for the school would be noted.

David Wright, who had once said that equal pay for women would be a curse to the community, gave Martha more leeway in her reform work than Frances received from Henry, a supporter of women's rights. Martha noticed this bit of hypocrisy. David didn't object when she went off to work with Stanton and Anthony, as long as Eliza was at home to help. Martha liked to think that her independence made David somewhat more self-sufficient at home, which was sure to benefit Willy and Frank. The Fourth National Woman's Rights Convention was to take place in October 1853, in Cleveland, the center of western reform movements, and she spent the summer helping to set the agenda and invite the speakers.

Martha, working closely with Stanton and Anthony, had changed her mind about Anthony, whose sternness masked her vulnerability. Anthony once confessed that she had moments of faintheartedness: "There is so much, amid all that is so hopeful, to discourage & dishearten—and I feel *alone*." She had her own bedroom in the Stantons' house, where she helped with the children as she and Stanton conferred. The two formed a smoothly functioning team: Stanton was the writer and thinker, Anthony the organizer and campaigner—hiring lecture halls, pasting up flyers, making travel arrangements for speakers, and giving talks herself. Anthony, like Martha, found public speaking an ordeal. Her lectures, delivered in a hammer-on-anvil style, lacked Stanton's flair, but they were hard to ignore. As Henry Stanton characterized the partnership, Susan stirred the puddings, Elizabeth stirred up Susan, and Susan stirred the world. Late in life, Stanton found a metaphor she preferred: she forged the thunderbolts, and Anthony fired them.

Martha's common sense checked Stanton's and Anthony's more extreme impulses, and she defused disagreements with humor. Anthony later said that she and Stanton always knew they had made the right decisions once Martha gave them her blessing. Given Henry's edict that Frances keep a low public profile, and her own disinclination to step out of bounds, Frances did not attend what Stanton called the women's "councils of war," but she sent her ideas through Martha, "and sometimes," Stanton said, encouraging suggestions from Seward himself, "from whose writings we often gleaned grand and radical sentiments." When Lucretia was visiting, she "added the dignity of her presence at many of these important consultations," but she "was uniformly in favor of toning down our fiery pronunciamentos. For Miss Anthony and myself, the English language had no words strong enough to express the indignation we felt at the prolonged injustice to women."

The framers had shown in 1787, when they gathered in Philadelphia for the Constitutional Convention, that such conclaves could be tools of revolution. Martha enjoyed that notion, as she did the conduct of business and the camaraderie at the women's annual meetings—even if she was bored by some of the sessions. By now she could rattle off every issue, telling Lucretia that she had heard so often how "the law classifies women with children and idiots, and that the man has the *custody* of the wife, and that the men who enforce the laws are mean men, but not meaner than the laws, that it is not quite so fresh as when I first listened to it."

Martha was an officer at the Cleveland convention, which drew fifteen hundred people. Garrison, one of the featured speakers, said, "The boasted human rights that we hear so much about are simply the rights of woman of which we hear so little." Lucretia, able to still the anticipatory buzz in the hall simply by walking to the front of the platform, calmly attacked the power of "Church and State" and "priest craft" for oppressing women. The *New York Herald* reliably weighed in, describing the convention as "a gathering of unsexed women, unsexed in mind, all of them publicly propounding a doctrine that they should be allowed to step out of their appropriate sphere to the neglect of those duties which both human and divine law have assigned to them."

After the convention, Martha accompanied the Motts to Cincinnati, where Lucretia and Lucy Stone, the young Oberlin graduate and activist, had been asked to speak. They packed a lecture hall with thirteen hundred people, who applauded Lucretia's startling description of the Bible as "a giant scarecrow, across the pathway of human progress." From Cincinnati, Martha, Lucretia, and James took a steamboat up the Ohio River to Maysville, Kentucky, the town where, decades earlier, young Harriet Beecher had witnessed the slave auction that inspired her book. That stretch of the river, with Kentucky to the south and Ohio to the north, was familiar to every reader of *Uncle Tom's Cabin*. Maysville also happened to be the home of John Pelham, one of Martha's two slaveholding brothers-in-law from her first marriage. Lucretia was to give a talk at the Maysville courthouse, and John invited Martha and the Motts to stay with him and his unmarried sisters.

Martha looked forward to the visit. She had kept up with the Pelhams after Peter's death, and she encouraged her daughter Marianna to exchange letters and visits with her aunts, uncles, and cousins, sure that the ties between the two families were strong enough to weather the tempest over slavery. The steamboat was delayed, but when they arrived late that night, John was waiting patiently at the landing with his carriage, and at the end of their moonlit drive, his sisters had a large fire going in the parlor. Lucretia didn't know the Pelhams, but wrote to her family in Philadelphia, "We were made so entirely at home by their Kentucky hospitality, that we soon felt like old acquaintances."

The next morning, John told Martha that he hoped Mrs. Mott would not allude to slavery in her talk. Martha replied that the anti-slavery cause was eminently religious, that Lucretia felt herself called by God, and that it was not for her to come between her sister and her sense of duty. At the courthouse, Lucretia chose a common abolitionist theme—the effects of slavery on slavers as well as slaves. A correspondent for *The Liberator* reported, "No crying evil of the day escaped exposure and condemnation." Nonetheless, to the Pelhams' relief, Lucretia—grandmotherly, devout, and accompanied by her congenial husband—was well received, and she consented to give another talk that evening, "On Woman." She said, to general approval, that women had every right to be shown the same respect as men, including the right to be heard in public. Writing to her family, she said: "A great gathering & apparent satisfaction."

Martha reveled in her freedom to travel. Rather than return home, she accompanied the Motts to Philadelphia and stayed with them for two months, long enough to attend the American Anti-Slavery Society's twentieth-anniversary convention in December. During that time, Eliza, who had married a young Auburn entrepreneur and had a baby to care for, was responsible for eleven-year-old Willy and nine-year-old Frank, and for all the meals. Martha wrote to David saying she hoped that he did not need her or miss her at all, and that Eliza would not "sink under her accumulated duties."

She worried about Tallman. When he was sixteen, she had sent him to live temporarily with the Motts, hoping that they would be a steadying influence, and that he would find a job in Philadelphia. He had abandoned an early dream of going to sea like his Coffin ancestors, but become dazzled by stories of the California gold rush, and in 1851, at nineteen, he had set off for the West Coast. Having no luck panning, he had turned to raising cattle and then hogs, but each venture met with misfortune. "I guess he will come out right after a while," Martha noted dubiously, "& learn a great deal from experience—that best of teachers they say," adding that she would have preferred a gentler instructor.

The abolitionist and women's rights movements remained closely linked. Garrison, Douglass, and Phillips spoke at the women's conventions, and Lucretia, Lucy Stone, and Ernestine Rose at the American Anti-Slavery Society. In Philadelphia, Martha went to a convention-sponsored debate, between a Presbyterian minister who supported retrograde biblical teachings about women and a radical British lecturer who opposed them. It quickly turned nasty. When Martha saw Garrison that evening, she humorously reported to him about the sorry behavior of both debaters. He appreciated Martha's "keen sense of the ludicrous," and asked her to write up her account for *The Liberator*. Martha, now a reformer of some note herself, was gripped by her old insecurities. She told him she hadn't taken notes and couldn't depend on her memory. Garrison persisted. Believing that women too often, "through a misconception of duty," excused themselves from fully engaging in abolition, he told her that he would like her to be a regular correspondent for the paper. She replied, "I should have nothing to correspond about."

Although Martha did not write the article, she gave Garrison a copy of a letter she'd written to David about the debate, which Garrison published. She made quick work of both speakers. The Presbyterian spluttered, "Am I to be put down by an Englishman?," but he managed to rouse "the mob spirit." The Englishman, faced with a crowd of menacing Americans, had to make a hasty retreat. "Protected by the police and a few of his friends," Martha wrote, he "escaped in safety."

On Christmas morning, 1853, Henry woke up in Washington to a crystalline day, all alone. He wrote to Frances, "There is neither doll, riding-whip, watch, or watch-dog, bon-bon, or sugar-plum in all this vast house, from kitchen to garret. I am a bachelor, without wife or children." Frances was in Auburn with Fanny, who had a bad cold and a worrisome ache in her side. She feared—accurately, as it turned out—that her daughter had inherited Hannah Miller's weak lungs. Frances herself was experiencing one of her undiagnosable disorders, describing it to Henry as a "deranged state of my nervous system." Frederick was there for the holiday, with his fiancée, Anna Wharton, a nineteen-year-old society girl from Albany.

Anna was the eldest child of a prominent druggist. People gossiped about the match, saying that the very ambitious Mrs. Wharton had ensnared Frederick for Anna. Frances had met Anna only once before, and she observed to Henry a few days before Christmas that although she was not pretty, she was quiet and gentle, adding archly, "I believe these are esteemed desirable qualities for wives in general." Fanny, who was nine, old enough to understand the message of *Uncle Tom's Cabin*, wrote to her father that she was reading the book, and that her mother had given her a clever puzzle, "Uncle Tom's Cabin Dissected," which became a three-dimensional cabin when assembled.

Like Martha and other abolitionists, Frances was indoctrinating her younger children in the ideas driving the two predominant reform movements. *Uncle Tom's Cabin* had inspired stage adaptations in New York City, Philadelphia, Chicago, and other cities—introducing many more thousands of people to the evils of slavery. Garrison, after seeing the play performed in New York, wrote that abolitionism was no longer a creed for the very few: "O, it was a sight worth seeing, those ragged, coatless men and boys in the pit (the very *material* of which mobs are made) cheering the strongest and the sublimest anti-slavery message." Thirteen-year-old Ellen Wright, who was visiting her mother and cousins, saw the play with Martha in Philadelphia. Martha found the stage version didactic and mawkish, but she told David, "One is glad to hear such good sentiments & to see Anti Slavery patiently listened to where it would not have been borne a few years ago."

But not everyone praised *Uncle Tom's Cabin*. One South Carolina aristocrat, who ran her family's cotton plantation, wrote a review in a southern quarterly attacking Stowe for her "gross vulgarity and absolute falsehood," and her risible misunderstanding of southern manners and idiom. There were good Christian slaveholders, she said, who owned slaves because they thought it right to do so, "for the good of the slave—for the good of the master—for the good of the world." Harriet Tubman was one of the few abolitionist critics. She was grateful to white opponents of slavery, especially those, like Stowe, who, as a young woman in Ohio, had sheltered freedom seekers, and who now subjected herself to scathing put-downs by southerners. Harriet, who was still living and working in Philadelphia, objected to the book because it didn't go nearly far enough in its condemnation of slavery. Nor did she like the idea of turning it into a form of entertainment. Refusing to see the play, she said, "I've heard *Uncle Tom's Cabin* read, and I tell you Mrs. Stowe's pen hasn't begun to paint what slavery is as I have seen it at the far South. I've seen the real thing, and I don't want to see it on no stage or in no theater."

10

Harriet Tubman's Maryland Crusade

1851–1857

"MOSES" ARRIVES WITH SIX PASSENGERS.

"NOT ALLOWED TO SEEK A MASTER;"—"VERY DEVILISH;"—FATHER "LEAVES TWO LITTLE SONS;"—"USED HARD;"—"FEARED FALLING INTO THE HANDS OF YOUNG HEIRS," ETC. JOHN CHASE, ALIAS DANIEL FLOYD; BENJAMIN ROSS, ALIAS JAMES STEWART; HENRY ROSS, ALIAS LEVIN STEWART; PETER JACKSON, ALIAS STAUNCH TILGHMAN; JANE KANE, ALIAS CATHARINE KANE, AND ROBERT ROSS.

The coming of these passengers was heralded by Thomas Garrett as follows:

THOMAS GARRETT'S LETTER.

WILMINGTON, 12 mo. 29th, 1854.

ESTEEMED FRIEND, J. MILLER MCKIM:—We made arrangements last night, and sent away Harriet Tubman, with six men and one woman to Allen Agnew's, to be forwarded across the country to the city. Harriet, and one of the men had worn their shoes off their feet, and I gave them two dollars to help fit them out, and directed a carriage to be hired at my expense, to take them out, but do not yet know the expense. I now have two more from the lowest county in Maryland, on the Peninsula, upwards of one hundred miles. I will try to get one of our trusty colored men to take them to-morrow morning to the Anti-slavery office. You can then pass them on. THOMAS GARRETT.

HARRIET TUBMAN had been their "Moses," but not in the sense that Andrew Johnson was the "Moses of the colored people." She had faithfully gone down into Egypt, and had delivered these six bondmen by her own heroism. Harriet was a woman of no pretensions, indeed, a more

From William Still's *The Underground Railroad*, Philadelphia, 1872

Harriet's life might have turned out differently if her husband hadn't been disloyal. She made her first trip back to Dorchester County from Philadelphia in late 1851, at the height of the furor over the Fugitive Slave Act. For two years, she had imagined sharing her life with John Tubman: having children and raising them in a free city. In anticipation of their reunion, she spent part of her meager savings on a new set of clothes for him, but when she got near their old home, and sent a message that she was there, she learned that he had taken another wife. Shattered, she later told her friend Ednah Dow Cheney, a Boston intellectual and philanthropist, that she was overcome with rage, and wanted to "go right in and make all the trouble she could," but then realized "how foolish it was just for temper to make mischief." Practical even in despair, she led a group of slaves to Philadelphia, reasoning that if John could do without her, she could do without him. She explained that she simply "dropped him out of her heart." Concluding that God had other plans for her, she dedicated herself to returning to the Eastern Shore as often as necessary, until she had brought away the rest of her family and as many other enslaved people as she could.

Harriet funded her operations through her day jobs in Philadelphia and Cape May, New Jersey, and through the contributions of anti-slavery societies and donors such as Cheney. In the 1850s, Harriet conducted a dozen forays to the Eastern Shore, guiding to safety about seventy people. She provided advice about escape routes and safe houses to some sixty more. Intrepid but exceedingly cautious, she concealed her identity to all but a few, whom she referred to as "confidential friends all along the road." Free and enslaved Blacks in Dorchester and Caroline counties talked among themselves about a woman who moved in and out of the state without detection, leading some to believe that she had supernatural powers, a gift they called "the charm." They called her "Moses," which had the advantage of keeping her identity hidden to those outside anti-slavery circles and burnishing her legend within them.

One of Tubman's most valued underground railroad associates was Thomas Garrett, whom she met around 1852. A genial middle-aged Quaker with a full, square face and a generously cushioned midriff, he ran a hardware and steel business in Wilmington, Delaware. Garrett fed, clothed, and gave money to freedom seekers and then sent them thirty miles north to Philadelphia, where William Still, the head of the city's Vigilant Committee, took over. Four years earlier, Garrett had been successfully sued by two slaveholders for stealing a family of eight from Queen Anne's County, Maryland. Court records show that Garrett paid a fine of $1,500 ($49,000 in 2020), which bankrupted him. He said of the sentence, "Judge, thou has not left me a dollar, but I wish to say to thee and to all in this courtroom that if any one knows a fugitive who wants shelter and a friend, send him to Thomas Garrett and he will befriend him." Harriet and Garrett had an affectionate relationship, and Harriet invariably stopped at his home on her way into and out of Maryland.

Garrett kept a running tally of the people he assisted, telling an associate in Ohio, "My slave list is now 2,038. Still they go. Love to thy wife and all the friends of suffering humanity the world over." Garrett wrote regularly about Harriet's sagacity and bravery, and her humility, telling his British patrons at the Edinburgh Ladies' Emancipation Society: "She does not know, or appears not to know, that she has done anything worth notice. Harriet has a good deal of the old fashion Quaker about her."

Working through intermediaries, Harriet issued detailed instructions for her expeditions about the time and place to meet, choosing Black graveyards and other sites unfrequented by whites. She usually traveled in the winter, when the long nights and frozen ground impeded tracking by dogs. The Christmas holidays were best, when slaves were permitted to visit their families on other farms, and owners, sluggish from heavy food and drink, were less likely to notice disappearances. Armed with a pistol, Harriet tried to leave with her passengers on Saturday nights, because newspapers, with advertisements for runaways, weren't printed until Monday; and she hired accomplices to tear down any reward notices posted in the vicinity. Harriet told Cheney she could tell time "by the stars, and find her way by natural signs as well as any hunter." She credited her success at eluding capture to God's protection, and to a sixth sense she said she had inherited from her father, who had prophesied the Mexican War. She explained, "When danger is near, it appears like my heart goes flutter, flutter." Cheney believed that Harriet's faith in God lifted her "up above all doubt and anxiety into serene trust and faith."

Cheney asked her what she did when someone had second thoughts and wanted to turn back. She replied that she imposed strict discipline on her followers: "If he was weak enough to give out, he'd be weak enough to betray us all, and all who had helped us; and do you think I'd let so many die just for one coward man?" One passenger, whose feet were sore and swollen, gave out on the second night. The others bathed his feet and tried to reason with him, but he said he'd rather go back, and die if he must. "I told the boys to get their guns ready, and shoot him," she said. "They'd have done it in a minute; but when he heard that, he jumped right up and went on as well as anybody."

Late in 1854, Harriet learned that Eliza Brodess intended to sell the three brothers she hadn't yet taken away. Arriving in Dorchester County, she was told that they were to be auctioned off the day after Christmas.

She got word to them to meet her on Christmas Eve in the corncrib by Ben and Rit's cabin at Thompson's Big House at Poplar Neck. She spent a cold, rainy day in the cramped space with Henry, Ben and his fiancée, and two other young men. Robert arrived late because his wife, Mary, had just gone into labor with their third child, a girl they named Harriet. Mary clung to Robert, begging him not to leave, but he promised to find a way for her and the children to join him later in the North.

Harriet had let only her father know of her plan, and she swore her brothers to secrecy—sure that her mother would cry out at the boys' departure and raise an alarm at the plantation house. Rit prepared a pig for Christmas dinner as usual, and Harriet watched through the chinks in the corncrib as her mother came outside repeatedly, looking down the road for her boys. Harriet's father found a moment to bring them some food, and after dark, she and her brothers crept up to the cabin to catch a final glimpse of Rit. She sat by the fire, her head on her hand, rocking and praying.

That night, Ben accompanied them for the first few miles, wearing a handkerchief over his eyes so that he could swear convincingly, when questioned, that he hadn't seen them. Harriet's brothers guided him, on either arm, to the end of the road. When they left him, he stood there until their footsteps faded, then took off the handkerchief and hurried back to tell Rit that their sons were heading north with Harriet.

One of her routes was along the Choptank River, to the Mason-Dixon line near Sandtown, Delaware. The trips took from three days to several weeks, depending on whether she was being followed. She hid her passengers in the woods and marshes during the days, living on berries and stolen chickens, cows' milk, and vegetables, proceeding over the Chesapeake and Delaware Canal and on to New Castle and Wilmington. Once, she and six freedom seekers hid in "potato holes" in a field, covering themselves with dirt, before their pursuers walked by, just a few feet away. Frostbite was a menace, as were the spiny seedpods of sweet gum trees on the forest floor. Their flax shirts chafed at their arms and torsos until they bled. Harriet felt a measure of safety only when she reached Garrett's house in Wilmington. On the trip with her brothers, Ben's fiancée, and a few others they picked up along the way, she and one of her passengers wore out their shoes. Garrett gave them two dollars for new ones, and hired a carriage, which took them to an agent in Chester County, Pennsylvania.

William Still welcomed the group at the Philadelphia Anti-Slavery

Society on December 29, 1854, and added the account of their lives to his underground railroad ledger. Ben, age twenty-eight, told him that Eliza Brodess was "very Devilish," forcing her slaves to "work hard and fare meagerly, to support his mistress's family in idleness and luxury." Robert, thirty-five, said that he had been treated no better than "a dumb brute." Harriet and her brothers continued on to Albany, then across New York State, and, finally, north to St. Catharines, Canada, arriving in time to celebrate the New Year in another country.

Five months later, in May 1855, Tubman traveled to Baltimore to rescue a young woman named Tilly who wanted to join her fiancé in Canada. After dropping off Tilly in Wilmington, she turned around and went back for her sister Rachel, who, aside from Harriet's sisters lost to the Deep South decades earlier, was her only sibling still enslaved. But Rachel wouldn't leave without her children, Ben and Angerine, who were on different farms, and Harriet, after waiting for ten days, finally left without them, escorting another group instead.

In Philadelphia in March 1857, when preparing to try again, Harriet confronted another crisis. Eight armed freedom seekers from Dorchester County had made a daring jailbreak in Dover, Delaware, and her father was suspected of having assisted them. "The Dover Eight," as the escape was known, was read by abolitionists as a tale of audacious resistance, and by Dorchester County slaveholders, who held an emergency meeting to "devise means for a better protection of the slave property," as evidence of the rising exodus of runaways. Six men and two women, carrying knives and pistols, reportedly had taken shelter with Harriet's father. The group had paid eight dollars to Thomas Otwell, a Black agent Harriet had recommended—a rare instance when she trusted a weak link in the railroad. Otwell was supposed to take them to a safe house in Camden, Delaware. Instead, he'd led them to the Dover jail, hoping for a share of the $3,000 in reward money. The eight overpowered the jailer, and found their way safely to the North.

Harriet, concerned about her father's suspected role in the escape, set out to rescue him and Rit, but she was delayed by increased slave patrols and bad storms, and didn't manage to get there until the end of May. The journey posed unusual challenges. The vast majority of freedom seekers were young men who were strong enough for the rigors of the trip. Ben and Rit were elderly. They had never left Maryland, and Harriet's father said he must take his broadaxe and other tools, and her mother, her feather bedtick. Harriet procured an old horse, and created a buggy from cast-off chaise wheels and two boards, placing one on the axle as a seat for her parents, and the other below, as a footrest. On June 4, they reached Wilmington, where Garrett gave Harriet thirty dollars.

William Still interviewed her parents in his office in Philadelphia. They gave him a full report about their treatment under the Brodesses, Anthony Thompson, and Thompson's son, and spoke about their sorrow over the "portion of their children" sold to Georgia. Still wrote: "These two travelers had nearly reached their three score years and ten under the yoke. Nevertheless, they seemed delighted at the idea of going to a free country to enjoy freedom, if only for a short time—not many of those so advanced in years ever got to Canada." Harriet deposited them safely in St. Catharines, where they joined their three sons and Ben Jr.'s fiancée.

When Harriet was in Maryland, she helped to plot the largest escapes yet from Dorchester County. In October 1857, seven months after the Dover Eight jailbreak, more than forty people fled over three weeks—a crisis derisively described in northern newspapers as one of many "stampedes of slaves." Among the freedom seekers were a couple from Cambridge: Nat and Lizzie Amby, who, presumably at Harriet's suggestion, went on to Auburn, where they chose to spend their lives. As the nation convulsed over slavery, Harriet kept returning to Maryland, methodically removing the foundations of slavery a few people at a time.

11

The Race to the Territory

1854

Lawrence, Kansas, pen sketch, 1854

Henry sounded troubled in his letters home early in 1854, confirming Frances's sense that the national turmoil over slavery could not be contained. On January 4, Senator Stephen A. Douglas, a Democrat of Illinois, introduced the Kansas-Nebraska Act. Douglas designed the bill in large part to ensure a northern route for the transcontinental railroad, but it also would repeal the Missouri Compromise of 1820 and extend slavery into the West. The locus of the debate was a windswept region called the Nebraska Territory, known to most people simply as "Indian Country." A wilderness that extended north from Kansas to the Canadian border, it included the future states of Colorado, Wyoming, the Dakotas, and Montana. The land was inhabited by the Kansa, Pawnee, Osage, and other tribes of the Great Plains who had been forced there under the Indian Removal Act of 1830. Now, as plans for the railroad accelerated, settlers were pushing farther west in greater numbers, and the indigenous people were again violently displaced. Under the lines drawn by the Missouri Compromise, Nebraska would enter the Union as a free state, which southerners would not accept. California's entry into the Union already had upset the balance between slave and free states. Douglas proposed that two territories be created—Kansas and Nebraska—and that the voters there decide whether their new states would be free or slave, under the policy of popular sovereignty.

Douglas, who had brokered the Clay Compromise of 1850, wasn't a southerner, but he could think like one, and as the chairman of the Senate's Committee on Territories, he had the influence to shape the nature of governance in the West. Introducing the Kansas-Nebraska Act, Douglas claimed that popular sovereignty was the only way to expand an empire based on democratic ideals, and that the law, once and for all, would dissolve the antagonism between the two sections of the country. In truth, it would nullify the Missouri Compromise, which prohibited slavery west of the Mississippi north of the 36°30' parallel, excepting Missouri. Seward, Sumner, and Chase—the three most vocal anti-slavery senators—said that the consequences to the country would be calamitous. A vote was scheduled for early March. Henry had assured Frances that there were enough anti-slavery men in Congress to beat back their opponents. Now he admitted that he was heartsick at the number of states in the North that seemed certain to vote for the "nefarious Nebraska bill": "Maine, New Hampshire, Connecticut, Rhode Island, Vermont!!! All, all in the hands of slave-holders."

The Kansas-Nebraska Act intensified the abolitionist furies unleashed by the Fugitive Slave Act and *Uncle Tom's Cabin*. Garrison, speaking in New York City, criticized those who protested only against the spread of slavery, rather than against the institution itself: "If it would be a damning sin for us to admit another Slave State into the Union, why is it not a damning sin to permit a Slave State to remain in the Union?" *The New York Times* printed Garrison's remarks in full. He remarked with satisfaction to his wife, Helen, that it was "a sign of the times."

Henry promised Frances to do his part to change minds, and he followed through in a vehement Senate speech against the bill on February 17. He reiterated what he had said in 1850 about the Clay Compromise—that no congressional measure could bridge the divide between free states and slave states: "You may legislate, and abrogate, and abnegate as you will; there is a superior Power that overrules your actions, and all your refusals to act." That power would propel the country toward "the equal and universal liberty of man." He reported to Frances, "Some happy spell seemed to have come over me and to have enabled me to speak with more freedom and ease than on any former occasion here." The speech was reprinted as a pamphlet, and praised even by some southern senators. Lazette wrote to Henry, knowing he was awaiting her response: "May I never cease to be thankful for your ever abiding affection and care of me—Yes, I have read your speech—and a proud and happy sister I was while so doing." It made her heart, and others', "bound with joy and gratitude."

Frances and Lazette also thought Sumner's speech was outstanding. He contrasted the North, which aspired to the ideals of the Declaration of Independence, with the South, which violated them: "And now, sir, when the conscience of mankind is at last aroused to these things; when, throughout the civilized world, a slave-dealer is a by-word and a reproach, we, as a nation, are about to open a new market to the traffickers in flesh, that haunt the shambles of the South." Frances wrote to Sumner praising the strength of his argument, Henry called it grand, and Senator George Edmund Badger, a Cotton Whig from North Carolina, said he considered it perfect in every respect, except that it was for the wrong side.

At 11:30 p.m. on March 3, 1854, Senator Douglas, famous for what one paper called his "brilliant, sledge-hammer speeches," gave his concluding address. He promised that popular sovereignty would achieve what the compromises of 1820 and 1850 had not: self-government in the territories would "destroy all sectional parties and sectional agitations." Lawmakers must allow the people "to regulate their domestic institutions in their own way." Douglas denigrated the "trio of abolitionist senators"—Seward, Sumner, and Chase. "His arrowy words," one correspondent wrote, "were keen and burning, and kindled as they flew," showering his foes with "a perfect torrent of invective, argument, satire, and ridicule." Sumner and Chase accused Douglas of an "atrocious plot" to prevent free labor in the national domain. Douglas replied, using the Democrats' most shaming insults, that they were "the pure, unadulterated representatives of Abolitionism, Free Soilism, Niggerism in the Congress of the United States."

Congress passed the Kansas-Nebraska Act on May 30, 1854, and President Franklin Pierce signed it into law. Five days later, Henry again addressed the Senate. The country had just closed a cycle in its history, he said, and he dared southerners to stick to the principle of majority rule: "Come on, then, gentlemen of the slave states. Since there is no escaping your challenge, we accept it in the name of freedom. We will engage in competition for the virgin soil of Kansas, and God give the victory to the side which is stronger in numbers, as it is in right." Private organizations formed, in Massachusetts and New York, to subsidize the migration of anti-slavery settlers to the Kansas Territory. Pro-slavery extremists, led by Senator David Rice Atchison of Missouri, from the slave state on Kansas's eastern border, welcomed the contest. Atchison said that Missourians would repel abolitionist invaders "with the bayonet and with blood." Good as his word, he organized bands of whiskey-fueled men who crossed the border, waving revolvers and Bowie knives, shouting that they would "keep the abolitionists out of Kansas."

Violence appeared imminent in Washington, too, and Frances wrote to Henry and to Sumner that she prayed for their safety. Sumner conceded that a southerner had insulted him in a restaurant: "The Administration organs tried to stir a mob against me, and some evil-disposed persons expressed a desire to put a bullet through my head; but I was never for a moment disturbed. At least there seems to be an awakening of the North. Good!" David Wright was tempted to join the settlers leaving for Kansas, but Martha told him that she could not be happy so far away from Philadelphia—Aurora had been Kansas enough for her.

Abolitionists and opponents of slavery in Congress ratcheted up their calls to form a new single-issue party. Frances, studying the speeches and articles by Boston activists, was especially interested in those of Rev. Theodore Parker, an "ultra" abolitionist who advised Henry to take the leap. Parker preached, in his words, "abundant heresies": abolition, women's rights, temperance, penal reform, and pacifism. Like other radical clerics, he did not regard the Bible as God's word, disavowing miracles and revelation, and rejected passages that condoned slavery and the abasement of women. Too freethinking even for Unitarians, Parker had established a "free church" in 1846—a racially integrated congregation of two thousand in Boston. In 1850, as the head of Boston's Vigilance Committee, he had coordinated the protection of two parishioners, William and Ellen Craft, freedom seekers from Georgia. During those weeks, he said, he wrote his sermons with a sword in the open drawer under his inkstand and a pistol in his desk. He was later tried, in connection with the case, for inciting a riot. Henry wrote to Parker about the resistance he faced in Congress: "If I sometimes seem to be less directly in the right way to the port, I pray you to remember . . . what violent gales I have had to encounter from that quarter."

Frederick Douglass tried to flatter Henry into action, arguing to him in one letter that it was the time for "a great new party of freedom, of justice, and truth," and that he must lead it. "You, my dear sir," he wrote, "have the organizing power, and have the voice to command and give Shape to the cause of your country, and to the cause of human Liberty," concluding, "May God give you Strength for the great work which is before you and Shield you from every hurtful influence. I am, dear sir, Most Truly your grateful friend. Fred Douglass."

To Frances's disappointment, Henry resisted their pleas, working instead with Weed to get a majority of Whigs elected to the state assembly in Albany, thus ensuring Henry's reelection to the Senate. And so the national movement for a new party gathered momentum without him. Conscience Whigs, Free Soilers, and anti-slavery Democrats came together in political meetings from Washington, D.C., to Wisconsin to discuss what could be done to prevent the spread of slavery. In July 1854, at a state convention in Jackson, Michigan, the Republican Party was born. Henry won a second term, and a year later, in Syracuse, he told the Whigs what most of them already knew: it was time to retire the party, and to join the Republicans. Sumner, an early Republican, wrote to Henry with less-than-fulsome enthusiasm, "I am so happy that we are at last on the same platform and in the same political pew."

In September 1854, Stephen A. Douglas set off on a lecture tour through northern states to try to persuade the people there of the merits of the Kansas-Nebraska Act, and Frederick Douglass followed him at every stop, attacking the law. Newspapers relished the stunt, publishing stories about the Black Douglass vs. the white Douglas. Greeley's *Tribune* published a bit of doggerel: "Let slavery now stop her mouth, / And quiet be henceforth: / We've got Fred Douglass from the South— / She's got Steve from the North." Douglass said mordantly, "Ebony and ivory are thought to look better standing together than when separated." Douglas, though, avoided any contact between them. When traveling through Central New

York, he stopped in Aurora, where a correspondent reported that he was seen "loafing about the hotel till noon." Hearing that "Fred" had arrived, "Steve," "knowing the severe handling he and his measures would receive," retired to his room, pleading illness, and remained "in magnificent seclusion" until the train departed at 5:00 p.m. He later admitted that his bill had made him a pariah in the North: "I could travel from Boston to Chicago by the light of my own effigy."

In October, when Douglass let Martha know he would be coming through Auburn, she asked him to spend the night at the house. She walked over to see Frances, who told her she looked forward to hearing Douglass dismantle the senator, and that she regretted Henry's absence. No white speaker was a match for Douglass on the subject of slavery. In his speeches on the tour, Douglass said that he was a citizen of New York and the United States, "clothed all over with the star spangled banner and defended by the American Constitution." The millions of people still in chains had no protections at all: "To utter one groan, or scream, for freedom in the presence of a Southern advocate of Popular Sovereignty, is to bring down the frightful lash upon their quivering flesh." The country had reached an impasse: "The South must either give up slavery, or the North must give up liberty. The two interests are hostile, and are irreconcilable."

After Douglass left Auburn, Martha attended a bridal party, where, she wrote, she was asked "with the slightest possible sneer after our recent guests." Her interlocutor emphasized the word, "wishing to be informed whether we gave them 'the best room.'" She replied, "Certainly," and said that "in conversing with a man of superior intellect one forgot whether he was black or white."

12

Bleeding Kansas, Bleeding Sumner

1854–1856

Sumner beaten in the Senate by Representative Preston Brooks of South Carolina, political cartoon by John L. Magee, 1856

The Kansas pioneers from New England saw themselves much as their English forebears had, as apostles of God and freedom in an untamed land. By the autumn of 1854, while Douglas and Douglass were delivering opposing speeches about the Kansas-Nebraska Act, 750 people from the northeast were taking possession of a pleasant prairie hillside and valley by the Wakarusa River in Kansas Territory. They called their future town Lawrence, after Amos A. Lawrence, secretary of the New England Emigrant Aid Company, which had subsidized their travel. The settlers staked claims, elected officers for a municipal government, and laid out a grid of future streets. One of the founders wrote about the lush prairie grass and the largest tract of woodland in the territory. They ordered components for a sawmill, and soon would have plenty of timber to build permanent homes, churches, and schools. In the meantime, they lived in thatched "hay tents." Two women from Massachusetts ran the Pioneer Boarding House out of the largest tent, which was converted on Sundays into the Congregational Plymouth Church. The pulpit was made up of trunks, and the pews of boarders' beds and boxes. The worshippers sang John Greenleaf Whittier's "Hymn of the Kansas Emigrant," reaching a crescendo with the final stanza, "Upbearing, like the ark of God. / The Bible in our van. / We go to test the truth of God / Against the fraud of man." One settler wrote, "All were cheerful, hopeful and full of energy, and the scene reminded me of Plymouth Rock."

The hope gave way to alarm as David Rice Atchison's bands of Missourians, dubbed "Border Ruffians" by the anti-slavery press, began staking their own claims and harassing the Kansans. A friend wrote to Atchison that pro-slavery Kansans were "the unwilling receptacle of the filth, scum, and offscourings of the East"—people who came "to preach abolitionism and dig Underground Rail-roads." Martha told an Auburn friend that she expected the pioneers to "maintain their ground manfully, and not be driven off by the idle threats of the Missourians." But the Ruffians meant what they said. As Atchison, newly retired from the Senate, founded a pro-slavery town fifty miles north of Lawrence, named after himself, the skirmishes commenced. A pro-slavery newspaper promised, "We will continue to lynch and hang, tar and feather, and drown every white-livered Abolitionist who dares to pollute our soil."

The first legislative elections in Kansas were scheduled for March 30, 1855. It was a defining event. The new legislature would write the state constitution, and decide the fate of slavery in Kansas. The day before the vote, a thousand armed men crossed into the territory on wagons packed with tents and supplies, and preprinted ballots. On election day, they fanned out to free-state towns, stuffing ballot boxes and accosting free-state voters and election judges. The besieged free-staters refused to recognize the pro-slavery governing body, in Shawnee Mission, calling it the "bogus legislature." They established a rival government in Topeka, which President Pierce called "revolutionary" and "treasonable." The Civil War effectively had begun.

Douglass wrote: "As a nation, if we are wise, we will prepare for the last conflict," in which "the enemy of Freedom must capitulate." Martha and Frances abandoned their strongly held pacifism as they followed the events in Kansas through *The North Star*, the *Times*, the *Tribune*, and the pugnacious speeches of Rev. Henry Ward Beecher, the pastor of Plymouth Church in Brooklyn and a brother of Harriet Beecher Stowe. Upon hearing Beecher speak at the Congregational Church in Washington, Henry noted to Frances, "It was a noble, mighty speech—sermon it was *not*." Lucretia, like Garrison, opposed armed retaliation in Kansas. Martha challenged her: "I admit that I don't quite take in the philosophy of non-resistance." She thought the "carnal sword" was more effective sometimes than the "sword of the spirit." "If you perish by it—never mind, if thereby you win freedom for a race."

In Washington in the early spring of 1856, Frances helped Henry polish a speech that argued for the admission of Kansas into the Union as a free state. The people of Lawrence had replaced their hay tents with log cabins and frame houses, built three churches, established three newspapers, and constructed a fine hostelry called the Free State Hotel. The town also had formed an eight-hundred-man militia, to protect itself from the Ruffians. Supporters back east shipped wooden crates to Lawrence, labeled "Books" and "Primers," which contained highly accurate, breech-loading Sharps rifles. After Rev. Beecher said he believed there was more moral power in one Sharps than in a hundred Bibles, the rifles came to be known as Beecher's Bibles. Confrontations multiplied, and at the end of 1855, after a land dispute south of town between two men on opposite sides of the slavery question, the county's pro-slavery sheriff, Samuel J. Jones, and an army of fifteen hundred, mostly Missourians, had surrounded Lawrence, intending to raze the town. Kansas's territorial governor negotiated a temporary truce. In Henry's speech, delivered on April 9, he blamed President Pierce for failing to protect the anti-slavery settlers from "armed masses of men," and said that Kansas was "in the very act of revolution against a tyranny." Frances's approval was reinforced by the *Times*, which described Seward as incarnating, more than any other man, the anti-slavery sentiment of the North.

But not all New Yorkers shared this pride in their senator. A few weeks later, Lazette wrote sadly to Henry that the family's adored bulldog, Watch, had died—poisoned by a malign critic of Henry. "Will has this morning buried him under a tree in the upper yard—& few human graves have had as many tears shed over them as poor faithful Watch's." Lazette explained that she was writing to him rather than to Frances, who'd referred to her state of mind in recent years as "very dark some of the time." Lazette hoped he would open the letter before Frances saw it, "so that you may tell her at a time you think most proper." Henry replied on May 2, saying that he had broken the news to Frances and Fanny, who were mourning Watch, but, he said, "The incident comes not without its consolations to me—In other times it would have been the Master's life, not merely the dog's, that would have been demanded as a penalty for non compliance with vicious and barbarous prejudices."

In mid-May, Sumner paid a call on the Sewards in Washington, asking for their thoughts about a major speech he was drafting about the Border Ruffians, titled "The Crime Against Kansas." He read the draft to them in its entirety. Describing President Pierce's complicity in "the incredible atrocity of the Assassins and of the Thugs," he compared Senator Andrew Butler of South Carolina to Don Quixote, and described "the harlot, Slavery" as Butler's mistress. Senator Douglas, the author of the Kansas-Nebraska Act, was "the squire of Slavery, its very Sancho Panza, ready to do all its humiliating offices."

Frances and Henry agreed with much of it, but they were disconcerted by the invective he leveled at his congressional colleagues. They implored Sumner to remove those passages, but he was seeking affirmation, not editing. It wasn't the first time he had asked Henry for advice that he then disregarded. Henry commented to Frances about Sumner on another matter, "He took my advice as usual, and as usual followed his own." Frances, concerned that they had offended Sumner, wrote to him to clarify her position: "Neither my heart nor my conscience would allow me to say that any words were too strong spoken in favor of a wronged and suffering people or against their oppressors. I objected only to the cutting personal sarcasm, which seldom amends, and is less frequently forgiven."

Sumner memorized his entire oration—112 pages—and delivered "The Crime Against Kansas" in the Senate on two sweltering days, May 19 and 20, 1856. The "crime," he said, was hatched with "the *One Idea*, that Kansas, at all hazards, must be made a slave State." As he delivered the lines about Senators Douglas and Butler, Douglas paced in the back of the chamber, muttering, "This damn fool is going to get himself shot by some other damn fool." It wasn't an exaggeration. Members of Congress were known to shove and slug one another when angered, and many attended sessions with pistols inside their jackets.

Senator Butler was not in Washington to hear Sumner's insult, but his thirty-six-year-old cousin, Representative Preston Brooks of South Carolina was, and he concluded that the southern code of honor required serious redress. Hesitating between a horsewhip and a cane, Brooks settled on his walking stick made of gutta-percha, a hard rubber made from the tree's sap. On May 22, Brooks waited for the Senate to adjourn and for the ladies to leave the lobby—a nod to southern "chivalry." Brooks approached Sumner, who was bent over his desk, franking a stack of printed copies of the speech, to be mailed to friends, newspapers, and party officials. Brooks spoke a few words, and witnesses later recounted that before Sumner could stand up, Brooks began to thrash him with his cane. Sumner's long legs were trapped beneath the small desk, which was bolted to the floor with iron plates. As he abruptly stood up, he tore it from its mooring. Blinded by blood, he had difficulty shielding himself from the blows to his head, shoulders, and back, which Brooks delivered so energetically that the cane splintered.

Several senators tried to stop Brooks, but one of his allies from the House reached for his gun and shouted, "Let them alone! Goddamn, let them alone!" Another man cried, "Give the damned Abolitionist hell!" Brooks said that he'd given Sumner "about 30 first-rate stripes. Towards the last he bellowed like a calf. I wore my cane out completely but saved the head which is gold."

Sumner was carried to his rooms unconscious. Over the past six years, he had become one of Frances's dearest friends. They addressed each other as Charles and Frances, and discussed personal matters as well as politics. Although Frances had anticipated some kind of attack on him, she hadn't imagined that he would be almost beaten to death on the Senate floor. That evening, Henry visited Sumner, and found him lying on his bed, still covered with blood, but awake, lucid, and calculating how to turn his victimhood to political advantage. Frances had long since corrected her early impression that Sumner was a literary man, not a politician. She wrote home that he was "recovered from the bewilderment of his faculties, and much in hopes that some benefit to the anti-slavery cause might accrue from the affair." Henry, too, found satisfaction in the thought that the murderous assault would strengthen the Republican Party in the fall elections.

On May 21, the day after Sumner's speech, the Border Ruffians—accompanied by Atchison, Sheriff Jones, a federal marshal, and several hundred militiamen—reconvened on the outskirts of Lawrence. Atchison announced, "This is the day I am a border ruffian!" He told the men to carry the war "into the heart of the country, never to slacken or stop until every spark of free-state, free-speech, free-niggers, or free in any shape is quenched out of Kansas!" The posse was led by Sheriff Jones, who'd been shot in an earlier attempt to arrest several citizens on drummed-up charges. After the deputy marshal arrested several free-staters, Jones ordered his men to raze the town. They looted stores, broke the printing presses of two newspapers, and, after helping themselves to the liquor supply in the Free State Hotel, set it on fire.

One person closely following the violence in Kansas was a failed businessman of fifty-six named John Brown. His crevassed face a topographical map of bitterness and resolve, Brown was a ferocious abolitionist with eleven children. He took literally the Old Testament's language of vengeance, and believed it was his God-given destiny to overthrow slavery. Brown had been scheming his entire life, as he said, to "help defeat Satan and his legions." The previous spring, living with his second wife and younger children in North Elba, in the Adirondacks, Brown had gotten a letter from his oldest son, John Jr., which indicated to him that the time had come to begin his mission. John Jr. , who had settled about forty miles south of Lawrence in Osawatomie, Kansas, with four of his brothers and their families, wrote that they were threatened by "hundreds and thousands of the meanest and most desperate of men, armed to the teeth with Revolvers, Bowie Knives, Rifles & Cannon"—all paid for by slaveholders. They needed arms and money to fund their newly formed militia, the Pottawatomie Rifles. Brown had answered the call, heading to Osawatomie with a wagonload of rifles.

Late on the night of May 24, 1856, Brown rode with four of his sons (Owen, Frederick, Salmon, and Oliver) and a few accomplices a short distance along Pottawatomie Creek. They broke into three homes and hauled out five men, whom they questioned and pronounced guilty of being proslavery. The next morning, a sixteen-year-old boy found his two brothers and his father dead outside their house. The father had been shot in the face. One of the brothers was grotesquely mutilated—his fingers and arms cut off and his skull split open. Two other men were discovered lying nearby with similar wounds.

Brown, who denied having any role in the murders, fled into the Kansas wilderness with his band, pursued by a pro-slavery militia and a posse. He and the sons who had participated in the attack remained at liberty; John Jr. and Jason, who had not, were charged with treason, tortured, and kept in chains for months. At the end of August, Brown returned to Osawatomie to defend it with some forty men against three hundred Ruffians, but they were forced to retreat, and the settlement was looted and burned. Garrison castigated John Brown's violence, but most of the New England abolitionists turned a blind eye to the Pottawatomie massacre, considering Brown the Kansas avenger.

Northerners and southerners could only see the attack on Sumner and John Brown's bloodshed through their own political lenses. Martha did not condemn Brown, and even Lucretia later called him "a moral hero" in "the glorious cause of human liberty." In a microcosm of the national divide, Martha's family in the North and the Pelhams in the South ruptured over the Sumner caning. Martha valued the right to free speech, but when her twenty-one-year-old nephew, Charles Pelham, wrote from Alabama to express approval of Brooks's act, she replied that he should know better: "I felt very sorry that you should justify the murderous attack on Sumner." She trusted that "mature reflection & the generous impulses of youth, will lead you to judge wisely on this momentous question wh. is destined to shake the Union from centre to circumference."

Brooks's supporters in Charleston ordered him a new cane, inscribed with the words "Hit him again." Students at the University of Virginia instructed another craftsman to make a gold handle in the likeness of a human head, "badly cracked and broken." Republicans distributed a million copies of "The Crime Against Kansas." Their 1856 presidential campaign had a new slogan: "Bleeding Kansas" and "Bleeding Sumner."

Frances, dumbfounded by the lawlessness of the Border Ruffians, was undone by the savaging of Sumner, who struggled to clear his mind and recover his ability to walk. His speech about Kansas may have been infelicitous, but he had told the truth about the South. Until the attack, Frances had opposed the death penalty. Now, when a friend asked if she thought Brooks would be hanged if Sumner died, she replied tersely that he should be hanged regardless—but that "none are punished here but the poor slaves who rebel against their masters." She had not believed that anything could make slavery more hateful to her, "but the events of this winter have deepened that furor in my soul."

In June, she got surprising news from Henry: Weed and other Republican leaders had decided to endorse John C. Frémont for president. She had shared the common assumption that Henry, the party's leader, would be the nominee. Frémont was a forty-three-year-old former major in the Mexican War who had led four explorations of the Rocky Mountains, mapping parts of the West still untouched by white men. No stranger to self-promotion, Frémont took credit for securing California for the United States, and served as one of the state's first two anti-slavery senators. Weed, Henry's cold-blooded strategist, told him that the Republicans, still a very young party, had little hope of winning the presidency that year. The Democratic candidate, James Buchanan of Pennsylvania, who supported the Fugitive Slave Law and popular sovereignty, was bound to win the White House, and it was better that Frémont be sacrificed than Henry. Frances, angry on Henry's behalf, wrote about Weed, "His abandonment seems to have been a matter of very cool calculation—Worldly vision certainly does impel a person to 'swim with the tide.'"

On the Fourth of July, Henry reported in a letter to Frances that he had visited Sumner, whom he doubted would ever fully recover—he moved like a man recovering from paralysis, and had lost his old spirit. That day, as the church bells rang in Auburn, Frances wrote to Sumner, "You have served the cause of Justice & Humanity faithfully, fearlessly and effectually," and to Henry, "Where is our boasted Freedom if Kansas is forced to become a slave state?" If the violence of the Missourians and the attack on Sumner had not forced the North to see slavery in its true light, "what is to open their eyes!"

13

Frances Sells Harriet a House

1857–1859

Harriet Tubman, carte-de-visite portrait, Auburn, 1868–1869

Frances found the social scene in Washington strangely unchanged that winter. Henry held his annual New Year's Day party, which was attended even by Senator Douglas, whom she considered persona non grata. Everyone was determinedly festive. A few weeks later, Frederick's wife, Anna, helped her arrange a dance at the house for guests. Congress conducted business as usual. Henry managed to get a bill passed to fund the transatlantic telegraph, a visionary venture that skeptics refused to believe could deliver virtually instantaneous communication with London. Frances sent Aunt Clara a weather report about heavy snows and below-zero temperatures, and offhandedly mentioned the untimely death, from croup, of Sumner's attacker, Preston Brooks.

The spell broke on March 4, 1857, when President James Buchanan took the oath of office, and the upheavals over slavery resumed. As foretold by Weed, Buchanan had easily defeated Frémont, along with the candidate of the nativist Know Nothing Party, the former Whig President Millard Fillmore. Before Buchanan even entered the White House, he fulfilled his critics' fears about him. In his Inaugural Address, he lauded Congress's wisdom in passing the Kansas-Nebraska Act, without a word about Bleeding Kansas, and he predicted that "all good citizens" would "cheerfully submit" to the pending decision from the Supreme Court on *Dred Scott v. Sandford*. Buchanan knew how the case would be decided because, disregarding the separation of powers, he had exchanged letters about it with two justices. At his inauguration, Buchanan was seen whispering with Chief Justice Roger B. Taney, the author of the opinion. Two days later, in the justices' ground-floor courtroom of the Capitol, Taney read out his ruling. Abolitionists, Republicans, and anti-slavery Democrats in the North regarded it as the most disgraceful decision the Court had ever issued.

The case had been making its way through the legal system for eleven years. In 1846, Dred Scott, then forty-seven, had sued for his freedom and that of his wife, Harriet, and their children, arguing that they had been illegally held in bondage in the free state of Illinois and at Fort Snelling in present-day Minnesota. Chief Justice Taney, a defender of states' rights and a confirmed racist, wrote that neither the Declaration of Independence nor the Constitution defined Black men and women as citizens—they were, in his words, "beings of an inferior order." Taney ruled that Scott had no standing to sue in the federal courts, and that his residence in a free state and in a territory that Congress deemed free had no bearing on his status: Congress controlled the admission of new states to the Union, but it could not infringe upon the rights of people or property. The decision ensured the expansion and perpetuation of slavery by nullifying the Missouri Compromise, giving slaveholders the right to take their property into any of the territories.

After *Dred Scott*, Frances felt more than ever that she was not doing enough to undermine slavery. In August 1857, she received a letter from the Reverend May, asking her to describe the accomplishments of Myrtilla Miner and her pupils. Hostile neighbors in Washington had forced Miner to repeatedly move her School for Colored Girls, but she finally had found it a permanent home in less densely populated northwest Washington, and she was raising money to hire another teacher. May said that Miner spoke gratefully about how supportive Frances had been, and in Frances's response, she detailed all that Miner had done. He found her tribute perceptive and beautifully expressed, and asked if he could make it public, to help him raise money for the school. Frances asked him not to share it with anyone—her husband did not think it wise. May couldn't understand why Seward forbade her from lending her name to such a benevolent enterprise.

Frances faced the struggle that confronted other political wives who were more opinionated than their husbands would like. Henry thought it was enough for her to quietly provide Miner with encouragement, money, and classroom supplies. If Senator Seward's wife became known in Washington as a spokeswoman for Black education, his enemies would use it as further evidence that he was a dangerous "Black Republican"—with a wife he could not control. Frances acceded to Henry's request that she defer to him in public, but in private company and with him alone, she said what she thought. One of their dinner guests in Washington wrote to his wife that Frances was "a dignified, simple, quiet person who has the marks of individual strength and who has clearly developed her own place and her own views—which are not always those of her husband. She is said to be much more thorough in her religious and political radicalism than he." During the dinner, Henry said playfully, "My wife doesn't think much of me." Frances replied, "You do very well as far as you go."

At home in Auburn, Frances shared Martha's frustrations about the inoffensive speakers who were invited to lecture, and she encouraged her to organize lyceum talks herself. The only way to force adjustments in people's thinking was to expose them to ideas they reflexively disagreed with. Frances commented to Lazette, "I am sorry the women of Auburn are so afraid of themselves—They will not be likely to grow very wise if they are afraid to have sensible men come among them"—let alone sensible women. After Susan B. Anthony attracted a sparse crowd at a Cayuga County women's rights meeting, Martha wrote a bruising letter to the *Auburn Daily Advertiser.* Why was it, she asked, when other cities attracted audiences clamoring to hear Emerson, Beecher, Parker, and Phillips, that "Auburn shuts itself tightly in its sectarian shell, and dares not listen to anything that savors of progress? It is a disgrace to our beautiful city."

Frances had wanted for years to meet Elizabeth Cady Stanton, and she finally did in November 1857, during a visit to an old friend who lived in Seneca Falls. As expected, she wrote to Augustus, she found Mrs. Stanton "a woman of great abilities," but then, sounding more like her grandmother than like the modern woman she considered herself to be, Frances observed that Mrs. Stanton's marriage, undertaken against the wishes of her father, Judge Cady, was not "one of the most fortunate kind." She didn't know how thoroughly Cady disapproved of Stanton's activism. Stanton confessed to Anthony, "To think that all in me of which my father would have felt a proper pride had I been a man, is deeply mortifying to him because I am a woman. I never felt more keenly the degradation of my sex."

Frances and Stanton began corresponding and seeing each other when Stanton visited Auburn, often joined by Lazette and Martha. Lazette's husband, Alvah Worden, had died, and Lazette moved back to town, into a small house she built on land inherited from Judge Miller. In an oblique statement about slavery, Lazette called her home Pisgah, the name of the peak from which Moses was said to have viewed the Promised Land. Frances had never forgiven Worden for his abusive behavior early in the marriage, and Lazette was at last nearby, living on her own. Stanton described the Miller sisters as "women of culture and remarkable natural intelligence, and interested in all progressive ideas. They had rare common-sense and independence of character." Stanton couldn't persuade either of them to enlist openly in the women's movement, but she valued their advice, and the direct line Frances provided to Senator Seward.

When Frances was not with Henry, his impulsive goodwill sometimes hindered his judgment. He wrote exultantly that fall that Stephen A. Douglas had parted ways with President Buchanan and with southern Democrats—seeing the break as a sure sign that "the Administration and slave-power are broken." Frances didn't believe it. Douglas was only upset that the pro-slavery politicians in Kansas were making a mockery of popular sovereignty. They had issued a pro-slavery constitution without fairly presenting it to voters, causing Douglas to complain that a small minority had "attempted to cheat & defraud the majority by trickery & juggling." Frances, certain that Douglas would support slavery again in an instant if it would further his ambitions, replied to Henry, "I wish I could with your hopeful disposition see as much good in prospects from the change of course in Stephen A. Douglas as you do, or that I could as generously forget all that he has done heretofore—but I cannot." Douglas never, she said, would make any sacrifice to advance the progress of truth.

Frances was even more taken aback by a letter she received from Henry a few days later. Writing about a sixty-five-mile excursion to Culpeper, Virginia, to visit a former Whig congressman, John S. Pendleton, and his wife at their plantation, he sounded like a wealthy slaveholder himself. The Pendletons used the word *hands* rather than *slaves*, who, Henry claimed, "are treated with kindness, and they appear clean, tidy, and comfortable." He arrived during a husking "frolic"—a "merry and noisy scene." He thought that Mrs. Pendleton was a lady Frances would respect and love. Frances was incredulous. Henry knew that ever since their 1835 southern trip, she had seen Virginia as exemplifying the evils of slavery: the elderly woman whose family had been stolen from her, and the weeping children tied by a rope, being herded toward Richmond for sale.

So when Frances returned to Washington with Fanny and Will at the end of January 1858, she was relieved to find Henry drafting a slashing speech about the *Dred Scott* decision. He charged that Buchanan had overstepped his bounds by asking how the Court would rule: "In this ill-omened act, the Supreme Court forgot its own dignity." The Court had attempted to "command the people of the United States to accept the principles that one man can own other men," but the people "never can, and they never will, accept principles so unconstitutional and so abhorrent."

On March 3, 1858, Frances followed her practice of staying at home when the others went to the Capitol to listen to Henry speak. The response was predictable. Senator James Henry Hammond of South Carolina cried, "You dare not make war on cotton. No power on earth dares to make war upon it. Cotton is king." The North had manual laborers, he said. The South had slaves who, "hired for life, are well compensated . . .

yours are hired by the day, not cared for." President Buchanan was so offended by Henry's speech that he banned him from the White House, and Chief Justice Taney said that if Seward ever won the presidency, he would refuse to administer the oath of office.

The presidential election was still more than two years away, but there was a closely watched midterm race in 1858 between Senator Douglas and Abraham Lincoln, a Republican lawyer from Springfield, Illinois. Lincoln, who was forty-nine, had served in the House from 1847 to 1849. He, too, was a withering critic of the Kansas-Nebraska Act and of *Dred Scott*, arguing that Negroes were among the people for whom the Declaration of Independence and the Constitution were written. In five of the thirteen original states—New Hampshire, Massachusetts, Maine, Vermont, and Rhode island—free Black men had the right to vote without any restrictions. On June 16, accepting the Illinois Republican Party's nomination for the Senate seat, Lincoln warned, "A house divided against itself cannot stand. I believe this government cannot endure, permanently, half slave and half free."

A masterful rhetorician, Lincoln carefully calibrated his remarks about race. In a series of seven debates with Douglas in the summer and fall of 1858, he said that he did not favor social and political equality, but he did not hold back on the subject of slavery. Calling popular sovereignty "nothing but a living, creeping lie," he issued a distinctly American comparison between the principles of right and wrong: "The one is the common right of humanity, and the other the divine right of kings. It is the same principle in whatever shape it develops itself. It is the same spirit that says, 'You work and toil and earn bread, and I'll eat it.'" People who made excuses for enslaving others were following "the same tyrannical principle." Every man, Lincoln said, had a right to life, liberty, and happiness. Douglas spoke not about the unfulfilled promises of the Declaration of Independence, but about the limited rights in the Constitution. He impugned Lincoln as a "Black Republican" and defended the Kansas-Nebraska Act, arguing that the United States government "was made by white men for the benefit of white men and their posterity forever."

On October 25, ten days after the last of the Lincoln-Douglas debates, Henry delivered his own unvarnished speech in Rochester. The battles over slavery, he said, were not the work of zealots, as southerners claimed. That mistook the severity of the danger. He called slavery "an irrepressible conflict between opposing and enduring forces." The United States, sooner or later, would become either entirely a slaveholding nation, or entirely a free-labor nation: "I know, and you know, that a revolution has begun. I know, and all the world knows, that revolutions never go backward."

Although Lincoln lost the election to Douglas, who won a third term, the four-year-old Republican Party won five other Senate seats, and Republicans took control of the House. As Weed had predicted in 1856, Henry was well positioned for the presidency in 1860. A Republican friend from New York told him that he would certainly be the party's nominee, and suggested Lincoln as a suitable vice president. Frances agreed that Henry had earned the candidacy, and that Lincoln would be an ideal running mate, but she could not bear the thought of serving as First Lady. She wanted to participate in the anti-slavery revolt. If Henry became president, he would be even more inconvenienced by her activism, and she would be almost as mercilessly dissected as he was.

On Christmas morning 1858, Fanny went to St. John's Episcopal Church, a butter-yellow sanctuary with six white pillars and a tiered white bell tower at the north end of Lafayette Square. It was known as "the Church of the Presidents" because every occupant of the White House since James Madison had worshipped there. On Fanny's way home, she ran into Emily Howland, the new teacher Myrtilla Miner had hired to help at her school. Frances had befriended young Miss Howland, seeing her as a kindred spirit from Central New York. Ascertaining that Howland had no holiday plans, Fanny invited her to the Sewards' Christmas dinner.

Thirty years old, Howland was the Quaker daughter of the underground railroad conductor in Sherwood, a village near Auburn. Frances told Fanny that Howland was someone to emulate: a single woman who had no desire to mingle with the city's social elite, and devoted herself to the neediest. With Frances's help, Howland was developing a private aid channel for freedom seekers. Howland wrote in one note about a woman who had collected nine hundred dollars to buy her children. "The market value of humanity must have risen in Virginia," Howland commented. The "owner," after setting a price for the children, had doubled it. Frances had helped the woman once, and made a second donation toward the children's freedom.

After dinner at the Sewards', Howland read aloud to the family. Fanny, who was fourteen, wrote earnestly in her diary that evening that her Christmas was marred only by the southern custom of firing guns, pistols, and crackers—"On the day of all other sacred to 'peace and good will toward men,' thus celebrating the era of peace with the emblems of war."

Fanny modeled herself on her mother. Shy and painfully sensitive but already unshakable in her political beliefs, she supported women's rights and opposed slavery, and was herself an advocate of temperance and animal rights. She watched the servants in the downstairs kitchen as they prepared for her father's 1859 New Year's Day party. They set out a dozen lemons for a whiskey punch, but her father came in to say that Mrs. Seward thought it best not to have it. Fanny wrote in her diary, "So the punch is dispensed with, how glad I am!" She was upset to see the cook scald to death "eight unfortunate terrapins—poor things, if I could influence everyone by doing so, I would never taste animal food, but I cannot. At any rate I will not eat turtle, terrapins, lobsters, eels, and frogs."

By noon that day, the dining room table was laden with turkey, ham, tongue, and oysters, chicken salad garnished with hard-boiled eggs and celery, and delicacies from Henry's favorite bakery in New York, including a white-frosted plum cake decorated with the state coat of arms and a banner emblazoned with Seward's name. To Frances, Henry's opulent entertaining and his courtesy toward slavery's apologists felt even more offensive than in previous years. At the reception, as southerners laughed and filled their plates, she could think only of the woman Howland was helping, collecting pittances from strangers in the hope of buying back her own children. After the final guests departed, Henry called the party a great success, telling Frances that they must have entertained four hundred people.

During Henry's decade in Washington, an internal rebellion had been steadily gathering force in Frances. She wrote to Lazette a few days later that she couldn't abide by his rules any longer: "There are so many things that Henry and I cannot think alike about." She blamed herself, too. "It would be better for me to be away—You say you do not feel fitted to 'shine in fashionable society.' I am not only unfitted to shine but I am so ill accepted to its requirements as to be a positive drag on others—this is much more lamentable." At fifty-three, after thirty-five years of marriage, Frances told Henry that she would no longer serve as his hostess. Caught by surprise, he tried to cajole her, but she was adamant, and then they disagreed about who should take her place. Henry had once chillingly said about Frances to Sumner, "She is too noble a woman to think of parting from and too frail to hope to keep for long." He saw her decision as an admission of physical weakness, not an assertion of independence.

In mid-February, as the Seward household prepared for yet another formal dinner, followed by a ball at Willard's Hotel, Frances came down with influenza. Henry wrote in exasperation to their son Frederick, who was working in Albany at Weed's *Evening Journal*, saying that he was "left in straits." He needed someone to act "as and for Mrs. Seward, who is too feeble to preside." Emphasizing that Frances's duties were almost as onerous as his, he said that Frederick's wife, Anna, who helped Frances organize his parties when she was in Washington, was the only family member who was qualified. "I want her to come, stay, and do it." Fred couldn't join her right away, but they always complied with the wishes of "Father," as Anna called Henry, and she went at once to Washington. She took to the job—writing and dropping off invitations, accompanying Henry to parties, planning his receptions and dinners. Frances showed no hint of regret—only an immense unburdening.

Back in the North in the months that followed, Frances began to think more daringly about her life. Emily Howland had her personal aid network. Martha was a force for women's rights. Harriet Tubman was bringing dozens of people out of bondage. A few years earlier, Harriet's Philadelphia landlord had died, and his widow had left town with her money and belongings. Since then, between her trips to the Eastern Shore, Harriet had been scraping together funds for her rescue operations and living with her family in St. Catharines, Canada. Her father, Ben, had rheumatism; her mother, Rit, querulous in her old age, blamed Harriet for depositing them in a remote village in a frigid foreign country and leaving them for months at a time.

Harriet made it clear that she would not stop going back to Maryland until she had returned with her entire family and as many others as possible. It was suddenly apparent how Frances could make her own contribution to abolition. Auburn, midway on Harriet's underground railroad route across the state, would be a far more convenient location for her and her parents. On her journeys, Harriet was hungry and exposed to the elements for weeks at a time. Responsible for the lives of people utterly dependent on her, she had to be constantly alert to the rustle of branches, the barking of bloodhounds, the muted exchanges among slave catchers on horseback. She needed a home of her own to come back to. One of the parcels of land that Frances had inherited was about a mile from her house on South Street, just over the town border in Fleming. It included seven acres of farmland, a new frame house, a barn, and a few outbuildings. She decided that Harriet should have it—resettling herself, her parents, and other family members there.

It was a brazen idea. Under the Fugitive Slave Act, anyone found assisting a "fugitive" could be charged with "constructive treason," and sent to prison. Frances would be breaking that law just as Henry was beginning his run for president. Yet the property was Frances's, and it would be hard for him to argue against the plan. For years, they had been selling land in Auburn to free Blacks and immigrants, and, with Henry's assent, she was hiding freedom seekers in their basement. In that sense, the transaction would be just a more assertive act of conscience. As Henry had always advised others, it was a moral act to provide shelter for fugitive slaves.

Harriet was in no financial position to buy the property, and if it had been up to Frances, she might have made it a gift. But Harriet, who gratefully accepted contributions for her underground railroad work, refused outright charity. Twenty-year-old Will Seward, who was starting a banking career in Auburn, helped Frances draw up the paperwork for a twelve-hundred-dollar mortgage. Harriet made a twenty-five-dollar down payment, and agreed to quarterly remittances of ten dollars with interest.

The sale was completed while Henry was on an eight-month tour of Europe, Palestine, and Egypt. His closest political friends thought it was better for him to be away during the campaign, unable to do anything that might jeopardize his nomination. Weed, the ideal proxy, was confident he could deliver Henry as the Republican nominee. The two had once objected to Martin van Buren's stranglehold on Albany. Now Weed, known with fear, admiration, and hatred as "The Dictator," had the same control. He was friendly with the Republican governor, Edwin D. Morgan, ran one of the state's most influential newspapers, and had, one newspaper said, "oceans of money" to dispense.

• • •

As Weed was attacking the Buchanan administration and ensuring that Republicans won a majority of legislative seats in the state elections that year, Henry was greeted warmly in the salons, legislatures, and courts of Europe. He wrote to Frances about meeting Queen Victoria, describing her as a "sturdy, small, unaffected and kind person," who spoke with him about the modern wonders of railroads, steamships, and the new transatlantic cable Henry had endorsed, which would soon send its first message between North America and Europe.

While in England, Henry traveled to the Lake District, where he looked up Harriet Martineau, the erudite author of numerous books on laissez-faire economics and sociology, a discipline she helped to create. She also wrote about abolition and women's rights, and Frances had been reading her for years. In 1839, in *The Martyr Age of the United States*, Martineau had praised American women of different classes, creeds, and races for working together in the female anti-slavery societies. Martineau's home, shaggy with overgrown ivy, sat by Lake Windermere, a sheet of blue water flanked by terraced green hillsides and overlooked by mountains.

Henry found Martineau to be florid and good-looking with "matronly ways and manner." They spoke chiefly about slavery, "the great American question." Martineau said that she despaired of a peaceful solution. Henry explained his own "more practical views": war could be avoided if there was careful action on two fronts—organizing the anti-slavery movement and disarming the pro-slavery forces. Martineau called him a politician. He responded that even the great abolitionists Theodore Parker and Wendell Phillips were content that he act in his own way, introducing legislation when the time was right.

Frances regretted that she had only Henry's account of the conversation. Typically, he emphasized the reasonableness of his argument, and gave short shrift to one of the great intellectuals of the age.

14

Martha Leads

1854–1860

responsibility for any sentiments of his — This hue & cry about Free Love in New York, of all places in the world, is too contemptible & hypocritical to be worth a moments notice — that a steady persistence in the course already marked out, will ensure ultimate success, even tho' misrepresentation & abuse should continue to the end of the chapter, to discourage the wavering, and frighten the timid from our glorious platform —

"This hue & cry about Free Love in New York, of all places in the world, is too contemptible & hypocritical to be worth a moments notice." Martha Coffin Wright to Susan B. Anthony, July 17, 1860

At forty-seven, Martha never had felt more energetic. Stanton thought of her as "one of the most judicious and clear-sighted women in the movement," and Martha, like Stanton, saw her work as giving "soul and zest" to her life. It was never easy. One of the lyceum speakers she hosted, Sara Jane Lippincott, was the first female correspondent for *The New York Times*.

Lippincott wrote about abolition and other social justice issues under the pseudonym Grace Greenwood. In Auburn, she addressed the needs of the homeless population. A reporter for the local *Daily Union* couldn't bring himself to cover the talk seriously, and Martha had to write Greenwood a letter of apology. He roguishly praised her strong, vigorous mind, adding that it was "encased in a very handsome body," and saying he rejected the idea "that woman should not be permitted a place upon the platform unless she is about to be hung."

Martha carried on even after she and David learned in September 1854 that Tallman, while working on a schooner off the California coast near San Francisco, had been knocked overboard one night by a swinging boom, and his body was swept out to sea. He was only twenty-two—their eldest son and second child to die in five years. Still, rather than withdraw, as she had when Charley became fatally ill, Martha followed Lucretia's advice to pursue her work even while coping with her anguish.

She got the news while helping thirteen-year-old Ellen and eleven-year-old Willy pack their trunks for boarding school. Martha had persuaded David that it would be worth the expense to send them to Eagleswood, in Perth Amboy, New Jersey. They would send Frank, too, in a few years. Recently established by the abolitionist Theodore Weld to educate the next generation of activists, Eagleswood was on the grounds of the Raritan Bay Union, an American utopia of the day—a biracial community of artists, mechanics, and farmers sworn to "a freer, more harmonious form of human existence."

Eagleswood was nothing like the rigid Quaker day school that Martha had attended. It was coeducational and racially integrated, with a curriculum that included literature, science, art, and religion, along with instruction in industrial fields. Girls were required to take sports and lessons in public speaking, and students engaged in formal debates. Martha reported complacently to David: "The bigoted and narrow-minded chose other schools for their children—those who had not emancipated themselves from the prejudices of education & circumstance." Knowing how keenly the children felt Tallman's death, she liked thinking that Ellen and Willy couldn't help being happy in that stimulating environment. Eliza, who was twenty-four, was even more despondent than her younger siblings: "I hope Eliza will not suffer herself to dwell so constantly on her sorrow, but will open her piano and in practicing forget."

After leaving Willy and Ellen, Martha stayed with the Motts in Philadelphia, where she was to be an officer at the Fifth National Woman's Rights Convention, in October. She was gratified to work alongside women of different races, faiths, and classes. Lucretia's friends Harriet Forten Purvis and Margaretta Forten, Black co-founders of the Philadelphia Female Anti-Slavery Society, organized the program; and Ernestine Rose, a Jewish atheist, chaired. Still, racial and strategic tensions periodically erupted. Douglass criticized Lucy Stone for speaking at a segregated gathering in Philadelphia, and for accepting fees to lecture in the South to slaveholders. Stanton, who was an abolitionist, couldn't see her own prejudices. She was at her best and her worst when addressing her area of expertise: women's "legal disabilities." At a meeting in Albany that year, she said: "Would to God you could know the burning indignation that fills woman's soul when she turns over the pages of your statute books and sees there how like feudal barons you freemen hold your women." But she had in mind middle-class white women, not Black women. Stanton continued, crudely making a point about the inequities of the legal system: "We are moral, virtuous and intelligent, and yet by your laws we are classed with idiots, lunatics, and negroes." It seemed to her a statement of fact, not an assertion of racial superiority.

Before the Philadelphia convention opened, Martha declined her officer's role, admitting in a letter to David that in her current dismal state, she feared losing her self-control. Then, watching the bungling efforts of the woman who took her place, she was sorry she hadn't done it. The highlight of the three days was Lucretia's takedown of another clergyman, Rev. Henry Grew, over the supposedly holy rationale for the subordination of women. Lucretia objected, saying that first ministers had attacked temperance people, then they went after anti-slavery advocates. Now they cited passage after passage of the Bible to justify the oppression of women: "The pulpit has been prostituted, the Bible has been ill-used." Rev. Grew had no viable comeback, and the convention passed a resolution stating that the clergy's "teachings of the Bible are intensely inimical to the equality of woman with man." Martha wrote to David, who was beginning to come around to the importance of the movement, that the public seemed astonished that women could hold a respectable meeting and speak so well.

• • •

Martha's children knew how unpopular she made herself with her activism. One of her least favorite duties was collecting signatures on suffrage petitions, a dispiriting slog from house to house where most people shut the door before she could speak. One man, a doctor, let her in, but he refused to sign, telling her that women would stop at nothing: before you knew it, they would expect to serve as senators and foreign ministers. Martha, the dangerous woman her neighbors had always thought she was, replied that women certainly claimed, along with the right to vote, the right to be voted for, and that surely the doctor could think of women who were as competent to fill such offices as some men.

In October 1855, Martha was elected president of the next convention, in Cincinnati. She admitted to Ellen that the thought of chairing was "a perfect nightmare," and joked that she felt like a Quaker minister who went to meeting because he was curious about what he was going to say. But she'd learned from Stanton, Anthony, Lucretia, and "the beautiful and efficient" Ernestine Rose how to do the job, and she performed flawlessly. Referring to the changes wrought in her and others in only seven years, she told delegates that the Seneca Falls convention had convened "in timidity and doubt of our own strength, our own capacity, our own powers."

Ellen didn't find her mother's joke particularly funny. She herself was clever, amusing, and popular, but overwhelmed by self-doubt. At Eagleswood School, Ellen attended Sunday evening lectures by Anthony, Thoreau, Emerson, Garrison, and Abigail Kelley Foster, and she was asked to organize a debate about "woman's proper sphere." Rather than feeling like a member of the Eagleswood elite, she had a panicked sense of her shortcomings, feeling she could never measure up to her mother's expectations. She had frequent headaches, and that spring, she'd succumbed to an attack of "hysteria," after the Greek word for uterus, "hystera"—the all-purpose diagnosis for women afflicted with anything from toothaches to feelings of hopelessness. Martha regarded Frances's complaints about disordered nerves with pity and some impatience, and she brusquely warned Ellen not to indulge in what could become "a most undesirable habit."

Even so, she was uneasy enough to send her over the summer to Clifton Springs Sanitarium, west of Auburn, under the supervision of Ellen's calm, capable older sister, Eliza. Clifton Springs, a sanitarium offering the "rest cures" that became popular later in the century, provided a daily regimen of rest, exercise, healthful foods, and hydrotherapy in the mineral springs. Afterward, Martha expected Ellen to pull herself together, telling her, "You can never be what I hope to see you become without steady persevering effort, & there never will be a better time than now to begin."

Martha assumed that Ellen would attend college, an opportunity that hadn't existed for Marianna and Eliza. It was a privilege Martha had always envied young men more than any other. If college had been an option for her in 1826, she would not have rushed into her early marriage to Peter Pelham. Oberlin—Lucy Stone's alma mater—had been admitting Black students since 1835 and women since 1837, and some dozen female academies had sprung up to meet a rising demand. But to Martha's dismay, Ellen was more interested in her succession of suitors than in her studies. Martha told her that she shouldn't assume she would one day marry, and that if she pursued a single life, she would need a disciplined mind and a source of income. Moreover, Ellen must "prove the equality of men and women." Martha came up with what seemed an inspired solution: she asked Susan B. Anthony to prepare Ellen to be Anthony's successor in the women's rights movement.

Anthony, childless and lonely, welcomed the plan. In coming years, Ellen began attending anti-slavery and women's rights meetings with her mother, and spending time with "Aunt Susan" in Rochester, where she helped with organizational duties and socialized with Anthony's reformer friends. Anthony tried, without success, to get her to take on the job of secretary at one of the annual woman's rights conventions. Ellen enjoyed Anthony's company, describing her in her journal as "neither graceful nor beautiful nor rich nor winning to strangers," but "strong-hearted and a friend indeed." Nonetheless, she wrote miserably, "She is disapptd. in me—Of course she is—isn't everybody?—I am a nonentity, *after all*."

Martha talked with Frances about her hopes and fears for Ellen, and Frances confessed her concerns about Fanny, who had serious health problems: chronic racking coughs and high fevers. Four years younger than Ellen, Fanny wanted to be a writer, an idea her mother encouraged. Fanny was not well enough to go to boarding school, and Frances, with the help of a governess, taught her at home. She designed a classical education like the one Frances had received at Miss Willard's—supplemented by her own ideas about abolition and women's rights. In Washington over the winter of 1858–1859, Frances guided Fanny through Herodotus,

Thucydides, and Xenophanes, and hired tutors for French, music, painting, and dance lessons. Fanny, the daughter of a senator, would have a coming-out party in Washington when she was eighteen, but Frances saw her exposure to the arts not as a way to increase her value as a debutante, but as a necessity to becoming a well-rounded adult. She also hoped the lessons would help Fanny conquer her timorousness at Henry's dinners, and with young men. One day in Auburn, after Fanny ran into Martha's son Willy, a childhood playmate who had grown up to be intimidatingly attractive, she laughingly admitted to Frances and Aunt Lazette that she was so flustered she could barely speak.

Frances, too, thought that marriage should not be the only secure option for young women. She told Martha that when an acquaintance commented that it must be difficult to prepare Fanny for courtship while also overseeing her lessons, she'd replied that she was educating Fanny "not to be married." She and Henry established a fund for Fanny so that she would be able to live independently, and Henry commented to a dinner guest that he didn't want his daughter "to marry some scamp & be ill-treated." Perhaps alluding to his own marital tensions, he said that even marriage for love was as likely to prove unhappy as not.

Ellen and Fanny admired smart, independent women, but saw how they were ridiculed. Fanny didn't tell anyone outside her family about her writing, knowing that she would be mocked as a "bluestocking." She later noted in her diary that most men didn't meet her standard of "intellect, heart, and morals." No one measured up to her brothers or to her father, who always took "the woman's side of the question without identifying himself with the absurd & ultra woman's rights theorists." She meant the proponents of free love, such as the residents of the Oneida Community, sixty miles east of Auburn, who had as many sexual partners as they liked, and whose children were raised communally. Fanny's role models, after her mother and Lazette, were Martha C. Wright, Elizabeth Cady Stanton, Susan B. Anthony, Emily Howland, and Charlotte Cushman—a friend of the family and a favorite of Fanny's. Cushman, who had a successful transcontinental acting career, confidently talked about politics with Henry, and encouraged Fanny's literary interests. Fanny, sheltered by Frances, didn't know about Cushman's tempestuous love affairs with women in the United States and abroad. When Cushman asked Fanny about Augustus's bachelorhood, she replied that it was due to Gus's "remarkable diffidence."

She saw these women as demanding for themselves and Black Americans the rights that white men claimed for themselves.

Martha spent much of 1860 organizing both for abolition and for women's rights. In January, she convened an anti-slavery meeting in Auburn, and, in February, presided at another one in Albany. While she was there, she went with Stanton and Anthony to the state capital to lobby legislators to expand the Married Women's Property Act of 1848. They succeeded: both houses voted to pass the new bill, and the governor signed it. Three months later, starting on May 10, Martha chaired the most noteworthy women's rights meeting yet: the tenth anniversary of their national conventions. It took place at Cooper Union, a coeducational arts and sciences school in lower Manhattan, and it was scheduled, as usual, back to back with the annual gathering of the American Anti-Slavery Society, so that people could attend both. Until 1840, women were not allowed to be members of the anti-slavery society; now they held positions as officers and as members of the executive committee, and Lucy Stone and Abigail Kelley Foster were among its most popular lecturers.

At the tenth convention, the New York State women were in full cry. Anthony counted the advances women had made—lobbying to get bills passed in state legislatures, organizing petition drives, and entering formerly all-male preserves. She cited one outstanding example: Elizabeth Blackwell, who in 1847 had dared to pursue a career in medicine. Rejected by sixteen medical schools, Blackwell was finally accepted at Geneva Medical College, west of Auburn, only after the dean asked the all-male student body to put it to a vote. Thinking it was a practical joke, the students unanimously voted "Aye." Doctors' wives in town refused to speak to Blackwell, and people thought she must be lewd or insane. In 1849, Blackwell graduated at the top of her class, and she became the first licensed female physician in the United States. Eight years later, she and her younger sister Emily, who followed her in earning a medical degree, opened the New York Infirmary for Women and Children.

Stanton introduced resolutions on women's right to divorce. Like Wollstonecraft, she regarded loveless marriage as a daily hell that shriveled women's inner lives. For many women, it also posed the dangers of assault. Few people thought that way—even their reliable old friend Wendell Phillips. Nine years earlier, at the women's 1851 convention, Phillips had said,

"Throw open the doors of Congress, throw open those court-houses, throw wide open the doors of your colleges." Now, unwilling to approve changes to an institution that most men found perfectly satisfactory, he moved that Stanton's resolutions be struck from the record: the discussion should concern only "the laws that rest unequally upon women, not those that rest equally upon men and women." The women of New York had just achieved stronger guarantees of their right to their property and their children—why couldn't they leave it at that? Anthony, rising to Stanton's defense, said that marriage was a one-sided matter, in which man gained all and woman lost all: "Tyrant law and lust reign supreme with him—meek submission and cheerful, ready obedience, alone befit her." The convention voted down Phillips's motion to purge the record.

The press seized on the divorce plank, describing the women as advocates of free love—the kind of charge that scared off would-be disciples who found financial security and companionship in marriage. Stanton noted to Martha: "We have thrown our bombshell into the center of woman's degradation and of course we have raised a rumpus." Martha commented to Anthony: "This hue & cry about Free Love, in New York, of all places in the world, is too contemptible & hypocritical to be worth a moment's notice." She vowed to push on, despite "misrepresentation & abuse" meant to "discourage the wavering, and frighten the timid from our glorious platform."

As president, Martha left it to her friends to expound on the purposes and achievements of "this great movement." Avoiding solemnity, which was not her strength, she poked fun at an orthodox Presbyterian publication, *The New York Observer*, which featured headlines such as "Religion the Only Safe Basis of Popular Education," and "Why is there a Hell?" She knew the women's most daring goals would not be achieved in their lifetimes—their children and grandchildren would have to pursue them after they were gone. But that realization would deflate new followers, so Martha claimed that, before long, even their foes would see their cause as legitimate: "After all that we demand has been granted, as it will be soon, The New York Observer will piously fold its hands and roll up its eyes and say, 'This beneficent movement we have always advocated,' and the pulpits will say 'Amen!' " As the laughter and applause subsided, she asserted, "Then will come forward women who have gained courage from the efforts and sacrifices of others, and the great world will say, 'Here come the women who are going to do something.' "

15

General Tubman Goes to Boston

1858–1860

John Brown, 1859

Early in the spring of 1858, Harriet Tubman had an unsettling dream. She was in "a wilderness sort of place, all full of rocks and bushes," as she put it, where a serpent rose up and became the head of an old man with a long white beard. He gazed at her "wishful like, just as if he were going to speak to me." Then two younger heads appeared. A crowd of men rushed in and knocked them down, before attacking the older man, who continued to gaze at her in silence. He had an urgent message to convey, but what was it?

She couldn't make any sense of the dream until April, when her underground railroad contact in Syracuse, Rev. Jermain Loguen, arrived in St. Catharines to say that John Brown was with him, and that he wanted her to gather a group of trusted men to listen to what he had to say. Rather than meet at Brown's hotel, Harriet told Loguen to bring him to her home on North Street, where he would be safe. She had heard the stories about Brown's crimes, but she saw him as a godly man who was risking his life for the freedom of her race. When she opened the door, she recognized him as the figure in her dream. He was traveling under an alias, and had grown a flowing white beard.

Brown had been frenetically busy in the past few years, ducking the authorities and crisscrossing the country in search of funds for his personal war against slavery. In January 1857, eight months after the Pottawatomie massacre, Brown made his way to Boston, looking for wealthy supporters. He went straight to Franklin Sanborn, a well-connected twenty-five-year-old Harvard graduate and radical idealist whom Thoreau approvingly saw as the type that "calmly, so calmly, ignites and then throws bomb after bomb." Sanborn ran an experimental private school in Concord attended by the children of Nathaniel Hawthorne and Ralph Waldo Emerson, but he was consumed by his work as secretary of the Massachusetts State Kansas Aid Committee in Boston, founded to raise money for "the oppressed Free State Settlers of that Territory."

Brown had a hypnotic effect on abolitionists who lacked his fire-breathing pugnacity. Sanborn was awestruck by Brown's "blending of the soldier and the deacon," his "masculine, deep and metallic voice," and his unflinching commitment to a free Kansas. He rushed to introduce Brown to other members of the Kansas committee—the chair, George Luther Stearns, and Dr. Samuel Gridley Howe—and to his friends Rev. Theodore Parker and thirty-four-year-old Thomas Wentworth Higginson, the pastor of the racially diverse Worcester Free Church. All of them had given up on equivocating politicians and overcome any squeamishness about violence in the cause of justice, and they agreed to subsidize Brown's project. After Sanborn arranged for Brown to address the state legislature, it passed a $100,000 appropriation for Kansas free-staters. The Kansas Aid Committee provided Brown with two hundred Sharps rifles and several boxes of caps and cartridges, plus $500 for expenses. In New York City, Brown hired a British mercenary to train his men, and in Connecticut he got an edged-tool manufacturer to make a thousand pikes of his own design: Bowie knives affixed to six-foot poles.

At first, Brown kept his Boston donors guessing about his exact plans, writing to Higginson in February 1858 to request another $500 to $800, saying that he was perfecting "BY FAR the most *important* undertaking of my whole life." Higginson asked if he was referring to underground railroad operations. Brown replied: "Rail Road business on a *somewhat extended* scale; is the *identical* object for which I am trying to get means." The next month, Brown finally explained to the Boston men and to Gerrit Smith, whom he enlisted at a stopover at his home in Peterboro, that he was not talking about fighting the Border Ruffians in Kansas, but about a plot he had been perfecting for decades: starting at Harpers Ferry, then part of Virginia, he planned to overthrow the entire institution of slavery. The cabal eventually became known as the Secret Six.

Brown culminated his travels in St. Catharines, where he intended to raise troops for his incipient army, and to recruit Harriet Tubman as its commander. As requested, Harriet assembled a group of men she had helped to escape from Dorchester County, and a few friends she'd made in town. Brown told them he was planning a series of raids on southern plantations that would extend into the Deep South, liberating hundreds of thousands of slaves. The caves and forests of the Appalachian Mountains, stretching from Georgia to Canada, would provide cover for people heading north along a guarded "Subterranean Pass-Way." Two of the famous Dover Eight, who had broken out of the Delaware jail, signed on, as did three men Harriet had rescued in 1856, and two friends she had made in Canada.

After the meeting, Brown wrote feverishly to his son John Jr., "I am succeeding *to all appearance* beyond my expectation." Persuaded that Harriet had found his plot irresistible, he assured John that she had "hooked on" her whole team. Referring to her as General Tubman, he said she was "the most of a man naturally; that I ever met with." It didn't occur to Brown that Harriet might not take orders from anyone, and that she ran a very different kind of insurgency from the one he had in mind—removing freedom seekers from harm's way, not leading them back into the heart of slavery. In any case, she had her own plans. Brown assumed he was putting her to work for him; instead, she got him to do something for her.

She had strong friendships and underground railroad contacts in Wilmington, Philadelphia, New York, Auburn, Syracuse, Rochester, and towns in between, but she wanted to extend her reach into Boston. Seeing how generous the moneyed abolitionists were with Brown, she asked Gerrit Smith to send a letter of introduction to Franklin Sanborn, and in May 1859, just after buying her house from Frances Seward, she traveled to Boston to raise some money. Sanborn, curious to meet the woman Garrison called "Moses" and Brown called "General," visited Harriet at her boardinghouse at 168 Cambridge Street. She greeted him cautiously. Because Harriet couldn't read or write, Sanborn observed, "she was obliged to trust to her wits." To ascertain that he truly was Franklin Sanborn, she produced daguerreotypes of mutual friends, asking if he recognized their likenesses. Only when he had identified them did she speak freely. Sanborn again made the rounds of his friends in Concord and Boston, this time to introduce Tubman to Thoreau, Emerson, the Alcott family, and the philanthropist Ednah Dow Cheney. Harriet's stay in Boston intersected with one of Brown's trips there, and she asked him to introduce her to the great abolitionist Wendell Phillips. Brown took her to Phillips's house, and said, "Mr. Phillips, I bring you one of the best and bravest persons on this continent—General Tubman, we call her." Phillips and Ednah Cheney became lifelong benefactors.

Harriet remained in Boston that spring and summer, where she began speaking at Cheney's house to reformers interested in hearing about her underground railroad work and ready to offer financial support. As word about her spread, she talked before larger audiences and raised more money. Small, animated, clad in a homespun dress and kerchief, she entranced white audiences by acting out her life, interspersing scenes of violent abuse with bits of Scripture, baritone renditions of Negro spirituals, and wry anecdotes about outwitting former "masters." Cheney wrote that she played all the parts, and "The scene rises before you as she saw it, and her voice and language change with her different actors." Among women, Harriet encouraged a perception of her as a warrior who defied presumptions about sex, race, and education. She even turned John's betrayal into a humorous tale about how she had attained autonomy—returning from that trip with John's clothes, but without the man himself.

Playing to her audiences' enthusiasm for hair-raising first-person accounts of slavery and escape, she talked about a time she and four passengers were about thirty miles south of Wilmington, where they were closely pursued by slave catchers who had posted advertisements identifying the four men and offering large rewards for their capture. God told her to leave the road, she said, and take a route that would require them to cross a rushing tidewater stream. Neither she nor the men could swim, and the water came up to Harriet's armpits. Her followers refused to venture in until she was safe on the other side. Soaked and shaking from the cold, they eventually crossed a second stream, then walked on until they reached the cabin of a Black woman, who took them in, put them to bed, and dried their clothes. A few days later, they reached Thomas Garrett's house in Wilmington. Garrett was concerned that Harriet was sick. She was so hoarse she could barely speak, but she was more bothered by a toothache, which she dispensed with by picking up a rock and knocking out the damaged tooth.

In Boston, Harriet also met Thomas Wentworth Higginson, who became another lasting friend. Higginson, who said he liked to "pitch right into people and show them how foolish they are thinking and acting," had entered Harvard at the age of thirteen, studied theology at the Divinity School, and wrote poetry and articles supporting temperance, abolition, and women's rights. His reedy voice, neatly combed hair, and high, starched collars betrayed his social class, but he yearned to break the bounds of convention. He saw Tubman and other fugitive slaves as his teachers, writing, "We learned to speak because their presence made silence impossible." They "arrived from the South as if they still bore a hundred pounds weight of plantation soil on each ankle."

On July 4, 1859, Harriet appeared before her largest audience yet, at the Massachusetts Anti-Slavery Society, in Framingham. Higginson introduced her as a conductor on the underground railroad, and as a dutiful daughter. She had brought her father and mother out of slavery, and she was looking to raise a few hundred dollars to pay for a "little place" she had bought them—and then would "resume the practice of her profession." Garrison characterized her style as one of "quaint simplicity," saying that "she excited the most profound interest in her hearers." She raised thirty-seven dollars at the talk, and enough money during her months in Boston to make a $200 payment on her mortgage.

While John Brown was making the final preparations for his insurrection, Harriet was coping with the prosaic burdens of daily life. She had moved her family into her new home in Auburn that spring, but her brother John had trouble coping when she was away. That fall, when Harriet was in New York, John wrote in a dictated letter, which she had read to her, that their father wanted to return on foot to St. Catharines to retrieve some of his things—a distance of almost 140 miles. John reminded her: "Seward has received nothing as Payment since the 4th of July that I know of. Write me particularly what you want me to do as I want to hear from you very much."

On October 16, Harriet had a premonition. She told a friend she was staying with in New York City that Captain John Brown was in trouble, and that soon they would hear bad news about him. The next day, newspapers reported that Brown, leading a ragtag army of sixteen white and five Black men, had seized the federal arsenal at Harpers Ferry and was holed up in the engine house, where Lieutenant Colonel Robert E. Lee and his troops surrounded them. Brown was wounded and arrested, along with six of his men. Two of his sons, Oliver and Watson, were killed. Another son, Owen, escaped with four others. Harriet finally grasped the full meaning of her dream: the mute plea of the white-bearded man in the wilderness, about to be struck down by his enemies.

John Brown, seen by most Americans as a delusional fanatic, was executed in Charles Town, Virginia, on December 2. His admirers, though, cast him as a martyr. Longfellow wrote in his diary, "This will be a great day in our history; the date of a new Revolution—quite as much needed as the old one." In a speech at Tremont Temple, Emerson predicted that Brown would "make the gallows glorious like the cross." Harriet felt compelled to help finish the work that Brown had started. As she later told Martha, Brown "done more in dying than 100 men would in living." She'd said to Ednah Cheney on the day he was captured, "It's clear to me that it wasn't John Brown that was hung on that gallows. When I think how he gave up his life for our people, and how he never flinched, but was so brave to the end; it's clear to me that it wasn't mortal man, it was God in him." Referring to the prospect of universal emancipation, Harriet went on, "When I think of the prayers and groans I've heard on them plantations, and remember that God's a prayer-hearing God, I feel that His time is near."

• • •

Four months later, in April 1860, Harriet was on her way to Boston after a series of fundraising talks across New York. She stopped in Troy, eight miles north of Albany, to see a cousin and several other relatives and friends who were local underground railroad operatives. Troy was a city of 40,000 people, heavily populated by abolitionists. On the day of John Brown's execution, a local paper had described the mood: "Dull and sombre clouds, weeping with rain, obscured the light of day and cast a gloom upon the very air." Hundreds of people paid their respects when Brown's casket, on its way from Virginia to North Elba, New York, was placed in a roped-off section at Troy's Union Station.

Harriet's brief time in Troy coincided with a fugitive slave rescue that turned out to be as spectacular as the 1851 Jerry Rescue in Syracuse. On the morning of April 27, a man was arrested outside a bakery at Fulton and Fifth streets in Troy where he'd gone to buy bread for his employer. A father of six in his early thirties named Charles Nalle, he had fled Culpeper, Virginia, eighteen months earlier, after his enslaver refused his request to hire himself out so that he could live with his free wife. Nalle now worked as a coachman in Troy for a wealthy merchant and philanthropist, saving most of his earnings so that he could buy freedom for himself and his children. He was handcuffed by a Virginia slave catcher and taken into custody by a deputy federal marshal, who escorted him to the federal commissioner's office in the Mutual Bank Building on State Street.

Harriet rushed to the scene and assessed the crowd: free Blacks and people who had escaped from slavery, white laborers and businessmen, ladies with parasols, young ruffians, and defenders of public order. Correspondents covering the event reported that Nalle could be seen standing in front of a window on the second floor. Some protesters said that he should be taken from the authorities and safely sent to Canada, others that they should help buy his freedom. A few shouted that the law should be permitted to take its course. Harriet, using a ruse that had served her well in some of her rescue operations in Maryland, impersonated a stooped old woman. Her face obscured by her sunbonnet, she passed the crush of men on the stairs, and stood outside the door of the commissioner's office, pretending to be deep in prayer.

Nalle raised the window and tried to clamber out. A chorus of conflicting demands ensued—"Drop him! Catch him! Stop him!"—until someone pulled him back inside. As officers escorted him down the stairs,

Harriet leaped up, pushed past them, and, grabbing Nalle, fended off the constables' blows as she guided him through the crowd. One participant in the rescue later said that "it seemed a miracle that she appeared just at that time."

Determined to prevent Nalle's recapture, Harriet shouted: "Drag him to the river! Drown him! But don't let them have him!" His head was battered and his wrists were cut and bloody from the handcuffs. Harriet's coat was torn off, and her shoes were ripped from her feet. People closed protectively around them, propelling them down Congress Street toward the dock, where a skiff was waiting. As she ran, she later told Ednah Cheney, a little boy cried out, "Go it, old aunty! You're the best old aunty a fellow ever had." Nalle got into the skiff, and he was rowed across a narrow stretch of the Hudson to the town of West Troy. Harriet boarded a crowded ferry, and learned on the other shore that Nalle had been rearrested. She was directed to a judge's office. The crowd broke open the barricaded front door, Harriet and other rescuers rushed in, and a man inside the office was heard shouting, "Throw that damn nigger out of here, or we'll all be killed!" Nalle was hurled out, and Harriet followed him into the street. Three armed Black men in a wagon lifted up Nalle and galloped away, and Harriet disappeared into the crowd. Nalle was taken to Schenectady, and northwest to Amsterdam, where he remained in hiding for almost a month, until the people of Troy and West Troy raised $650 to buy his freedom. The residents of New York State had again outmaneuvered the authorities, with fugitive slaves leading the way.

Harriet resumed her trip to Boston, where she was due to speak at a series of anti-slavery and women's rights meetings. In early July, *The Liberator* published a brief piece about "a colored woman of the name of Moses" who talked about "her adventures in a modest but quaint and amusing style." A newspaper in Maryland, where Eliza Brodess still had a price on her head, featured a story under the headline "A FEMALE CONDUCTOR OF THE UNDER-GROUND RAILROAD," describing the talk by "Mrs. Harriet Tupman," who had brought into freedom no fewer than forty people, including her aged father and mother. "She had a prolonged and enthusiastic reception."

The story of the Nalle rescue became one of Harriet's favorites. As an older woman, she held the children of Auburn spellbound, telling them that as she pulled Nalle away from the authorities, a policeman clubbed her, but "I knocked him squawkin'." She then attacked the marshal's deputy, offering a graphic demonstration of how she choked him, "'til his tongue stick out like that." As she fought, she said, Nalle was hit so hard he lost consciousness. The children shouted with relieved laughter as she told them that she threw him across her shoulder "like a bag o' meal and took him away out of there."

16

The Agitators

1860

We have been expending our sympathies, as well as congratulations, on seven newly arrived slaves that Harriet Tubman has just pioneered safely from the Southern part of Maryland - One woman carried a baby all the way, & brot two other children that Harriet & the men helped along, - they brot a piece of old comfort & blanket, in a basket with a little kindling, a little bread for the baby with some laudanum, to keep it from crying during the day - They walked all night, carrying the little ones, and spread the old comfort on the frozen ground, in some dense thicket, where they all hid, while Harriet went out foraging, & sometimes cd. not get back till dark, fearing she wd. be followed - Then if they had crept further in, & she couldn't find them, she wd whistle, or sing certain hymns, & they wd. answer.

"One woman carried a baby all the way, & brot two other children that Harriet & the men helped along." Martha Coffin Wright to Ellen Wright, December 30, 1860

The Republican National Convention opened in Chicago on May 16, 1860, Henry's fifty-ninth birthday. He was in Auburn with Frances, working on an acceptance speech for the presidential nomination while Weed managed the delegates in the meeting hall. Frances, like just about everyone, assumed that Henry was about to be awarded the prize of his long antislavery career. She kept up a façade of excitement, but she had been quietly dwelling on threats to his safety ever since John Brown's raid, which Henry's southern foes blamed on him. An advertisement in a Richmond paper had offered five hundred dollars for "the head of William H. Seward," and someone poisoned Fanny's German Shepherd, Neptune, with arsenic—the second family dog to die for Henry's beliefs. If he should win the presidency, would a crazed Fire-Eater attempt to take his life? Would southerners rally the region to fight a civil war? How would she cope with being First Lady when she couldn't bear her role as a senator's wife?

Two days later, Frances was in her room when Henry, relaxing in the garden with their friend Rev. John Austin, got word of the final balloting in Chicago. The family doctor, Theodore Dimon, rushed to them exclaiming, "Oh, God, it is all gone, gone, gone! Abraham Lincoln has received the nomination!" The news, devastating for Henry, also brought into acute focus the conflict of Frances's entire married life. Secretly relieved for herself, she was irate when she learned what had taken place. Lincoln loyalists from Indiana and Illinois had printed counterfeit tickets and packed the hall—preventing the entry of many of Henry's supporters, who were up late the night before prematurely celebrating. Horace Greeley, a convention delegate, had been nursing a years-long grievance against Henry for not supporting him when he'd made a bid for lieutenant governor of New York. At the convention, Greeley lobbied hard against Henry, arguing that he could not carry New Jersey, Pennsylvania, Indiana, or Iowa. Lincoln, who did not have Henry's controversial political history, was a safer choice. Greeley was right, but Frances saw his defection as an act of pure vindictiveness. She told Henry that Greeley had outraged his oldest friends, and, "At the age of 50 he will not be likely to find new ones."

Martha returned from the women's rights convention at Cooper Union just as the Republican convention in Chicago was ending. She wrote to Stanton, "It was almost like a funeral in town, when the news of the nomination was rec'd." Seward had the same thought, but he somehow managed a witticism: "I had the rare experience of a man walking about town, after he is dead, and hearing what people would say of him."

After Henry left for Washington to resume his senatorial post, Frances regretted not going with him. He confessed in his first letter home that he felt deposed by his party, and that his house seemed sad and mournful. In the Senate, even Jefferson Davis greeted him sympathetically. Other friends assured him that his day would come. Neither Henry nor Frances believed that. He would be too old if the opportunity came again.

Charles Sumner, one of those who commiserated with Henry, had returned in December 1859, three and a half years after the attack by Preston Brooks. From France, where he spent much of his recovery, he had kept Frances up to date about his medical treatments, which included regular swims in the Mediterranean Sea and three months of daily "cuppings"—a heated glass placed on injured areas to stimulate blood flow and reduce pain. He still relied on morphine, and had difficulty walking without a cane. Nevertheless, on June 4, he was back on the floor, in full evening attire, giving a long, splenetic speech titled "The Barbarism of Slavery." Frances wrote, after reading it in Auburn, that he had made a "true exposition of unparalleled wickedness."

Henry promised Frances that when his term ended in March, he would retire, and she believed that he meant it. Fanny wistfully told her actress friend Charlotte Cushman that, with her father seeming to accept his defeat and her mother talking about them all living together in Auburn, "we were the happiest family imaginable." But others close to Henry did not believe he was ready to give up his career. Weed and Charles Francis Adams, the son of John Quincy Adams, told Henry that it was his duty, to the party and the country, to overcome his disappointment and campaign for Lincoln. Frances emphatically disagreed. She was surprised, she wrote, that so few of his friends placed any value in a life free of "the wranglings, the envy hatred & malice" of politics. "Twenty-five years of the best part of a man's life is all that his country can reasonably claim. You have earned the right to a peaceful old age." Henry, though, admitted to Weed that he was "not insensible to the claims of a million of friends, nor indifferent to the opinion of mankind."

Frances hoped to have a long talk with him when he returned that June for the wedding of their youngest son, Will Jr., to an intelligent, thoughtful local girl, Janet Watson, but she could not find the right time. Henry arrived just before the ceremony, which was nothing like the simple reception Judge Miller had held for her and Henry. Carpets were spread around the garden, lanterns strung in the trees, and townspeople strolled by for a glimpse of young Seward and his bride. Martha wrote to Lucretia,

"Church crowded, a perfect jam in the house, boys and girls perched on every picket and the street thronged, near the house, to hear the music, and 'take a smell.'"

There was not a moment after the reception either. Heeding Weed and Adams, Henry left immediately to campaign for Lincoln in Maine, New Hampshire, Vermont, and Massachusetts. Frances allowed Fanny, who was fifteen, and a friend to travel with her father and a small retinue on the second leg of the trip, which included, over the course of a month, a dozen states. Fanny was awed by the theatrics at every stop: torchlight parades, fife-and-drum corps, giant bonfires, and military-style parades performed by "Wide-Awakes"—Republican enthusiasts in black enameled cloth uniforms that reflected the lights of the torches, as Lincoln's aides John G. Nicolay and John Hay wrote, "like a beautiful serpent of fire."

Henry was reinvigorated by the adulatory turnout. In Lawrence, Kansas, rebuilt after its sacking in 1856, he bowed to his listeners, with "profound reverence" for their courage in pursuing a free state. In Springfield, Illinois, Lincoln boarded Henry's train to greet him and to discuss strategy. Henry had met Lincoln only once, at Tremont Temple in 1848, when both were Whigs, stumping for Zachary Taylor. Lincoln, until recently a little-known former representative, was tall, shambling, homely, and good-natured. Henry asked himself again how he had lost to this man. Charles Francis Adams thought that Lincoln appeared aware "that properly the positions should be reversed." Nonetheless, Lincoln gave Seward clear instructions for his speech at Chicago: the Republican Party would abide by the Constitution on states' rights and not interfere with slavery in the South. Henry entirely agreed. In an expansive mood as he spoke, he predicted that in coming years, the young men who voted the Republican ticket would say with pride, "I, too, voted for Abraham Lincoln."

Frances knew that she had lost Henry again. After the tour, she replied bitterly to a letter from Sumner, who praised Henry's skill as a speaker: "Yes, Henry is very popular now. He is monopolized by the public and I am at last—resigned." She was also disturbed by the note of moderation he was striking in his speeches, even in their own state, which had led the opposition to the Fugitive Slave Law.

Elizabeth Cady Stanton wrote to Frances after hearing Henry speak in Seneca Falls. Claiming not to understand the national political scene, Stanton said that she had asked a Republican luminary to parse Henry's words for her. The man explained that the party remained opposed to slavery, but that during election season, its leaders had to watch their language, telling her, "'Mr. Seward must of course keep the Pharaohs quiet until the children of Israel can peacefully walk out of bondage.'" Stanton assured Frances that she continued to "claim him for an out and out abolitionist." Frances, who never criticized Henry to others, did not correct that notion. But a few days before the election, when he declared that the party intended "to leave things to go on just exactly as they have gone on hitherto," she thought he sounded more like an old Cotton Whig than like a true Republican.

The nation never had been so politically engaged—or so divided. In November, 81 percent of eligible voters went to the polls. The Democratic Party, unable to agree on a presidential nominee, had chosen two candidates: Stephen Douglas of Illinois and Vice President John C. Breckinridge of Kentucky. Lincoln handily won the election, even though he lost the entire South. Of the fourteen states where Seward had campaigned, Lincoln carried all but slaveholding Missouri. South Carolina announced its intention to secede, and Georgia, Alabama, Mississippi, Louisiana, and Florida began considering whether to join a new confederacy.

Until 1933, U.S. presidents were not inaugurated until March, four months after being voted into office. Lincoln stayed in Springfield until he was due to be sworn in, which left Henry to take charge of the party in Washington: dissuading Radical Republicans from further roiling the South, and calming senators from the slaveholding border states—a ragged belt across the country's midsection consisting of Delaware, Maryland, Virginia, Kentucky, and Missouri. If enough states seceded, the North would have only two options, acquiescence or war, and if the border states sided with the South, the United States would cease to exist.

Henry promised Frances that he was not contemplating any fatal compromises with the South, and pleaded for her loyalty: "I have faith that my good angel wont desert me, as long as you and I keep together." He soothingly detailed his domestic routine: going to the market, eating breakfast, talking with a reporter, and answering letters. "I would not have believed it," he said, "but my pretty cat remembered me, and was wild with joy at my return. She attends me constantly, sitting on my shoulder when I write, and following me when I move." Turning to the tense political scene, he said with his new note of accommodation that the best response to the Fire-Eaters, who were threatening secession, was "restraint and kindness."

Many of Henry's supporters were confused by his public posture, and thought that Weed had virtually gone over to the other side. In his *Evening Journal*, he lauded a measure proposed by Senator John Crittenden of Kentucky, known as the Crittenden Compromise—the last gasp of those who still believed in bargaining with the South. The bill would allow slavery into the western territories south of the Missouri Compromise line—a position Henry and Lincoln explicitly opposed. Frances, receiving one letter after another from constituents who assumed that Weed spoke for Seward, wrote to Henry, "The air is filled with such strange tales of compromise and concession that I myself do not know what to believe."

Henry was a member of the Committee of Thirteen, a group of senators formed to examine various plans, including Crittenden's, to save the Union and to give the incoming administration some time to organize. Frances wrote, "There is the feeling here that this is the time to speak bluntly to the South and not to make concessions—You will of course do as you please, as you must, but I thought it my duty to tell you of the atmosphere here and the way I have been besieged by letter writers who think they can influence you through influencing me." Henry said that he did not agree with Weed, and reiterated that he would not act unwisely, but Frances wondered what deal he might strike in order to avoid war.

In mid-December, Lincoln asked Henry to serve as his secretary of state, the highest post in the administration, and Henry returned to Auburn to consult with Frances. Given the parlous state of the country, she couldn't advise him not to take the job. Like most Americans, she assumed that a self-taught lawyer from the West who had served only two years in the House would be out of his depth in Washington. Henry knew everyone in the House and Senate, and understood the powers of the White House as well as he did those of Congress. Frances planned a family Christmas in Auburn, but Henry was home for barely a week when he was called back to work with the Committee of Thirteen. It was too late. On December 20, 1860, South Carolina seceded.

Henry told Lincoln he would accept the position. "It is inevitable," he wrote to Frances. "I will try to save freedom and my country." On New Year's Eve, he added, "I cannot think of myself in this emergency of probable Civil War and Dissolution of the Union. I could not be well or happy at home, refusing to do what I can, when called to the councils of my country." She prayed that he was right to think he could shape events of such magnitude. Kindness and restraint toward the South had never worked before, and they certainly wouldn't now.

On the day that South Carolina seceded, Martha responded to a letter from her nephew Charles Pelham, who practiced law in Talladega, Alabama. Charles had infuriated her in 1856 with his callow response to the caning of Sumner. Now he tried to put southerners in the role of the country's founders, fighting against a tyrannizing majority. Martha corrected him again. "I am astonished," she wrote, "at the blindness that leads you to speak of the spirit of our forefathers to resist *oppression*, and to *throw off* the *chains*." Charles's spiteful remarks about Lincoln and the future of slavery caused her to remark that Jefferson himself had seen the conflict over slavery as between injustice on one side, "and the eternal and unchanging principle of right, on the other." Martha added that she was not as pleased about Lincoln's election as Charles imagined. She feared he might, "by a mean spirit of compromise," postpone the day of emancipation "for the *masters* as well as the slaves of the south." She signed the letter, "With much love to yourself, and affectionate remembrance to your father, — whether in a united or divided confederacy, Affectionately Yr. Aunt Martha C. Wright."

About a week later, Harriet arrived at Martha's house with six underground railroad passengers. She had gone to Dorchester County hoping at last to rescue her sister Rachel and Rachel's two children, but she had waited in vain throughout the night in a blizzard at the agreed-upon location in a wood. She later learned that Rachel had died just days before. It was a terrible blow—her fourth sister lost to slavery. Adding to her sorrow, she couldn't take Rachel's two children, Angerine, who was thirteen, and Ben, eleven. She told Ednah Cheney that she had to leave them there "for want of $30"—the cost of paying someone to bring them to her. Harriet couldn't linger. After the mass escapes of 1857, authorities and slaveholders had caught and imprisoned several underground railroad agents. Still, she managed to spirit away a couple, Stephen and Maria Ennals, and their young children. At one point, sensing they were being followed, they had trudged through a swamp to a small island, where they hid in the wet grasses. Around twilight, a man appeared in Quaker garb, slowly walking along a path by the edge of the swamp. Harriet thought he was talking to himself, but as he drew closer, she heard him say, "My wagon stands in the barnyard of the next farm along the way. The horse is in the stable; the harness hangs on a nail." That journey north took more than a month.

Martha, after listening to Harriet describe the trip, wrote to her youngest daughter, Ellen, impressing upon her the torments faced by freedom seekers on the run. Ellen, who was completing her education at Mrs. Sedgwick's School for Young Ladies in Lenox, Massachusetts, never forgot it. "We have been expending our sympathies, as well as congratulations," Martha noted, to a group of six "newly arrived slaves that Harriet Tubman has just pioneered safely from the Southern part of Maryland." A woman had held her baby in her arms the entire way, while Harriet and the men helped along the other two children. "They walked all night, carrying the little ones, and spread the old comfort on the frozen ground, in some dense thicket, where they all hid, while Harriet went out foraging & sometimes could not get back till dark, fearing she would be followed. Then if they had crept further in, & she couldn't find them, she would whistle or sing certain hymns, & they would answer." It was Harriet's final underground railroad rescue. After that, she took her war against slavery to South Carolina's Lowcountry.

PART THREE

WAR

(1861–1864)

Lieutenant Colonel Will Seward, 138th New York Infantry, 1865

Two Brothers in Arms, ca. 1860–1870

17

"No Compromise"

1861

Frances A. Seward in her garden, 1862

Henry grandly called himself the "premier" of the new administration, but it seemed to Frances that he was assuming a crushing burden—one that voters had not seen fit to entrust to him. While President-elect Abraham Lincoln remained in Springfield, working out his choices for his other top advisers and his policy toward the South, Henry hired his own first aide—their son Frederick, to be his assistant secretary of state. In a city riddled with disloyal southerners and spies, he wrote to Fred that he needed "a confidential friend and scribe," adding, "It is revolutionary times here." Henry's immediate task, in his final senatorial address on January 12, was to make one last attempt to avert war. According to the *Chicago Tribune*,

"Never in the history of the American Congress has there been witnessed so intense an anxiety to hear a speech as that which preceded the delivery of Mr. Seward's." The *Washington Evening Star* speculated that if he extended the olive branch, the Union might escape destruction. Hopes were high that Henry had some solution to a conflict he had unambiguously described a few years earlier as "irrepressible."

Frances wasn't with him in Washington to offer her usual advice, and she was unsure what to expect. In his first address to the Senate a decade earlier, he had refused to bend to southern demands, and in recent months, he had repeatedly promised her that he would act wisely. When Frances read the speech, she was appalled. Henry again cited Jefferson, though not to proclaim the rights of all men. "In political affairs," he said this time, "we cannot always do what seems to us absolutely best." As the governor of New York, he had protected fugitive slaves from pursuers, by signing personal liberty laws; he now advised northern states to repeal such laws. He even pledged that the administration would approve a constitutional amendment stating that Congress could not "abolish or interfere with slavery in any state." Admitting that he didn't personally endorse all of the measures, he stated weakly, "We must be content to lead when we can, and to follow when we cannot lead."

Frances accused Henry of abandoning anti-slavery convictions he'd held his entire life: "Compromises based on the idea that the preservation of the Union is more important than the liberty of nearly 4,000,000 human beings cannot be right." Giving half of the territories of a free country "to the curse of slavery," she continued, "cannot be approved by God or supported by good men."

Henry tried to assure her that she would soon see that he was not offering compromises but explanations, "to disarm the enemies of Truth, Freedom, and Union of their most effective weapons." Reminding her that she wasn't there to witness what he confronted every day, he wrote: "Mad men North, and mad men South, are working together to produce a dissolution of the Union, by civil war. The present administration, and the incoming one, unite in devolving on me the responsibility of averting those disasters." There were said to be two thousand armed conspirators in the city, including the mayor. He hoped to get home for a visit, but without him, he said, the government would succumb to chaos and despair: "I am the only *hopeful, calm, conciliatory* person here."

Frances wrote blisteringly about their eldest child, Augustus, who, promoted to major, had left his sinecure at the U.S. Coast Survey, a government agency that mapped the Atlantic shoreline, and now worked with the Paymaster Corps, at Fort Defiance in New Mexico Territory. The previous spring, the Navajos had nearly overrun the fort, which was built on their sacred ground. She blamed Henry for encouraging Gus to attend West Point, and then allowing him to fight in the Mexican War—a conflict they both saw as an exercise in rank imperialism. She sympathized with the Navajos, just as she had with the Mexicans. For sixteen years, she had prayed that Gus "might be spared the misfortune of raising his hand against his fellow man." Now she accepted the onset of civil war, if it would bring an end to slavery. In a final thrust, she likened Henry to the former secretary of state who had died disgraced for executing the Fugitive Slave Law: "You are in danger of taking the path which led Daniel Webster to an unhonored grave."

The next morning, after mailing the letter, she regretted that line, writing again to say that she'd had a violent headache—she had exaggerated, and she hoped he would destroy it. The onus was partly on her. If she had been in Washington, she might have persuaded him not to deliver the speech.

Lazette, who usually defended Henry, couldn't do it this time. Running into Martha at a church fair, Lazette admitted she was disappointed in the speech, and said that she supported dissolution of the Union. So did Lucretia, who believed that the administration should let the slave states secede, sure that the South could not survive as a separate country. She wrote from Philadelphia, articulating what she, Martha, Lazette, and Frances all thought: she didn't like Henry's tendency to "*allay*, rather than *foment* the National excitement." Martha was with Frances when an abolitionist friend from out of town criticized the speech, and she noticed Frances's cheeks redden in response. Frances, excruciatingly torn between her loyalty to her husband and the position she held along with her friends, felt that Henry had discredited himself, perhaps permanently.

As the nation prepared for war, Martha and Stanton, hoping to put pressure on the new administration, thought that they must suspend the annual women's rights conventions and help their allies push for immediate emancipation. Anthony resisted the idea, arguing that constant pressure was necessary to protect women's gains. Stanton, though, felt indebted to Garrison for his early advocacy for women. In 1840, he had opposed more conservative members of the American Anti-Slavery Society, saying that women's rights were a central part of abolitionist doctrine, which prompted the conservatives to stalk off and form their own group. Garrison's society was the first organization, Stanton said, to recognize "the humanity of woman," and its members as "the only men who have ever echoed back her cries for justice and equality." She assumed that once emancipation was achieved, Garrison and his followers would join them in a united push for full citizenship for women.

In the winter of 1861, Martha, Stanton, and Anthony organized half a dozen anti-slavery meetings across western New York. They took up Garrison's slogan, "No Union with Slaveholders! No Compromise with Slaveholders!," a position many felt was just as seditious as that of the southern secessionists. Stanton's husband, now a reporter for *The New-York Tribune*, warned her: "The mobocrats would as soon kill you as not."

In Buffalo, where the women rented St. James Hall, a venue used for everything from poultry shows to opera, they drew a large audience that included opponents bent on shutting down the event. By 1861, mobs in the North no longer dragged men through the streets with ropes around their necks, broke up women's prayer meetings, or, as Stanton put it in a memoir, dipped "the apostles of reform" in barrels of tar and feathers: "They simply crowded the halls, and with laughing, groaning, clapping, and cheering, effectually interrupted the proceedings." To maintain order, the mayor sent fifty policemen to the hall, but rather than restrain the catcalls of Democrats and young "roughs," the police joined in. Stanton objected that the hecklers—the "northern buffaloes"—had trampled the right of free speech. In Rochester, when demonstrators shouted down their meeting in Corinthian Hall, the proprietor called a halt to the gathering, which reassembled at the African Methodist Episcopalian Zion Church. In Syracuse, protesters forced the leaders to retreat to a private home, then marched through the streets to Hanover Square, where they burned effigies of Susan B. Anthony and Rev. Samuel J. May.

Martha had turned her house, now empty of children and more centrally located than Stanton's, into a regular gathering place for women's rights organizers and out-of-town speakers. On the night of the anti-slavery meeting in Auburn, Stanton, Anthony, and May stayed with her and David. Anthony had learned the art of making impromptu remarks onstage. When she was booed that evening, she called out, "Why, boys, you're nothing but a baby mob—you ought to go to Syracuse, and learn how to do it." Martha, who had soured on Seward after his speech in January, wrote to Willy that the responsibility for the disturbance "must rest on our public men, who are continually preaching up compromise & concession toward our *Southern brethren*."

Martha was elected president of the 1861 Annual New York State Anti-Slavery Convention, which was to meet in Albany. Expecting another melee, she asked the mayor to make sure that no one was harmed. It was 14 degrees below zero on February 4, as Martha and Lucretia crossed State Street, buffeted by heavy winds and snow. The mayor sat next to them with a loaded gun on his lap. After Martha delivered the opening remarks, Lucretia gave a brief history of abolitionism, raising her voice above the stamping and hissing. Stanton spoke about the right to free speech. One of the resolutions, read by Anthony on the next afternoon, stated baldly why abolitionists objected to the Lincoln administration: "Resolved, that the government of this country is, and ever has been, a cruel, bloody and unmitigated despotism," which crushed "the souls of millions of human beings." It would remain so "under Republican rule."

When Anthony mentioned the martyrdom of John Brown, the hissing resumed. The mayor ordered quiet, and Martha told her, "Repeat." Martha wrote to Ellen, "It was grand for those rough creatures to be compelled to hear so much for their edification." Most of them had gone for the fun of it, not to make a political statement—or, as she said, out of "any vicious *union saving* sentiment."

As Douglass rose to speak, a group of men tried to storm the stage, but they were blocked by the police. Six feet tall, he buttoned his coat and called out, "Let them come on!" The men were ejected, and order was restored. Martha later wrote to a friend, "I shall always remember the manly bravery of Frederick Douglass, as he stood on the edge of the platform with folded arms, & dared the mob to come on, as they threatened to attack him." It was a demonstration of Douglass's earlier observation "If there is no struggle there is no progress. . . . Power concedes nothing without a demand. It never did and it never will." After the meeting concluded, the police officers formed lines on either side of the front doors, holding back demonstrators, and then escorted Douglass and the women to their hotel, along with the Albany mayor, trailed by two or three hundred hooting and yelling men and boys.

The threats seemed everywhere. While in Albany, Martha learned from David that a slaver who had traveled to Syracuse had been overheard talking about the planned arrest of fugitive slaves in Auburn. Both of them thought of Harriet, who had returned from Maryland just a few months earlier with her six passengers. David got word to Ben and Rit of the danger. Harriet was in Peterboro staying with Gerrit Smith, who insisted, over Harriet's objections, that they leave immediately for Canada. She knew she could count on Martha and David to provide for her family in her absence, and sent a request asking them to order a barrel of flour for her family, saying she would reimburse them when she returned. Martha supplied the flour, along with two baskets of provisions.

After Martha got back to Auburn, she walked over to the Sewards' house to tell Frances about the raucous week of meetings. Lazette was there, and so, unexpectedly, was Seward, having decided that he could be spared in Washington for a few days. Although Frances was amazed by Martha's bravery before the mobs, she was disconcerted by the resolution passed in Albany that predicted the "unmitigated despotism" of the Lincoln administration. Henry was tired and pinched, but, displaying what Frances called his "generous spirit," he showed no resentment as Martha spoke—only genuine interest in her account.

In Washington, amid the political turbulence, Henry, Fred, and Anna were preparing to move into a three-story brick mansion on Lafayette Square, across from the White House. Frances had overseen Henry's previous moves, but this time Anna was in charge. Henry loved the pomp of high office, and Anna indulged him in his belief that his home should be commensurate with his title. Once owned by the Washington Club and now called the Old Club House, it had a wide center hall, a library, and several parlors, which were well suited to entertaining. Unlike their house in Auburn, which was softly lit by candles and lamps, Henry's new home, like most urban residences, was plumbed with gas lighting. Anna wrote to Frances that the home had windows on all sides, which would allow for the circulation of fresh air in the spring. She and Fred were planning a garden for the large back yard. Henry had asked her to hire a steward for his dinners, and Anna was contemplating an Englishman who served

Lord Lyons, the British ambassador. What did Frances think? It had never been clearer that she and Henry lived two disconnected lives.

Frances was consumed by the prospect of secession, and by Fanny's worsening health. Fanny rarely complained, but that winter she contracted one of her bronchial infections. Fanny also had some of her mother's ailments, writing in her diary about "derangements of the stomach" and "attacks of the blues, a species of mental nausea." Frances understood the connection between mental and physical health. Wendell Phillips rightly said that society conspired to keep women frail, turning them into "such a hothouse plant, that one-half the sex are invalids." In a sad commentary about the suffocating constraints of indoor routines, Frances copied a passage in her scrapbook from an essay in *The Westminster Review* pointing out that women "would be thought mad to run, leap, or engage in active sports" or to "search the sea-cliffs for flowers" with their children. Many of women's maladies, the writer said, could be traced to the "want of fitting employment—real purpose in their life."

Hoping to strengthen Fanny, Frances excused her from her afternoon lessons that winter so that she could go ice-skating, part of a physical fitness craze in the North. Learning that Martha was hosting a talk by Harriet's Boston friend Thomas W. Higginson, on "Physical Culture," Frances sent Fanny with Lazette and Will's wife, whom they called Jenny. Returning that night, Fanny jotted down Higginson's remarks. He was an amateur boxer and an adherent of the dietary reformer Rev. Sylvester Graham, who promoted his famous crackers and a balanced consumption of nutritious foods. In Higginson's lecture, he took aim at Americans' sedentary ways and indulgent eating habits. Fanny was amused by his droll description of the contents of schoolchildren's dinner pails, packed by loving mothers: an unwholesome piece of mince pie, a cold sausage, a pickle, a piece of pound cake, and two doughnuts. She approved of Higginson's politics, too: "I liked Mr H. for one thing that he never mentioned the human race as '*men*'—but always '*men & women*' as was right."

Frances, reading reports in late February that southern conspirators were plotting to thwart the presidential transfer of power on March 4, noted to Henry, "Attempted and threatened assassination seem the order of the day." He replied: "I have brought the ship off the sands, and am ready to resign the helm into the hands of the captain whom the people have chosen." Then, switching to his determination to deal gently with the South, he declared, "The Republicans must give up their ultra sentiments." Frances replied no less emphatically. She presumed she did not get his meaning when he said that the task of saving the Union meant a less determined fight against slavery—"That would be clearly wrong."

Lincoln left Springfield on February 11 on a meandering thirteen-day, two-thousand-mile train trip to Washington, stopping briefly at towns and cities in Indiana, Ohio, New York, New Jersey, Pennsylvania, and Maryland. Despite repeated threats against his life, he declined Henry's pleas to go straight to the capital, insisting that the tour would help unite the North behind him. His itinerary was widely published, including the dates and times of arrival in many cities. Frances and Fanny read the papers together each day to assure themselves that no one had done him harm—unaware that detectives with the Pinkerton Agency had alerted Henry to a conspiracy to assassinate Lincoln in Baltimore.

Shortly after noon on February 21, Henry summoned Frederick from the Senate gallery giving him a letter he had written to the president-elect about the plot, urgently advising him to change his travel plans. He asked his son to take the first train to Philadelphia, to intercept Lincoln there.

Frederick arrived that night at about 10:00 at the Continental Hotel on Chestnut Street, which was ablaze with lights and music. Elbowing his way through a giddy crowd that spilled into the street, he saw Lincoln surrounded by well-wishers. "Clearly, this was no time for the delivery of a confidential message," Fred later recalled thinking. He asked Ward H. Lamon, Lincoln's bodyguard, to direct him to Lincoln's bedroom. An hour later, Lincoln entered. Fred, who never had met him, saw that although campaign posters had accurately reproduced his angular features, they had failed to convey his careworn look and kindly smile.

Lincoln asked politely after Fred's father, and then read the letter under the gaslight. He said he, too, had received intelligence from Allan Pinkerton "about an attempt on my life in the confusion and hurly-burly of the reception at Baltimore." Lincoln had wanted to make a dignified arrival in the capital, but the next morning he agreed to the plan to change the final leg of his route. Fred was surprised when Lincoln, in a speech that day at Independence Hall, drew attention to the threat, saying he would rather be assassinated on the spot than surrender the principle of freedom. Lincoln then raised a brand-new American flag, with thirty-four stars, reflecting Kansas's admission into the Union just weeks earlier as a free state.

As planned, Lincoln went to Harrisburg, and telegraph lines were cut to prevent any news about his whereabouts. He then went back to Philadelphia, where he boarded an 11:00 p.m. train to Washington, arriving before dawn on February 23. Lincoln, wearing a nondescript felt hat and overcoat, hunched over with Pinkerton by his side, was met by Henry at the station. Henry reported to Frances, later that day, "The President-elect arrived *incog*, at six this morning."

After having breakfast together at Willard's Hotel, Lincoln and Henry rode in the president's carriage, as Lincoln told him about his other cabinet choices. It was an eclectic group. Gideon Welles of Connecticut would be secretary of the navy, and Montgomery Blair of the slave state of Maryland, postmaster general—both former Democrats. Senator Salmon Chase of Ohio was the new treasury secretary. Chase, who once had thought so well of Henry, was now a Radical Republican who blamed him for diluting the party's message. Lincoln, though, wanted men who would challenge him and one another. Seward, Chase, and Edward Bates—a lawyer and former U.S. Representative from Missouri, who became attorney general—all had been candidates for the 1860 Republican nomination. Lincoln was sure he could manage their ambitions and maintain their loyalty.

The next morning, after attending services at St. John's Church, where the parishioners all knew Henry but few recognized Lincoln, Henry took him on a tour of the House and Senate. A correspondent for the *New York Herald* wrote about the "irrepressible senator," who introduced Lincoln to everybody, "on the same principle which leads children to display their new toys." Henry wrote to Frances about the president, "He is very cordial and kind toward me—simple, natural, and agreeable."

Lincoln asked Chase and Seward to vet his inaugural address. Chase advised him to take an assertive tone with the South. Seward offered six pages of revisions, arguing for words of affection, of "calm and cheerful confidence." He objected to Lincoln's final passage: "With you, and not with me, is the solemn question of 'Shall it be peace, or a sword?'" Henry, certain that it was his reassuring words in recent months that had preserved the Union thus far, warned that if the address were presented as drafted, Virginia and Maryland would secede.

He crossed out the offending paragraph and suggested some flowery language of his own: "Although passion has strained our bonds of affection too hardly they must not, I am sure they will not be broken. The mystic chords which proceeding from so many battle fields and so many patriot graves pass through all the hearts and all the hearths in this broad continent of ours will yet again harmonize in their ancient music when breathed upon by the guardian angel of the nation." Lincoln liked the idea but thought the rhetoric needed work, and he rewrote the passage.

On March 4, 1861, the crocuses and spring foliage in the parks formed a bright backdrop for the American flags floating along Pennsylvania Avenue between the White House and the Capitol. Squads of riflemen crouched on housetops, at the windows of the Capitol, and under the steps that led up to the ceremonial platform. Batteries of light artillery stood by in case of riots. Speaking on the East Portico before 25,000 people, Lincoln said that he did not intend to interfere with slavery in the southern states, and that he would abide by the Fugitive Slave Law. Following Henry's advice, he said, "We are not enemies, but friends. We must not be enemies." And in a few closing sentences that came down through history as one of the most stirring expressions of the American promise, he transformed Henry's clumsy locution into soaring prose: "Though passion may have strained, it must not break our bonds of affection. The mystic chords of memory, stretching from every battlefield and patriot grave to every living heart and hearthstone all over this broad land, will yet swell the chorus of the Union, when again touched, as surely they will be, by the better angels of our nature."

Frances, unmoved by the talk of affection, wrote to Henry on March 9 to say that the address, with its recommendation of gradual emancipation, would satisfy only conservatives: "I am sorry for this." Other abolitionists also raised objections. Douglass condemned the speech as a "double-tongued document"—with its description of secession as unlawful, but its defense of the South's right to buy and sell other human beings. To Lucretia, it was "infernal & diabolical."

Henry dashed off a note to Frances, saying that the political troubles facing the administration were enough to tax the wisdom of the wisest. "Fort Sumter in danger. Relief of it practically impossible." Until that spring, Frances had never heard of Fort Sumter. The three-story, five-sided brick-and-wood fort occupied an island just inside Charleston Harbor, and for months the governor of South Carolina had been demanding that Major Robert Anderson surrender it to the Confederates, threatening all-out war if Lincoln did not comply. On April 1, as the soldiers ran through their provisions and the administration debated whether to relinquish the fort or to send in reinforcements, Henry warned Frances that he could no longer write as candidly as he would like, fearing his letters might be opened, revealing state secrets. He wished that she were there to comfort him, he said, and to share his thoughts about the dangers ahead.

Seward argued that they should give up Fort Sumter, but Lincoln didn't think it would be enough to prevent more states from seceding, and he directed the commanding general of the U.S. Army, seventy-four-year-old Winfield Scott, to order more troops and supplies. The Provisional Confederate Congress was prepared for the move. In February 1861, it had authorized a call for volunteers for its army; by April, 62,000 young men from six states had signed up. President Davis appointed Brigadier General Pierre G. T. Beauregard to take command of Charleston.

South Carolina promptly put up batteries and mounted guns at Charleston Harbor. On April 12, 1861, five hundred Confederate soldiers bombarded the eighty-five-man garrison, setting fire to its wooden portions. Anderson's men withstood the assault for thirty-four hours before saluting, lowering, and packing up the United States flag. Frances, who had not yet heard the news, wrote to Henry, "I feel condemned for sleeping peaceably while you are so disturbed—Every ring of the bell suggests the bearer of some evil tidings. Every body feels uncomfortable from this state of suspense, but few seem to apprehend the dreadful consequences of the inauguration of a civil war."

After the fall of Fort Sumter, Lincoln issued his own order for troops, requesting 75,000 volunteers to serve ninety-day rotations in the Union Army. But it took time to enlist and train soldiers. Washington was surrounded by states in open or prospective revolt, and army and navy officers were resigning in large numbers, taking up arms against the government. Confederate campfires could be seen across the Potomac. Although the District of Columbia had ten volunteer companies, many men refused to swear an oath of allegiance to the United States. The capital's sole defensive structure, Fort Washington, was twelve miles south. Frances beseeched Henry, "It is so sad to be away from you and feel that you are environed with difficulties and dangers—May I come to you." She repeated the offer five days later, but he had moved on, saying he could think of nothing at the moment but the South's treason and his duties as secretary of state.

Virginia seceded on April 17. Two days later, in Baltimore, as the soldiers of the Sixth Massachusetts Regiment changed trains, they were surrounded by two or three thousand men who hurled paving stones at them. Soldiers fired muskets into the crowd, setting off a riot; twelve civilians and four soldiers were killed. Baltimore officials cut the telegraph lines and burned bridges to block northern troops from passing through. Frances wrote to Henry: "The true, strong, gracious North is at last fairly roused, and you may rely upon all you hear about the enthusiasm of the people—high & low, rich & poor"—all enlisted at last in the cause of human rights. She knew that many northerners did not think they were fighting "for the liberty of enslaved Africans, far from it." But, she continued, "I see the hand of God no less plainly in the matter, and no peace can be established which does not give promise of liberty to all." Anticipating the woes to come, she thought of women sending sons and husbands "to the field to fight as of old in a Holy cause."

The early days of the war were marked by public exhilaration and private apprehension. In Auburn, flags flew from merchants' shops and people's homes, and townspeople wore pins of the Stars and Stripes. Within a week of Lincoln's call for troops, nine companies were formed in Cayuga County, six of them at Auburn, where the sounds of military drills became commonplace: the early-morning bugle call, the order to get in formation, the officers' shouts barking out the nine-step process of loading and firing muskets. Fanny wrote to her father about the ritual marking a young man's designation as captain: the presentation of a Bible or a sword. Martha's Willy had enlisted, and Frances knew that before long, so would her own Will. Her war fervor briefly wavering, she wrote on April 30 to Frederick, "Will is talking of raising a company—Is it necessary?" Jenny's mother begged Will not to go, telling him that his enlistment would kill her daughter. Will's unmarried business partner in the new Seward Bank of Auburn, Clinton D. MacDougall, was commissioned as a colonel in the 111th New York Volunteer Infantry, and he urged Will to stay and oversee the bank. But the mood of patriotism prevailed. The pastor at the Church of the Holy Trinity delivered a sermon pronouncing any able-bodied man who did not sign up "a traitor and a coward." After church, he marched fifty men to the recruiting office.

Women quickly made themselves indispensable. That spring, Dr. Elizabeth Blackwell, who twelve years earlier had become the country's first licensed female physician, founded the Women's Central Association of Relief in New York City, which organized four thousand women to collect and distribute medical supplies, clothing, and food for Union hospitals. Dr. Blackwell also persuaded several male physicians to help her to train women to work as nurses on the front. Nursing, a grisly, indecorous profession, had formerly been restricted to men. An old friend of the Sewards', Dorothea Dix, took the idea further. A well-known spokeswoman for humane treatment of the mentally ill, Dix traveled to Washington to propose to Lincoln a national corps of female nurses.

Lincoln signed an executive order establishing the United States Sanitary Commission, the progenitor of the Red Cross. Frederick Law Olmsted, the landscape architect who designed New York's Central Park, ran the commission, and Dix was named superintendent of women nurses. Dix received Blackwell's trained nurses at her house on Fifteenth Street, along with the supplies gathered by her association—an efficient assembly line run and staffed by women. Thousands of ladies' aid societies made donations, which Dix dispersed as the supplies poured in: shirts and socks, dried fruit, jars of jelly, crates of canned fruits and vegetables, scraped lint for bandages.

Frances started the Ladies' Aid Society of Auburn. She wrote to ask Miss Dix what was most needed, while Lazette worked with the local female Samaritan Society, which provided much of the clothing for a company of soldiers in Canandaigua. Fanny and a friend raised money by selling refreshments at the county fair. Will's wife, Jenny, organized the painting of a flag of blue silk with gold-colored silk fringe and a gilt eagle on the top for the Cayuga regiment. One ladies' group in western New York produced more than twelve hundred Havelocks, a cloth headdress to protect soldiers' necks from the "tropical" summer sun, causing Ellen Wright to remark to Martha that the luckiest man in the U.S. Army was the one with the fewest female relatives and friends.

Fanny joined thousands in Auburn who went to the station to watch four of the new companies depart. Looking at the prison walls and railroad bridges crawling with spectators, she thought they "seemed alive." Crammed amid the well-wishers, she couldn't get near the train, but by standing on tiptoe, she could see the recruits leaning out of the train windows, cheering and waving their hats. That evening, she wrote in her diary about the look on the boys' faces as the train pulled out of the station: "the sadness at parting and the joy of engaging in a noble action."

18

A Nation on Fire

1861–1862

Frederick Douglass, ca. 1855

Most northerners assumed that the war would be brief, almost bloodless. One national statesman predicted it would blow over in sixty days; the mayor of Brooklyn said that the rebels would "be at once so effectually squelch'd, we would never hear of secession again." Postmaster General Blair, from Maryland, thought that the Fire-Eaters of the Deep South had little fight in them, and would collapse when confronted with the soldiers of the North. On May 24, 1861, the day after Virginia seceded, Union troops crossed into the state from Washington, taking control of Alexandria and Arlington Heights. There was only a single casualty on each side.

Frances did not share that blithe expectation of a quick victory, but she was encouraged by reports of the rapid remaking of the capital. Five forts were under construction, and sentries stood guard at all entry points—bridges, railroads, and the Chesapeake and Ohio Canal. By June, when Washington normally sank into the torpor of a southern town in summertime, the city was taken over by more than thirty thousand troops. Earthworks bristled with cannon, and infantry, cavalry, and long trains of army wagons trundled down Pennsylvania Avenue. Men seeking commissions in the army or jobs in the civil service filled Willard's Hotel. Soldiers settled into public buildings and erected tents on city squares, and in outlying fields and forests. New York's 12th Regiment found a picturesque spot by a stream in the woods outside Alexandria, quartering itself in bush huts and an abandoned cotton factory. Seven thousand soldiers slept inside the Capitol. Soldiers of the 6th Massachusetts, who had been stoned by Confederate partisans in Baltimore, wrote letters home from senators' desks. Regiments held afternoon and evening parades, and the Marine Band played concerts on the South Lawn of the White House. As Henry wrote: "It begins to be a camp."

His letters were full of unexpected praise for Lincoln's political acumen and executive skills. Although Henry complained that he was "a chief reduced to a subordinate position," he and the president evidently enjoyed each other's company. They met almost every day at the State Department and White House, and regularly rode out together in Lincoln's carriage to visit army camps. On many evenings, Lincoln walked across Pennsylvania Avenue to sit and talk with Henry at the Club House. Their political ideas and instincts were remarkably similar, and they shared a penchant for long-winded stories that others found tiresome. Lincoln, afflicted by periods of extreme melancholy, found in Henry's sanguine nature the same sort of relief that Frances did. According to Lincoln's secretaries, John Nicolay and John Hay, their boss fully appreciated Seward's "unreserved and undeviating devotion." Other cabinet members, Henry wrote to Frances, seethed about his intimacy with Lincoln: "But I have said too much already. Burn this, and believe that I am doing what man can do."

Frances got a scribbled note in mid-July: "We are on the eve of a conflict on the Virginia side of the Potomac, probably some day this week. It will be very important." On July 21, Lincoln, under public pressure to engage the rebels, ordered Brigadier General Irvin McDowell to attack the Confederates at Bull Run, near Manassas. Northern loyalists, wanting to witness what they thought would be the signature encounter of the war, packed picnic lunches and rode to the battlefield on horseback and in carriages. William Howard Russell, a British war correspondent, wrote in the London *Times* that one lady with an opera glass, beside herself with excitement after one heavy discharge of musketry, cried, "That is splendid, Oh my! Is not that first rate? I guess we will be in Richmond tomorrow."

Union troops fought well for much of the day, but Confederate General Beauregard received reinforcements late in the afternoon. They broke McDowell's right flank, and forced his army to retreat. Henry spent the evening with Lincoln at the War Department and at General Scott's headquarters, receiving successively dire reports from the field. When he got home at midnight, he told Frederick and Anna, "What went out an army is surging back toward Washington as a disorganized mob." In the panicked flight, infantrymen had thrown aside their rations and their arms, and walked into the city in a soaking rain without greatcoats or shoes, their feet raw and blistered. The Union toll was some three thousand troops. It was another four years before Richmond was conquered.

Frances, learning of the rout, thought about the stricken families of the young men who had "given their lives for the maintenance of liberty." Lincoln ordered the enlistment of another million men, this time for three-year tours of duty. Henry wrote, "One great battle has been lost, and nothing remains but to reorganize and begin again." Lincoln turned to him, rather than to Secretary of War Simon Cameron, who tried to run the war from behind a desk, and lasted less than a year in the job. It was Henry who accompanied Lincoln as he visited the troops, and delivered speeches that promised arms and victories in the days ahead.

Lincoln chose thirty-four-year-old George B. McClellan, a charismatic graduate of West Point and a Democrat, as the commander of the new Army of the Potomac. McClellan excelled at training recruits, but he was flagrantly insubordinate. Sharing the common view that Seward dictated White House policy to a weak president, McClellan described him as "a meddling, officious, incompetent little puppy" who had done more than any other man to get the country into its scrape. Henry was stung by the incessant criticism over Bull Run, and in September he escaped briefly to Auburn.

Out of the maelstrom, and with Frances again, he could see that she was falling into a depression. Feeling superfluous in her own family, she also felt she had no clear identity outside it. While Henry was consumed by the war in Washington, the boys were living their own lives. Augustus was serving at Fort Defiance and Frederick was working for Henry. Will now would feel obliged to enlist. Fanny, at sixteen, would soon be an adult. The underground railroad had ceased operating when the war began. Frances, greeting an old friend after many years, noticed how he had aged, commenting to Frederick, "I almost dread seeing any one I used to know 10 or 12 years ago, presuming that I have degenerated equally myself. I feel incapable of giving or receiving pleasure." Some weeks earlier, Henry had brushed aside her suggestion that she might be of some help to him in Washington. Now he told her she should return with him, persuading her to bring Fanny and Jenny on a two-week visit. The night before they left, Henry addressed a few hundred people gathered in front of the Sewards' house, the *Auburn Daily Advertiser* sentimentally reported, "beneath the deep shade of the trees his own hands had planted." After the cheers subsided, Henry told them of the three thousand men each day who marched to the battlefield: "You could never fight for a cause more glorious; you could never fall for a country more worthy of sacrifice."

The Sewards stayed overnight in New York City at the luxurious Astor House, across from St. Paul's Chapel on Vesey Street. On the train to Washington the next day, they were given the directors' car, outfitted with a parlor, bedroom, and dressing room; sleeping berths; a sofa, table, chairs, and a stove; and a basin and looking glass. In Philadelphia, La Pierre House supplied a full dinner, complete with tablecloth and silver, and a waiter who served them. As the train drew closer to Washington, the Sewards saw military encampments dotting the hills, and they passed squads of picket guards and "Blue Coats" in an almost continuous line for more than a hundred and fifty miles. The rituals of camp life, viewed through the train window, looked like scenes from a play: men building blockhouses, washing, cooking, sleeping, and cleaning their rifles around small fires.

Frances ruefully wrote to Lazette that the palatial Club House was suited to Henry's "tastes & habits—such as they are at this day." Anna and Frederick had planted clematis, passionflower, and scarlet beans to shade the piazza, where Henry smoked his cigars. He had brought their servant Nicholas Bogart with him, and through the evergreens in back, Frances could see Nicholas standing by the stable, showering a fine bay horse with water from the canal: "The horse seemed, from his perfect quietness, to enjoy the operation." That evening, Frances chose to rest rather than to be introduced to the president along with Fanny and Jenny. As Henry conferred with Secretary Chase and other officials, Lincoln went out of his way to be kind to Fanny, showing her two kittens Henry had given to his sons Willie and Tad, and telling her that they climbed all over him. Frances met Lincoln a few days later, on an afternoon visit with her family to several camps outside the city. She found him "amusing and friendly, with a manner like an unassuming farmer's—not awkward & ungainly but equally removed from polish of manner."

Frances woke each morning to the sound of drumbeats, and went to bed to the rumble of wagons. Occasionally the boom of a cannon could be heard across the Potomac. At about eight o'clock one night, a cavalry regiment passed the Club House, on its way to the Chain Bridge, some three miles northwest of Georgetown; it was followed a few hours later by an entire infantry brigade—about twenty-six hundred soldiers. Henry went outside to wish them Godspeed, but Frances felt an indescribable sorrow, knowing that many of the boys would not return. Another evening, the Sewards heard a single voice sing out, "John Brown's body lies a-moldering in the grave," followed by the chorus: "But his soul goes marching on!" Gradually more voices picked up the lyrics, written by members of a Massachusetts militia battalion and set to the hymn "Say, Brothers, Will You Meet Us?" The sound of boots and song could be heard as the troops marched down Pennsylvania Avenue, passed the Treasury Building, and continued into Virginia.

Henry had been right to encourage Frances to come. Relieved by Anna of the stress of party preparations, she took an active interest in some of his guests. One evening, Henry invited General Benjamin Butler and the London *Times* correspondent William Howard Russell to dinner. Butler, a Democrat from Massachusetts, had endorsed the *Dred Scott* decision, and was not someone Frances normally would have warmed to. But Butler had become an unexpected cause célèbre among abolitionists. He was the commander at Fort Monroe, the sixty-three-acre stone citadel at Old Point Comfort, on the southern tip of the Virginia Peninsula, where the first ship of enslaved Africans had arrived in 1619. Several months earlier, when three freedom seekers had sought protection at the fort, Butler had decided that, rather than return them, as the Fugitive Slave Law required, he would hire them to work in his quartermaster's department.

Butler's command decision impressed Frances: a general in the field was making policy, as demanded by circumstance. Fort Monroe guarded a prized harbor: warships could sail up the Chesapeake Bay to Washington, or, once the James River was under Union control, follow it to Richmond. On the night of May 23, 1861, the three enslaved men, who had been digging rebel trenches and building gun platforms on the mainland, rowed across the James, and presented themselves to the pickets guarding the fort, providing Butler with valuable information about the Confederates' activities. Butler refused a rebel officer's demand that he return the men, as required by the Fugitive Slave Law, replying that Virginia claimed no longer to be part of the Union, and that he was under no constitutional obligation to a foreign country. With impeccable logic, he reasoned that by robbing the enemy of crucial manpower, he could buttress his own. He called the men "contraband of war," a term that northerners began to use for enslaved people who surged into Union camps, seeking protection.

Butler's order forced Lincoln's hand. Abolitionists and Republicans in Congress recognized the significance of the migration: former slaves were proving how useful they could be in the war. In early August, less than three months after Butler's order, Lincoln signed the Confiscation Act of 1861, which stated that because the Confederacy was using its slaves to wage war against the United States, they could be legally confiscated.

Later that month, General John C. Frémont, who headed the Department of the West—most of the area from the Mississippi River to the Rocky Mountains—issued an edict from St. Louis that went even further. Missouri's Border Ruffians had become Confederate guerrillas, murdering and marauding in their own state. On August 30, Frémont declared martial law and pronounced the slaves of rebels in his region "free men." Lincoln countermanded the measure, calling it unconstitutional, and fearing its effects on the four barely loyal slaveholding border states, including Missouri.

Frances concluded that the Union generals were in a better position to assess the army's needs than the president and his cabinet. In September, she sent a forthright letter to Henry from Auburn saying she was sorry that Lincoln had interfered with Frémont's proclamation: "It was a measure so universally approved at the North that the President's action must give great dissatisfaction." Moreover, it was evident that the army needed manpower, and that nothing but prejudice stood in the way. As Douglass wrote that month, "The national edifice is on fire. Every man who can carry a bucket of water or a brick is wanted, but those who have the care of the building, having a profound respect for the feeling of the national burglars who set the building on fire, are determined that the flames shall only be extinguished by Indo-Caucasian hands, and to have the building burnt rather than save it by means of any other."

On November 7, the North celebrated a significant military victory. In the Battle of Port Royal, a joint operation of the army and navy, federal troops took control of the Sea Islands off South Carolina and Georgia, and the coastal town of Beaufort—the first southern city to fall into northern hands. A day later, Henry faced his first major challenge of international diplomacy, in an incident that threatened to start a war with Britain. Charles Wilkes, the captain of a Union ship off Cuba, ordered his men to fire on an unarmed British mail packet, RMS *Trent*, suspecting it of blockade-running. Two former U.S. senators—James Mason of Virginia and John Slidell of Louisiana—were aboard the British boat. They were heading to Europe, Mason as an envoy to Britain and Slidell to France, to try and persuade the two nations to support the Confederate cause. Wilkes arrested Mason and Slidell and delivered them to Boston, where they were imprisoned.

Wilkes was celebrated in the North as a patriot who had captured two traitors, but the British prime minister, Lord Palmerston, called the arrests illegal. He issued an official dispatch demanding that the administration apologize and release the prisoners, threatening to go to war if the Americans did not comply. Early in the Lincoln administration, Henry had warned the European nations about the consequences of not declaring loyalty to the Union. Now he dropped his bellicose posture, assuring the British and French ambassadors in Washington that he was pursuing a peaceful resolution to the confrontation. Frances, angry that Britain had refused to support the Union, wrote to Lazette, "The signs of the Times are so dark that my heart fails me I cannot write what I would say. Just as all things were tending to a consummation of our domestic difficulties the selfish course of England promises to derange if not destroy all." Henry had to remind her that the administration could not afford to antagonize Britain.

Frances, who went to Washington for the holidays, saw that he was right. Finding little to praise in the administration, she felt relieved to trust Henry on foreign affairs, where his diplomatic skills were invaluable. In a cabinet meeting Lincoln called on Christmas morning, Henry argued that they should accept Britain's terms: an apology and a return of the two prisoners. Postmaster General Blair agreed, as did Senator Sumner, who was in attendance as the new chairman of the powerful Senate Committee on Foreign Relations. Treasury Secretary Chase objected, declaring that he would "sacrifice everything I possess" before consenting to a return of Mason and Slidell. Lincoln said he was not inclined to give up the prisoners without getting something in return, but he wanted to think about it overnight.

At home after breakfast on December 26, Henry read aloud a draft of his proposal, which explained his rationale for conceding to Britain's demands. Frances was persuaded, writing to Lazette, "Unpalatable as the conclusion is, it is impossible for a reasonable mind to come to any other." Henry said that the administration must act upon American principles, citing as a precedent Secretary of State James Madison's handling of a case in 1807, when the British had fired on an American ship, boarded, and taken prisoners. Madison had avoided war by successfully demanding a return of the men.

Frances had long, fulfilling discussions with Henry those weeks on all sorts of military, political, and social topics. "I have not talked with Henry so much & so satisfactorily in a year," she reported to Lazette. The concession to the British was one compromise she could accept: "We have always denied the right of search, and what we deny to others we must not take ourselves." She assured Lazette that there was no truth in reports of dissension in the cabinet. As Henry had told her: "All goes on harmoniously though every man has his own opinion of affairs." Lincoln and the others had no better solution to offer, so they accepted his argument on the *Trent* stalemate.

Seward's plan was seen on both sides as a breathtaking act of diplomacy. It appeased Britain and assured the northern public that the prisoner release was preferable to an international war that would doom the Union. In return, Britain agreed to maintain its neutrality in the Civil

War. Even Judah Benjamin, the Confederates' secretary of war, praised the resolution: "It is impossible not to admire the sagacity with which Mr. Seward penetrated into the secret feelings of the British cabinet and the success of his policy of intimidation." It was the kind of maneuver Lincoln liked to practice: extracting concessions from both sides while persuading each that it had gained more than it had lost. Writing to Lazette, Frances said, "If any thing were wanting to convince me of Henry's exceeding magnanimity this would supply it."

At Henry's 1862 New Year's Day reception at the Club House, Frances took stock of their military guests, whose erect bearing, polished black boots, and crisp epaulettes denoted the growing professionalism of the army. Arrogant young McClellan was turning ungainly farm boys into a disciplined fighting force of 120,000 soldiers. The Navy too was showing new strengths. At the start of the war, the United States had fewer than forty warships, but on the orders of Secretary Welles, dozens more were built, and hundreds of sailing ships and ferryboats were purchased and rapidly converted for war service. Henry, in the face of carping inside and outside the administration, maintained his professionalism. He had argued successfully for a naval blockade against the southern states, to cut off the trade in cotton and other commodities, and at the reception, members of the diplomatic corps praised him for the resolution of the *Trent* affair. Frances wrapped up her commentary to Lazette that night on a note of nationalist pride: "The Americans have more true greatness than any of those powerful European nations which . . . seize every opportunity of trespassing on the rights of others."

19

"God's Ahead of Master Lincoln"

1862

Harriet Tubman, ca. 1868

Harriet wanted to join the war, and the Union victory at Port Royal made it possible. A humanitarian catastrophe was unfolding on the Sea Islands of South Carolina, territory now controlled by the U.S. Army. Plantation owners and other white residents had fled as the army advanced, leaving behind fine furniture, private libraries, outsized oil paintings of family aristocrats, and ten thousand slaves. In peacetime, those people, from about two hundred plantations across sixty thousand acres, had comprised 90 percent of the population. They were now "contrabands" under the protection of the army. Harriet heard that her friend Ednah Cheney and Governor John Andrew of Massachusetts were looking for volunteers to send to Port Royal to provide social services and to teach school and trades. They worked in tandem with Treasury Secretary Chase, whose department was responsible for abandoned and confiscated property in the South. Union officials also were in charge of the cultivation of cotton and rice. The crops, worth millions of dollars, would be shipped north, to help pay for the war. The federal government provided transportation and some living expenses for the volunteers. Harriet intended to go to Port Royal to help them, and to serve in the Union army as a guerrilla operative—work she told Martha was a kind of "secret service."

Early in the spring of 1862, Harriet appears to have used her friendship with Cheney to meet with Governor Andrew. Abolitionists and Radical Republicans had been saying all along that freed slaves would be highly motivated to become self-sufficient, and to work and fight for the nation. This was an unforeseen chance to prove it. The first order of business was establishing schools for children and adults—one of the central premises of abolition. Responding to the Treasury Department's call for teachers of "talent and enthusiasm," Governor Andrew, Cheney, and fifteen other Bostonians formed a commission dedicated to advancing the moral, religious, educational, and employment needs of the freed people of Port Royal. Governor Andrew knew Harriet by reputation, and he needed little convincing to write the letters of introduction she would need to travel into a military zone. Most of the missionaries he was interviewing were gently reared white pastors, teachers, and businessmen. Harriet Tubman had more than ten years of experience infiltrating enemy territory.

In Philadelphia, Lucretia Mott's friend J. Miller McKim started a group similar to Governor Andrew's, called the Port Royal Relief Society. Lucretia and the Philadelphia Female Anti-Slavery Society helped McKim gather supplies and interview volunteers, sending several of their young members. The first African American schoolteacher to sign up was twenty-four-year-old Charlotte Forten, the granddaughter of one of the society's co-founders. Laura Towne, a white abolitionist volunteer from Philadelphia, was assigned to St. Helena Island, just east of Port Royal. Towne wrote to McKim soon after her arrival to say that she had too many students to continue her lessons in the Baptist church. He ordered a schoolhouse to be shipped in pieces to the island. It was assembled across from the church, and named the Penn School, which Towne ran with her Quaker friend Ellen Murray. Secretary Chase's exercise in public-private welfare reform was called the Port Royal Experiment.

Before Harriet left Auburn, she made sure that her family was provided for. She had saved enough money to sustain her parents through the winter, and asked her brother John and her sister-in-law Catherine to care for them. Harriet counted on two of her Boston-area friends, Franklin Sanborn and Ednah Cheney, to provide financial assistance if needed, and on Martha and others in Auburn to check in regularly. She had a more significant request of Frances and Lazette, regarding her beloved ten-year-old niece, Margaret Stewart. Determined to see Margaret's upbringing overseen by women whose political, educational, and religious beliefs were close to her own, Harriet asked if they would care for Margaret for the duration of the war.

Frances and Lazette regarded the Port Royal Experiment as a just, humane blueprint for postwar reconstruction, and welcomed the opportunity to help Harriet on a matter of such personal importance. Lazette ran the Seward household in Auburn when Frances was in Washington, and she would be responsible for Margaret in her absence. Harriet, a pragmatist in all she did, was idealistic about America's future, and she wanted Margaret prepared for adulthood in a more egalitarian nation. Martha thought of Harriet's arrangement with Frances and Lazette as a logical extension of her friends' years of anti-slavery work. Frederick Douglass had made a similar plan when he was in Britain in the 1840s, leaving his eldest daughter, Rosetta, with James Mott's cousins Lydia and Abigail Mott, who educated her in their home in Albany.

Margaret was a mysterious figure in Harriet's life. Almost a century after she died, one of her biographers discovered that Margaret had been raised by a free Black couple, neighbors of Ben and Rit at Poplar Neck in Caroline County. Margaret had a twin brother and two younger siblings. Harriet knew the family well, and became obsessively attached to the little girl. In one of the only immoral acts ever attributed to Harriet, in late 1860, she secretly made off with Margaret, taking her to Canada to live with the Rosses. She never spoke about what she had done, and decades later, Margaret told her daughter, Alice Lucas Brickler, that Aunt Harriet had "kidnapped" her from a comfortable home before the Civil War. Alice said that "sorrow & anger were there," and that she wondered what Harriet's thoughts could have been "as she & her little partner stood side by side on the deck of the steamer looking far out over the water." Some of Harriet's descendants speculated that Margaret, who resembled her, was actually her daughter. Why else would Harriet, who acutely valued family ties, have done something so dangerous and wrong? Alice surmised that when Harriet looked at Margaret, she "saw the child she herself might have been if slavery had been less cruel," and that "she longed for some little creature who would love her for her own self's sake." Alice saw Margaret as Harriet's "dearest possession." Indicating how highly Harriet regarded Frances, Alice said, "She gave the little girl, my mother, to Mrs. William H. Seward, the Governor's wife. This kindly lady brought up Mother not as a servant but as a guest within her home. She taught Mother to speak properly, to read, write, sew, do housework and act as a lady." Whether Margaret was Harriet's niece or her child, Harriet must have told herself that, with Frances's assistance, she could give Margaret opportunities that she couldn't possibly have had in Maryland.

Harriet helped her white friends to see the war as she did. Discussing with Ednah Cheney the staggering notion of white men fighting for Black freedom, she said that the blood of her race had called for justice in vain, and that now white sons must be taken from their parents "to bring the call for justice home to their hearts." She cited the book of Exodus to explain her decision to go to South Carolina: "The good Lord has come down to deliver my people, and I must go and help him." Frances used the same passage when writing to Henry in March, just before Harriet departed, "I think we may safely assume that the cry of the oppressed has reached the ear of God and that he has 'come down to deliver them.'"

It was only a matter of time before twenty-three-year-old Will Seward enlisted. Easygoing, charming, and loving, he was Frances's favorite son. She forgave him a boyhood marred by disreputable behavior and lack of interest in his studies. When he was twelve, he'd been sent home from a tavern where he was found sitting on a bar stool drinking beer and eating oysters. Henry, mostly absent from Will's life, found him maddening, but Frances defended him, saying he was like any other lively boy; he just attracted more attention because of his family's prominence. She noted to Lazette, "That his heart is uncorrupted I have not the shadow of a doubt." She put her foot down only once, when, at age fifteen, Will said he wanted to go to West Point. Frances wrote to Augustus, emphasizing, not for the first time, her displeasure with his military career: "He will not." In 1858, at age twenty, Will had gone to Washington, where his father had expected him to succeed Frederick as his private secretary, but Henry soon concluded that Will wasn't cut out for the work. Finally, as Henry was leaving for his European trip in the summer of 1859, he'd left Will in charge of the family finances, and Will rose to the occasion. Will was almost as attached to Auburn as Frances was, and with a $5,000 loan from a friend of his father's, he'd opened his bank with Clinton MacDougall.

Frances drew resolve from Martha, who had seen her own Willy depart for Washington in December 1861, as a second lieutenant in the Auburn First Independent Battery of Light Artillery. Martha had told Willy to die before ever helping to return a slave to the South. Frances commented to Lazette that although Martha had not been free from worry since Willy's departure, "Her patriotism is stronger than her maternal instincts." She prayed that she could show that kind of fortitude when Will's turn came.

In January 1862 in Washington, Frances had her first disagreement with Charles Sumner, who, unmarried and childless, could not grasp how parents felt when they sent barely grown sons into battle. She told him that she had no patience with old men who stayed at home and told young men to fight. Watching regiments marching unfaltering to battle brought tears to her eyes. Every one of those boys, she said of the families they had left, "had some sore heart watching their movements."

That spring, the Lincoln administration and Congress enacted changes that were extraordinary by the standards of Washington. Under Henry's leadership, the United States and United Kingdom agreed to a treaty that halted the international slave trade, and on April 16, Lincoln signed a bill ending slavery in the District of Columbia, a goal that Henry had pursued since his early days as a senator thirteen years earlier. It was the first time the government officially had liberated slaves, but the measure came with strings attached: Washington slaveholders were offered financial compensation for their loss of "property," and the newly freed men and women were encouraged to emigrate to Liberia and Haiti, their expenses paid. For the first two years of the war, Lincoln remained peculiarly attached to the idea of colonization—one of his few significant points of disagreement with Henry, who argued, "I am always for bringing men and States *into* this Union, never for taking any *out*."

Frances wanted Henry to go further, drawing his attention to a problem triggered by the emancipation bill, which had freed more than three thousand people in Washington. She had read that some were being forced out of the District, and she asked whether there was some way that Congress or the president could protect those who needed immediate assistance—as the government was doing in the Port Royal Experiment. She asked Lazette to talk to Martha, to look into whether Auburn could serve as a sanctuary for refugees, by taking in some two or three thousand people. Trying to reawaken Henry's conscience about people who had been victimized for generations, Frances quoted Jefferson, Henry's favorite founder, who wrote: "I tremble for my country when I remember that God is just."

Harriet arrived in Beaufort, on Port Royal Island, with no experience of slavery in the Deep South. Although she had lost three sisters to the region, it remained an abstract terror, a place of vast plantations where most slaves were born, lived, and died, cut off from any exposure to the world outside. The freed slaves of Port Royal, the Gullah, were wholly unprepared to take control of their lives. They made a strange sight—the women in skirts made of burlap sacks tied around their waists with the bags' ravelings, and the men in jackets fashioned from strips of old carpeting and bits of blankets. They spoke an almost unintelligible blend of English and the West African dialect of their ancestors. Harriet later said, "Why, their language down there in the far South is just as different from ours in Maryland, as you can think. They laughed when they heard me talk, and I could not understand them, no how."

Harriet's first job, while learning the dialect and exploring the outer reaches of areas under Union control, was to work in the Christian Commission house, established by the YMCA to provide clothing, books, and other supplies to Union soldiers and the locals. She also began to serve as an army nurse for the acting assistant surgeon, Dr. Henry K. Durant, who ran one of the Beaufort hospitals and authorized her to place orders for hard liquor, which dulled surgical pain. That spring or summer, she was introduced to General David Hunter, the recently arrived head of the Department of the South—the Union-occupied coasts of South Carolina,

Georgia, and Florida. Hunter, an abolitionist, was known among his soldiers as "Black Dave." Harriet presented herself to him as the woman sent by Governor Andrew, uniquely qualified to serve as a scout and spy. It was the sort of job she had sought ever since the death of John Brown.

Rebels controlled the Charleston and Savannah Railroad, some thirty miles north, and their pickets pressed in on the Yankees from north, south, and west. Harriet reported to Hunter and other generals intelligence she picked up from the locals and from contrabands coming into the area, about the movement of Confederate troops and materiel, the river tides, and the locations of torpedoes floating under the surface of the water. As she had on the Eastern Shore, she availed herself of Black mariners and other locals who knew the Lowcountry's unique topography. Deploying the leadership talents that Ednah Cheney had spotted early on, Harriet soon had half a dozen scouts working under her direction. With funds from the relief societies, she built a washhouse on Craven Street, where she oversaw women doing laundering and sewing for the army. At night she baked pies and gingerbread and made root beer by the cask, then had the women sell the provisions in the camps—teaching them the fundamentals of a market economy. She paid them for their work, saving what remained for her mortgage and for her own and her family's living expenses.

In Washington, before leaving for Port Royal, General Hunter had asked the new secretary of war, Edwin M. Stanton, to give him wide latitude in his job. Without explicitly saying so, he intended to establish the Union's first regiment of Black soldiers. Hunter convinced himself that he had Stanton's tacit acquiescence, and on May 9, 1862, he decreed all slaves in the Department of the South "forever free." Hunter, likable and generous in private, was overbearing in command. He ordered his men to round up for training all Black men in the Port Royal area between the ages of eighteen and forty-five. The inductees had been told by departing plantation owners that Union officers intended to ship them to Cuba to be sold, and when white soldiers appeared, many attempted to flee. Few of Hunter's troops shared his enthusiasm for establishing the country's first Black regiment, and they cruelly added to the panic by telling the women that their men would be sent to the front lines as cannon fodder. Husbands were forcibly separated from their wives and children, as they had been under slaveholders. Secretary Chase's civilian superintendent on the plantations, Edward L. Pierce, wrote to Chase that the violent seizure of the men must stop—it would take time to convince a people who had been enslaved for two centuries that "they have a country to fight for."

Lincoln revoked Hunter's emancipation order, stating that only the president could declare freedom for slaves. He also repeated his standing offer to the border states of Delaware, Maryland, Kentucky, and Missouri: the government would pursue gradual emancipation and provide compensation for owners' loss of slaves. The changes "would come gently as the dews of heaven, not rending or wrecking anything." That beguiling image was accompanied by an ultimatum: if the states did not accept his offer, they would face military emancipation, and receive no money for the people they considered their property.

Harriet, noting that the field hands were "as much afraid of the Yankee Buckra as of their own masters," found Hunter's brutal methods regrettable, but she agreed with him and other abolitionists that the only way the Union could win the war was by abolishing slavery and enlisting Black men. As she fervently told her Boston friend Lydia Maria Child, there would be no victory until the president ordered emancipation: "They may send the flower of their young men down South, to die of the fever in the summer, and the ague in the winter." They could send them year after year, until they used up all the young men. "All no use! God's ahead of master Lincoln. God won't let master Lincoln beat the South 'til he does *the right thing*. Master Lincoln, he's a great man, and I'm a poor Negro, but this Negro can tell master Lincoln how to save the money and the young men. He can do it by setting the Negroes free."

20

Battle Hymns

1862

President Lincoln and General McClellan
at Antietam, October 3, 1862

The cacophony of war was inescapable in Washington—the supply wagons and artillery, cavalry, and infantry slogging forward in late-winter rains and heavy mud, the constant comings and goings at the Club House: messengers from the telegraph office, statesmen, and nocturnal visits from the president. While Frances was in the city with Henry, she argued with him about emancipation. Republicans in Congress had been discussing the idea of a presidential proclamation ending slavery, but Henry opposed it. Invoking the southern states' constitutional rights, he said that in his position he had to consider three possible consequences: it would reinvigorate southerners, perhaps turn the border against the Union, and conceivably precipitate a full-scale slave revolt. Frances could see the war only as a test between good and evil. As she read the Constitution, she wrote to Lazette in March 1862, humanity and liberty were paramount: "I have felt all along that God could not give us a permanent peace while we supported slavery and I grow more and more sure of it every day."

In Auburn, talking to Martha and Lazette and reading Garrison's and Douglass's newspapers, Frances dispensed with any effort to see the war as Henry did, writing to him that it would be as well to let the slaves "take their chance for starvation as to leave them exposed to such horrible cruelty as is sometimes their fate." According to his position, she said, "the mere keeping together a number of states is more important than human freedom."

What's more, Lincoln's prosecution of the war was failing. Since the Battle of Bull Run in July 1861, the Union had suffered incomprehensible human losses—at Ball's Bluff, in Virginia (1,002 casualties), at Mill Springs, in Kentucky (262), and Hampton Roads, in Virginia (369). In early 1862, General McClellan appeared paralyzed by the thought of seeing more of his men die, lingering all winter with his army in Washington, despite Lincoln's repeated orders to move out and engage the enemy. On March 11, Lincoln stripped McClellan of supreme command, but left him in charge of the Army of the Potomac.

Six days later, McClellan finally launched the Peninsula Campaign, vowing to march into Richmond and end the war. He had 120,000 troops at his disposal, outnumbering the rebels by ten to one. But, facing a formidable-looking line of defensive works along the Warwick River, he stalled outside Yorktown. Refusing the president's command to strike at once, he set about building his own elaborate fortifications. For a second time, he was tricked by the Rebels' use of "Quaker guns," logs placed to resemble lines of artillery pieces. At the end of May, by the time McClellan judged his troops ready to engage, the rebels were retreating to safety in Richmond.

As the war lurched into its second year, Susan B. Anthony saw her fears for the women's rights movement confirmed. In the spring of 1862, the New York legislature revoked statutes it had passed two years earlier: mothers' rights to equal guardianship of their children and widows' rights to their husbands' property. It was a serious setback, and all the more problematic with men away fighting and widows badly in need of financial protection. Stanton recorded the move as the "dastardly law-makers" of New York exploiting the country's consuming absorption in the war, "stealing the children and the property of the white mothers in the Empire State!" Anthony tried to revive the women's rights conventions, causing David to snap at Martha, "Susan B. must be insane to think to interest people in Womans rights at this time—all nonsense." Martha could not fault Anthony's zeal, but she wrote to her, "As to calling a National Woman's Rights Convention, I would have felt that it would be very unwise, at this time when the nation's whole heart and soul are engrossed with this momentous crisis." Anthony complained in a letter to Lydia Mott, a cousin of Lucretia by marriage, that Garrison, Phillips, Mrs. Mott, Mrs. Wright, and even Mrs. Stanton were all telling her to wait until the war excitement abated: "I am sick at heart, but I can not carry the world against the wish and the will of our best friends."

Other women's rights activists were frustrated that they weren't doing more to help the beleaguered troops. The Boston poet Julia Ward Howe recalled that after watching a review of McClellan's troops at Bailey's Crossroads, outside Washington, she was ashamed at having so little to offer: "Something seemed to say to me, 'You would be glad to serve, but you cannot help any one; you have nothing to give, and there is nothing for you to do.'" Howe's abolitionist husband, Samuel Gridley Howe, who had been one of John Brown's Secret Six, was too old to fight, and their sons were too young. She lacked the "practical deftness" required for making shirts and preparing bandages for Dorothea Dix at the Sanitary Commission. In the carriage on the way back from Baileys Crossroads, she and her minister sang "John Brown's Body." The minister, knowing that the marching song had originated as a hymn, encouraged Howe to compose some loftier lyrics to "that stirring tune."

Howe woke up before dawn the next morning, and as she later wrote, the lines of a poem "began to twine themselves in my mind." She jotted down the stanzas before she forgot them, thinking, "I like this better than most things that I have written." In February 1862, *The Atlantic Monthly* published "Battle Hymn of the Republic," which made even Frances feel more hopeful about victory:

I have seen Him in the watch fires of a hundred circling
camps
They have builded Him an altar in the evening dews and
damps
I can read His righteous sentence by the dim and flaring
lamps
His day is marching on . . .

In late May, Frances received a long, detailed letter from Frederick, offering the most vivid picture she'd had of occupied Virginia. It was based on an excursion with his father and Anna, headed by Navy Secretary Welles, who had invited the Sewards and Attorney General Edward Bates and his family on a six-day river trip along the coast. The party set off on May 13, on the *City of Baltimore*, a steamboat adapted for patrol and blockade duty, traveling down the Potomac into Chesapeake Bay, and then up the York River, stopping at McClellan's field headquarters, thirty-five miles east of Richmond. Frederick evoked the vast tent city along the water: "At night, the long lines of lights on the shore, the shipping and bustle in the river, made it almost impossible to believe we were not in the harbor of Philadelphia or New York." As Henry, Welles, and Bates reviewed the troops, McClellan said that if he was sent the men he asked for, he could conduct "one of the great historic battles of the world." Henry, one of the few members of the administration who retained any confidence in McClellan, sent Lincoln a telegram urging him to order General Irvin McDowell's I Corps to the York River. The president agreed, but the next day, learning that "Stonewall" Jackson had attacked Union forces in the Shenandoah Valley, he sent the corps there instead.

Near Norfolk, the successful naval Battle of Hampton Roads, in March, had left acres of wrecked vessels. As Frederick walked through a forlorn assemblage of roofless brick buildings, he came upon a Massachusetts regiment camped in the ruins. He showed his eye for small encounters that told larger truths, confirming Frances's belief that he was a writer, not a politician. A soldier standing guard asked him if he remembered reading in the newspapers eighteen months earlier about a Boston shoemaker in Savannah who had been beaten and tarred and feathered, for supposed "abolitionism." Frederick replied that he had published the story while working at Weed's *Evening Journal*. The soldier said, "I am that shoemaker." He had enlisted with the goal of returning to Savannah, "to see those gentlemen again."

After the *Baltimore* stopped by Jamestown, the officers spotted a rowboat approaching from the direction of rebel lines. They pulled out their spyglasses, and one announced, "I think they are all black, sir." The boat contained thirteen men, one woman, and two children, who silently pulled up to the gangway. Frederick wrote that an officer called down, "Who are you? Where are you going?" The leader replied: "Going along with yous, Massa!" They explained that they were enslaved by two colonels in the Confederate Army. Learning that they were to be sent to North Carolina to work for the rebels, they had crept out one night, carried the boat to the James River, and set forth, looking for a ship flying the Stars and Stripes. Henry had told Frances that Union commanders got their most reliable intelligence from Black men and women, many of whom had been forced to work as cooks and manual laborers, and some to fight, for the Confederate Army.

Virginia was split in two, a fate its people could have avoided if they had decided, like the border states, not to join the Confederacy. Frances recalled Henry's glowing description of his visit, in 1857, to the Pendleton plantation in Culpeper, when he had imagined a possible reconcilation with the South. His account of the river trip was bleaker than Frederick's. He wrote that he'd found an entire society falling into ruin—houses ransacked, storehouses and barns empty: "Slaves are deserting the homes entrusted to them by their masters, who have gone into the southern armies or are fleeing before ours." He wrote to Fanny, "We saw war, not in its holiday garb, but in its stern and fearful aspect. We saw the desolation that follows, and the terror that precedes its march."

The prospect of a quick, successful end to the war looked worse still after Robert E. Lee was appointed commander of the Army of Northern Virginia. McClellan had consistently overestimated the strength of the enemy, but that summer he made the mistake of underestimating fifty-five-year-old, white-haired General Lee. Even southerners were dubious, calling Lee "old stick-in-the-mud" for his tendency to fall back rather than push forward. But he was fighting to regain control of Virginia, his own state, and he proved to be a decisive commander and a brilliant strategist. Well aware of McClellan's failings, Lee didn't fear the Army of the Potomac's superiority in numbers. Over seven days, from June 25 to July 1, Lee's army engaged Union troops in seven battles that resulted in sixteen thousand northern casualties. The rebel toll was considerably higher, at twenty thousand, but both sides saw the week as a victory for Lee, who forced McClellan's army to retreat. McClellan blamed Lincoln and Secretary of War Edwin Stanton for not sending more men, wiring Stanton, "You have done your best to sacrifice this army." The shocked telegraph supervisor had the sentence deleted before the message was delivered.

Northerners were losing faith in the administration's conduct of the war. While Henry asked Congress to authorize the nation's first national conscription, Radical Republicans and abolitionists, Frances included, said that the war could not be won without emancipating and enlisting enslaved men. Henry wrote testily to her about that argument: "If it were not painful to reflect that you are misled, when you have a right to know accurately the condition of the country, I should almost be glad that you escape the painful anxieties that oppress me, and so are able to occupy yourself with more pleasant matters."

Congress, though, was moving toward emancipation, and, unbeknownst to Frances and the public, President Lincoln was, too. The Confederates made extensive use of slaves to support their armies—in the trenches, in the hospitals, in the fields, and in the kitchens—and he now thought that he could use the emergency powers the Constitution granted a wartime president to define emancipation as a "military necessity." The First Confiscation Act, passed in August 1861, had permitted Union commanders to seize the slaves of Confederate officials. On July 17, 1862, Lincoln signed the Second Confiscation Act, which freed all escaped slaves in areas under Union control, and gave officers the authority to enlist the men in ancillary military positions.

Five days later, on July 22, the president gathered his cabinet, and told them that he had drafted a bolder act still—a preliminary emancipation proclamation for slaves in Confederate states. He read aloud from two sheets of paper. The language was stiff and legal: "I, Abraham Lincoln, President of the United States of America, and Commander-in-Chief of the Army and Navy thereof, do hereby proclaim and declare that hereafter, as heretofore, the war will be prosecuted for the object of practically restoring the constitutional relation between the United States, and each of the States, and the people thereof, in which States that relation is, or may be, suspended or disturbed." In the third paragraph he got to the nub: on January 1, 1863, "all persons held as slaves within any State, or designated part of a State, the people whereof shall then be in rebellion against the United States shall be then, thenceforward, and forever free." It was not the immediate, universal freedom that abolitionists wanted: slavery would continue in the border states, emancipation would not be put into effect for five months, and slaveholders would be paid for relinquishing the people whose freedom they had stolen. The proclamation, though, conclusively redefined the purpose of the war. Lincoln's order was an announcement to the world that he intended to save the Union by ending slavery.

Secretary of War Stanton advised announcing the proclamation immediately, and other cabinet officials expressed a range of objections and opinions about its political ramifications. Seward, thinking about the effects of emancipation both in America and abroad, voiced the worry he had expressed to Frances about a possible racial war in the South. He told Lincoln that emancipation would lead Britain and France to intervene, expanding the conflict rather than bringing it to a close. But seeing that the president had made up his mind, he advised that Lincoln wait for a moment of strength, not after a series of military defeats. As he later said, a proclamation of freedom must be "borne on the bayonets of an advancing army, not dragged in the dust behind a retreating one."

The agreement remained confidential, when such a thing was still possible in Washington, and Henry even kept the news of the historic decision from Frances, as he continued to emphasize the limited usefulness of emancipation. "Proclamations are *paper*," he explained, "without the support of armies." It wouldn't help the slaves of southeastern Texas, which the Confederacy controlled; and even in the parts of Virginia occupied by the Union, troops were under attack and the freed slaves in danger. He asked her to consider the possible ruin of the republic. The United States represented "the best hopes of all mankind," and its salvation was "of vastly more consequence than the destruction of slavery." Frances, refusing to believe that he meant that, wrote: "You owe it to yourself & your children & your country & to God to make your record clear." If the president did not repudiate slavery, Henry should resign rather than continue giving "countenance to a great moral evil."

He turned to Fanny for solace. "Blessed, my dear child, is the cheerfulness of the young," he wrote, implicitly chiding Frances for her severity. "Your letters are pleasing to me, because they bring no alarm, no remonstrances, no complaints, and no reproaches." Feeling the public anger as if it were being poured directly into his heart, he pleaded, "Write to me then cheerfully, as you are wont to do, of boys and girls and dogs and horses, and birds that sing, and stars that shine and never weep, and be blessed for all your days, for thus helping to sustain a spirit that loves to contend with crime, and yet is sensitive to distrust and unkindness."

The Republican press continued its criticism of the administration. Horace Greeley wrote an open letter to Lincoln in the *Tribune*, castigating him for his "mistaken deference to Rebel Slavery," for being "disastrously remiss" in enforcing the Confiscation Acts, and for his obsequious treatment of the border states, noting that slavery everywhere was the "inciting cause and sustaining basis of treason." Lincoln—looking ahead to the midterm elections, and knowing there would be opposition to an emancipation proclamation—carefully replied in an open letter to Greeley: "My paramount object in this struggle is to save the Union; and is not either to save or to destroy slavery." If he could save the Union without freeing any slave, he would do it. If he could save it by freeing all the slaves, he would do that.

On August 4, after Secretary of War Stanton called for an additional 300,000 volunteers, Will told Frances he would be among the new recruits. Her terror vying with her pride and patriotism, she found his decision almost unbearable. Martha said she opened the paper each morning with trembling fingers, knowing that Willy was fighting in Virginia, and that the long casualty lists might include his name. The chances of Willy surviving intact seemed to dwindle every day. By the end of the war, New York State had sent more than 448,000 men to serve, and some 53,000 of them had died.

Within a month, Will Seward was commissioned as the lieutenant colonel of the 138th New York Infantry. Regiments, composed of a thousand or so men, were raised locally, and Will was the secretary of the committee overseeing recruiting in Cayuga and Wayne counties. The mustering area and the barracks were on Camp Street in Auburn, already occupied by the 111th New York Volunteer Infantry. As in the early weeks of the war, young men occupied all the hotel rooms, spare bedrooms in private homes, and the empty floors of businesses. Will, in charge of the overflow, asked a few of his recruits to sleep temporarily in dry goods boxes in the street. Flags hung from the windows, and the men performed drills to the sound of church bells, cannon, and the cheering and clapping of spectators along Genesee Street. One day, half a dozen soldiers appeared at the Sewards' door politely asking for apples from their orchards, which Fanny rushed to supply. She wrote to her father that "they expressed themselves glad that this was 'Mr. Seward's residence.'"

The timing of Will's departure made it still more difficult. His wife, Jenny, whom Frances saw as a second daughter, was expecting a baby. And Aunt Clara's health was failing. But Frances, like Jenny's mother, concluded that she could not ask Will to spare himself when every family they knew with boys who qualified to serve were making that sacrifice. She wrote to Frederick, "As it is obvious all men are needed I made no objection."

Henry came home to welcome his first grandchild and to see Will off. The military situation in Virginia was alarming. After the Seven Days Battles, the Peninsula Campaign had ended in failure, and General Lee was moving steadily north. Soon after Henry arrived in Auburn, Frederick wrote with news that was reminiscent of the Battle of Bull Run the previous summer. McClellan had delayed responding to Lincoln's order to merge his army with General John Pope's, and Lee surrounded Pope's army at Manassas. The Second Battle of Bull Run ended with fourteen thousand Union casualties.

Henry returned at once to Washington, arriving the day after a September 2 cabinet meeting in which Stanton, Chase, Attorney General Edward Bates, and Secretary of the Interior Caleb Smith told Lincoln that he must dismiss McClellan. He refused, saying that he had just ordered McClellan's army to Washington to secure the city, and that he trusted him to do so. Chase, who was emotional even when not facing an immediate crisis, announced that the order would result in a "national calamity." Bates wrote in his diary that the president was "wrung by the bitterest anguish—said he felt almost ready to hang himself." Henry did his best to shore up Lincoln's spirits and to offer tactical advice, writing to Frances that he didn't blame anyone, saying that it was his duty "to look forward, not backward."

The rebels were poorly fed and clothed and outnumbered—but even so, Lee appeared all but indestructible. On September 5, his army crossed the upper Potomac and entered Frederick, Maryland, putting Confederate soldiers for the first time on northern soil, in a position to threaten Washington and Baltimore, or to proceed into Pennsylvania. Radical Republicans predicted that if the administration continued its current course, conservative northern voters would favor a negotiated peace. The midterm elections were only two months away.

Henry became a scapegoat for the administration's failures. The *Chicago Tribune* described McClellan in the field and Seward in the cabinet as "the evil spirits that have brought our grand cause to the very brink of death." There was talk about forcing Henry's resignation as well as McClellan's, and on September 10, four men from New York, led by James A. Hamilton, a son of Alexander Hamilton, visited Lincoln at the White House, part of a committee that claimed to be proposing how to better prosecute the war. It was an unsettling act of disloyalty by citizens of Henry's own state. Lincoln told the New Yorkers, "You, gentlemen, to hang Mr. Seward, would destroy the government," and he dismissed them.

Will's regiment stayed in Auburn until the birth of his daughter, on September 11. He and Jenny named her Cornelia Margaret, and called her Nelly. Frances was touched. Will was the most sensitive of her sons, attentive to her when she was sick and able to lift her spirit when no one else could. Cornelia had died before Will was born, but he knew that Frances had never fully gotten over the loss.

Before dawn on September 12, Jenny awoke to the tramp of boots passing the house, and "no other sound," she recalled, "but a few words of command in a lowered voice that I knew so well." Will's regiment was marching to the depot, to take the train to Washington, where they would reinforce the capital's defenses. Jenny, lying in bed with her newborn, thought it was the most mournful sound she had ever heard. "No drum, no fife, nothing but the quick firm steps; and all the stillness was for my sake." The men, after arriving in Washington, called their quarters at Fort Mansfield, near Tenleytown, "Camp Nelly Seward." Fort Mansfield was one of sixty-eight gigantic structures built to protect the capital from a Confederate invasion. Connected by military roads, the forts eventually had more than eight hundred cannon, ninety-three batteries with more than fourteen hundred emplacements for field guns, twenty miles of trenches, and officers' headquarters, storehouses, and construction camps. Three months after Will arrived, he wrote to Jenny asking her to bring Nelly and live with him in his log cabin for the winter, as officers' families often did when they were in camp. The family doctor in Auburn told her that if she went, she would bring home a dead baby, but now resolute about Will's service, Jenny's mother encouraged Jenny to go. Frances, thinking of her grandmother during the Revolutionary War, said, "Nonsense; think of all the babies that have been born and brought up in log-cabins."

On September 17, at Antietam Creek in Maryland, about sixty miles northwest of Washington, McClellan at last won a major battle. It was the bloodiest day yet of fighting, with combined casualties of 23,000. To Lincoln's frustration, he did not pursue Lee as the Confederate army retreated across the Potomac into Virginia, but it was victory enough. He told his cabinet that he had made a vow to God: if the army forced the rebels out of Maryland, he would consider it "an indication of Divine will"—a sign that God "had decided this question in favor of the slaves."

Five days later, on September 22, 1862, the president issued his preliminary Emancipation Proclamation, with the official order to follow on January 1, 1863. Those hundred days gave any slave state a final chance to rejoin the Union. Frances responded to Henry: "The Proclamation is so eminently good & right that I cannot fear the ultimate consequences—God is just." Martha wrote to Willy, "The Emancipation Proclamation, tho' far less than we hoped, & had a right to demand, after the expenditure of so much of the best blood of the nation, is still an advance, which we hail with joy, as the forerunner of a proclamation of Liberty throughout *all* the land."

Nonetheless, the Union's losses against Lee continued, and on November 5, Lincoln removed McClellan, naming as his successor a peer of Augustus's from West Point, Ambrose E. Burnside. If McClellan was too slow, Burnside was too hasty. On December 13, at the Battle of Fredericksburg, he ordered a hundred thousand men to cross the Rappahannock and march straight up Prospect Hill and Marye's Heights. By the end, some 12,500 Union troops were killed or wounded, to Lee's 5,000. Lincoln said, "If there is a worse place than Hell, I am in it." In the aftermath, venomous ill will toward Henry resurfaced. That month, the abolitionist *Boston Commonwealth* published an article headlined "Remove Him!," describing Henry as "the enemy of the public."

Frances was in Washington for her usual winter visit, and nursing Will back to health. His regiment, redesignated the 9th New York Heavy Artillery, was at Fort Mansfield helping to defend the city. He'd come down with a mild case of typhoid fever, an illness caused by flies that had come into contact with feces or contaminated food, and he was sent, with Jenny and Cornelia, to the Club House to recover. On the night of December 17, Henry faced another crisis. His friend Senator Preston King of New York rushed from Capitol Hill to tell him that thirty Republicans had just met in the Senate reception room to discuss forcing his removal from the cabinet. One senator charged that Henry had "never believed in the war," and that as long as he remained in the cabinet, only "defeat and disaster could be expected." Senator King and several others objected to the unorthodox proceeding, but the next day, Charles Sumner proposed that a committee of nine senators call upon the president, to suggest changes in the conduct of the war and the cabinet.

It turned out that Frances's dear friend Charles had been quietly conspiring against Henry since the start of the administration. A close adviser to the president on foreign affairs, he was certain that he would have been a far better secretary of state than Seward. He'd advised Lincoln, "You must watch him and overrule him." Throughout his scheming, he'd written to Frances in all seriousness that there was so little true principle in Washington, "I feel more and more alone."

Henry told King, "They may do as they please about me, but they shall not put the President in a false position on my account." He wrote to Lincoln, "Sir, I hereby resign the office of Secretary of State, and beg that my resignation may be accepted immediately." Frederick delivered Henry's note to Lincoln, along with his own letter of resignation.

Lincoln saw the accusations against Seward as "a lie, an absurd lie," and he found a way to quash the senatorial rebellion. At 7:00 p.m. on December 18, he received the committee of nine senators at the White House. Listening to them lecture him about the conduct of the war, and to their demand that Seward be removed from the Cabinet, he said he would carefully consider their resolutions. Senator Zachariah Chandler of Michigan, thinking they had succeeded, said that the "millstone around the Administration" would soon be gone.

The president summoned the senators back the next evening, asking the members of his cabinet, except Seward, to attend. While admitting that he hadn't consulted regularly enough with them, he defended his secretary of state as neither improperly meddlesome nor less committed to winning the war than any of them. He then asked Sumner and each cabinet member in turn if he thought Seward should be fired—hoping to shame them by calling them out individually. The strategy worked. Sumner harrumphed about Seward's diplomatic dispatches, citing one that purportedly blamed Congress and secessionists alike as foes of the Union. Chase, who'd been organizing his own anti-Seward conspiracy, grumbled that he wouldn't have come if he knew he was going to be "arraigned before a committee of the Senate," but he fell in line. The following morning, he, too, offered his resignation.

Lincoln knew exactly what motivated and rankled ambitious men, and how to use their weaknesses to suit his needs. He sent letters to Henry and Chase, informing them that he had concluded the public interest would not be served by their resignations. "I, therefore, have to request that you will resume the duties of your departments respectively. Your obedient servant, A. Lincoln." Henry replied, "My Dear Sir—I have cheerfully resumed the functions of this department in obedience to your command. With the highest respect, Your humble servant, William H. Seward." Chase had no choice but to do the same. Henry, benevolent in his triumph and hoping to mend frayed ties, invited Chase to dinner. Chase declined, saying he was ill.

In late December, Frances heard from Elizabeth Cady Stanton, who was curious about the White House intrigues. Frances replied that she was glad of Mrs. Stanton's continuing faith in the goodness of her husband. "He is worthy of your esteem." Implicitly contrasting him to the nine disloyal senators and to Secretary Chase, she said that Henry was "too generous to allow his shortcomings to be imputed to another, and too just not to feel that every human being should bear the responsibility of his own conduct." She was disenchanted with Chase, but Sumner's duplicity was a burning personal affront, and she severed their friendship. Frances confessed to Stanton, "I dare not look the war squarely in the face since my last son went into the army. I wish I could talk with you, which I will try to do when I next go to New York."

Fanny and Lazette joined the rest of the family in Washington for the New Year. For the first time in nineteen months, all four Seward children and their families were reunited with their parents. They shared their delight in the baby, and their relief and gratitude that Lincoln had stood by Henry. Best of all, freedom was coming for millions of enslaved people. Howe's "Battle Hymn" again came to mind:

In the beauty of the lilies, Christ was born across the sea
With a glory in His bosom that transfigures you and me
As He died to make men holy, let us live to make men free
While God is marching on . . .

On December 30, Lincoln made copies of his draft of the final Emancipation Proclamation for each member of the cabinet. Although the issue of allowing Black men to bear arms was not addressed, they were being admitted into the military, and the obvious next step was the authorization of Black enlistment. By the end of the war, almost 200,000 African American men were fighting for freedom and for the restoration of the Union. The only emendation Lincoln accepted was a concluding statement, originating with Sumner and proposed by Chase, which encapsulated Lincoln's belief that emancipation was both constitutionally and divinely sanctioned: "And upon this act, sincerely believed to be an act of justice, warranted by the Constitution, upon military necessity, I invoke the considerate judgment of mankind, and the gracious favor of Almighty God."

21

Harriet's War

1863

Combahee River Raid, *Harper's Weekly*, July 4, 1863

On New Year's Day 1863, as the country prepared for the announcement of a national proclamation that would begin the process of overturning 244 years of slavery, Fanny Seward made her debut in Washington society. Diffident even when she was not the center of attention, she didn't mind that her coming-out was eclipsed. She duly recorded her attire in her diary: a new light blue silk gown and a white hat trimmed with navy-blue flowers, which she wore to the president's annual morning reception at the White House, and a plum-colored dress for her party that afternoon. Pained by all of the suffering and sacrifices, Fanny and her mother had not found much pleasure in shopping for the fabrics and her new beaver cloak. To Frances, presenting her daughter to the ruling class at a time of civil war felt like a distasteful artifact of a defunct society. Well-born

Washingtonians might carry on with rituals that separated high from low, white from Black, and men from women, but their way of life was coming undone.

There were two signatories to the Emancipation Proclamation: Secretary of State Seward and President Lincoln. After the president's reception and Fanny's party, Henry and Frederick picked up the final copy from the State Department calligrapher and carried it in a portfolio to the White House. Alone with Lincoln in his study, they spread out the broadsheet on the table where the cabinet met. He paused before signing. The New Year's reception was always an exhausting affair, and never more so than that year: the secretary of state presenting the diplomatic corps, followed by civil and military officials, and, at 2:00 p.m., greeting the throngs of citizens who had waited for hours on the porch and along the carriageways and avenue for the honor of shaking the president's hand. Lincoln told Henry and Frederick that he never had felt more certain that he was doing the right thing, but his arm was numb, and he feared that he would tremble. Frederick remarked that the signature was steady. His father then signed and affixed the seal.

In the North, there were anticipatory celebrations throughout the day. Garrison spent the afternoon at Boston's Music Hall, with Whittier, Emerson, Longfellow, Stowe, and other New England abolitionists. Emerson read his "Boston Hymn," composed for the occasion, and the orchestra played Mendelssohn's "Hymn of Praise." Nearby, at Tremont Temple, Douglass spoke, noting that two years earlier, he had been forced off the same stage by a mob. Now he talked hopefully about emancipation, and about Black enlistment.

Harriet Tubman, in Beaufort, did not share in the euphoria. The proclamation would do nothing for people enslaved in the four border states, including Maryland, her birthplace. She told her biographer Sarah Bradford that when she was asked at Port Royal why she was not celebrating, she'd replied, "I had my jubilee three years ago." During a prewar visit with her friend Rev. Henry Highland Garnet in New York, she'd had a vision that augured an end to slavery. "My people are free! My people are free!" she shouted, as she came downstairs to breakfast. Garnet, too, had liberated himself from slavery on the Eastern Shore, and he scoffed, saying that his grandchildren might see the day of emancipation, but that he and Harriet never would. She replied, "I tell you, sir, you'll see it, and you'll see it soon." On the nation's official day of emancipation, she went about her duties as usual, saying, "I rejoiced all I could then. I can't rejoice no more."

She and others at Port Royal were hastening the day of universal freedom. On August 9, 1862, General Hunter, lacking support from the War Department, had disbanded the First South Carolina Volunteers and taken a sixty-day leave of absence. Brigadier General Rufus Saxton had more luck, with a far more ambitious undertaking. Saxton was the new military governor of the Department of the South, a job that was part ranking commander and part social services administrator. A soft-spoken Unitarian abolitionist from Greenfield, Massachusetts, he had a way with the local people and with the Lincoln administration that Hunter did not. Wanting to prove that even men who had spent their entire lives enslaved would make fine soldiers, he informed Secretary of War Stanton that he intended to conduct a series of guerrilla river raids along the coasts, to drive off plantation owners, appropriate food and other goods, rob them of their slaves, and enlist qualified men. On August 25, Secretary Stanton issued orders permitting Saxton to enroll enough men for five regiments—five thousand Black soldiers.

Saxton asked some of the teachers with the Port Royal Experiment to help him recruit at the plantations and in the churches, where he assured families that the men would be treated and paid exactly as white troops were—thirteen dollars a month. He appointed Harriet's Boston friend Thomas Wentworth Higginson, a captain in the 51st Massachusetts Volunteer Infantry, to lead the reconstituted First South Carolina Volunteer Infantry Regiment (Colored).

Harriet had welcomed Higginson with a brace of ducks. It was he who had introduced her at her first large speaking event in Boston, and Higginson and his wife, Mary, had often welcomed her into their home. He was stationed with his soldiers about four miles south of Beaufort at Camp Saxton, where the regiment's tents were arrayed in neat white rows on the grounds of an old cotton plantation. The main house, set high above the Beaufort River, was pillaged and weed-choked, but the soldiers' dusty grounds were swept clean each day, and majestic live oaks draped in gray Spanish moss provided a welcome heavy shade.

Higginson's smooth cheeks and starched collars were gone, replaced by a full beard and the blue double-breasted uniform of a colonel. His tent had a latch on the door, the only one in camp, and his quarters were outfitted with a fireplace, a fragrant wreath of oranges on the wall, and a desk that held his writing utensils and a copy of Victor Hugo's *Les Misérables*, published that year. He wrote emotionally about the melancholy beauty of his surroundings and about how his men performed their drills with determination and discipline. He found one soldier's expression of patriotism more affecting than any he'd ever heard: "Our masters, they have lived under the flag, they got their wealth under it, and everything beautiful for their children. Under it they have grind us up, and put us in their pocket for money. But the first minute they think that old flag mean freedom for we colored people, they pull it right down, and run up the flag of their own." The soldier told Higginson that the regiment had never lost their faith in the old flag, "and we'll die for it now."

The First South Carolina Infantry was the advance guard for Black regiments in other states. Governor Andrew of Massachusetts, heading up recruitment for the first two Black regiments in the North, asked Douglass and other Black abolitionists to travel to other states seeking volunteers. Douglass's recruits included his sons Lewis and Charles. Emancipation was the first step to citizenship; Black enlistment was the second. Most white troops did not welcome the development, but as a soldier from Michigan said, "A black man could stop a bullet as well as a white man." Black troops and their advocates knew that once they had served their country, it would be difficult to deny them their full rights.

The officers of Port Royal relied on Harriet Tubman for the success of their river raids. Her scouts helped her explore the coast to locate Confederate pickets and to seek vulnerable points of attack—intelligence she relayed to Higginson, Saxton, and others. Saxton had initiated the first incursion in early November 1862, dispatching to Georgia sixty-two Black soldiers serving under Lieutenant Colonel Oliver T. Beard of the 48th New York Infantry and two other white officers. In five days, they conducted four raids, skirmishing with the enemy, destroying nine saltworks, and returning with barrels of corn and rice. More significant, they brought back ninety-four Black recruits and sixty-one women and children. Saxton wrote to Secretary Stanton that he intended "to prove the fighting qualities of the negroes (which some have doubted)." The river raids were designed, too, as a form of psychological warfare: plantation owners were haunted by the specter of musket-bearing freedmen liberating slaves.

With Secretary Stanton's approval, Saxton increased the numbers of boats and men. In the raids, armed steamers, each carrying about a hundred Black troops, landed at a plantation's dock. Advance men waded into the water and onto the land, fighting off or capturing rebel pickets. When the whistle blew on a Yankee steamer, enslaved laborers dropped their work and rushed to the landing. As overseers and rebels appeared, Union men opened fire, giving the fleeing slaves cover as they boarded the boats. There was no time for the enemy to coordinate a counterattack. Within the year, Higginson had more than 550 soldiers in his regiment.

On Emancipation Day, Beaufort was unnaturally quiet. General Saxton had organized an all-day celebration for the Black soldiers and their families and participants in the Port Royal Experiment. A marching band from Maine played hymns and patriotic songs as Saxton's steamer, *Flora*, and other boats ferried thousands of guests from outlying islands to Camp Saxton. The local women wore bright holiday kerchiefs, and the teachers their Sunday dresses. Each company was given a barrel of molasses water, and lemonade was provided for civilians. The ten companies feasted on skeletal oxen roasted over oak fires. The army's ubiquitous hardtack, which vaguely resembled Scottish shortbread but had the color and consistency of petrified wood, was in plentiful supply. Black troops marveled at their sudden change of fortune. One of Higginson's soldiers told him: "I think myself happy, this New Year's Day, for salute my own Colonel." Only a year earlier, he had been doing forced labor for a Confederate officer.

Everyone gathered under the live oaks for a reading of the Emancipation Proclamation and the presentation of regimental colors. Dr. William H. Brisbane, a former slaveholder from Beaufort who had converted to abolitionism, read the Proclamation aloud, concluding with the names of President Abraham Lincoln and Secretary of State William H. Seward. As Higginson was presented with the flags for his regiment, an elderly Black man started singing "My Country 'Tis of Thee," and others joined in—their first declaration of allegiance to their nation. Some white officials on the platform started to sing, but Higginson motioned to them to stop. "It seemed the choked voice of a race at last unloosed," he wrote in his journal. "History will not believe it."

The effects of the Emancipation Proclamation were immediately apparent in abolitionist Port Royal. On January 7, Harriet obtained a letter from a military officer ordering that she be issued one hundred dollars in "secret service money." She used it to pay her scouts as they prepared for more river raids. A few weeks later, she went to General Hunter, who had returned from his furlough to his headquarters on Hilton Head. She needed to buy flour and sugar at the U.S. Commissary for her baking, and she requested permission to move around the region more freely. He gave her a military order stating: "Pass the Bearer, Harriet Tubman . . . wherever she wishes to go, and give her free passage at all times."

In late January, Higginson led his first raid, along St. Mary's River, between Georgia and Florida, returning triumphantly with loads of brick, iron, and lumber. Higginson reported to the War Department that his men had more than proved themselves: "No officer in this regiment now doubts that the key to the successful prosecution of this war lies in the unlimited employment of black troops." He praised the "fiery energy" of his men as they loaded and fired, shouting to one another the soldier's rallying cry "Never give it up!" Everything, Higginson said, "even to the piloting of the vessels and the selection of the proper points for cannonading, was done by my own soldiers."

Another abolitionist officer, Colonel James Montgomery, soon arrived in Beaufort with orders to raise a second Black South Carolina regiment. Montgomery had fought in Kansas with John Brown against the Border Ruffians, and Harriet made herself useful to him, too. He was a tall, weather-beaten evangelical preacher, of whom Brown had said, "Captain Montgomery is the only soldier I have met among the prominent Kansas men. He understands my system of warfare exactly." Montgomery, whose eyes had their own unnerving intensity, sat for one photograph with long tufts of hair standing on end as if he had been struck by lightning.

The insurgent Montgomery and the Boston Brahmin Higginson, both Brown enthusiasts, had very different ideas about battle. Higginson said of his troops, "They are all natural Transcendentalists," and he conducted his raids as ordered: recruiting soldiers and gathering needed supplies. Montgomery engaged in lawless "western brigand practices," burning and pillaging enemy property. Higginson haughtily wrote to his mother: "I will have none but civilized warfare in *my* reg't."

• • •

In early May, Harriet learned from her scouts that the rebels had withdrawn their heavy cannon and most of their soldiers from the breastworks along the Combahee River, north of Beaufort. It was "sickly season," when yellow fever and malaria set in. She told Hunter, who used the information to plan a major raid along the Combahee River, where some of the largest rice plantations in the country were located. He assigned the expedition to Montgomery, who asked Harriet and three pilots and scouts she worked with—Samuel Hayward, Charles Simmons, and Walter D. Plowden—to go with them. She was elated. A forty-one-year-old woman, once enslaved herself, Harriet had been asked to take part in the most ambitious military operation yet in Port Royal.

After dark on the night of June 1, 1863, a contingent of 250 men from the 2nd South Carolina regiment and a company from the 3rd Rhode Island Heavy Artillery set off from Beaufort on three boats. The moon wouldn't begin to rise until midnight, giving them several hours before they would be visible to Confederate pickets. Harriet and the scouts were with Montgomery on the lead vessel, the *John Adams*, an old ferryboat from Boston equipped with two Parrott guns and two howitzers.

They proceeded up the Beaufort River, past Lady's Island, entering St. Helena Sound and then the mouth of the Combahee. The snaking river was hard to navigate, clogged in spots with rotting logs and matted grass. When the second steamer, the *Sentinel*, ran aground, Montgomery ordered its men into the other two boats. The silence was broken only by whispered commands and the chugging of the engines. At dawn, the *Adams* and the third boat, the *Harriet A. Weed*—from New York, named after Thurlow Weed's daughter—arrived at Fields Point, a sentry lookout, where Montgomery ordered a captain and a contingent of troops to go ashore. They drove the rebel pickets inland, and kept up a skirmish for most of the day.

The *Adams* and the *Weed* continued to the Nicholls Plantation, where the field hands had begun their day. Harriet conveyed the scene to Sarah Bradford. As the fog rolled off the water and the steamers became visible, some workers rushed to the woods, "coming to peer out like startled deer," but most dropped what they were doing in the cabins and the fields, and ran toward the dock, grabbing whatever was at hand to take with them. Union skirmishers provided cover for dozens of soldiers whom

Montgomery ordered to set fire to barns, rice storehouses, and the plantation house. They opened the rice trunks—the wooden floodgates that controlled the water levels—and ruined the harvest, then destroyed the trunks. Word quickly spread, as Harriet said, that "Lincoln's gun-boats come to set them free."

She told Bradford, "Here you'd see a woman with a pail on her head, rice a smoking in it just as she'd taken it from the fire, young one hanging on behind, one hand 'round her forehead to hold on, the other digging into the rice-pot, eating with all its might; 'hold of her dress two or three more; down her back a bag with a pig in it. One woman brought two pigs, a white one, and a black one; we took 'em all on board; named the white pig Beauregard," after the Confederate general, "and the black pig Jeff Davis." The pigs squealed, the chickens clucked, the babies squalled. Harriet called them "the children of Israel, coming out of Egypt."

She helped them to the rowboats, tearing her skirts on the dense briar patches along the shore. The rowboats quickly filled, and people waded into the water, holding on. To avoid capsizing, the oarsmen beat their hands with the paddles, trying to force them back until the next run. They wouldn't let go, and Montgomery called out, "Moses, you'll have to give 'em a song." He referred to them as her people, but as she recalled, they "wasn't my people any more than they was his—only we was all Negroes—'cause I didn't know any more about them than he did." She did what she could, improvising lyrics and a melody to generate calm, "Come along, come along, don't be alarmed, Uncle Sam is rich enough to give you all a farm."

Harriet proceeded on the *Adams* upriver; the *Weed* stayed at the Nicholls Plantation, taking on passengers. At Combahee Ferry, Montgomery blew the steamer's whistle. Several dozen men from the 3rd Rhode Island proceeded to the Middleton Plantation, looting and burning the house and outbuildings, while a contingent of Montgomery's 2nd South Carolina got off on the mile-long causeway above the rice fields and advanced in double file toward one of the largest properties, the Heyward Plantation. Totally exposed on the flat, watery stretch, their black skin visible, the men marched forward in formation. Meeting no resistance at the plantation, they torched Heyward's house and outbuildings, crops, rice mills, and cotton warehouses. Heyward escaped, but the troops made off with his horse and sabre. Further inland, they spared the Lowndes Plantation house and slave quarters, but burned the rice mill and the barns. In the yard, as a few dozen slaves ran toward the landing, a small girl was shot by a rebel; an adult lifted her up and took her along with the others. Montgomery's men gave protection to hundreds from the two plantations as they fled across the causeway to the *Adams*.

A few Confederates fired a field cannon from the base of the causeway, but retreated when the *Adams* returned fire. The boats, filled beyond capacity, couldn't take everyone. William Apthorp, a captain in the 2nd South Carolina, wrote, "Remembering the treatment that these poor people would suffer for their attempt to escape the Yankees, it was hard to leave them. But it was impossible to take another one, and sadly we swung away from the landing." Downriver, the *Adams* met the *Weed*, which had also reached capacity. A Rhode Island captain said, "This was the saddest sight of the whole expedition—so many souls within sight of freedom and yet unable to attain it."

The boats docked at Beaufort the next morning. Harriet walked through cheering crowds along Bay Street to the Baptist church with her scouts, the colonel, the troops, and the contrabands. Those who couldn't squeeze inside the church stood outside the open doors and down the front steps. Montgomery gave a speech, then everyone sang a spiritual. Harriet, her skirt in tatters, spoke exultantly. Alone, in Maryland, she had never been able to rescue more than a dozen people, and most of her groups were far smaller. On the Combahee River raid, she had helped free 750 people. She caused a great sensation, one onlooker said, with her speech of "sound sense and real native eloquence."

On June 30, Harriet dictated a letter to her friend Franklin Sanborn, who had become the editor of the Boston *Commonwealth*. She had some advice about how to cover the raid: "Don't you think we colored people are entitled to some credit for that exploit, under the lead of the brave Colonel Montgomery?" Montgomery's Black troops, aided by Harriet and her scouts, had weakened the rebels by bringing away, she said, punctuating each point, "*seven hundred and fifty-six* head of their most valuable live stock, known up in your region as 'contrabands,' and this, too, without the loss of a single life on our part, though we had good reason to believe that a number of rebels bit the dust." Harriet herself escorted about a hundred men to the local recruitment office.

She said of her ruined skirts: "I made up my mind then I would never wear a long dress on another expedition of the kind." With her women's rights friends in mind, she asked to be sent a utilitarian "bloomer dress, made of some coarse, strong material to wear on expeditions." And she made a case for the Port Royal Experiment. Arguing that the program would lead quickly to self-reliance, she said that she was trying to find jobs for some of the freed people, to lighten the burden on the government and help them to respect themselves by fending on their own.

Harriet ended with a mention of her parents. She had been away from Auburn for almost two years, and Ben and Rit were in feeble health, but she would consider herself a deserter if she went home before the war was over. She reminded Sanborn of his promise to contribute a small sum of money every year to help her carry on her work. She relied on him, as she did on Martha and Frances and others in Auburn, to help out a little longer: "I hope the good people there will not allow them to suffer, and I do not believe they will."

Sanborn had read about the Combahee River Raid in a Wisconsin newspaper that had a correspondent in Port Royal. The story told of a "Black She 'Moses'" dashing into enemy territory with Colonel Montgomery's "gallant band of 300 black soldiers." Sanborn, knowing that the "She Moses" could only be Harriet, couldn't resist the scoop. On July 17, he reprinted part of the article, identified the mysterious savior as Harriet Tubman, and wrote the first account of her life ever published, based on interviews he had conducted with her before the war. Responding with alacrity to Harriet's plea, he appealed to his readers for donations, so that she could stay on in South Carolina. Money rolled in, and three days after his piece appeared, Frances received a hundred dollars, to be credited to Harriet's mortgage account.

Harriet's joy about the Combahee Raid was heightened later on the day of her return by the arrival in Beaufort of the eleven-hundred-man 54th Massachusetts Infantry. General Hunter had asked Governor Andrew to send the 54th to Port Royal, believing that the educated colored men from the North would set a high standard for South Carolina's "brigade of liberated slaves." The commanding officer was Colonel Robert Gould Shaw, a twenty-five-year-old former captain in the 2nd Massachusetts Infantry, who had fought at Antietam. Shaw's parents were prominent Boston abolitionists, and Governor Andrew believed that Shaw would have no "vulgar contempt for color." When Mrs. Shaw learned that her only child was "willing to take up the cross," she said it was the proudest moment of her life.

Even overrun by troops, officers, and the paraphernalia of war, Beaufort was a very small town—a miniature Charleston, with a neat grid of streets composed of sand and crushed oyster shells. Pillared white mansions lined the waterfront and extended a few blocks back, some occupied by Saxton and other officers, others converted into hospitals. Roses and crepe myrtles bloomed in untended gardens, and bougainvillea spilled over broken fences. The entire town turned out to welcome the 54th. Teachers and officers' wives dressed up for the occasion, bands played, and detachments from the 1st Massachusetts Cavalry galloped down Bay Street.

Shaw, small and slight with a wispy blond goatee, looked like a boy dressed up as a colonel, but he had the full respect of his soldiers. He had trained them hard, and now demanded that they receive equal treatment. Although Secretary of War Stanton had pledged to pay Black soldiers thirteen dollars a month, Congress had only agreed to ten, from which three was subtracted for their clothing allowance. Shaw wrote to Governor Andrew to object, and Andrew wrote to Lincoln and Stanton. Many of Shaw's troops refused to be paid at all until the matter was settled, as did a third of Higginson's men, who said they were willing to give their soldiering to the government, but they wouldn't despise themselves enough to take less than they had been promised. The complaints eventually were addressed: in June 1864, Congress changed the law, retroactively granting equal pay to Black troops.

Harriet, privy to the controversy and a firm advocate of equality, had an idiosyncratic position when it came to her own wages. She was not an official army employee, and followed her own accounting system. Saving the written orders she received from Hunter and other officials as proof of service, she also kept track of the days she spent as a scout. After the war, she expected to file for her pay retrospectively, and to be reimbursed at the going rate for scouts of $2.50 per day.

About a week after the 54th Massachusetts arrived in Beaufort, Montgomery asked Shaw and his men to accompany him on a raid up the Altamaha River in Georgia. Both had the rank of colonel, but Montgomery—Shaw's senior in years and experience—wanted to show

Shaw and his men how war was waged along the coast. As the steamer approached the port of Darien, Montgomery lobbed a few shells among plantation buildings. Discovering that the town was deserted, Montgomery and Shaw ordered the soldiers to load all furniture and movable property onto their boats. Then Montgomery turned to Shaw and said with a smile, "I shall burn this town." When Shaw objected, Montgomery said he would take full responsibility, and explained that Darien—a source of cotton, rice, turpentine, and timber—had been harboring blockade runners. Southerners must feel that the hand of God had descended to sweep them away.

In the Combahee River Raid, far more property had been destroyed, but that was an act of war. The thefts and burning of Darien, an abandoned village, were seen by Shaw as "this dirty piece of business," which he feared would tarnish all Black troops and their officers. As expected, the southern and northern press condemned the 54th as "cowardly Yankee negro thieves."

After the Darien affair, Brigadier General Quincy A. Gillmore replaced General Hunter as head of the Department of the South, and in early July, he moved most of the Port Royal troops up the coast in preparation for a major attack on Charleston. Nurses and doctors accompanied soldiers to the front, and although there is no record of Harriet's location, she appears to have been sent to Folly Island, where a supply depot, advance headquarters, and a field hospital were located. The islands off the coast of Charleston look on a map like pieces of a jigsaw puzzle, separated from the mainland and one another by inlets and creeks. Folly was about six miles south of Fort Wagner on Morris Island, the first target of the offensive.

General Gillmore instructed the 54th regiment to stay behind, prompting Shaw to object to his brigade commander, General George C. Strong, saying that his men must prove how capable they were by fighting alongside white troops. On July 11, Strong had led an unsuccessful attack on Fort Wagner, and, needing every man available, he agreed to Shaw's request to join a second assault. The 54th first proved itself on July 16 on James Island, to the west of Morris: three companies, on picket duty for a division from Connecticut, beat back a two-hour charge by rebels who vastly outnumbered them. A Connecticut soldier wrote to his mother, "They fought like heroes." The regiment evacuated James Island that night, marching in a thunderstorm across earthen dikes and narrow plank bridges and arriving before dawn at a beach on Cole's Island, adjacent to Folly. The men waited under a burning sun throughout the day for the *General Hunter* to take them to Folly. Upon their arrival, around 5 p.m., they marched six miles, then took another steamer to Morris Island and General Strong's temporary headquarters.

On the morning of July 18, the Union commenced its second assault on Fort Wagner with a naval bombardment. General Gillmore had a daunting battle plan: after taking the fort, the soldiers would capture Battery Gregg at the northern tip of Morris, and, finally, win back Fort Sumter, move into Charleston Harbor, and overrun the city. The USS *New Ironsides*, accompanied by five smaller monitors, issued a volley of shells from the cannon, demolishing barracks and storehouses at the fort and sending volcanic eruptions of sand into the air. General Strong praised Shaw for his troops' performance on James Island, and asked him if he would lead the infantry charge on Fort Wagner that evening—an honor that was little more than a suicide mission. One division commander told Gillmore, "Well I guess we will let Strong lead and put those d——d negroes from Massachusetts in the advance: we may as well get rid of them one time as another."

Shaw's advance began at dusk, the sky clogged with smoke from the monitors' shelling. The men hurrahed, one soldier recalled, "as if going on some mirthful errand." The strip of sand was narrow, and the tide was coming in. The soldiers on the right splashed through the water; on the left they were pressed up against the marsh. Fort Wagner loomed up before them, made not of brick and wood like Sumter, but of earth, sand, and palmetto logs, with thirty-foot parapets and fourteen cannon—an army's version of a child's castle on a beach. Land mines, sharpened palmetto stakes, and a ten-foot moat hindered the men's progress. Some could free themselves from the mud only by cutting off the legs of their pants. When they were two hundred yards from the fort, Shaw ordered the charge. Grapeshot, shells, and hand grenades dropped on them in a deadly hail. Some drowned in the moat's water, others in the incoming tide. "Our men fell like grass before a sickle," one lieutenant commented. As darkness descended, the colors of the soldiers' coats could be seen only in the flashes of light from bursting shells and howitzer and musket fire. Shaw, leading from the center, scaled the embankment and was shot and killed as he reached the parapet.

Harriet watched the battle from her vantage point. "And then we saw the lightning, and that was the guns; and then we heard the thunder, and that was the big guns; and then we heard the rain falling, and that was the drops of blood falling; and when we came to get in the crops, it was dead men that we reaped."

By 10:30 p.m., the battle was lost. Sergeant William Carney, a onetime slave from Norfolk, had rushed to catch the American flag after its bearer fell. Shot in his right arm, chest, and legs, he somehow managed to carry the flag back, becoming the first Black man to be awarded the Congressional Medal of Honor. The 54th Massachusetts suffered 281 casualties: 54 killed, including Shaw, 179 wounded, and 48 missing—about 45 percent of the regiment. The total Union toll was 1,515; the Confederate toll, 174. The rebels threw Shaw into a pit along with his troops. When General Gillmore later sought to retrieve his remains, Shaw's father wrote: "We hold that a soldier's most appropriate burial-place is on the field where he has fallen."

Harriet was accustomed to frightful hospital conditions, especially in the warm weather, when disease was rampant, but she had never seen anything like the aftermath of Fort Wagner. In Beaufort, thirty-six hours after the battle, she was nursing the Black wounded, many of them teenagers. A hundred and fifty men were taken to an old mansion on Washington Street, converted into Hospital #10, the first general hospital designated by the War Department for Black soldiers. They were laid out on blankets as beds were prepared. The rooms soon smelled of sweat, feces, blood, and, overpoweringly, of gangrene.

The people of Beaufort formed an ad hoc relief committee, distributing buckets of broth and gruel, pitchers of lemonade, vegetables, and fruitcake. The next day, the army's Sanitary Commission came through with cots and fresh clothes. Esther Hawks, a doctor from New Hampshire, organized the intake at Hospital #10. She was officially on the Sea Islands as a teacher, but she often worked at the hospital, where her husband was a surgeon, and ran it when he was not there. Hawks wrote of a twenty-year-old Black man who told her he'd lived in Syracuse after liberating himself from slavery in Maryland. As soon as the government was willing to take him on, he joined up—not to fight for his country, as he'd never had any, but to gain one.

Harriet said of her hospital duties: "I'd go to the hospital, I would, early every morning. I'd get a big chunk of ice, I would, and put it in a basin, and fill it with water; then I'd take a sponge and begin. First man I'd come to, I'd thrash away the flies, and they'd rise, they would, like bees round a hive. Then I'd begin to bathe their wounds, and by the time I'd bathed off three or four, the fire and heat would have melted the ice and made the water warm, and it would be as red as clear blood. Then I'd go and get more ice, I would, and by the time I got to the next ones, the flies would be round the first ones, black and thick as ever."

In September, Lincoln harshly addressed northerners who still opposed emancipation: "You say you will not fight to free Negroes. Some of them seem to be willing to fight for you. When victory is won, there will be some black men who can remember that, with silent tongue and clenched teeth, and steady eye and well-poised bayonet, they have helped mankind on this great consummation. I fear, however, that there will also be some white ones, unable to forget that with malignant heart and deceitful speech, they strove to hinder it." They were prophetic words, foreshadowing a question that the freed people of the South and Republicans often asked in the postwar decades: would Reconstruction have succeeded if Lincoln had lived?

Shaw's valor made a lasting impression on Harriet. On July 17, Shaw wrote to his wife, Annie, that he and his men had consumed nothing but coffee, hardtack, and water for two days. In coming decades, as the Battle of Fort Wagner took shape in Harriet's memory, she always said that before the assault, she served Robert Shaw his last meal.

22

Willy Wright at Gettysburg

March–July 1863

William and Martha Coffin Wright, 1861

On March 15, 1863, Martha got a glimpse of Willy in Philadelphia, where he spent the day with her while enjoying a brief furlough. She had not seen him since December 1861, when he'd come home to recuperate from typhoid fever. She wrote in her diary, "Felt very sad to part with him, with all the dread possibilities of the future but proud that he appreciated & was willing to take part in the struggle for National life." Notwithstanding the enormous effort it took to say goodbye, Martha noted determinedly to David, "I would not have him anywhere else than at his post of duty"—

even if it ended in his death. They had lost Charley to illness when he was barely a year old, and Tallman to the sea when he was twenty-two. If Willy didn't survive, she told herself, he would die in the service of creating a new America.

She next heard from him in May, when she was in New York City, and David forwarded her a letter about his participation in the Battle of Chancellorsville, under General Joseph Hooker. It was one of the worst Union defeats yet, delivered by an army half the size of the Army of the Potomac, but luck was with Willy's battery, which escaped almost unscathed. Martha wrote to him that his letter was an inexpressible relief: "My heart is so constantly with you, and in this great struggle, that I find it difficult to interest myself in anything else."

Willy was a sporadic, terse correspondent, and in the last weeks of June, Martha and David waited uneasily for another letter. General Lee seemed unstoppable. He had beaten McClellan at the Seven Days Battles, Pope at the Second Battle of Bull Run, Burnside at Fredericksburg, and Hooker at Chancellorsville. He'd been forced out of Maryland in the Battle of Antietam, but now Lee's army had invaded Pennsylvania, and Major General George Meade, who had just replaced Hooker, was calling for reinforcements. Willy was certainly among those sent. Martha remembered how excited he had been when issued his uniform two years earlier: while showing off his saber practice, he had almost brought down the parlor chandelier. They all had thought that by now the war would be long over.

Martha felt Willy's fatigue and apprehension about coming battles as if they were hers. She saw him in her mind's eye, not yet twenty-one, sweating and spent in his now-worn jacket and filthy trousers marching straight toward tens of thousands of enemy soldiers. When she and Frances visited or ran into each other in town, they talked of nothing but the war and their two Williams. Frances's confidence in a Union victory collapsed when she wasn't with Henry. She wrote to him that month, "I need it in these disastrous times. The loyalty of the people is now to be put to the test—God grant that it may not fail."

Martha affected a breezy tone in her weekly letters to Willy, updating him about friends and family as a way of masking her fears for his safety, sometimes enclosing notepaper and stamped envelopes, lightly scolding him for not writing more often. Noting the changes in Auburn, she said that many people were hiring former slaves who had come north looking for work. Martha and David were boarding a boy named Sam, and they'd planned to enroll him in the district school for Black children, but an army captain had just hired him as an orderly. Sam wanted to live in Auburn after the war, and Martha had spoken with a friend who ran a nursery with her husband and said they would hire him on his return.

On June 25, Willy's battery began a forced march from Manassas, about a hundred miles south of Gettysburg. The men rested on July 1, and started again at 9:00 p.m., arriving eighteen hours later, with a few ten-minute stops for coffee. Early in the morning, villagers stood by the road with buckets of water and baskets of bread torn into pieces. Soldiers took sips of water and the bread without breaking stride.

The fighting at Gettysburg began on July 1, three days after Meade's promotion and two days before either army was fully assembled. Lee's troops forced Union men through the streets to a defensive position on Cemetery Hill, south of town. On Friday, July 3, Willy wrote in a diary entry, "Morning cloudy and cool. Received orders and started at 4:30 a.m. Marched about one mile. Came into park in rear of Cemetery Hill, remaining there until 10:00 a.m. then ordered to the front. Marched down the turnpike towards Gettysburgh, turning to the left up the Taney Town road. Received orders to park a short distance behind the line of battle in a small wood at the left of the turnpike facing Gettysburgh." His battery, led by Captain Andrew Cowan, who was twenty-one, just a year older than Willy, was attached to the Army of the Potomac's VI Corps, which had been ordered to join the II Corps at Cemetery Ridge, north of Little Round Top, overlooking a grove of peach trees.

The clouds lifted, and the Auburn men were so close to a rebel battery below that they could see the sun's rays flash on the brass buttons of enemy cannoneers lounging around their guns. As the morning wore on, still, windless, and increasingly hot, Cowan's horses stood motionless in their heavy harnesses; nearby, wild hogs feasted on the mangled carcasses of soldiers killed the previous day. The minty aroma of pennyroyal permeated the air. Willy Wright and a companion caught some sleep in the shade. "It was like a calm Sabbath day in some village," one Auburn man wrote. "The two armies lay like tigers waiting for a victim."

At one o'clock on July 2, a mile west, the initial bombardment from rebel artillery commenced. For two hours, exploding shells caused a booming and screaming that was said to be heard in Baltimore, fifty-two miles away. Shells pouring from a hundred guns crashed through the trees, ripping off enormous branches and tearing up the ground. Cowan's men moved to their posts under terrific fire and a burning sun. The Confederates attacked the Union's right flank, at Little Round Top, the Wheatfield, Devil's Den, and the Peach Orchard—resonant names for every survivor and for the families of those who died there. The Union men suffered heavy casualties, but they held their position as the rebels charged their right flank, at Culp's Hill and Cemetery Hill.

Willy's battery, on the other side of the ridge with reserves and an ambulance unit, waited for orders to engage. He could feel the ground rock beneath him, noting, "Most of the shells passed over the troops & came crashing all around us in the woods." The exchange of fire ceased in midafternoon. During the lull, the reserve artillery guns were ordered to the front and men took their places, so low to the ground and so veiled in smoke that an observer would not have guessed that an army was spread across the hillside. The Auburn battery was moved south on the ridge to replace a Rhode Island light artillery battery that had been virtually expunged. The position put them at the center of the rebel offensive, in one of the pivotal battles of the war. The commanding officer rode down the line ordering the batteries to hold their fire until the Confederates drew near.

On Lee's orders, his second-in-command, General James Longstreet, reluctantly coordinated a risky frontal assault against the Union line, which stretched for half a mile across Cemetery Ridge. The attack began at about 3:00 p.m., as 12,500 rebels, led by Major General George Pickett, advanced in two lines, in parade-ground formation. A company captain in the 118th Pennsylvania Infantry, in reserve near Big Round Top, wrote to his aunt: "It was a beautiful sight to see, as far as the eye could reach, regiment after regiment in mass, with colors unfurled, upon a line as straight as a die." Confederate Brigadier General Lewis Armistead, a Virginian, told his brigade just before the charge, "Remember what you are fighting for—your homes, your friends, your sweethearts!" Then he attached his hat to the tip of his sword and ordered, "Forward!"

The Union men could hear the piercing rebel yell above the cannon fire. The Auburn chronicler wrote, "It was a glorious spectacle." Quoting from a poem about the Battle of Waterloo, he continued, "'Twas worth ten years of peaceful life' to witness such a sight. On they came at a sharp double quick, and all the guns in that crest of hills poured upon their ranks a terrible rain of shrapnel, shell, and solid shot, ploughing great furrows through the living lines so bravely rushing on to death."

Some of the infantrymen, crouching behind a stone wall in front of the battery, had a less inspired reaction. Fearing certain death, they abandoned their positions. Willy's captain, Cowan, wrote in his account of the battle that their corporal swore at them like a pirate and pranced like a mad bull, smashing a large tin coffeepot over one soldier's head. Cowan ordered the battery to switch to canister rounds for close-range firing, and when the rebels got within thirty yards, Willy waved his cap and called, "Give it to 'em!" They blew holes in the approaching ranks, but the rebels closed up and came on. At ten yards, with little ammunition left, Cowan ordered the men to load the guns with double charges of canister for the final round.

A reporter for *The New York Times*, Samuel Wilkeson, had just discovered that his nineteen-year-old son had died at Gettysburg. Wilkeson, positioned with the Auburn men, recounted of Pickett's Charge, "The rebels were over our defences. They had cleared cannoniers and horses from one of the guns, and were whirling it around to use upon us. The bayonets drove them back. But so hard pressed was this brave infantry that at one time, from the exhaustion of their ammunition, every battery upon the principal crest of attack was silent except Cowan's." The men rapidly fired grapeshot and canister at the oncoming rebels. General Alexander Webb, whose Philadelphia Brigade had taken heavy casualties, backed up the Auburn battery, despite an injury in his thigh, and Cowan's guns enabled the Union line, outnumbered two to one, to charge Armistead. He was mortally wounded, and the federal troops captured him and two thousand of his men.

One Auburn man was loading a charge of canister when he took three balls in his head. A rebel at close range fired at Cowan, but the shot went through his coat; he tore it off and worked a cannon himself. Willy was hit in his chest, and the bullet exited through his back, below his shoulder blade. The battery doctor saw Willy as he fell backward, a hand on his breast, and heard him say, "I'm—not—ashamed—of—this—wound." He was caught by two of his soldiers, one of whom, George Reed, cradled Willy in his lap until the horse-drawn ambulance arrived, and rode with him to a barn on a farm that had been fashioned into a field hospital. As Reed tended to Willy, Cowan shouted, "Come on, boys! Come on quick and give it to 'em! Sweeten 'em! I'll give every one of you a gold medal." The rebels turned and fled across the field. The men in the Auburn battery, blackened with powder, their tongues cleaving to the roofs of their mouths, drank from the dirty sponge buckets and a basin where the wounds of others had been washed. Reed, in the barn, ladled water into Willy's mouth.

On July 6, Frances read in Weed's *Journal* that Willy Wright was among the injured at Gettysburg and she took the report to Martha, knowing how anxiously she was waiting for news. Two days later, it was confirmed in the *Times*. Willy's was the first name on the list for Cowan's battery: "Lieut. Wm. P. Wright—right breast, probably mortally." Martha and David soon received a penciled note from Cowan, written on the field. He said that Willy's injury was severe, but that he was receiving every possible attention, and that the battery had covered itself with honor. David forbade Martha from traveling with him to Gettysburg. She knew he wanted to spare her a gruesome and possibly tragic scene, but she wrote to Lucretia, "If I had not been over-ruled, I should have gone, & I shall always be sorry I didn't."

David did stop in Philadelphia to pick up their eldest daughter, thirty-eight-year-old Marianna. Their train was jammed with families and volunteers carrying medical supplies. They changed depots in Baltimore, where David learned that Will Seward's banking partner, Clinton MacDougall, also had been wounded at Gettysburg and was recovering at a hotel in the city. David went to see him, and MacDougall said that he had sent an orderly to the VI Corps field hospital for information; the orderly returned with the news that Lieutenant Wright had died.

Clinging to the hope that MacDougall had been misinformed, David and Marianna took a military freight train on the branch line to Gettysburg. "It was a rough, untidy affair, without seats," David recalled. The floors were covered with wood chips. Marianna scrutinized some of their travel companions—twenty nurses, of whom she wrote, "Their hands though gentle and willing as they may have been, were not invariably clean." Incongruously, they wore oversized hoops, dresses of faded cotton or flimsy silk, "and petticoats not snowy in their whiteness." That night, the train broke down, and the Wrights slept in a meadow under a walnut tree, where, Marianna wrote, "a carpet bag was your pillow, and stars shone from your ceiling."

David and Marianna arrived in Gettysburg on July 10. The small brick and frame houses were pocked with holes, and the country village of twenty-four hundred was overrun with medical personnel, the wounded, and families seeking their sons and brothers. Men moved toward the depot swinging on crutches or limping in obvious pain. Others, Marianna noticed, "step actively in spite of ghastly wounds in face or head or throat, or arms in slings." Muddy mules, strung together, pulled ambulances and wagons loaded with supplies. There were only a hundred medical officers to care for fourteen thousand wounded Union men and seven thousand Confederates left behind. David secured breakfast and a room for the night in a private house that already had more guests than beds, and then set off alone on his trip to the hospital. He found it a few miles down a rutted country road, spotting the VI Corps's yellow flags flying across a field.

Directed to the guest room in the farmhouse, he found sluggish black flies, fat from feasting, covering the walls and ceiling. Willy was awake, sitting straight up in bed, supported by pillows. A silk handkerchief had been placed on his right chest and shoulder, covering a ragged wound. The ball had entered between the second and third ribs, and in exiting had shattered Willy's shoulder blade. The open laceration emitted bubbles each time he drew a breath. George Reed, the battery boy nurse, was caring for him. Willy calmly told his father that he'd been expecting him. The surgeon took David aside and said that someone must be in the room at all times—if Willy dozed and fell from his upright position, he would hemorrhage and strangle in his own blood. Even with scrupulous care, the surgeon had little hope of saving his life.

David returned to town to report to Marianna and to send a telegram from the local office to Martha. They were offered a ride back to the farmhouse, and as they bumped along, they imagined the agonies of the wounded making the trip from the battlefield to the hospital. David engaged a room connected to the house for Marianna, and he asked that a cot for him be put in Willy's room. For the next eleven days, he went to bed early each night, rising at 1:00 a.m. to allow George Reed to sleep until breakfast. Each morning, David took a walk among the tents, sadly observing the sheet-shrouded bodies of the soldiers who had died overnight.

Marianna shared her room with four other women, all caring for their wounded. She wrote to Martha about the gravity of Willy's condition, but knowing that her mother was seeking any reassurance, said that his appetite was good, and that the doctors believed that "his youth and health and good habits and temperament are all in his favor, and above all his strong determination to live." Lightening the mood, she reported of her room: "I found in my bed with me this morning a woman, a grasshopper, a spider, many smaller creatures which 'graze upon the human body,' and a moving canopy of flies." The soldiers slept more haphazardly—in tents, on barn floors, under sheds, and in the grass, soaked by heavy dew and fog. They "rose when they were ready, like the beasts that perish, giving themselves a little shake in their woolen garments."

On one of Marianna's excursions around the field hospital, she spoke to two injured rebels from Georgia who told her that slavery was divinely sanctioned, a notion that always infuriated her mother. The sight of the wounded was something Marianna hoped never to repeat. In a large tent one man, burned a reddish black by powder, lay "scorched and seamed with blinded eyes." When he heard her footsteps, he cried out, "I am all torn and bruised and tortured and nobody comes near me."

Marianna's youngest brother, Frank, traveled from Harvard University to relieve her, followed by Eliza on July 17. David stayed until the twenty-first, when—exhausted and feverish—he went home. At the end of the month, after Willy was stabilized, but his condition still dire, Frank and Eliza took him back to Auburn. His damaged lungs made breathing shallow and painful, and he couldn't move his shoulder. Infection would pose a mortal threat until the wound closed.

The evisceration of Pickett's men dealt Lee a defeat from which he never fully recovered. The Auburn battery lost four men and fourteen horses. Eight men, including Willy, were wounded. The location was identified as the "High-Water Mark" of the Confederacy. A monument there reads: COWAN'S FIRST NEW YORK BATTERY ARTILLERY BRIGADE—SIXTH CORPS. DOUBLE CANISTER AT TEN YARDS JULY 3rd 1863. And, on the other side, ending with Lincoln's words: ERECTED IN MEMORY OF OUR COMRADES, JULY 3, 1887. "THE WORLD CAN NEVER FORGET WHAT THEY DID HERE." Willy Wright was a hero, but it took months of Martha's constant care to ensure that he didn't die a martyr. In December 1864, she was relieved when the army declined Willy's offer to return as a staff officer, but wrote to Ellen that she was "proud for one so desperately wounded to be willing to give further service."

23

A Mighty Army of Women

1863–1864

Elizabeth Cady Stanton and Susan B. Anthony, ca. 1870

Frances was far from the war planning in Washington and the action on the battlefields, but she experienced firsthand the political effects of the administration's policies. The mood across New York State was volatile. Governor Horatio Seymour, a leader of the Democratic Party's noisy Copperhead faction, opposed Lincoln and pushed for a negotiated settlement with the South. Seymour objected to the nation's first draft law, scheduled to go into effect in New York City on July 11. The law contained an ill-advised provision that allowed wealthier conscripts to pay a "commutation fee" of three hundred dollars—sparing them the horrors of battle. New York City was heavily Democratic, and its poor Irish and German immigrants, already the victims of discrimination, low wages, and unemployment, felt coerced into fighting in a war they did not support. They anticipated tens of thousands of former slaves streaming in when it was over, offering cheap labor. The draft lottery was soon to take place in other towns, and there was talk of violence in Auburn, Troy, Seneca Falls, and Albany.

Irish factory workers in Auburn were said to be planning an uprising against the Black population, and there were threats to burn down the Sewards' house because Henry was "a friend of the Negro." When Martha learned that her house might be targeted, she asked the mayor to assure her family's safety. Frances thought about Harriet's family and about her other Black friends in town, writing to Henry, "As to personal injury I fear more for the poor colored people than for others—They cannot protect themselves since few persons are willing to assist them." She sent Nicholas and Harriet Bogart into the country until the danger was over, and, glad for the first time in her life to have firearms in the house, supplied their coachman William Johnson with a pistol. She wrote to Frederick, "I wish all the coloured people were armed."

On the Fourth of July, in Manhattan, Governor Seymour gave a speech on the steps of City Hall, which Frances saw as an outrageous attempt to incite the public to rise up against the Lincoln administration. Seymour called the draft unconstitutional, forcing men into an "ungodly conflict" for Black freedom, and he suggested that the public interest could be proclaimed by a mob as well as by a government. Twenty thousand men from the state militia had been sent to fight at Gettysburg, and the municipal police were not in any way equipped to put down a large citizens' revolt.

The riots began on the morning of July 13. Hundreds of men, women, and boys marched to the draft office on Third Avenue and Forty-Sixth Street, where they accosted the police with bricks, stones, and clubs. They broke the windows and doors, broke the lottery wheel, and set the place on fire. The other draft offices in town were closed, but the mobs, some numbering in the thousands, grew and spread. The Colored Orphan Asylum on Fifth Avenue was burned. Although most of the two hundred children were rescued, a little girl found hiding under a bed was clubbed to death. The staff of the *Times* rolled in several Gatling guns borrowed from the army, and the editor, Henry Raymond, took charge of one. The *New York Daily News*—a Democratic paper the Lincoln administration had banned for sedition for eighteen months—was spared. A Black cartman was beaten senseless as he was leaving the stable for the evening, then hanged from a tree and set on fire—one of eleven recorded lynchings in New York during the rampage. Lincoln ordered troops from Gettysburg to be sent to the city. Three days later, the revolt was over, but it took six thousand men to put it down, and left a hundred and twenty people dead.

When Henry was governor, two decades earlier, he had tried to bring people together, not pit them against one another. Frances wrote about a "disturbed and fearful week in Auburn," saying, "Our state is disgraced before the civilized world—if there was any civilization in the world, which I sometimes doubt." He replied that the ignorance and cruelty were painful, but, in times of revolution, unavoidable, and that surely no one would be desperate enough to harm her. Thinking about the presidential election in the fall, he calculated that the draft riots would help Lincoln, who needed every possible advantage. Even after General Meade's definitive victory at Gettysburg and General Ulysses S. Grant's a day later at Vicksburg, Mississippi, many voters were tempted by the Copperheads' calls for a negotiated peace. Overlooking Frances's extreme attachment to her house, Henry counseled her not to give a thought to rumors that it would be destroyed. Even if it were, the sacrifice would be a small one for the country, "and not without benefit."

During the perilous spring and summer of 1863, Stanton and Anthony, after consulting with Garrison, Greeley, and Governor Andrew of Massachusetts, created a group called the Women's National Loyal League. Undertaking the most ambitious petition campaign ever attempted on either side of the Atlantic, they meant to ensure the passage of the Thirteenth Amendment to the Constitution, which would forever end slavery in the country. They believed that once the amendment passed, abolitionists would help them achieve the vote for women. In the summons to the founding meeting of the league, on May 14 at the Church of the Puritans in upper Manhattan, they announced that women must look beyond their work in ladies' societies: it was time for the "daughters of the Revolution" to "lay hold of their birthright of freedom, and keep it a sacred trust for all coming generations."

Women could not fight for their country, but they could petition. The Loyal League aimed to secure one million signatures on its strategically named Women's Emancipation Petition. Stanton had moved with her family to New York the previous year, and she'd befriended Greeley. In his *Tribune*, Greeley congratulated the women for pursuing the sole object of abolition, and for their courage in aiming so high. The conservative *Herald* had a term for them that was meant to be stinging: "revolutionary women's rights movement."

Martha took Ellen with her to the meeting, and by midsummer, they were distributing "half an acre of petitions" around Auburn. Anthony was more concerned than ever about regaining momentum for women's rights after the war. Black men, who were now fighting for their country, would rightly demand all the benefits and protections that white men had, and northerners would be far readier to heed them than the cries of middle-class women. Stanton proceeded as if success were imminent, telling Martha that they must prepare to enter the political sphere, advising her to become familiar with the political issues of peacetime: canal tolls, free trade, homestead and squatter sovereignty, and military affairs. She recommended *Les Misérables*, which had given her "a new pang for the miseries of womankind, and a fresh resolve that the weal and the woe of humanity shall be all and everything to me." Stanton subsequently saw the cancellations of the annual women's conventions as a "blunder," pledging thereafter to follow "my beloved Susan's judgment against the world." The vow foreshadowed the hostile split a few years later between Stanton and Anthony and their abolitionist friends.

The Loyal League needed an ally in Congress, and Garrison contacted Sumner, telling him in November 1863 that, as the Senate's foremost antislavery senator, he should lead the effort in Washington to abolish slavery. Sumner, whose political fortunes were at a low ebb, did not hesitate. He had riled the British by constantly attacking them for their neutrality in the war, and other senators were fed up with his harangues about the South and his refusal to listen to anyone more moderate than he was. In December, Anthony contacted Sumner, asking for his advice about when and how to present their petition to Congress. He replied, "Send on the petitions as fast as received. They give me opportunities for speech."

Stanton employed three of her five young sons at the Loyal League's office in Cooper Union. They rolled up the petitions state by state, and she wrote the numbers of signatures on each roll. In late January 1864, she packed the petitions in a trunk and shipped them to Washington, where they were tied with regulation red ribbons, indicating they'd been officially logged. Over nine months, the League had procured a hundred thousand signatures. Petitioners in New York had collected 17,706 names; in Illinois, 15,380; in Massachusetts, 11,641. Garrison instructed readers of *The Liberator* that there was no time to lose if they were to roll up a million endorsements in the current session.

The Thirteenth was the first constitutional amendment passed by Congress in sixty years. Shepherding it was the responsibility of the chairman of the Senate Judiciary Committee, Lyman Trumbull, but Sumner saw the Loyal League's petition as his chance to determine the shape of the most consequential law in his lifetime. In a shameless attempt to subvert Trumbull, he established and chaired the new Select Committee on Slavery and Freedom, designed to consider all matters related to slavery and the treatment of the freed people.

Sumner had given careful thought to staging the presentation of the petition. On February 9, at his direction, two Black men entered the Senate carrying the rolls, which had the heft of large logs, and placed them ceremoniously on his desk. Sumner rose and said the petition represented a critical moment in the history of slavery, and in the war. Commending the women for their work, he called them a mighty army, "without arms or banners; the advance-guard of a yet larger army." Then, reconsidering that martial image, he added that because the document was the work of women, it was only a petition. It didn't even rise to the level of an argument: "I need not remind the Senate that there is no reason so strong as the reason of the heart. Do not all great thoughts come from the heart?"

Sumner went on to propose his own wording for the amendment, including the phrase, "all persons are equal before the law." The Senate rejected it—disliking the echo of the French Revolution, and fearing that it could open the way to women's suffrage. Trumbull's committee retained full control of the process, marginalizing Sumner in the framing and passage of the amendment.

Stanton wrote to Frances in mid-February. Enclosing a copy of the petition, she asked if Frances and Lazette would help Martha collect more signatures in Auburn, pointing out, "You have quite a circle of acquaintances among the coloured brethren & sisters!! Could you not hire some bright mulatto boys & girls to canvass your city & send us 10,000 from that region round about."

Frances responded as she had to the British women's abolitionist petition in 1852, when Henry was a senator. Now he was secretary of state, and a constitutional amendment abolishing slavery was at issue. In Auburn, she had been covertly supporting abolition for decades. It could have been a clear-cut opportunity to work at last with Martha and the other "women's rights women." Instead, accepting her husband's decree against overt activism even as she objected to it, Frances asked him for his advice: "I enclose Mrs Stanton's letter, and would like you to suggest the answer." If she were living alone, she said, she would not hesitate to sign and circulate the petition, but she knew that her name would be used for purposes beyond the signature. Given its importance, she thought it was his right to determine where her name should appear in public.

Henry's reply was as expected, and it conveniently shifted the burden of the decision to him. Frances knew from Martha how humiliating it was to petition, and she did not have Martha's experience or her toughness. She also had pressing duties as a mother. Her Will, too, was at home, finally recovering from a second, far more serious, onslaught of typhoid. Willy Wright's wound showed how a bullet could tear apart a strong young man, but illness—typhoid, malaria, yellow fever, dysentery, cholera, measles, pneumonia, tuberculosis, chicken pox—was an even worse menace. Will's infantry had moved from Fort Mansfield to help finish the construction of Fort Foote, about ten miles south of Washington. The new fort, set high on Rozier's Bluff, had an extensive view of the Potomac River, but it was backed by a marsh known as the Graveyard of Prince George County. Three hundred of the six hundred men there were sick. Frances and Jenny nursed Will for three months as he fought off high fevers, crippling stomach pain, diarrhea, and loss of appetite. They feared he might die in bed—a fate they hadn't previously considered. In March, Will at last regained most of his weight and strength, and as he resumed his duties, his one wish was that Jenny and one-and-a-half-year-old Nelly live with him in camp again for several weeks. Jenny agreed to go, and Frances accompanied them to Washington; then Will and his family went on to the fort.

Jenny was comfortable in Will's board-and-batten officer's house, which had a large central room, two small bedrooms, a loft, and a wooden floor. At Fort Mansfield, where they'd had cruder quarters, she'd been awakened one night by the strange sensation of her hair whipping around her face, blown by wind through the cracks between the logs. At Fort Foote, the roof leaked when it rained, but Jenny and Will lived far better than lowly soldiers, who were jammed together in log huts with dirt floors and slept in hard, narrow bunks. Will's cook, Banty Fowler, prepared meals in a tent at the back. Jenny loved his buckwheat cakes, and said the oysters and shad that he bought from the fishermen along the river were the best she ever ate: "The shad were so fresh that Banty used to say they turned over in the pan while he was cooking them."

She missed only Frances, who had been helping to raise Nelly in Auburn, and whose calm oversight as they'd coaxed Will back to health had kept Jenny from despair. Despite all of the precautions she took to keep Nelly healthy, late one night she became feverish. A young army surgeon, confronted with the flushed little creature, confessed that he had never cared for a baby, and Jenny wanted her mother-in-law to come. Will traveled by tugboat to Washington to ask Frances and the Sewards' personal physician to return with him. He found Henry at breakfast when he arrived, but learned that Frances was in her room upstairs recuperating from her own weeklong illness. Will was distraught, saying he and Jenny had hoped his mother could help, and Henry predicted, "She will go."

Sure enough, Frances dressed and packed, and in less than an hour she and Henry's doctor were heading with Will in the tugboat to Fort Foote, tossed and drenched in a heavy storm. Jenny wrote gratefully, "Such was her beautiful, unselfish character, putting aside her own ills when she could help the other members of her family. You can imagine how relieved I was when she and the doctor came in at the door."

24

Daughters and Sons

1864

Burning of the Wooden Covered Bridge—
Battle of Monocacy

During Willy's long, uncertain recovery, Martha offered him the comforts she had when he was sick as a young boy—changing his sheets and plumping his pillows, reading to him, and cooking his favorite meals. Each morning and evening, she examined his shoulder and studied his face for any sign of improvement. Ellen, her only other child at home, spent much of her time in Boston visiting the second-generation Garrisons, whom she had gotten to know the previous winter. The Garrisons had four sons and one daughter. Martha had been amused by Ellen's initial impressions of two of the sons: Wendell, who was "nice only dolorous, with a frequent and deep sigh, which speaks a world of grief & experience," and George, who was "good, but uninteresting as a prairie." Of twenty-six-year-old William Jr., Ellen said only that he was a most pleasant man, and that she liked him better than anyone else she had met in a long time.

In mid-February, Martha and David received a short letter from young William Garrison, dated the fourteenth, Valentine's Day. He wrote: "My dear Mr. & Mrs. Wright, It has been my misfortune not to know you—my great good fortune to know your daughter Ellie. To know her has been to love her. How could I help it? Why she returns my love I cannot tell you—that she does, renders me happy beyond expression. I pray that your approval may bless us both." A few days later, they heard from Ellen, who had failed to mail her letter when William mailed his. Martha tore it open, and Ellen giddily confirmed that she had accepted his proposal of marriage: "Please do not fancy that I have acted impulsively, & blindly in this, nor that I do not strive to appreciate how serious, and irrevocable the next step is." She begged her parents to share her happiness. When William learned about the confusion over the letters, he rushed to apologize, and said that he had a good job as a clerk at the wool business of an abolitionist friend, Richard Hallowell, with a starting salary of $1,200 (about $20,000 in 2020). Until he had sufficient savings, he and Ellen would live with his parents.

Martha was hurt that Ellen, who normally could not contain her emotions, had revealed nothing to her about her feelings for William. She also was brought up short by her own willful blindness. Ellen had repeatedly said that she was not cut out to be an activist, but Martha had thought she just needed further encouragement. In fact, Ellen was determined to avoid what she saw as her mother's mistakes. In a letter to William later that year, Ellen wrote that Martha had suffered more than most women, and never had achieved peace and happiness. Martha, supremely competent and good-natured, would not have recognized herself in Ellen's sketch of her and David: "The children came too fast, the purse was too slender." The consequence was plain, at least to Ellen: "the father nervous & overworked—no time to get acquainted with his family—the mother poor soul—half dead."

Martha could hardly object to Garrison's son and namesake joining her family. William sounded like a serious, thoughtful young man with his parents' values—a very good match for irresolute Ellen. The younger Garrisons, like the offspring of the Motts and most of their friends, were full-fledged reformers. It was difficult, though, for Martha to accept that her three daughters had chosen to be traditional wives and mothers. Ellen ceded to William the role of social activist, including his advocacy for women's suffrage. Writing to Susan B. Anthony, Ellen said that she intended "to keep in my corner, & raise up children, who perhaps might do better service for the world."

Martha had been friendly with William Lloyd Garrison for three decades. They reconnected regularly at anti-slavery and women's rights conventions and at the Garrisons' home in Boston, the Wrights' in Auburn, and the Motts' in Philadelphia. Although she and David shared most of the Garrisons' values, the war had put them somewhat at odds. After considerable internal struggle, Garrison had come out in support of the war, saying that freedom was worth the toll, but he and Helen still thought that conscientious objection represented "a higher plane of moral heroism and a nobler method of self-sacrifice." The Wrights had no such reservations. They saw Willy's wound as a badge for having enacted the most honorable form of national service.

When the Garrisons' eldest son, George, was commissioned as a second lieutenant in the second Black northern regiment, the 55th Massachusetts, they tried to convince him not to go. The losses of Fort Wagner fresh in mind, Garrison told George that he respected his convictions of duty, but he asked him to consider the vicious racism his regiment would be subject to, and to understand that if he was taken prisoner, as the son of the most hated abolitionist in the country, he would be treated unmercifully. Prison camps were notorious for the ruthlessness and deprivations inflicted by the guards. Those arguments failing, Garrison begged George to consider his mother: "Her affection for you is intense; her anxiety beyond expression." Ellen, who had seen Willy return from Gettysburg close to death, did not argue with her fiancé when he told her that he and his younger brothers were "grounded in the faith of a different duty," and that he would not enlist. She told him that although she respected George's bravery in going to war, it seemed "unnatural for a Garrison to wield a sword."

Ellen's wedding was set for September 14, and that summer Martha plunged into a frenzy of cleaning, preparing menus, and making room assignments for relatives. She calmed Ellen by suggesting the guest list and deciding on the furniture she would take with her to Boston. As the day approached, Ellen came down with a cold in her lungs and a sick headache. Martha disguised her concern, telling Ellen that she would feel better in Boston, away from the damp lake air, and that she shouldn't worry: "It will all come out, somehow, such things always do." Most critically to both of them, she agreed that William was "the right one."

She decorated the parlor with autumn flowers and branches, but on the wedding day, after a hot, dusty summer, a chilly rain fell outside. Ellen was so weak that her closest friend, Lucy McKim, and William's sister, Fanny Garrison, had to prop her up as she got dressed. At Ellen's request, Susan B. Anthony was one of the few guests invited from outside the two families. The Reverend May was the officiant, as he had been thirty years earlier at the wedding of Helen and William Lloyd Garrison. Wendell Garrison, who was engaged to Lucy McKim, wrote to George in South Carolina about the brief ceremony, expressing surprise at seeing their father's eyes filled with tears.

After it was over, and Martha had cleared her desk of dirty plates and champagne glasses, she sat down to write to her new son-in-law. Her memory of the preceding month was like a confused dream, she said—her unease about Ellen's health overshadowing every other feeling. Now that Ellen was well again, and Martha had accepted a future for her of domestic contentment, Martha liked thinking about her setting up house. Weddings brought a sense of renewal. Martha told William: "I should like to look in upon you this morning and see how you have arranged everything and how the little wife looks among her household gods." But that would have to wait. She was hurrying off to see Eliza, who had recently given birth to her fourth child, a girl named Helen. Martha was good with babies, and Eliza often called upon her mother's expertise. As Eliza recalled, she would "take up a poor little fretting morsel into her arms, smooth out its clothes, perch it upon her knees, jolt it softly, and the little creature would drop off to sleep almost immediately, soothed by the magic of her touch. She loved children devotedly."

In that third year of the war, Frances remained perpetually apprehensive about Will. In March 1864, Ulysses S. Grant had assumed command of the Union armies, and there was no question that Will would be sent to the front. Grant, a small man of forty-six with clear blue eyes and a trimmed graying beard, had performed superbly at Vicksburg and in other western battles. He didn't have McClellan's swagger, or his scruples about using the full strength of the military to eradicate the enemy. When Lincoln met Grant at the White House, he commented, "He's the quietest little fellow you ever saw," but "where he is, things move!"

Two months later, Grant initiated the Overland Campaign, an operation in Virginia between the Rapidan and James rivers north of Richmond. He announced that he would hammer ceaselessly at Lee until Lee had no choice but to rejoin "the loyal section of our common country." He told his generals to destroy all points of support for the Confederacy: railroads, crops, and private homes. Soldiers were called from all the forts around Washington, and Will's regiment was among them. Frances wrote to him, "I cannot yet bring myself to the contemplation of your death or of your suffering." Thinking of his tenderness during her spells of sickness, she said, "your strong hand, and your ability to help all who are weak and dependent, it seems impossible that you should be called away—I love Jenny & Nelly as a part of yourself."

In her tranquil garden, she could barely imagine the scenes of slaughter in Virginia. Reinforcing her strength of will, she wrote to Augustus on May 15 that this was a moral war, unlike the one he had fought in Mexico, and that the difference was a great relief to her. At the same time, she admitted to Anna, "I do not like this mode of warfare—it too nearly approaches the barbarian." At least Frederick and Augustus were safe. Once Gus had finished serving at Fort Defiance, he'd declined to continue in the field, taking instead a job as a paymaster in Washington, where he lived with Henry, Frederick, and Anna.

For weeks after Will left camp, no letters arrived for Jenny. Then, at twilight one evening in early June, in their house at Fort Foote, she heard him twice call her name. In the loft with Nelly, she jumped up, looking over the railing and expecting to see him coming up the stairs. "There was no one there," she later wrote, "and I went back disappointed, thinking how strange it was. Afterwards, I found that this occurrence took place at the very hour that he was in the Battle of Cold Harbor, and came very near losing his life."

At Cold Harbor, one of the most ill-considered Union assaults of the war, Grant's determination to liquidate the enemy got the better of his tactical judgment. Unfamiliar with the marshy, woodsy territory, he thought that he could coax out a seven-mile line of rebels, who were dug in behind a heavily fortified network of rifle pits. At 4:30 a.m. on June 3, Grant ordered sixty thousand troops to advance. As the men fell, their comrades used their bodies as sandbags. Seven thousand troops were lost that day, to Lee's fifteen hundred casualties. Several days later, Frances and Fanny got a heart-stopping report that Will had been one of the first men to enter the rifle pits. He had received a heavy blow on the head from the butt of a rebel musket; within moments, the rebel was riddled by Union bullets. Will's uniform was shredded by shot, and the leg of his boot torn open. Many of the soldiers, expecting to die, had pinned their names and addresses to their coats. The bloodied slips of paper would be returned to their families along with the boys' other effects—relics from a death that could have been avoided with more cautious leadership.

Still, Grant had achieved his larger objective—forcing a badly weakened rebel army back to Richmond. Cold Harbor marked the end of the Overland Campaign and the start of the Siege of Petersburg, a pitiless war of attrition. On June 12, Will marched with the Army of the Potomac toward the outskirts of Petersburg, near Grant's field headquarters at City Point. The village, abandoned by its residents early in the war, sat at the confluence of the James and Appomattox rivers. From City Point, Grant could move troops easily, by rail or water, and Fort Monroe and Washington were easily accessible. In a matter of weeks, the becalmed outpost had become one of the busiest ports and supply depots in the world.

Frances continued to write to Will a few times a week, even though he changed camp so frequently she doubted her letters would catch up with him. It was another form of prayer—sending him thoughts of devotion and safety. She later learned that he had been ordered from his camp outside Petersburg, not to the front with Grant's troops, but to Maryland, fifty miles north of Washington, where he would take part in a critical defensive operation, designed to keep the rebels from conquering Washington.

Will's 9th New York Heavy Artillery, woken at midnight on July 6, joined a VI Corps division of several thousand men, marching fifteen miles to City Point, where they boarded transport ships to Baltimore, then cattle cars to Frederick. They arrived on the night of July 8, and had some coffee before marching southeast, to Monocacy Junction, four miles south of Frederick.

General Lee saw an opportunity to attack Washington while the forts were feebly manned. He ordered General Jubal A. Early, a cold, solitary man he called "my bad old man," to leave Richmond and Petersburg with twelve thousand Confederate soldiers and thirty-six cannon, clear out Union troops in the Shenandoah Valley, move into Maryland, and advance on the capital. If Early entered the city, there would be little to stop him from seizing the U.S. Treasury and the White House, perhaps taking President Lincoln and his cabinet as prisoners of war. At Monocacy, Major General Lew Wallace had fewer than six thousand troops and only seven cannon. He couldn't possibly defeat Early's men, but he wagered that he could delay them long enough to give Grant time to send fresh troops up the Potomac from City Point in Virginia to defend Washington.

After a night of rain, a sunny day broke on July 9—hot, bright, and breezy. Some of the golden wheat fields were waist high; in others, the crop had been gathered, tied in sheaves, and stacked in tall rows. Wallace, joined by Brigadier General James B. Ricketts's five thousand men, formed a battle line along the east side of the Monocacy River, abutting farmers' fields. At 9:00 a.m., amid skirmishing and artillery barrages, Will detached a company, ordering them, "at all hazards," to hold a covered bridge straddling the river along Georgetown Pike, the road that led directly to Washington. A few hours later, in preparation for an attack, a few members of the company gathered bundles of wheat, put them under a corner of the bridge's roof, and set them ablaze. One of Will's privates, watching the bridge burn, said the fire "wrapped the roof in flames like magic."

Monocacy was a smaller engagement than Gettysburg, but soldiers who survived both battles found the combat equally harrowing. The fighting culminated that afternoon near the Thomas farm, which Union troops had taken earlier in the day. Will's regiment was in the field behind a post-and-rail fence, alongside men from New Jersey, Pennsylvania, Ohio, and Vermont. At 3:30, they watched three Confederate brigades, from Virginia, Georgia, and Louisiana, advance in staggered formation, their battle flags fluttering. The Union men entered the fight with nothing more for protection than hedges, fences, and the shocks of wheat, but a rebel private from Georgia later wrote that as he advanced, he couldn't see a single Yankee: "All we could shoot at was the smoke of their guns, they were so well posted."

On July 10, Frances received a telegram from Henry saying that Will had been wounded and taken prisoner. In an agony of uncertainty, she waited twelve hours for further word. Finally, Henry wired again to say that Will was injured, but not captured. He was carried off the train in Washington, worn and thin, his pale cheeks sunken. At the Club House, he told his father, Frederick, Anna, and Augustus about his escape. Amid the helter-skelter of retreat, his horse was shot, and as it fell, he was thrown to the ground, the weight of the horse fracturing his ankle and injuring his arm. His officer's uniform had been destroyed in the fighting at Cold Harbor, and he was dressed as a private. Will's change of clothing almost certainly saved him from being taken as a prisoner of war—officers were often traded for their Confederate counterparts. After the rebel line passed by, Will dragged himself through the dust and smoke into a wood by the road. He saw a stray mule and a Union straggler, who helped him to mount. Devising a bridle out of his red silk pocket handkerchief, he rode the mule through the night until he caught up with his regiment at Ellicott's Mills, about forty miles east. More than 50 men in his regiment had been killed, and another 254 were wounded or missing—about a quarter of its strength. In total, there were 1,300 Union casualties at Monocacy. General Wallace said of the troops who didn't survive, "These men died to save the National Capital, and they did save it."

Will's orderly soon paid a visit to Henry's house, with his own plucky story to tell. Riding another mule as he made his escape, the orderly recognized Will's horse. Shot in the neck, the horse had struggled up and begun following the retreating soldiers. The orderly stanched the flow of blood with tobacco, got onto a military train with the horse, and returned it to Will. The horse was treated at Henry's stable, to resume duty once he and Will were restored to health. The two mules were sent to Lazette's daughter's farm in Canandaigua, where Will's savior was called Jenny.

When Frances heard the good news, she admitted to Henry that she hadn't wept during the long hours after his first telegram, but when she got the second, "tears came with it." She feared Early's advance on Washington, "but joy at the escape of our boy preponderates now—May God preserve you all—and save our country."

General Wallace's maneuver worked as planned. Grant had time to send extra troops from City Point, and they began landing at the Seventh Street Wharf in Washington on the evening of July 11, just hours after Early reached the northern outskirts of the Capital. The Union men marched north, past the Smithsonian along the Mall and up to Fort Stevens, now between Fort Stevens Place and Georgia Avenue, Early's point of attack the next morning. Early on July 12, Lincoln, suddenly confident of victory, arranged an outing to the fort with the First Lady. Mrs. Lincoln didn't like Seward, resentful of his closeness to her husband, but Lincoln invited Henry and Frederick to join them. The president, on the front parapet, was easy to spot in his stovepipe hat and long black coat. A soldier begged Lincoln to descend before rebel sharpshooters started firing. Moments later, a bullet whistled overhead, hitting a surgeon standing nearby. As darkness fell, Early ordered his men to retreat.

Will returned to Auburn to spend the remaining month of his medical leave recuperating at home. He was commended for gallantry at Cold Harbor, and promoted to brigadier general after the Battle of Monocacy, receiving a letter from Secretary of War Stanton that praised his "gallant and meritorious services." Martha and Frances, who knew many of the boys called from Auburn, counted themselves among the most fortunate mothers of the war. The 111th New York Volunteer Infantry Regiment, which had been organized in town, had lost seventy soldiers at Gettysburg; of its two hundred wounded, at least fifty died. One was Colonel Hugh Watson McNeil, thirty-two years old, who had studied law at Henry's firm and became part of Pennsylvania's famous "Bucktail" regiment, known for its troops' prowess as riflemen. At Antietam, McNeil was hit in the chest by a Minié ball just as he raised his sword, and he died within the hour.

The war brought a change in the focus of the collaboration between Frances and Emily Howland. Howland had left her teaching post at Miner's School for Colored Girls to work at Camp Todd, in Arlington, Virginia, one of five camps built by the government to house former slaves. It was understaffed, overcrowded, and poorly managed, and Howland worked as a teacher, a volunteer nurse, and a liaison with the National Freedman's Relief Association, founded in 1863 to provide aid and education to freed people. She also operated her own job placement service, connecting Black war refugees with employers in the North. Howland enlisted Frances in Auburn and friends in Philadelphia and New York, to participate.

In June 1864, Howland sent Frances a garrulous boy named Joseph whom Frances taught to read; William Johnson was showing him how to drive the carriage. Many in town objected to the influx of Black refugees, and they made their displeasure known. After Joseph was roughed up, first by some local Irish boys, and then by a man who assailed him when he went to the depot to pick up a woman arriving from Washington to work for Lazette, Frances thought about giving him a pistol for self-protection. Late one night, someone threw a stone through a window of a room where Frances liked to read. The next morning, examining the damage outside, she could see a muddy footprint on the slate walk. She wrote to Frederick, "These are lawless times."

That summer, Harriet returned to Auburn on a military furlough, her first trip north in nearly three years. She regaled Frances, Martha, and other friends with war stories about the Port Royal Experiment, the Combahee River Raid, the Battle of Fort Wagner, and her experiences in Fernandina, Florida, where, a few months earlier, she had served briefly as a nurse. She'd arrived in camp to find almost everyone incapacitated with dysentery—a bacterial infection that caused loose, bloody bowels, killing more soldiers than any other illness or wound. She recalled that "they was dying like sheep." The standard treatments ranged from "blue mass" (a blend of chalk and mercury) to cauterization of the anal opening. The army surgeon was ill, and Harriet indicated that she cured him and all the others: she "dug some roots and herbs and made a tea for the doctor and the disease stopped on him. And then he said, 'Give it to the soldiers.' So I boiled up a great boiler of roots and herbs and the General detailed a man to take two cans and go round and give it to all in the camp that needed it."

Harriet was transported with pleasure at being reunited with Margaret, who had been a child when Harriet had entrusted her care to Frances. Now Margaret was a poised, book-smart young woman. Frances knew how to raise and tutor girls, and, through Harriet's eyes, she could see the progress that Margaret had made. When Harriet came to visit Margaret, she would not accept Frances's offer of a carriage ride: she walked the mile and a half up South Street. But when Margaret visited Ben and Rit and Harriet, Frances made sure she rode in the Sewards' carriage. Harriet liked fine clothes, and the sight of Margaret, in her stylish hat and dress and her dainty shoes as she lifted her skirts to step down into the yard, must have been profoundly stirring.

It was clear that Harriet lived on next to nothing. When she needed cash for personal spending, she did domestic work for officers in Port Royal. That February, Martha had learned from Ellen's fiancé, William Garrison Jr., that while Harriet was cooking and washing for General Alfred H. Terry on Folly Island, William's brother George had paid her a visit. She loved her friends' children, and they reciprocated. As a boy,

George had thrilled to Harriet's stories at his parents' house about the underground railroad, and she was now occupying the same narrow strip of South Carolina sand as he was. George, a second lieutenant in the 55th Massachusetts, and his men were performing fatigue duty on the island—the dull, heavy work of building fortifications and repairing trenches, unloading freight and ammunition from incoming ships, and drawing cannon to the front. He rushed over to see Harriet, he wrote to William, saying that he found her ironing a large pile of clothes, and that when she turned around, she gave him a hearty hug. She said that she needed to pay off "some debts that she owed," and told him about her spying duties for the army. George said enviously, "She has made it a business to see all contrabands escaping from the rebels, and is able to get more intelligence from them than anybody else."

Although Harriet tried to keep up with her mortgage payments, the Sewards covered the costs of her property's upkeep. Harriet said she trusted in God to provide for Ben and Rit, but she relied on a few earthly patrons as well. She left for Boston in early August to see Franklin Sanborn, who published another notice in the *Commonwealth* about Harriet's work: "Her services to her people and to the army seem to have been very inadequately recompensed by the military authorities, and such money as she has received, she has expended for others as her custom is. Any contributions of money or clothing sent to her at this office will be received by her, and the givers may be assured that she will use them with fidelity and discretion for the good of the colored race."

By the end of the summer of 1864, Lincoln was virtually certain he would lose the election to the Democratic nominee—his aggrieved former commanding general, George McClellan. The president said as much to Frederick Douglass, whom he invited to the White House for a private consultation. They had first met the previous August, when Douglass had complained about discrimination against Black soldiers. He had left unsatisfied, after Lincoln told him that the inequality the soldiers faced was "a necessary concession" to those who didn't believe they should serve at all. A year later, Lincoln was consumed with worry about the future of the millions of people who were still enslaved. McClellan opposed emancipation, and Douglass remarked on the president's "alarmed condition" as he pondered how to get large numbers of enslaved people into Union-held territory. Lincoln said, "The slaves are not coming so rapidly and so numerously to us as I had hoped." Astonishingly, the president proposed a guerrilla operation modeled on John Brown's Harpers Ferry scheme. Lincoln suggested that Douglass gather "a band of scouts, composed of colored men," who would penetrate rebel states, spreading the word about emancipation to the slaves who hadn't heard of it, and urge them to seek protection within Union-held territory—exactly the work that Harriet Tubman was doing in South Carolina. Douglass never had undertaken anything like it, but he wrote that on that day, he saw in Lincoln "a deeper moral conviction against slavery than I had ever seen before in anything spoken or written by him."

Frances, too, had dropped her criticism of Lincoln, and of Henry. A McClellan victory would be ruinous to the country, and she found some reassurance in Henry's certainty—virtually alone among Republicans—that, if the army had just one indisputable military success before the election, Lincoln could win. Almost miraculously, there were two. On September 1, General William Tecumseh Sherman marched into Atlanta, and a few weeks later, General Philip Sheridan defeated Jubal Early in Winchester, Virginia. Sheridan, following Grant's orders to reduce the Shenandoah Valley to "a barren waste," drove the Confederates out of the valley, burning and plundering across four hundred square miles.

On November 8, Lincoln was reelected in a landslide. Two days later, Jenny Seward delivered her second child. Frances wrote to Henry that their resilient daughter-in-law had passed safely through her confinement at one in the morning, and that she was more comfortable than Frances could imagine anyone else being after that experience. Will, now a brigadier general, on a fifteen-day leave of absence, was there with Jenny, Frances, Fanny, and Lazette to greet his new son, William Henry III. In December, Will wrote to Jenny from Martinsburg, Virginia, where he was commanding four thousand men. Predicting the war would be over by the coming spring, he said, "Since my return this time I have been much like a boy anticipating the coming of some holiday." He added, thinking about the changes of four years: "My little wife the mother of two children and myself occupying a position which I should have as soon thought of filling as going to the moon."

The northern public's expression of confidence in the president seemed to Frances a harbinger of national healing. Lincoln's capacity for forgiveness was much like Henry's, but even Henry would agree that Lincoln was the greater statesman. Called by a crowd outside the Club House to speak, Henry paid tribute to a president who was "benevolent and loyal, honest and *faithful*"—the word he'd applied to himself in the 1846 Freeman case, about his support for the rights of all men. Lincoln eventually would join Washington, Jefferson, and Adams, Henry said, as "among the benefactors of his country and the human race."

PART FOUR

RIGHTS

(1864–1875)

Lucretia Mott and Martha Coffin Wright, 1860s

25

E Pluribus Unum

1864–1865

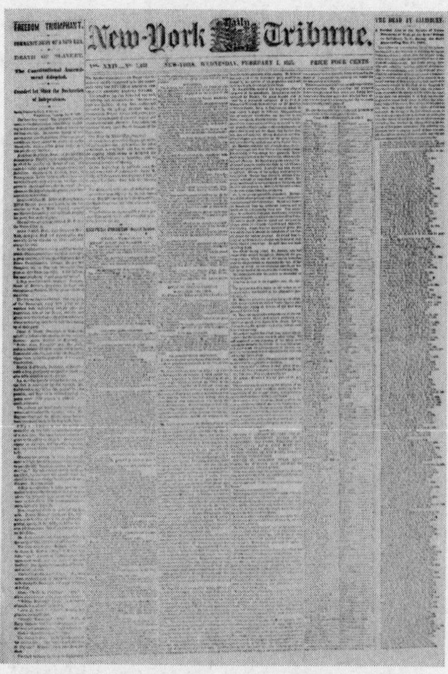

FREEDOM TRIUMPHANT.

New-York Daily Tribune.

PRICE FOUR CENTS

"Freedom Triumphant . . . Death of Slavery"
New-York Tribune, February 1, 1865

Frances felt blessed as Christmas 1864 approached. One morning in the Club House, unable to write because her fingers were too cold to hold her pen, she watched as Henry stoked the fire in the library and Augustus stood by the mantel reading the morning newspapers. Gus was even more reclusive than she was, and whenever Henry had a large party, the two of them fled as soon as they could to the small office behind the library, where they kept each other company. The charms of eligible young women were lost on Gus, and Frances was grateful to Frederick and Anna, who went out of their way to include him in their lives. The war was drawing to a close. Lee's army was trapped behind its fortifications around Petersburg and Richmond, and on December 22, 1864, Lincoln received a telegraph from Sherman: "I beg to present you, as a Christmas gift, the city of Savannah, with 150 heavy guns and plenty of ammunition, and also about 25,000 bales of cotton." Sherman's troops were resting and resupplying before moving north to capture Columbia, the capital of South Carolina.

Henry was working closely with Lincoln and Weed to lobby undecided members of the House, promising campaign contributions and government jobs if they agreed to vote for the Thirteenth Amendment. The women of the National Loyal League had not reached their goal of a million signatures, but they had made their mark. The Senate had passed the amendment in April—after a coarse debate about how it might lead to "racial cross-breeding." One of its authors, Senator John B. Henderson of Missouri, emphasized, not the historic import of the amendment, but how little it granted to the Black man, giving him "no right except his freedom," saying that it left the rest to the states. Lincoln said, "We are like whalers who have been long on a chase: we have at last got the harpoon into the monster, but we must now look how we steer, or with one 'flop' of his tail he will send us all into eternity."

There was a new comity between the administration and the abolitionists. Garrison publicly thanked the president for his role in supporting the amendment; Lincoln gave the credit to others: "The logic and moral power of Garrison and the antislavery people of the country and the army, have done it all." In Congress, the Radical Republicans, led by Sumner in the Senate and Thaddeus Stevens in the House, argued that the amendment didn't go far enough, emphasizing that Black Americans must be afforded the same political and economic opportunities as whites; without legal protection from the federal government, they would face retaliation in the South.

One afternoon in December, Frances found Henry talking with Sumner in the parlor. Henry had forgiven Sumner for attempting to oust him from the Cabinet, and Sumner was reenlisting him as an ally. Sumner's immediate goal was to force the Washington and Georgetown Railroad to desegregate its streetcars. The company required African Americans to ride outside on the trolleys' narrow platforms, or in sporadically provided "colored cars." Under pressure from Black ministers and the press, the railroad had provided ten new cars, but they, too, were strictly segregated, a decision condemned by the National Freedman's Relief Association as an effort to resuscitate the "carcass of slavery." Sumner had joined the outcry when a conductor forced off a car a Black major in the 7th United States Colored Infantry Regiment.

Frances greeted Sumner politely, but without her former fondness. At fifty-three, mostly recovered from his caning in the Senate, he was heavier and slower on his feet, his still-copious hair was graying, and the pouches beneath his eyes were darker. He was courting twenty-six-year-old Alice Mason Hooper, a socially prominent widow. Henry invited Sumner to stay for dinner, but he said he was dining with Mrs. Hooper. Frances had doubts about the relationship, ending a letter to Lazette with Edmund Burke's words, "What shadows we are, and what shadows we pursue."

By the time the House voted on the Thirteenth Amendment, on January 31, 1865, Frances had left Washington. A two-thirds majority was required to pass an amendment to the Constitution. The galleries were full, and members of the Supreme Court and the Senate joined the representatives on the floor of the House. Tally sheets were distributed to keep track of the votes. Finally, Speaker Schuyler Colfax stood and gaveled the room to order. He announced in a quavering voice that the ayes on the passage of the joint resolution to amend the Constitution of the United States had 119 votes; the noes, 56. The ayes included five Democrats who had succumbed to Lincoln's, Henry's, and Weed's blandishments—just enough to pass the amendment.

For a moment there was silence in the chamber—then, pandemonium. Members threw their hats in the air, cheering and roaring. Women waved their handkerchiefs. People hugged each other and sobbed. Artillery at the Capitol fired a hundred-gun salute. The *Tribune* declared the next day: "FREEDOM TRIUMPHANT. COMMENCEMENT OF A NEW ERA. DEATH OF SLAVERY. The Constitutional Amendment Adopted. Greatest Act Since the Declaration of Independence." No attempt was made to restore order. Thaddeus Stevens later found a few well-chosen words to explain the success of the amendment: "The greatest measure of the nineteenth century was passed by corruption, aided and abetted by the purest man in America."

Frances, although hopeful, believed it was too soon to celebrate. The war continued, and the amendment had to be ratified by three quarters of the states. Sherman was moving through the Carolinas, and Grant was eight months into his siege of Petersburg. There was speculation that rebels might attempt to abduct or assassinate the president. Frances wrote a remarkably subdued note to Henry: "I congratulate you on the passage of the Constitutional amendment which I know you had much at heart. The prospect of abolishing slavery throughout the United States is indeed cheering."

On Inauguration Day, March 4, 1865, tens of thousands of spectators traveled by foot and carriage from Pennsylvania Avenue to Capitol Hill in a windy morning rain. It had been pouring for weeks, and the mud in the streets was several inches deep. Douglass, invited by Lincoln to attend the swearing-in, recalled, "I felt then that there was murder in the air, and I kept close to his carriage on the way to the Capitol, for I felt that I might see him fall that day." The cast-iron dome, painted white, had been completed at the end of 1863. It was topped by a nineteen-foot bronze Statue of Freedom, a classical female figure in a helmet cast in the likeness of an eagle's head. "E PLURIBUS UNUM" was carved into the pedestal.

Lincoln emerged on the East Portico to the cheers of forty thousand people, and the sun breaking through the clouds. His address was marked by certitude but no triumphalism. Four years earlier, the insurgents had gone to war to ensure the continued enslavement of one-eighth of the country's population. They had failed, Lincoln believed, because God was demanding an end to slavery.

One of his bodyguards wrote, "They seemed to hang on his words as though they were meat and drink. And when he concluded the last paragraph, beginning, 'With malice toward none, with charity for all,' which fell like a benediction from heaven, the shout of the people seemed to rise to the very sky." At the White House reception, when Lincoln was told that Douglass was present, he asked to see him, and wanted to know what he thought of the speech. Douglass called it "a sacred effort," eliciting a delighted smile from the weary president.

Harriet was in Washington, too, awaiting authorization from the War Department to travel back to Port Royal on a government ship. During her stay, she volunteered at the Home for Destitute Colored Women and

Children, in Georgetown, a charitable organization established in 1863 as a residence and school for war refugees. The night after the inauguration, Harriet attended a service at the Fifteenth Street Presbyterian Church, a few blocks from the White House. Her friend Henry Highland Garnet was the pastor, and Douglass was the featured speaker. She had last seen Douglass the previous fall, when she was in upstate New York, and had stopped by his house in Rochester. The different paths they had taken for the same goal had brought them together again at this church fifteen years later, to give thanks to God and the president. Douglass centered his remarks on words from Lincoln's inaugural address: that if God willed that the war continue until "every drop of blood drawn with the lash shall be paid by another drawn with the sword, as was said three thousand years ago, so still it must be said 'the judgments of the Lord are true and righteous altogether.'" In simpler language, Harriet had said something similar to Lydia Maria Child in Boston in 1862, when she remarked that God wouldn't let Lincoln win the war until he set the Negroes free.

Harriet regretted passing up her own chance to meet the president. Sojourner Truth, who had campaigned for Lincoln's reelection, had invited Harriet to go with her to the White House three months earlier. She had declined, not yet persuaded that Lincoln was fully committed to emancipation. Harriet told a friend, "'Twas Sojourner Truth told me Master Lincoln was our friend. Then she went to see him, and she thanked him for all he had done for our peoples. Master Lincoln was kind to her, and she had a nice visit with him, but he told her he had done nothing himself. He was only a servant of the country. Yes, I'm sorry now I didn't see Master Lincoln and thank him."

At the Fifteenth Street Church, Harriet felt compelled to speak. She had served in the Department of the South for three years under Generals Hunter and Saxton, and under Colonel Montgomery, she had helped to liberate almost eight hundred slaves. She had cared for sick and maimed soldiers in South Carolina and Florida. Yet, just an hour or two earlier, on her way to the church from the Home for Destitute Colored Women and Children, a conductor had attempted to order her off a segregated streetcar. Harriet, already embarking on the next phase of her career as a resistant, stood up and said: "They tried to keep me out tonight when I came from Georgetown, but I wouldn't go out."

26

Retribution

1865

"Blood, blood, my thoughts seemed drenched in it—I seemed to breathe its sickening odor."
Entry from Fanny's diary, April 14, 1865

The Civil War ended almost precisely four years after it began. On hundreds of battlefields and in hospitals from Florida to Missouri, more than half a million men had died. No one could predict how much animosity remained, but the opposing generals acted with grace. On April 2, General Robert E. Lee ordered the evacuation of Richmond, and the next day the United States flag flew again above Virginia's capitol. Grant and Lee agreed to meet in the coming week to discuss the terms of surrender. In

Washington, on the balmy afternoon of April 5, Henry, Frederick, Fanny, and one of Fanny's friends, finally able to relax after the unspeakable traumas of the war, went out for a carriage ride. But the horses took fright, and Henry, jumping out to seize the reins, took a bad fall, dislocating his shoulder and breaking his lower jaw. Frances, receiving the news, left immediately, arriving thirty-four hours later to find him patient and uncomplaining, but his face so swollen and discolored that he was almost unrecognizable.

Lincoln had gone to Richmond to visit the fallen capital, and he was aboard the steamship *River Queen* at City Point, on his way back to Washington, when he learned about the accident. Arriving at the Sewards' on the evening of April 9, he climbed the stairs in the hushed house and sat down gingerly on Henry's bed. His neck was swathed in bandages.

"You are back from Richmond?" he whispered.

"Yes," Lincoln replied, "and I think we are near the end, at last."

The president stretched out, resting his cheek on his elbow, with his face next to Henry's. Fanny came in, said good evening, and as she walked to her chair, Lincoln reached his long arm around the foot of the bed to shake her hand. Lincoln talked quietly with Henry about his trip to Richmond, like a father telling a sick child a bedtime story. He had been accompanied by his bodyguard, twelve marines, and his son Tad, who was celebrating his twelfth birthday. Departing rebels had set fire to the tobacco warehouses, and much of the city was destroyed. The presidential party disembarked at the edge of town, where Lincoln had listened as a group of freed people joined hands and sang a hymn of thanks. As word spread, hundreds came forward to see "the great Messiah," as one elderly man described Lincoln, who had "come at last to free his children from their bondage."

Lincoln called out: "My poor friends, you are free—free as air. You can cast off the name of slave and trample upon it; it will come to you no more. Liberty is your birthright." Then, surrounded by marines, he proceeded through the heat and smoke, as white residents watched silently from their windows. Arriving at the top of a hill overlooking the Shockoe Valley, he entered the Confederate Executive Mansion, a three-story gray stucco house. It, too, was battle-scarred. An elderly house servant told them that before Mrs. Davis departed, she had instructed him to keep it in good order for the Yankees.

In the parlor that Jefferson Davis had used as his office, Lincoln sat down, remarking, "This must have been President Davis's chair." He asked, "I wonder if I could get a glass of water." He met with Major General Godfrey Weitzel, the Union officer in charge of the city, and two representatives of the Confederate government, to discuss repealing the ordinance of secession, the disbanding of the Army of Northern Virginia, and the surrender of the other rebel armies. He assured them that his administration would deal fairly with the South. After lunch, he rode in an ambulance to the state capitol, perched above the city's tumbledown remains. Inside the chambers, Lincoln's bodyguard William Crook recalled, they found the destruction wreaked by relic hunters and Confederates in flight: members' tables overturned, and the floor littered with official documents and worthless bales of Confederate money.

Back at City Point, Lincoln visited sick and wounded soldiers at the two-hundred-acre Depot Field Hospital. The hospital was composed of twelve hundred tents, ninety log buildings, and support facilities including kitchens, dining halls, laundries, dispensaries, and offices. As Lincoln continued to describe his trip to Henry and Fanny, he said that he had shaken the hands of seven thousand patients. Men who were ambulatory waited patiently in lines outside; he greeted the more seriously wounded at their cots. Fanny wrote, "He spoke of having worked as hard at it as sawing wood, and seemed in his goodness of heart, much satisfied at the labor."

Lincoln left after Henry fell asleep, but soon Edwin Stanton, the secretary of war, arrived for the third time that day, and said he must be woken up. Stanton told Henry that at four o'clock that afternoon, General Lee had surrendered himself and his army to General Grant at Appomattox Court House. Fanny wrote that her father took Stanton's hand and said, "God bless you Stanton—I can never tell you half . . ." Stanton gently interrupted: "Don't try to speak." Henry finished the thought: "You have made me cry for the first time in my life, I believe."

Frances was buoyed by reports of the courteous conclusion to the monstrous war, hoping that Lincoln and Henry were right that southerners would reenter the Union amicably and that northerners would welcome them back. In the parlor of a private house in the village of Appomattox Court House, the two generals greeted each other and sat down at two small tables flanking the fireplace. Grant drafted the conditions of surrender, not in the form of a treaty between two nations, but as a letter to "Genl. R. E. Lee, Cmdg. C.S.A.," written in pencil on a single sheet of stationery. He requested the Army of Northern Virginia to stack its weapons and flags, park its artillery, and turn over its munitions. Officers would be permitted to keep their personal effects—swords, pistols, sidearms, horses, and mules. Soldiers and their commanders could then return to their homes. Lee, grateful for the lenient terms, wrote a brief letter of acceptance. He told Grant that his men were hungry, and Grant ordered the distribution of rations to men who only days earlier he had been starving into submission. Lee left the room with his adjutants, followed by Grant and his entourage. The two generals tipped their hats.

On April 11, Frances, tending to Henry, heard cheers outside, as a crowd moved toward the White House lawn, to hear Lincoln speak. Mary Lincoln's dressmaker, Elizabeth Keckley, who had grown up enslaved in Virginia, saw it as "a black, gently swelling sea," and the president walking to the North Portico "with pale face and his soul flashing through his eyes." He acknowledged the people's "gladness of heart," but reminded them of the great difficulties ahead. During the presidential campaign, he had not spoken publicly of the vote for Black men. Now he said, to signal moderation, "I would myself prefer that it were now conferred on the very intelligent, and on those who serve our cause as soldiers." One of the spectators, the actor John Wilkes Booth, told a companion, "That means nigger citizenship! Now, by God, I'll put him through. That is the last speech he will ever make."

April 13 was a holiday in Washington. Buildings were festooned with flags, and Union loyalists celebrated throughout the day. After dark they placed candles and lanterns in their windows, and General Grant rode out with Mrs. Lincoln in the presidential carriage to see the illuminations. At the Sewards' house, Henry's condition was improving, but the gaslights were kept dim, and Frances and Fanny watched a fireworks display on Lafayette Square through Henry's bedroom window. Frances, ready at last to celebrate, welcomed the hubbub. Fanny noticed that her mother was bright and cheerful.

On April 14, the fourth anniversary of the surrender of Fort Sumter, Frederick attended a morning cabinet meeting in his father's place. Lincoln was sitting in his threadbare writing chair by the south window of his study, with an expression, Frederick said, "of visible relief and content upon his face." Fred recalled that a few weeks earlier, the new postmaster-general, the former Ohio governor William Dennison Jr., had commented, "Well, I should think the Presidential chair of the United States might be a better piece of furniture than that." Lincoln replied, "You think that's not a good chair, Governor. There are a great many people that want to sit in it, though. I'm sure I've often wished some of them had it instead of me!"

Lincoln had invited General Grant to attend the meeting, and he entered to applause. Grant talked about his final pursuit of Lee, and about the surrender ceremony. Lincoln mentioned that the previous night, he had dreamed he was in a vessel, moving rapidly toward an unknown shore. He had woken from the same dream before the battles of Fort Sumter, Bull Run, Antietam, and Gettysburg. One cabinet member sensibly suggested, "Perhaps at each of these periods there were possibilities of great change or disaster; and the vague feeling of uncertainty may have led to the dim vision in sleep." Lincoln replied, "Perhaps. Perhaps that is the explanation."

Stanton outlined each department's duties in coming months. Treasury would take the customhouses of the South and collect revenues. War would garrison or destroy the forts, take possession of arms and munitions, and maintain the public peace. Navy would occupy the harbors and assume control of ships and ordnance. State would repair strained relations with Europe. The laws of the United States would once more apply throughout the country. As the meeting disbanded, Lincoln asked Grant to accompany him and Mrs. Lincoln to Ford's Theatre that night for a performance of *Our American Cousin*, but Grant said that he had promised his wife they would leave immediately for their home in Burlington, New Jersey. Stanton advised Lincoln against going to the theater, saying that he was needlessly putting himself in harm's way. Lincoln chided him for his lack of faith in human nature.

At the Club House, the Sewards prepared for the nighttime vigil. Frances, Fred, and Anna had stayed up on recent nights, so Fanny took her turn, sitting with her father and picking up where they had left off in Bulfinch's *Legends of Charlemagne*. Augustus was to relieve her at eleven. The doctors checked in on Henry, promising to return in the morning. The nurse, George Robinson, stayed on. When Henry began to doze, Fanny closed the book and turned down the gaslight. At a little past ten o'clock, the Sewards' nineteen-year-old doorman, William Bell, answered the front door to a tall young man in a light hat and long overcoat. Holding a small parcel wrapped in butcher paper and twine, he said that he had some medicine from Dr. Thomas Verdi, Henry's physician. Bell told him that he would take it, but the man pushed past him, rushing upstairs.

Fanny heard people talking outside the room, and she thought the president had returned, to see how her father was getting along. She opened the door and looked into the hall, where Fred was arguing with a stranger. The man asked her if the secretary was asleep. Fred interrupted, saying that he was Seward's son, shutting the door, and telling him to leave the package with him. The man began to walk down the stairs, then turned, drew a navy revolver from his coat, and pulled the trigger. The gun misfired, but he used it to beat Fred on his skull, hitting him so hard, he broke the ramrod.

The assailant then pushed into Henry's room, holding the pistol in his left hand and a Bowie knife in the right. He stabbed at Robinson, the nurse, landing a few glancing blows on his forehead, before turning toward the bed. Fanny, standing between her father and the man, screamed, "Don't kill him!" Trying to protect Fanny, Henry awkwardly tried to sit up, but the man pushed her aside and pressed Henry to the bed. Later that night, Henry said he knew the man meant to kill him, but that he feared more for Fanny. He felt the cold blade of the knife as it split open his cheek, then torrents of blood, like a warm, heavy rain. Robinson, bleeding from his head wound, grabbed the man from behind, but he fought back, stabbing Robinson in the shoulder and striking him with the gun.

Woken by Fanny's screams, Augustus rushed into the room, and shoved the man toward the door. The attacker lunged at him with the knife, shouting, "I'm mad, I'm mad!," then fled, trailing his victims' blood on the stairs. Coming upon a messenger from the State Department, he plunged the knife into the messenger's back, and ran from the house.

Frances and Anna, who had been asleep in the back of the house, arrived on the landing. They couldn't make out much in the murky light, and were confused by Fanny's question, "Is that man gone?" Fanny ran back into her father's room, where she found the mattress soaked in blood and pierced by the knife in several places. Her father was on the floor on the far side of the room, and for the second time in less than two weeks, she was sure he had been killed. As Fanny walked toward him, she slipped in a pool of blood. Robinson tore back Henry's nightclothes to listen for a heartbeat, then lifted him back onto the bed, instructing Fanny how to stanch the blood. He worked on the right side while Fanny knelt on the bed on the left, pressing another neck wound. Her father, still conscious, told her to send for surgeons and to ask for a guard to be placed outside. In the hallway, Frances, in a state of shock, bent over Fred. She looked up at Fanny and said she was afraid he could not survive.

Henry's right cheek, slashed from ear to neck, was nearly severed from his face. Dr. Verdi arrived and, after a quick examination, told the family that the wounds were not mortal. Henry, seeing Fanny's stricken look, reached out to soothe her. She wrote in her diary: "Blood, blood, my thoughts seemed drenched in it—I seemed to breathe its sickening odor. My dress was stained with it." The bedclothes were stained a dark red, "the blankets & sheet chopped with several blows of the knife." The drugget on the stairs was splattered with blood, all the way down to the floor below.

To Frances, the attack was a ghastly reminder of William Freeman's murderous rampage on the Van Nest family two decades earlier, and her fear of a nighttime intruder intent on murdering her family. As Dr. Verdi applied cold-water compresses to Fred's head wound, he asked, "For Heaven's sake, Mrs. Seward, what does all this mean?" She led him to Augustus, who had superficial wounds, but he was alert and asked about his father. Robinson, the nurse, was next. His wounds were relatively light.

Fanny found the other night nurse, Donaldson, sitting with his face in his hands, sobbing. Fanny asked him if he was hurt, and he replied, "No, Miss Fanny, I wasn't here. If I had been here this wouldn't have happened."

Stanton and Welles arrived, with the news that President Lincoln had been attacked at Ford's Theatre. They were on their way to the boardinghouse where he had been taken, across the street from the theater. At 10:15, John Wilkes Booth had entered the president's box, fired a derringer at the back of his head, leaped to the stage, and escaped on horseback. Stanton had issued orders to investigate the plot, close all bridges and roads out of the city, and organize a manhunt. Frances asked with her usual solicitude, "Are *you* safe, Mr. Stanton?"

The next morning, Stanton returned to tell Frances that Lincoln had died at 7:22 a.m.—the first assassination of a U.S. president. Henry's doctors wanted to keep the news from him until he was stronger, but Frances disagreed, gently telling him, "Henry, the president is gone." A few hours later, the Sewards' old friend Dorothea Dix, the superintendent of army nurses, came by. Henry could communicate only with a slate and chalk, and Fanny read his shaky handwriting to Dix: "The friends of America ought to have watched Mr Lincoln better. His life, however, is forfeit. The Nation will do him Justice."

Henry's attacker was arrested, and identified as Lewis Powell, one of Booth's conspirators in a plot against Lincoln, Seward, and Vice President Johnson. A twenty-one-year-old Confederate veteran and member of the Confederate Secret Service, Powell had been wounded at Gettysburg and lost two brothers in the war. A third man, George Atzerodt, assigned to murder Johnson, lost his nerve and got drunk instead. Members of the 16th New York Cavalry hunted down Booth, finding him twelve days after the assassination at a farm near the Rappahannock River in Virginia. When he refused to surrender, they shot and killed him. Powell and Atzerodt were found guilty, and executed on July 7.

Vice President Johnson was sworn into office, in a ceremony performed by the new chief justice, former treasury secretary Salmon Chase. In 1864, Lincoln had chosen Johnson, a former Democratic senator from Tennessee, as his running mate. He'd thought that Johnson—a southern Unionist who alone among his colleagues from Confederate states opposed secession—would be helpful in the difficult process of reconstruction.

Lincoln's funeral service took place in the East Room of the White House on April 19. Major General Weitzel, ordered to send "one of the best regiments of colored troops," dispatched the 22nd United States Colored Infantry. Its band struck up a dirge, and met the procession at Seventh and Pennsylvania Avenue, church bells tolling, cannon firing every sixty seconds, and drummer boys tapping out muffled beats. Mourners lined the streets, and as the hearse passed by, the casket resting on a high platform, men took off their hats and wept.

The Sewards could barely process the events of April—Lee's surrender, Henry's carriage accident, the attacks on Henry, Augustus, and Frederick, the assassination of Lincoln. Will, who had almost lost his life at Cold Harbor and Monocacy, was called from Martinsburg to help his shattered family. In a letter to Jenny, Will wrote that his father was very weak and not entirely in his right mind. Augustus was up and about, but Fred's skull had been cracked in two places: "The slightest unfavorable turn may end his life." Frances had thought that Fred's civilian job would protect him from being wounded; instead, Fred was one of the war's final casualties. Will located a dentist in New York who, he was told, could make a rubber mold to hold together Henry's jaw. The dentist came to Washington and spent three days setting the jaw and putting the splint-like contraption in place. On April 21, Will remarked that his father's constitution was as resilient as his spirit. Henry demanded that they carry him downstairs each morning for a short carriage ride.

Five of the best surgeons in Washington were brought in to operate on Frederick. When they opened the wound, they discovered that pieces of bone were causing pressure on the brain. He didn't have the strength to undergo the surgery without chloroform, but the doctors warned that the anesthesia presented its own dangers. Frances and Anna—unable to think clearly—asked Will to decide. He ordered the surgery, telling Jenny, "I felt that there was no hope for him as he was. After this you may imagine with what anxiety I watched for the result."

Three pieces of bone were removed, the bleeding was stopped with ice, and Frederick briefly opened his eyes and spoke. By early May, he was well enough for Frances to read *David Copperfield* to him. He asked frequently about his father, but had no recollection of the attacks, and she didn't tell him about the president's death. She wrote to Weed, "It seems as if I had two hearts, one throbbing for Henry, and the other for Frederick," and she confessed to an Auburn friend that the constant, wearing anxiety consumed her strength. Henry was in pain from the splint, but the surgeons saw no cause for alarm. Frances said that "this baptism of blood" had obliterated much of her previous life. "But our calamities do not make us unmindful of the great loss our country has sustained in the death of our good President."

Initially, even Republicans thought that President Johnson would follow Lincoln's plan for Reconstruction, but he was heard to say, "This is a country for white men, and by G-d, as long as I am president it shall be a government for white men." When Congress was out of session, he issued an executive order to readmit the governments of the southern states that swore allegiance to the nation. Henry approved of the policy, and, confident that he could steer Johnson away from his most extreme tendencies, agreed to remain as his secretary of state. On May 9, three and a half weeks after the attack, Henry received the new president and the cabinet in one of his parlors, and a few weeks later, he asked to be carried to his desk at the State Department. Henry confidently told one visitor to his office, "These Southern people will come back in peace, and in obedience."

As for the North, he advised, as Lincoln had: "Patience, forbearance, magnanimity."

Frances became ill from the strain of nursing Henry and Frederick. In early June, she wrote to Lazette that she could only manage to sit by Frederick's side for an hour in the morning and again in the evening: "His pale, patient face is never out of my mind." Will and Fanny were more distressed about their mother than they ever had been. Languid and sleeping much of the time, she seemed to be fading away.

Frances knew she was dying, in a city she hated, away from Lazette and Martha and other friends, and far from her cherished home in Auburn. During the war, she had objected to Frederick about an extension he and Henry were planning for the south side of the house, which would double the size of the front, destroying its rural character and turning it into a formal city residence. Some of the oldest trees would have to be destroyed—the towering locust and horse chestnut, and the flowering cherry tree that her father had planted, "home of the robin for nearly forty years." She preferred houses like Dickens's Bleak House, where, she wrote, "you go up and down steps, out of one room into another, & where you come upon more rooms when you think you have seen all there are, & where there is a bountiful provision of little halls & passages, & where you find older rooms in unexpected places with lattice windows & green growth peering through them." Despite her pleas, the plans for the renovation went forward.

But she accepted that disappointment, and others that were deeper and more long-standing. Frances's early expectations about growing old harmoniously with Henry had been a naïve fantasy of marriage, and of a society, she'd soon learned, that was built on intolerable inequities. Despite all their disagreements and separations, they had sustained their love for each other. As a politician, Henry had succeeded, more honorably than not—condemning slavery across four decades, and he was sure to leave behind the reputation he sought. Frances was reassured by the thought of Lazette's fast tie to Fanny. Picturing her garden in its June splendor and the summerhouse she and Henry had built after his 1833 European tour, she told him that she would like to see the flowers and hear the birds just once more.

On the night of June 17, Augustus sat beside his mother, gently fanning her face and exchanging whispers with Will while Fanny slept on the camp bed in the room. The next day, only Fanny took note of Will's twenty-sixth birthday, describing him as "good, & gentle, & strong & considerate & kind!" In coming days, Frances contracted a fever, which weakened her heart. She told Fanny that she wasn't in any pain. "I am so comfortable. I only want to see you all look happy."

Lazette, on her way to Washington, got a telegraph when she stopped in Albany. On June 21, scarcely two months after the assassination of the president and the near-lethal attacks on Henry, Frederick, and Augustus, Frances died at fifty-nine. She had lived just long enough to see that they would survive. Fred called it "the longest and saddest day of that long sad year." Fanny, who had spent her life at her mother's side, wrote to a friend that Frances "lay still and beautiful, only breathing more and more lightly till she ceased to breathe at all. It comforts me to think that she can never suffer any more." But she was devastated. In her diary, Fanny wrote down passages from the Bible: "Thou shalt not be afraid for the terror by night, nor for the arrow that flieth by day," and "this God is our God for ever and ever: he will be our guide even unto death."

Martha went to see Lazette at the Seward House, where she found her lying on a sofa, a maid applying cold water to her head and rubbing her feet. Her hands and arms were purple. The doctor arrived and said her circulation was failing—Lazette's own heart constricted with grief. Martha had feared for Frances ever since hearing about the attacks. Seeing Lazette, she was frightened for her, too. Her combativeness gone, she looked and sounded like an old woman. Lazette was indebted to Seward for his many kindnesses, and she had defended him even when Frances had not. That day, Lazette told Martha that the lives of politicians were bound to be vexed, even dangerous—the closest she ever came to regretting her sister's marriage. Martha ached for Fanny, too, writing to Ellen after the Powell assaults, "Think what a horror this will be to Fanny Seward, all her life, as she recalls the dreadful scene." Now Fanny had lost the person she loved most.

On June 23, Frances's casket arrived on a special train from Washington. Seward, Fanny, Will, and Augustus followed. Fred was still too weak to travel. All the shops in town were closed. Seward, his face disfigured by the wound, looked startlingly diminished. Martha observed that he was "very pale in a plaid cap fitting close to his head, with loops at the corners for the semi-circular supports for his jaw."

The coffin was placed under one of the old trees in Frances's garden, where Henry received hundreds of mourners before the funeral at St. Peter's Church. He had asked two old friends—David Wright and Thurlow Weed—to lead the pallbearers. Seward, Lazette, and Fanny leaned on one another as they slowly made their way to the front. Weed wrote in the *Times* that the attempted assassination of Seward and Frederick "has, whatever their fate may be, caused this death." An Auburn newspaper, reported that more mourners attended Mrs. Seward's funeral than almost any previously held in New York. They were there to show their love for Mrs. Seward, the reporter wrote, more than their high regard for the secretary of state. According to the obituary in the *New York Times*, at Fort Hill Cemetery during the burial, a bird perched in a tree over the grave, its song mingling with the clergyman's "Ashes to ashes, dust to dust."

Henry was touched by the personal tributes to Frances. Sumner wrote to say that he grieved with him: "With sincere and most affectionate interest I followed that funeral procession from Washington to Auburn with the remains of one that I loved and honored much. Mrs. Seward was a noble woman—all that you once told me she was, when you first spoke to me of her, before I ever saw her. I shall never forget her goodness to me, her kind counsels when I was an invalid, and her sympathy in my trials."

The *Chicago Journal* published a long appreciation by the publisher, Charles L. Wilson, who had been secretary of the American Legation in London during the war. Wilson portrayed Frances as Henry liked to see her: "She believed that woman would be accorded a wider and freer action in the future than was usual in the past; yet she did not feel called by this conviction, to eccentricities in dress, nor to haranguing public assemblies." Wilson was praising Frances's wisdom in accepting her sphere. He didn't know about her work on the underground railroad, her sale of family property to Harriet Tubman and her mothering of Harriet's niece, or her strenuous disagreements with Seward over emancipation. Nor was he aware that Seward, a friend of the women's rights movement, had told her not to join it. Wilson thought Frances was a woman who "might have been a social power had she not chosen to consecrate all her energies to the duties of home." Her "influence was always given to the side of justice, humanity, and freedom, but noiselessly and without heat, acrimony, or contention." Thankfully, in his view, not a dangerous woman. Henry told Fanny, "It was a friend that mourned in those beautiful lines."

Martha didn't share Douglass's and Garrison's newfound respect for the Lincoln administration. The day before the Confederates abandoned Richmond, she had written to Lucretia that she wished the war would continue until every last rebel was dead. Full of sorrow for Fanny and Lazette, she blamed Seward for Frances's unhappiness. Martha credited him for his years of speeches condemning slavery, but she had come to find him hungrier for power than for principle. Looking back on Frances's life, her friend of three decades, citing the "1000 anxieties that have pressed upon her," Martha told Lucretia how much she would "miss her gentle presence and the earnest interest she felt in the right." Frances was relieved at last of the "honorables & the Gents. & the Majors, & the never failing attendants on the great. Poor Mrs. Seward sleeps well, untortured by the restless ambitions of others."

27

Civil Disobedience

1865

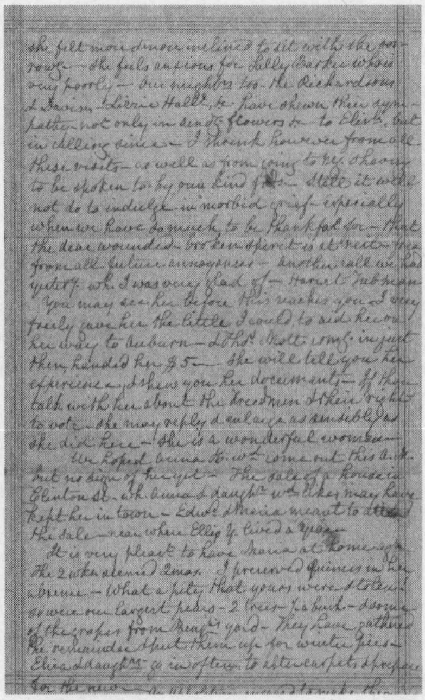

she felt more & more inclined to sit with the sor-
rowing— she feels anxious for Lilly Barker who is
very poorly— our neighbors too— the Richardsons
& Davis, Lizzie Hall &c. have shewn their sympathy not only in send^g flowers &c— to Eliz^h. but
in calling since— I shrink however from all
these visits— as well as from going to Mr. Shaw's
to be spoken to by our kind f[illegible]— Still it will
not do to indulge in morbid grief— especially
when we have so much to be thankful for— that
the dear wounded— broken spirit is at rest— free
from all future annoyances— Another call we had
yesterday wh. I was very glad of— Harriet Tubman
You may see her before this reaches you & I very
freely gave her the little I could, to aid her on
her way to Auburn— & Thos. Mott coming in just
then, handed her $5— She will tell you her
experience, & shew you her documents— If thou
talk with her about the Freedmen & their right
to vote— she may reply & enlarge as sensibly as
she did here— She is a wonderful woman—
We hoped Anna H. w^d come out this [illegible]
but no sign of her yet— The sale of a house in
Clinton St. wh. Anna & daught^r w^d like, may have
kept her in town— Edwd & Maria meant to attend
the sale— near where Ellis Y. lived a year—
It is very pleas^t to have Maria at home ag[illegible]
The 2 wks. seemed 2 mos. I preserved quinces in her
absence— What a pity that yours were stolen!
so were our largest pears— 2 trees— [illegible]— & some
of the grapes from Mary's yard— They have gathered
the remainder & put them up for winter [illegible]
Eliza & daught^r go in often to [illegible] carpets & prepare
for the new— [illegible]

"If thou talk with her about the Freedmen & their right to vote—she may enlarge as sensibly as she did here." Lucretia Mott to Martha Coffin Wright, October 2, 1865

Harriet got word of Frances's death while working at Hampton Hospital, on the Virginia mainland near Fort Monroe, Virginia. Nurses from the Sanitary Commission had told her that she was urgently needed at Hampton, where Black soldiers were being abysmally neglected and mistreated.

The Hampton complex consisted of the Chesapeake Military Hospital for officers, in the four-story former Chesapeake Female Seminary, and the United States General Hospital, Hampton, for the troops. Hampton resembled a tidy village, with thirty cottages arranged in a triangle around a large kitchen and dining room, along with the "dead house," the coal yard, the bathing houses, the storehouses, and the stables. It was well provisioned, with a hundred-acre vegetable garden, hot running water, a library of three thousand books, and—it was said—the most advanced treatment in the world for trauma and disease.

African American patients saw none of that. In early July 1865, after working at the hospital for five weeks, Harriet dictated a letter to *The Independent*, a weekly magazine edited by Henry Ward Beecher, to publicize "the sad and miserable condition of the men." The weakest were being starved. Little was expected from the enemy, she said, "but from our friends we looked for justice." The troops had fought at Petersburg and Richmond, endured frigid winters in their huts and tents, faced bombshells and cannon balls. Now they were dying hungry. The rations were cabbage and beef boiled in water, coffee and tea so weak that the water was hardly colored, and the portion of soup for two men, meat and all, barely enough to fill an ordinary tumbler.

The hospital surgeon was Eli McClellan, who, Harriet remarked, was a cousin of General George McClellan. He ignored repeated complaints about the soldiers' care. The conditions had been primitive in the converted homes and field hospitals of South Carolina and Florida, but soldiers were too valued to be left to die. Harriet said she had spent fifteen years pursuing liberty for her people, and she wanted readers to know that while they were enjoying the comforts of home, their friends were suffering in Virginia. "Is there no relief from these abuses?" She signed the letter, "Yours, affectionately, Harriet Tubman."

Harriet hated missing Frances's funeral, but she did not have the money for the trip to Auburn, and she couldn't be spared at the hospital. In mid-July, when the family returned to Washington, she went to pay her respects. Harriet found Seward sorely changed. His right arm hung limply by his side, there was a rheumy sadness in his eyes, and his mouth and neck were disfigured by scars. Fred's skull was mending, but caved in from the butt of Lewis Powell's revolver, and he moved with the halting step of the wounded. Fanny, noticeably frailer, bore all the signs of tuberculosis.

She was collecting Frances's letters, an idea her father encouraged, telling her, "They will be precious even now, and they will become more so every day." Fanny made sure the correspondence was preserved—a commentary on American racial, social, and marital unrest like no other. Referring to Frances's penetrating readings of Jefferson, Dickens, Martineau, and the many other public intellectuals they had discussed over the years, Henry said that she loved knowledge because "it disclosed the treasures of truth."

Harriet had come to mourn, but also to ask for Seward's help. She wanted to know what could be done about the situation at Hampton Hospital. He introduced her to the U.S. surgeon general, Joseph Barnes, who had overseen his care and Lincoln's, and was initiating reforms in the treatment of patients in army hospitals. Dr. Barnes wrote an order requesting that Harriet be appointed "Nurse or Matron at the colored hospital"—an official position of authority in the U.S. government—and Secretary Stanton's assistant adjutant general issued a pass for her return trip to Fort Monroe.

She asked, too, if Seward could help her secure her army pay. He wrote to General Hunter that Tubman "believes she has a claim for faithful services to the command in South Carolina with which you are connected, and she thinks that you would be disposed to see her claim justly settled." He emphasized their personal tie: "I have known her long, and a nobler, higher spirit, or a truer, seldom dwells in the human form."

Back at the hospital, Harriet could not get anyone to recognize the position that Dr. Barnes had promised. Out of money, and knowing she was needed at home, she left on October 1, stopping in Philadelphia, where she took a detour to see Lucretia at Roadside, a rambling farmhouse she and James Mott had bought in 1857, about eight miles north of the city.

Lucretia was grieving for her forty-year-old daughter, Elizabeth Cavender, who had died of cancer a few weeks earlier. She wrote to Martha that she avoided neighbors, but was very glad to see Harriet. It had been sixteen years since they first met in Philadelphia, when Harriet, a young freedom seeker, looked to her for guidance. Lucretia, who had a nuanced view of the bloody conflict, listened intently to Harriet's description of her work at Port Royal. Before the war, Lucretia had believed that the administration should let the slave states peacefully leave the Union, sure that the South could not survive as a separate country. Still, she had supported the troops, especially Black soldiers. In May 1863, when the government was finally ready to enlist Black men, recruits were trained at Camp William Penn, next to Roadside, on thirteen acres donated by Lucretia's abolitionist son-in-law Edward M. Davis. Lucretia liked the sounds of the bugle calls and the marching band as they drifted over the fields, and when the newly minted soldiers marched off across the Motts' lawn, she stood on the veranda, handing out gingerbread from her apron.

Lucretia saw emancipation as the result of the abolitionists' thirty-year "moral war" against slavery, a campaign that was far from over. When the Civil War ended, Garrison had meant to disband the American Anti-Slavery Society, but Wendell Phillips believed the group was entering a critical new phase, and he took over. In his first speech as president, he said that every effort must now be spent on protecting the Black people of the South: "This hour belongs to the negro." He tried to convince Elizabeth Cady Stanton that they must not "mix the movements" just then—it "would lose for the negro far more than we should gain for the woman." Southern states, with President Johnson's approval, had instituted a series of "black codes"—slavery by another name. Children who had been separated from their parents during the war were kept on plantations and made to work under "apprenticeship laws." Adults were severely restricted in their rights to buy or lease property and to move about freely. The unemployed were arrested on charges of "vagrancy," and assigned to compulsory labor.

Lucretia was still a dominating presence in the Philadelphia Female Anti-Slavery Society and the American Anti-Slavery Society. Like Sumner in Washington, she focused on equal rights in Philadelphia, pushing the city to integrate its railway lines. One day when she was on a streetcar, a conductor ordered a Black woman to ride on the car's platform in the pouring rain. Lucretia objected, and when he told her that he was only following orders, she went to stand with the woman outside, refusing to reenter until he allowed them both back in.

On Harriet's visit to Roadside, she and Lucretia discussed the importance of the vote for African American men. The Thirteenth Amendment, abolishing slavery in the United States and its territories, was about to be ratified, and Congress was drafting the Fourteenth Amendment, guaranteeing equal protection of the law, due process, and birthright citizenship. Lucretia wrote to Martha that Harriet was heading home, and that she had no money. "I very freely gave her the little I could, to aid her on her way to Auburn." Noting Harriet's account of her wartime service, and her rationale for Black suffrage, Lucretia continued: "If thou talk with her about the Freedmen & their right to vote—she may reply and enlarge as sensibly as she did here—she is a wonderful woman."

Martha agreed with Lucretia, Harriet, Phillips, and Douglass: if it proved politically impossible to simultaneously achieve two of the most profound changes in the Constitution ever undertaken—the vote for women and the vote for Black men—then women would have to wait a little longer. That put her at odds with her two closest colleagues. As drafted, the Fourteenth Amendment would grant the vote to "the male inhabitants" of each state—introducing the word *male* into the Constitution for the first time, and making no such provision for women. Stanton and Anthony, livid that after all of their labors to get the Thirteenth Amendment passed, women's rights once again were being shunted aside, were initiating a new petition, demanding that the Fourteenth provide equal protection of the law by sex as well as by race.

Martha had committed her career to women's rights, but to her it was inarguable that enslaved men were more wronged than white women. Although she agreed with Stanton that enfranchisement for one class should be extended to all, she now knew what Seward had meant in the January 1861 speech that she'd found so objectionable: "In political affairs, we cannot always do what seems to us absolutely best." Hoping to avoid choosing sides, Martha told Stanton that she would "rest on her oars" for a spell. Stanton blamed Phillips for Martha's abdication, telling him that even women such as Martha Wright wouldn't sign the petition because the abolitionist "priesthood"—Phillips, Douglass, and Garrison—opposed it. Stanton wrote to Anthony that once the word *male* was introduced into the Constitution, it would take a century to get it out again: "I have argued constantly with Phillips and the whole fraternity, but I fear one and all will favor enfranchising the negro without us. Woman's cause is in deep water."

Stanton then turned to her usually loyal associate: "Martha, what are you all thinking about that you propose to rest on your oars in such a crisis? I conjure you and Lucretia to be a power at this moment in taking the onward step." Unable to refuse Stanton when she issued a direct order, Martha agreed to rejoin the movement. Stanton was relieved that she remained "sound at the core," adding, "I have been out of patience with men, women, and fate."

• • •

Harriet left Roadside in time to board the 11:00 p.m. train to New York City. Black passengers were forced to sit in the smoking car, in the back of the train, but she was an army veteran, and had a discount ticket that allowed her to ride with white travelers. When she presented it to the conductor, she later told Martha, he said, "Come, hustle out of here! We don't carry niggers for half fare." Harriet informed him that she had the right to travel with the other passengers. He grabbed her arm, warning, "I'll make you tired of trying to stay here."

The conductor hadn't reckoned on Harriet's tenacity. Grabbing hold of the seat, she told him that he was a Copperhead scoundrel. Furthermore, she didn't thank anybody to call her a colored person. She said she would be called Black or Negro—she was as proud of being a Black woman as he was of being a white man. Harriet had large, strong hands, and it took the conductor and two passengers to wrench her loose, injuring her hand, arm, and ribs as they forced her into the smoking car.

Harriet stopped in Brooklyn, where she gave a talk at the African Methodist Episcopal Church on Bridge Street, her arm in a sling. The church was full of congregants, white and Black, who wanted to hear the famous "She Moses" speak. The pastor introduced her, and read aloud the letters she had collected from Secretary of State Seward and her army commanders, testifying to her valuable work in the war. She had an unrivaled American success story to tell. Speaking about her lack of education, she said she wasn't brought up, but "came up." Then, after claiming that she wasn't fit to mix in political matters, she mentioned her friendships with John Brown and William Lloyd Garrison. She talked about the bravery and suffering of the soldiers who had won the war, and about her experiences in South Carolina and Florida. Now she intended to pursue equality for Black Americans and for all women. Harriet traveled the rest of the way without incident, and settled permanently into her small farmhouse in Auburn, one of the few women in the country who owned a home of her own.

28

Wrongs and Rights

1865–1875

Harriet Tubman, ca. 1911

Martha, who had been overwhelmed in the 1840s and '50s by the "thousand annoyances of the nursery and kitchen," found contentment as a sixty-three-year-old grandmother. After Stanton's reprimand about resting on her oars, she resumed her position in the women's rights movement, but she excused herself when her children asked her to help with their offspring. She admitted to Ellen's husband, William Garrison Jr., that David was right to say she was constantly preoccupied by one child or another: who wouldn't be, "with 13 grandchildren all to have teeth &

mumps & Scarlet fever & measles & whooping cough & lovers & weddings & things!" Martha's sons- and daughters-in-law welcomed her involvement in their lives, and she had a particular bond with William, who met her standards as a correspondent, and had an off-kilter sense of humor similar to hers. In an afterthought to one long letter to him, writing sideways across the top of the crowded first page, Martha asked, "Did you read about that unlucky man who threw a stone at a dog, & it killed his mother-in-law?"

Harriet often stopped by Martha's house, where they shared news about family and friends, and talked about Republican plans for Reconstruction. On her first visit, in autumn 1865, her injured arm in its sling, she looked like a battle-scarred soldier—as she was, in all but the most literal sense. Telling Martha about the conductor's attack, she showed her a visiting card a young white man had given her as he got off the train. He had advised her to sue the railroad company, saying that he would serve as a witness. Martha, furious about the incident, told David that they should pursue a lawsuit. He contacted Wendell Phillips's son-in-law at the American Anti-Slavery Office in New York, paid for newspaper advertisements asking the man to come forward, and wrote to George W. Smalley, the chief war correspondent for the *Tribune*, hoping to interest him in a story about the incident. The witness did not appear, the story wasn't written, and the effort stalled.

Harriet began to restore her seven acres as a working farm, with a vegetable garden, chickens, hogs, and the apple trees—a reminder of the orchards of her childhood that had eased her hunger. But she had no income, and could barely make ends meet. She was responsible for a multigenerational family: her niece Margaret, who moved back from the Seward House; her elderly parents; a sister-in-law and her two children; a newly married niece and her husband; and a penniless boarder. As word got out about her generosity, she began to offer indigent people a temporary place to stay. She welcomed baskets of food as neighborly gestures, and responded in kind when she could. On one occasion, hearing that Ellen was visiting Martha with her first two children, Agnes and Charles, she rushed over with a gift of fresh eggs.

Martha and Harriet kept up with Lazette, and they found some comfort in sharing their memories of Frances while sadly witnessing Fanny's decline. Harriet had seen many soldiers die from tuberculosis, and knew that Fanny couldn't live much longer. Seward treated her with extra tenderness, while refusing to face the truth. Fanny asked him to instruct her in politics, but she lacked her mother's political acuity, and he told her that he didn't want to subject her to needless anxieties. Then, in a confounding erasure of Frances's counsel of forty years, he claimed, "So I always dealt with your mother, and she had an easier life for leaving political troubles to me; and I the easier life, by leaving the affairs of home and children, exclusively to her." Fanny had never found fault with her father, but the remark must have left her baffled and indignant.

On October 29, 1866, Harriet had one of her premonitions. She saw a chariot in the air, she told her minister, "going south and empty." When it returned, lying inside, "cold and stiff," was "the body of a young lady who had recently gone to Washington with her father." Fanny, twenty-one years old, died that day at the Club House on Lafayette Square, with Lazette and her father beside her. Lazette confessed to Emily Howland, who came to express her sorrow, that the loss of Frances and Fanny had left her with no desire to live. Howland couldn't understand how Seward carried on without the wife and daughter who had sustained him. As she looked at him "pale and feeble and old," she "wondered how he could turn back from the second grave to political schemes and tricks with any heart in them." Martha knew that if Frances had lived, she would have implored Seward to resign rather than serve under Andrew Johnson.

Martha spent the early months of 1866 helping Stanton and Anthony prepare for their long-awaited Eleventh National Woman's Rights Convention, to take place in New York City on May 10. It was the first time that women's rights activists had gathered since the start of the war, but they nonetheless had made themselves heard. After the Loyal League petition drive for the Thirteenth Amendment, they had collected thousands of signatures for women's suffrage, and sent them on to Congress. Stanton, reminding Wendell Phillips how much women had contributed to Black freedom, argued that abolitionists and women's rights activists must continue to "stand side by side in this crisis of our nation's history." Although Phillips disagreed about giving the two causes equal weight, he assured her that he would never put an obstacle in the way of women lobbying for the vote. In a show of good faith, he supported their call for the convention, as did Douglass and other champions of suffrage for Black men. It seemed conceivable that the disagreement between Stanton and Anthony and the abolitionist "priesthood" could be put to rest.

Instead, the normally controlled discord over race boiled over. Stanton knew that Black men, whose military service had made the Union victory possible, had the political advantage. She said preemptively in her opening address: "We press our demand for the ballot at this time in no narrow, captious or selfish spirit; from no contempt of the black man's claims." On the contrary, the women acted from "the purest patriotism, for the highest good of every citizen, for the safety of the Republic, and as a spotless example to the nations of the earth." But Phillips, their ally of many decades, was in no mood to be mollified. Yes, he conceded, "A vote is a great thing. Legislation is a large power." But at a time when the Black vote for men was within reach and the vote for women was not, women should concentrate on pushing their way into the business world and achieving equality in education. "When you come to the woman question," Phillips lectured his largely female audience, "the first great abiding difficulty is that woman is herself the obstacle." And, disregarding his promise not to get in the way of their work, he said, "Nothing can help you up at Albany. No ballot-box will help you." Phillips, the son of an influential Boston family and a graduate of Harvard College, went on, "Let woman know that nobody stops her but herself. She ties her own limbs. She corrupts her own sisters." Stanton's ally Matilda Joslyn Gage, not one to be patronized, shot back that from the earliest days of the republic, the men who wrote the laws had kept women out of public life. Generation after generation of women were forced to stay home, wash the dishes, and mend the stockings: "This hand of restriction was put around her brain, and every day it was tightened."

African American women, so often overlooked by abolitionist men and white women's rights activists, had their own scores to settle. One of the speakers, Frances Ellen Watkins Harper, a forty-one-year-old poet, abolitionist, and women's rights advocate, had long argued, "As much as white women need the ballot, colored women need it more." She made the audience take stock of America's worst injustices by talking about the train conductor's assault on Harriet Tubman: "That woman who had led one of Montgomery's most successful expeditions, who was brave enough and secretive enough to act as a scout for the American army," Harper said, "had her hands all swollen from a conflict with a brutal conductor, who undertook to eject her from her place. That woman, whose courage and bravery won a recognition from our army and from every black man in the land, is excluded from every thoroughfare of travel." Harper, too, in a recent trip between Washington and Baltimore, had been forced to move to the back of the train: "Aye, in the capital of the nation, where the black man consecrated himself to the nation's defence, faithful when the white man was faithless, they put me in the smoking car!" Martha, hoping to make headway with the lawsuit, informed the convention that the company responsible was the Camden and Amboy Railroad.

Harper stole Stanton's show. The nation, she said, "standing upon the threshold of a great peril, reached out its hands to a feebler race, and asked that race to help it." When the peril was over, Black men were told, "You are good enough for soldiers, but not good enough for citizens." She concluded, "You white women speak here of rights. I speak of wrongs." And, in an inspired flourish: "I do not believe that white women are dew-drops just exhaled from the skies."

Stanton and Anthony's goal was to formally unify the two movements with a new organization, which would demand universal suffrage, and Anthony introduced the key resolution: now that "the negro and the woman" had the same civil and political status, they needed only the ballot: "Hereafter we shall be known as the 'AMERICAN EQUAL RIGHTS ASSOCIATION.'" Martha seconded the resolution. Dismissing a snide remark from the audience that the name of the new group was an attempt to banish the odious phrase "woman's rights," Martha explained that every good cause once had been odious: "We desire the change, because we feel that at this hour our highest claims are as citizens, and not as women. I for one have always gloried in the name of Woman's Rights, and pitied those of my sex who ignobly declared they had all the rights they wanted."

Still, Martha saw the logic behind all three arguments: Stanton and Anthony's (for the woman's vote), Phillips's (for the Black man's vote), and Harper's (for Black women and men to be accorded every right granted to white people). Seventy-three-year-old Lucretia, who had spent half a century fighting for human rights for all, was elected president of the new association. She was tired at the thought of the difficulties ahead. After meeting privately with Stanton and Anthony in New York, she complained to her family that just listening to them made her ache all over. She sighed, "You see how little rest, this side of Jordan, there is for the aged."

Douglass too joined the new group, and he thanked Stanton for "the launching of the good ship 'Equal Rights Association.'" But at the association's first convention, six months later, he drew the same distinction that Phillips did: for white women, the vote was "a desirable matter"; for Black men, disenfranchisement was "a question of life and death." Stanton and Anthony could not accept that truth. In the 1840s and '50s, they had consistently argued that voting was a right. Now they said that it was a privilege of citizenship that people must be worthy to exercise.

In the fall of 1867, they expressed that new position in the most offensive way conceivable. In Kansas, the old proving ground over slavery, voters were considering two ballot initiatives: one to amend the state constitution by enfranchising Black men, the other by enfranchising women. Stanton and Anthony traveled 1,600 miles to canvass there. Betraying their own organization's pledge to support suffrage for both "the negro and the woman," they stumped only for the women's vote. Worse, they invited George Francis Train—a wealthy entrepreneur from Omaha, would-be presidential candidate, and unabashed racist—to join them. "Woman first, and negro last, is my program," Train said, adding that he was willing that intelligence should be the test. The two groups did little to convince voters, who defeated both measures.

Lucy Stone, who went to Kansas with her husband, Henry Blackwell, to campaign for both measures, wrote that Train was "a lunatic, wild and ranting." Garrison called him "one of the greatest despisers of the negro race living." Rather than heeding this response, Stanton and Anthony accepted Train's offer to subsidize a weekly suffrage newspaper, *The Revolution*, and began publishing it in January 1868. They printed his tirades and wrote their own. Stanton contrasted the "pauperism, ignorance, and degradation" of the freedmen with the "wealth, education, and refinement of the women of the republic." If the vote could only be granted to one group of people at a time, it should be given first to women, at least to "the most intelligent and capable."

Stanton ineffectually defended herself to Martha: "Mr. Train is a pure, high-toned man, without a vice." Yes, he had "some extravagances and idiosyncrasies," but "it seems to me it would be right and wise to accept aid even from the devil himself, provided he did not tempt us to lower our standard."

Martha saw that Stanton, normally so clear in her logic, was past the point of reason. Thinking that she could disabuse her and Anthony of their worst impulses, as she had in the past, Martha signaled her disapproval by saying only, "I am sorry for the idiosyncrasies of Mr. Train." Lucretia was less forgiving. Deciding she could no longer justify working with Stanton and Anthony, she wrote to Martha about their newspaper, "The Revolution is not satisfactory." She withdrew from the American Equal Rights Association at its May 1868 meeting, recommending that it be disbanded. Martha, despite her discomfort, maintained her loyalty, telling David that she found Train loathsome, but that she chose to stand by old friends, even when they did unwise things. She did not see the similarity between her decision and Seward's to stay on in the Johnson administration—trying to exert a conciliatory influence over a leader who had become intolerant and immovable.

Martha envied Harriet her singular ability to avoid the hostilities among their friends, and to unite people behind a common cause. Acquaintances in Auburn of all ages called her "Aunt Harriet." Martha could think of no one else so free of animus. Harriet was still pledged to help the freed people of South Carolina remake their lives, and in 1868, she followed the prewar example of the female anti-slavery societies: orchestrating a Christmas fundraising fair. She made sure that articles were published in the *Auburn Daily*, and deputized Martha to make aprons, pincushions, and rag dolls; Martha's daughter Eliza to offer her house as the drop-off location for clothing donations; and other women to make their own crafts, cakes, and pies. She asked men for financial contributions.

Seward refused, thinking that Harriet carried Christian self-denial to an unhealthy extreme. He told her, "Harriet, you have worked for others long enough." If she asked for a donation for herself, he would give it to her, "but I will not help you to rob yourself for others." Charles P. Wood, a local banker, was more helpful. He wrote a detailed account of Harriet's "Services as a Scout," appending copies of the testimonials and notes she had saved from Seward, General Hunter, Colonel Montgomery, Brigadier General Saxton, and the two doctors she had served under, Dr. Durant and Surgeon General Barnes. By Wood's estimate, she was owed several thousand dollars.

In the meantime, Rev. Samuel Miles Hopkins, a professor at Auburn

Theological Seminary, and his sister, Sarah Bradford, aware that the gears of the government bureaucracy turned slowly, had come up with a different way to provide Harriet with some income. During the war, Bradford had taught Sunday school at Auburn's Central Presbyterian Church, where she'd gotten to know Ben and Rit Ross and some of the young women Harriet had brought north. Bradford was a successful children's book author, and, after conducting several interviews with Harriet, she wrote a biography along the lines of the slave narratives that had been popular in the antebellum years. She called the slim book *Scenes in the Life of Harriet Tubman*, admitting that she made "no claim whatever to literary merit," hoping only that its sales would "secure a little fund for the relief of this remarkable woman." Bradford included copies of the testimonials from the Union officers, and she asked Douglass to write one of his own.

Douglass's contribution, written in the form of a personal letter, contrasted his life as a newspaper editor and anti-slavery spokesman with Harriet's treacherous undercover work. Denied the privilege of literacy, she acted on her beliefs, in the face of incalculable physical pain and personal danger. "I have wrought in the day—you in the night," Douglass said. "I have the applause of the crowd and the satisfaction that comes of being approved by the multitude, while the most that you have done has been witnessed by a few trembling, scarred, and foot-sore bondmen and women, whom you have led out of the house of bondage, and whose heartfelt 'God bless you' has been your only reward. The midnight sky and the silent stars have been the witnesses of your devotion to freedom and of your heroism. Much that you have done would seem improbable to those who do not know you as I know you. Your friend, Frederick Douglass."

William G. Wise, the treasurer of the Auburn Woolen Company, undertook a subscription drive to cover the cost of printing *Scenes*, to which Will Seward Jr., David Wright, Gerrit Smith, Wendell Phillips, and a few dozen others contributed. J. C. Darby & Co. of Auburn produced a woodcut for the frontispiece depicting Harriet as a scout in a striped skirt, oversize jacket, and kerchief, a haversack across her chest, her hands resting on the barrel of a rifle, soldiers' white tents visible in the background. The Reverend Hopkins's grandson, the muckraking journalist Samuel Hopkins Adams, later wrote, "She was inordinately proud of that woodcut. Reference to it never failed to loosen her tongue."

The Bradford book was launched at Harriet's Christmas fair, where

Harriet was asked to speak about her life—a performance that a friend of Martha's said was as good as a play. Martha shipped copies of *Scenes* to Boston, asking William Garrison Jr., to sell them out of his office on Channing Street. Franklin Sanborn gave it a generous review in the *Springfield Republican*, saying that Tubman was providing clothes and books to two schools for the freed people of the South. The proceeds of the book sales enabled Harriet to pay an installment on her mortgage and to cover taxes and improvements on her home, and the fair raised the significant sum of $500 ($9,000 in 2020).

At the fair, Martha tried to take advantage of the holiday spirit by collecting signatures for Stanton's newest petition. The Fourteenth Amendment had been ratified that July, guaranteeing all citizens equal protection of the laws; it included the word *male*, but not the word *sex*. Congress was currently debating the Fifteenth Amendment, which guaranteed the right to vote, regardless of "race, color, or previous condition of servitude." Stanton and Anthony were hell-bent on accomplishing with the Fifteenth what they'd failed to do with the Fourteenth. But the people of Auburn, representing the wider resistance to the vote for women, were little more receptive than they'd been when Martha had begun petitioning decades earlier. She got only six signatures, and the usual snubs: "Suffrage—What's that?—Women vote? No!!! Perfect nonsense!!"

When it became clear that Congress would pass the Fifteenth Amendment unchanged, Martha supported it. Stanton and Anthony lobbied against it. Stanton said again and again, "Votes for all or votes for none." She occasionally conceded the difference between the "condition of the most fortunate women at the North" and the "living death colored men endure everywhere," and claimed that she and Anthony spoke "not for ourselves alone, but for all womankind." At the same time, she wrote in her most racially inflammatory language yet about the "unwashed and unlettered ditch-diggers, bootblacks, hostlers, butchers, and barbers" who would rule over women if Black men were granted the vote without them: "Think of Patrick and Sambo and Hans and Yung Tung" making the laws. "We object . . . we object . . . we object."

The Fifteenth Amendment was sent to the states for ratification after it was passed on February 26, 1869. A few months later, the American Equal Rights Association imploded. At its third annual meeting, Douglass said that when it came to women's rights and equal rights, there was no name greater than Elizabeth Cady Stanton's, but, he said, with nicely calibrated understatement, "my sentiments are tinged a little against *The Revolution,*" Stanton and Anthony's newspaper. It was a prelude to a scorching rebuttal: "When women, because they are women, are hunted down through the streets of New York and New Orleans; when they are dragged from their houses and hung upon lamp-posts; when their children are torn from their arms and their brains dashed out upon the pavement; when they are objects of insult and outrage at every turn; when they are in danger of having their homes burnt down over their heads; when their children are not allowed to enter schools; then they will have an urgency to obtain the ballot equal to our own." Martha, who was in Boston with Ellen, William, and their children, wrote to David: "I tho't Douglass' criticism on Mrs. Stanton good."

But Stanton and Anthony kept Martha close. The day after that disastrous meeting, the two formed their own group: the National Woman Suffrage Association, to pursue their strategy of obtaining a constitutional amendment and other radical reforms, such as changing divorce laws. Martha joined the national association, and in July, she traveled with Eliza to Saratoga Springs, to help form a state branch: the New York Woman Suffrage Association. The idea was proposed by their colleague Matilda Joslyn Gage, who believed in the efficacy of working at the state and local level, and in fighting for all the rights denied to women. Martha was elected president, and through intensive grassroots organizing, she, Gage, and their troops began to establish "political equality clubs" in nearly every county in New York.

Lucy Stone, trying to pull Martha out of Stanton and Anthony's orbit, wrote to her in August that she was founding her own group, the American Woman Suffrage Association, and she asked Martha to attend the first meeting. Stone supported ratification of the Fifteenth Amendment, and she was lobbying state-by-state for the woman's vote. Martha's decades of experience in New York and her philosophical affinity for Stone's approach would be great assets. Martha, though, replied that she didn't see how the single cause would be better served by two organizations: "In *union* there is strength," she implored. If women worked together, they would surely soon win the day, and "in our final triumph, forget all past differences." Stone got her husband, Henry Blackwell, to write to Martha, who reiterated that she stood above all "for the cause." Seeing that Stone's association was a fait accompli, Martha wished the couple every possible success, as she did Stanton and Anthony, who deserved "all the love & honor" for their "untiring devotion."

The next month, in January 1870, Martha went to Washington with a delegation from Stanton and Anthony's National Woman Suffrage Association to lobby for the vote in the District of Columbia. The territory of Wyoming had adopted suffrage for women in December 1869, and the association hoped that success would help its cause in the East. They were trying to do for women what John Quincy Adams and Seward had once tried to do for the enslaved people of Washington: make the case that the capital city should set a moral standard for the country. Stanton and Anthony spoke before Congress, at a two-hour joint committee hearing, an occasion, Martha wrote to David, that marked an era "in the history of our movement & of course the nation." Three months later, she published a rebuttal to an article in *The Nation*, by Lucretia's friend J. Miller McKim, who claimed that almost as many women as men opposed women's suffrage. Martha wrote curtly: "For more than twenty years, 'women duly authorized to speak' have reiterated their demands, which, except in a few instances have been denied or ignored. He who denies or ignores this fact reads our country's history to little purpose."

In 1874, Martha was elected president of the National Woman Suffrage Association. Unlike Stone's group, which included Henry Blackwell, Henry Ward Beecher, and Thomas Wentworth Higginson, Stanton and Anthony's organization was made up mostly of women—Martha, Matilda Joselyn Gage, and Ernestine Rose among them. Stanton and Anthony had always looked forward to Martha's turn chairing conventions. As Anthony said, "every word was to the point," and "her opinion on every question carried decisive weight" with officers and members of the audience. But even at that late date, Martha couldn't see it. She wrote to Stanton, "I dreaded inexpressibly the greatness thrust upon me, knowing so well my own limitations on the matter of speech making."

Before assuming her duties as chair, Martha went to Boston for the birth of Ellen and William's fourth child. They had one girl and two boys, and Ellen hoped for another girl, but after the baby was delivered, Martha wrote to Anthony, "Another scion of the House of Garrison was born." Ellen told William with feigned disappointment, "Another horrid boy."

William, a firm supporter of women's suffrage, wrote, "But he can vote!" They named the baby William Lloyd Garrison III.

On Martha's birthday, December 25, she made a notation in her diary: "Christmas—68 years old. Beautiful bright day." On the twenty-sixth, she sat with Ellen, knitting and helping with the baby, then went to see a play with William. Whenever she was in town, she attended lectures and other cultural events, but she had become jaded about the writing and talks by "the literary Lords" she'd once lionized. She wrote to Marianna about the Boston Radical Club, "Just between ourselves, I think these radical meetings a great humbug." Singling out Bronson Alcott, Louisa May Alcott's head-in-the-clouds father, she asked, "What do you think of Alcott's question? 'Is *is*, is, or is it isn't?' "

The next day, Martha came down with a fever and a cough, and when the doctor diagnosed probable pneumonia, Ellen telegraphed David and Eliza. David arrived two days later, on a Tuesday, and Eliza on Friday. By then, Martha was in a delirium. Ellen gratefully allowed Eliza to take over, noting to their cousin Maria Mott Davis, "She seemed so fresh and shiny—I believe the magnetism of her presence really affected Mother." David was undone by the sight of his stalwart wife unable to speak, and "so wearily struggling toward the end." Ellen sensed that Martha wanted her to hold her hand: "Even at the very last, when it was almost cold, she raised it & laid it across my lap." The family wrapped their hands in the blanket with hers, "for the touch of her flesh sent a chill to our marrow." Martha died on January 4, 1875.

Ellen contemplated how desolate the house in Auburn would be. "I don't know what my poor Father will do. It was sad enough to see him here so white and haggard. It seems as if we never could grow accustomed to her absence. I miss her regular letters already." David made a piercing confession in a memoir he wrote for his family: "Although you, my children, may not have any special reason to feel proud of the life work and memory of your father, you have great reason to feel a loving pride in the life work and memory of your mother."

Anthony wrote to Ellen about Martha: "So calm—So self-poised—so equal to every emergency." Saying that only one of Martha's daughters could take her place, she added, "What a tower of strength I always felt her to be on the platform with us." Ellen had declined to be a force in the movement, so it was Eliza who stepped up as Martha's successor, eventually becoming a leader of the New York State Woman Suffrage Association, working to amend the state constitution and broaden women's rights. Eliza's husband, Munson Osborne, had transformed his small business into one of the largest manufacturers of agricultural equipment in the country, and their palatial house at 99 South Street, built in 1879, replaced Stanton's and Martha's as "the center of the rebellion."

Eliza wished that her mother could have witnessed Frederick Douglass's final, ungrudging, tribute to what Martha had accomplished with Stanton and Anthony. In 1888, addressing the first meeting of the International Council of Women in Washington, a group the two had co-founded, Douglass said: "It was a great thing for humane people to organize in opposition to slavery; but it was a much greater thing, in view of all the circumstances, for woman to organize herself in opposition to her exclusion from participation in government." And, he said, "When a great truth gets abroad in the world, no power on earth can imprison it, or prescribe its limits, or suppress it."

Martha also bequeathed to Eliza her friendship with Harriet. Frances and Martha were gone, but Harriet, still in her early fifties, was as active as ever. Over the next few decades, Harriet and Eliza worked for the same causes, and considered each other family. Both belonged to Stanton and Anthony's association, and supported and spoke before Black and white women alike. In the 1890s, Eliza founded the Woman's Educational and Industrial Union in Auburn for the advancement of working-class women. Harriet visited Eliza each Sunday on her way to or from church, and Eliza fussed over her when she was plagued by headaches, seizures, and poor health. As Harriet got older, Eliza wouldn't allow her to refuse assistance. Learning that Harriet's cookstove had given out, she ordered a new one, and as the house fell into disrepair, she sent out a carpenter to replace some shingles and windows and put in a new cistern.

Ellen and Marianna saw Harriet less frequently, but they knew her almost as well as Eliza did, from the indelible written portraits their mother had left behind. Two of Martha's letters were especially memorable: the one to Ellen in 1860, when Harriet appeared at the house with seven fugitive slaves on her final underground railroad expedition; and another to Marianna, dated November 9, 1865, just after Harriet returned from the war. Harriet's physical courage and her dignified reproof to the train conductor had struck Martha as forcefully as any story she knew of wartime valor: a Black woman who had spent three years defending her country telling a white man of no particular distinction that he could insult and attack her, but he could not force her to demean herself.

Martha wrote to Marianna that by the time Harriet left, it was 28 degrees and a dry snow had fallen. The sun was low in the sky. A new load of coal had just been delivered to the house. As Martha walked Harriet to the door, thinking about stoking the furnace and preparing supper before David came in, she remarked that it was cold, and getting hard to see. Harriet told her she didn't care about that. She would just as soon go in the dark as in the light.

Epilogue

The First Wave, left to right: Stanton, Douglass, two unidentified participants, and Martha

Monuments always obscure more than they reveal. Although Frances's presence can be felt in the Seward House Museum, at 33 South Street, it is a shrine to her husband. The south wing, built soon after her death, in 1866, contains a drawing room adorned with a grand piano and a four-foot papier-maché globe, and a dining room that dwarfs the size of the room Frances helped design in 1848. The table, set with a white linen tablecloth, fine china, and heavy silver, seats twenty-four. In the original north-side parlor, portraits of Henry and Frances painted in 1843 hang on either side of the fireplace, depicting the rising young politician and his winsome wife. The other portraits are of John Quincy Adams and Thurlow Weed. The parlor leads into Henry's library, where three walls of heavily laden bookshelves display much of his 5,200-volume collection. Above a glass-fronted cabinet holding Fanny's books is a photograph of Henry and

Fanny taken by Mathew Brady in Washington in 1855. Frances's books are scattered through the house.

In 1877, a wide, curving staircase was built toward the back of the foyer, its banister made from the wood of local black walnut, butternut, and cucumber trees. The second-floor hallway is lined from baseboard to ceiling with portraits of the people Seward consorted with over his long career: kings, queens, and princes; emperors and empresses; counts, dukes, and lords; and the two presidents he served, Abraham Lincoln and Andrew Johnson, the best and worst of American leaders. Next to the door of Judge Miller's bedroom hangs an 1862 photograph of Frances reading in the garden, an image of apparent ease.

Martha and David's house, around the corner at 192 Genesee Street, was razed in 1880. A marker by the sidewalk reads: "MARTHA COFFIN WRIGHT, with sister Lucretia Mott, an organizer of the 1848 women's rights convention. Underground railroad stop." Martha herself is immortalized at the Visitor's Center at Seneca Falls in a nearly life-size bronze statue, standing alongside Stanton, Lucretia, Douglass, and others who planned and attended the convention. She is heavily pregnant, her bonnet tied under her chin, gloves in hand, her Empire dress cinched above her belly.

As Martha had expected, her descendants perpetuated her political legacy. Her daughter Ellen never did address suffrage meetings, but in the 1880s, she attended them with Martha's favorite son-in-law, William Garrison Jr., who was a frequent speaker. Ellen's and William's daughter Eleanor became an organizer for the National American Woman Suffrage Association, the group formed in 1890 by Stanton, Anthony, and Lucy Stone after they finally put aside their disagreements. Ellen's older sister Eliza was a leader in the state and national suffrage associations for the rest of her life. Eliza's daughter Helen Osborne Storrow chaired the international Girl Scouts association for eight years, and donated to causes ranging from land conservation to improving the lives of immigrants. Her son Thomas Mott Osborne chaired New York State's first commission on prison reform, then started the Mutual Welfare League, which grew into the Osborne Association—today one of the country's largest prison reform groups. As of 2020, Martha's great-great-granddaughter Lucretia Mott Osborne Wells was vice president of the board of directors.

• • •

By 1902, eighty-year-old Harriet Tubman was the only surviving member of the three original Auburn agitators. That November, Eliza invited six women to her house at 99 South Street. Elizabeth Cady Stanton had died the previous month, shortly before her eighty-seventh birthday, and Eliza wanted to honor her, and to discuss the next stage of the movement. Her guests included her sister Ellen; Susan B. Anthony; Emily Howland; Gerrit Smith's daughter, Elizabeth Smith Miller; and Rev. Anna Howard Shaw, a doctor who gave up medicine and her ministry at two churches in order to pursue temperance and the vote full-time. After five decades of organizing, women had achieved a great deal. They could attend college and become doctors, lawyers, and ministers, and they were speaking in growing numbers about suffrage. In half of the country, women could vote in school board elections, and women in Wyoming, Colorado, Utah, and Idaho had secured full voting rights. Eliza and her friends vowed to carry on until every adult woman in every state could go to the polls—a battle that was won nearly two decades later, in 1920, when the Nineteenth Amendment was ratified.

Eliza's sixth guest that day was Harriet Tubman. Walking up South Street from her house, almost a mile away, Harriet arrived a little late. She was a legendary figure from another era. Lucretia had died in 1880, and Lazette in 1875. Anthony herself was eighty-two. Harriet had survived her second husband, Nelson Davis, a much younger veteran of the Civil War. In 1897, Queen Victoria, moved by Tubman's underground railroad exploits, had invited her to attend her Diamond Jubilee. When Harriet politely declined, the queen sent her a silver medal, struck for the occasion, and a delicate white lace and linen shawl. Harriet eked out an existence with help from family and friends, and two small stipends from the government: eight dollars a month as Davis's dependent, and an additional twelve dollars a month for her wartime nursing duties. Harriet was now planning her "final work": a home for elderly, impoverished African Americans. In the course of a long, prodigious fundraising campaign, she acquired twenty-five acres abutting her property in Auburn, and formed a partnership with her place of worship, Auburn's African Methodist Episcopal Zion Church. As the women welcomed Harriet, she said in her fond, frank way that it was the last time they would all be there together.

Five years later, Frank C. Drake, a reporter for the *New York Herald*, which had changed ownership and its political stance, heard about Tubman's project, and in September 1907, as the home was nearing completion, he traveled to Auburn to interview her. Harriet was thin and stooped, but she retained her sense of command, and used the conversation to create one more record of her life. When Drake probed about her straitened circumstances, she said, "You wouldn't think that after I served the flag so faithfully I should come to want under its folds." But she wasn't asking for pity. She instructed him to write that she was a member of the Women's Auxiliary of the Grand Army of the Republic—a group of Union veterans who lobbied for their rightful benefits.

Then, thinking about the apple orchards of the Eastern Shore, Harriet asked, "Do you like apples?" The reporter said he did.

"Did you ever plant any apple trees?" He hadn't.

"No, but somebody else planted 'em. I liked apples when I was young, and I said, 'Some day I'll plant apple trees myself for other young folks,' and I guess I done it."

The Harriet Tubman Home for Aged and Infirm Negroes, at 180 South Street, opened to fanfare on June 23, 1908: a parade down South Street with a Black marching band from Ithaca, a formal dinner, and speeches. "I did not take up this work for my own benefit," Harriet said in her remarks. "All I ask is united effort, for united we stand, divided we fall." She housed ten residents in a brick building, which she named John Brown Hall. A photograph taken around 1911, when she was eighty-eight, shows her sitting in front of the hall, wrapped in a voluminous white throw. She looks ethereal but tenacious, her eyes clear and challenging, her powerful left hand gripping the arm of her chair.

Harriet spent her last few years as a resident of the Harriet Tubman Home. Her friend Mary B. Talbert, a founder of the National Association for the Advancement of Colored People, visited her in February 1913. As Talbert got up to leave, Harriet took her hand, asking her to "tell the women to stand together for God will never forsaken us." The following month, on March 10, gravely ill with pneumonia, Harriet quoted from the Gospel of John to her family and friends: "I go away to prepare a place for you, and where I am you may be also." She died that day at age ninety-one, and she was buried at Fort Hill Cemetery, with the silver medal from Queen Victoria, her casket draped in the American flag.

Shortly after Harriet's funeral, the Auburn *Citizen* published a letter to the editor from a resident, G. Howard Carter, who said he was writing "on behalf of the colored people of Auburn and the entire country for that matter." He wanted to honor one of Tubman's close friends. "Mrs. Seward," he wrote, was "directly interested in Harriet Tubman." Explaining Frances's silence "as to her many deeds of kindness to the colored people," he said that the great majority of them were never known. The Black community, though, had handed down the story of Frances's friendship with Harriet, and of her obdurate advocacy for Black education, emancipation, and equal rights. "Upon numberless occasions," Carter wrote, Mrs. Seward "has come to the rescue of the colored people in Auburn where her memory will always be kept green and her deeds will not die."

Auburn citizens raised money for a plaque honoring Harriet Tubman's "unselfish devotion to the cause of humanity." At the unveiling, Julia Ward Howe's, "Battle Hymn of the Republic" was played, and Booker T. Washington, president of the Tuskegee Institute in Alabama, gave the keynote address. Referring to Tubman's lack of any formal learning and the hardships she had overcome, he called her "one of the best educated persons who ever lived in this country." Harriet's grandniece Alice Lucas Brickler unveiled the plaque, which was nailed to the right of the doors of the Cayuga County Courthouse. To the left was a plate honoring William H. Seward.

In 2017, the National Park Service and the Thompson Memorial AME Zion Church announced the establishment of the Harriet Tubman National Historical Park, which includes a renovation of the church at 33 Parker Street and her thirty-two acre property at 180 South Street. The park is a companion site to the Harriet Tubman Underground Railroad National Historical Park in Church Creek, Maryland.

At Fort Hill Cemetery, due west and down several hills from the Seward and Wright family plots, Harriet's grave can be found under a towering Norwegian spruce. A tribute etched on the back of her tombstone reads:

> To the Memory of HARRIET TUBMAN DAVIS Heroine of the Underground Railroad. Nurse and Scout in the Civil War. Born about 1820 in Maryland. Died March 10, 1913 at Auburn, N.Y. "Servant of God, Well Done."

On the windy early-summer day that I was there, visitors had left offerings along the top of the curved stone: tiny pinecones, a handful of smooth stones, two bunches of wild daisies, and three pennies showing the gaunt profile of Abraham Lincoln.

Acknowledgments

I am a journalist, not a historian, but for any writer, ideas can take a long time to germinate, and they start with the passions and discoveries of those who precede them. My interest in the history of radical resistance in the Finger Lakes region began when I was a college student there in the 1970s, and my professor and friend Mary Gerhart took me to the Seneca Falls Visitor Center. A decade later, while I was a Nieman Fellow at Harvard, I joined a graduate seminar taught by David Herbert Donald, who was working on his now classic biography of Abraham Lincoln. One of the great Civil War historians, Donald fueled my fascination with Lincoln, and sparked an abiding interest in Frederick Douglass and Charles Sumner and the cutthroat politics of the nineteenth century. It wasn't until 2007, when I stumbled across the unexplored partnership of Martha Wright, Frances Seward, and Harriet Tubman, that I thought I had a story to tell.

I was in Auburn, at the Seward House Museum, researching my previous book, *Nothing Daunted*, about my grandmother and her closest friend. They had grown up in town in the 1890s, and I'd just learned that, as small children, they had seen Harriet Tubman, an elderly woman by then, make her way up South Street. That image stayed with me as I took a tour of the Seward House Museum. The animated young education director, Jennifer Haines, wanted to talk about Mrs. Seward, not about her illustrious husband—showing me the basement kitchen where Frances harbored freedom seekers, and talking about Frances's role in the famous Freeman case. When Jennifer said she had transcribed some of Frances's letters to Seward, I asked her to send me some of them. They felt eerily alive.

In the 1940s, an early Seward biographer, Glyndon Van Deusen, had discovered the family papers in the attic of the house, stuffed in trunks, valises, and armoires—to any researcher, the equivalent of buried treasure. In 1952, Frances and Henry's grandson, William Henry Seward III, donated the cache to the Rush Rees Library at the University of Rochester. I called a curator there, who told me that when the boxes were being sorted, Frances's correspondence was set aside as "worthless." Van Deusen had no interest in it, blithely dismissing Frances in his book as "a neurotic invalid." Subsequent biographers quoted selectively from the letters, but the vast majority of them had never been published or even read. Imagining the rare perspective they might offer on the most tumultuous decades in American history, I drove to Rochester to take a look. They were even more revelatory than expected, and I enlisted Jennifer in transcribing the entire lot. Her successor at the museum, Jeffrey Ludwig, shared Seward arcana with me by email, and volunteered several hidden gems. Many of the family papers are now accessible to the public through the Seward Family Digital Archive, an undertaking led by River Campus Libraries at the University of Rochester and the Digital Scholarship Lab.

Frances's letters led me to Martha. In 2004, an academic couple, Sherry Penney and James Livingston, published *A Very Dangerous Woman*, based on Martha's extensive correspondence. Their biography discussed her growing activism and touched on her friendship with Frances and Harriet. Martha's vibrant personality shone through her letters, which I began to examine in the Sophia Smith Collection at Smith College, with the help, over the years, of several students.

The legendary Harriet Tubman left no written record, and although Martha periodically wrote about her, Frances never did. Still, I had the accounts of other friends, many of whom wrote in detail about their conversations with Harriet. I also was lucky to have contemporary biographers to read and consult, especially Kate Clifford Larson, who published *Bound for the Promised Land* in 2004, after more than a decade of meticulous, wide-ranging scholarship. I met up with Kate on the Eastern Shore, and she drove me around Harriet's areas of operation in Dorchester and Caroline counties. She was extraordinarily generous with her time and contacts, and passed along some discoveries she made after her book was published.

Jeff W. Grigg was my guide to Harriet's work with the Union Army in South Carolina. The author of a compact, deeply researched book, *The Combahee River Raid*, Jeff lives just a few miles from Combahee Ferry. He spent a day driving me around the area, helping me to visualize the burning plantations, the causeway traversed by Colonel Montgomery's Black troops, and the brambles by the water's edge where Harriet tore her skirts as she helped people board the *Adams*.

I benefited from many others who preserve historic sites, homes, and archives. In Auburn, they include the staffs at the Harriet Tubman National Historical Park, the Seymour Public Library, and the Cayuga Museum of History and Art; and in Syracuse, the Onondaga Historical Association. Judith Wellman, the head of Historical New York Research Associates, has located underground railroad stations across Central New York, work that is essential to understanding the system's inner workings. The Harriet Tubman Underground Railroad National Historical Park in Church Creek, Maryland, and the Harriet Tubman annual Underground Railroad Conference in Cambridge were excellent resources, as were, in Charleston, the Fort Sumter National Monument and the South Carolina Historical Society. For information about Harriet's time in and around Beaufort, I made use of the Parris Island Museum, the Penn Center, and the Beaufort History Museum, and visited a mansion at 1001 Bay Street, which served as Union Hospital No. 15, where the pencil doodlings of soldiers are still visible on the plaster walls. Other collections include Houghton Library at Harvard, the Historical Society of Pennsylvania, the Friends Historical Library of Swarthmore College, and the Mabel Smith Douglass Library at Rutgers. In Washington, I availed myself of the National Archives, the Smithsonian National Museum of African American Art, and, at the Library of Congress, the division of Rare Books and Special Collections, and the Prints and Photographs Division. I'm very grateful to MacDowell for a fellowship in the fall of 2018, which gave me uninterrupted time to untie some knots in my narrative.

It is a big favor to ask busy people to read part or all of one's book, but many friends, old and new, gave crucial editorial guidance and support: David Remnick, Connie Bruck, Nick Trautwein, Mary Gerhart, Ann Hulbert, Ann McDaniel, Kate Larson, Adrian LeBlanc, Kate Walbert, Wanda Hendricks, Walter Stahr, Lori Ginzberg, Nancy Hewett, Jelani Cobb, David Blight, Jean Strouse, Sean Wilentz, Jennifer Haines, Jean Humez, Nell Freudenberger, Anne Garrels, Phillip Blumberg, Kylie Warner, Louise Knight, Carol Faulkner, Michael Long, Wayne Motts, Hal Higby, Barry Richardson, Tony Horwitz, David Grann, and Marc Leepson.

Thanks, too, for the insights and expertise of Anthony Cohen, Christopher Haley, Donald Ritchie, Catherine Clinton, Scott Christianson, Trudy Krisher, Virginia Cannon, Hendrik Hertzberg, Tom Mallon, Jeffrey Frank, Emily Stokes, David Connelly, Linda Frank, Amy Hague, Kate Long, Emily Kraft, Thomas Slaughter, Kenneth and Audrey Mochel, Laurel Auchampaugh, John Stauffer, Megan Marshall, Dori Gottschalk-Fielding, Charles Lenhart, Paula T. Whitacre, Linda Schwab, Norman Dann, Missy Warfield, Rev. Paul Gordon Carter, Kathleen Mackel, Ellen Mousin, Elizabeth Koenig, Barbara Connor, Lezlie Harper, Rosemarie Romano, Kristen Oertel, J.O.K. Walsh, Jayme Grodi, Amy Dru Stanley, Joanne O'Connor, Mike Connor, Susan Miller, and Susan Van Dyne.

I could not have finished this project without my painstaking, good-natured fact checker, Madeleine Baverstam, and the contributions of many industrious young transcribers and researchers: Veronica Oberholzer, Elyssa Spitzer, Tara Merrigan, Katie Mikulka, Marley Miller, Jaritza Sierra, Rebecca Ryder, Kimberly Garcia, Maxine Wagenhoffer, Hannah Wilentz, and Daniel Wenger.

The Agitators is in part about how families hand down their stories. I am beholden to the descendants of my three protagonists for discussing painful chapters of the past, and for allowing me to see some of the documents they have kept. From Martha's family: Frederik R. L. Osborne. From Frances's: Ray and Sue Messenger and Cornelia Rogers. From Harriet's: Judith Bryant and Pauline Copes Johnson.

Amanda Urban, the most patient and supportive of agents, retained her enthusiasm through several missed deadlines. Nan Graham, my rigorous editor and champion on *Nothing Daunted* as on this book, read more drafts than I like to remember, pointing out wrong turns and helping me create a lean, coherent narrative. Courtney Hodell made key structural suggestions and brought a sure sense of how to enliven the main characters. I'm also grateful to Nan's colleagues at Scriber, each of whom played a part in turning *The Agitators* from a raw manuscript into a handsome book, and in ushering it into the world: Erich Hobbing, Jaya Miceli, Dan Cuddy, Sarah Goldberg, Brian Belfiglio, Roz Lippel, Kate Lloyd, Brianna Yamashita, Zoey Cole, and Sabrina Pyun.

Above all, boundless thanks to my dear, long-suffering family, who countless times had to pull me away from my computer and out of the nineteenth century: Hermione Wickenden, David Wickenden, Cynthia Snyder, Dan Southerland Weiser, Norma Weiser, and, as ever, my husband, Ben: relentless investigative reporter, steely-eyed editor, and the staunchest partner conceivable. This book is dedicated to our daughters, Sarah and Rebecca. Their tough-minded observations about the country's continuing inequities are an inspiration, and they sustained me through the writing of *The Agitators*.

Notes

PART ONE: PROVOCATIONS (1821–1852)

1. A Nantucket Inheritance (1833–1843)

4 *Mary Coffin Starbuck*: Mary Coffin Starbuck's father was Tristram Coffin, Martha's great-great-great-grandfather. Mary Starbuck was the sister of Martha's great-great-grandfather, James Coffin. See Helen Stehling, "Mary Coffin Starbuck's Account Book with the Indians," Nantucket Historical Association, www.nha.org/history/hn/HN-fall1997-stehling.htm; www.womenhistoryblog.com/2008/10/mary-coffin-starbuck.html; Lydia S. Hinchman, *Early Settlers of Nantucket, 1659–1850: Their Associates and Descendants* (Philadelphia: Ferris & Leach, 1901), 160–61. The Wampanoags of Nantucket eventually perished of the plague and other imported diseases.

4 *A harpooned whale*: "Whales and Hunting," New Bedford Whaling Museum, whalingmuseum.org/learn/research-topics-overview-of-north-american-whaling/whales-hunting. *In 1800, Thomas*: Sherry H. Penney and James D. Livingston, *A Very Dangerous Woman: Martha Wright and Women's Rights* (Amherst: University of Massachusetts Press, 2004), 7–9. *But he was*: Carol Faulkner, *Lucretia Mott's Heresy: Abolition and Women's Rights in Nineteenth-Century America* (Philadelphia: University of Pennsylvania Press, 2011), 20–21.

4 *By 1789, the elderly*: "Founding of Pennsylvania Abolition Society, 1775," *Africans in America*, PBS; Eric Ledell Smith, "The End of Black Voting Rights in Pennsylvania: African Americans and the Pennsylvania Constitutional Convention of 1837–1838," Pennsylvania Historical and Museum Commission, *Pennsylvania History: A Journal of Mid-Atlantic Studies*, 1998. *Anna Coffin proudly*: famouskin.com/famous-kin-chart.php?name=8453+benjamin+franklin&kin=48707+lucretia+mott&via=8457+peter+folger.

5 *Anna, drawing on*: Penney and Livingston, 7–11; Eliza Wright Osborne, "A Recollection of Martha Coffin Wright by Her Daughter," thanks to Frederik R.-L. Osborne, Eliza's great-grandson.

5 *She had resented*: MCW to LCM, February 3, 1843, in Penney and Livingston, 15.

5 *Upon receiving a*: Penney and Livingston, 17–24.

6 *In 1826, not long*: Osborne, "Recollection of Martha Coffin Wright"; Penney and Livingston, 29, 31, 34–35.

6 *David Wright, the*: "David Wright," unpublished autobiography, part one, GFP; Theodore M. Pomeroy, "Sketch of the Life and Character of Mr. David Wright," May 17, 1898, GFP.

6 *"You complain of"*: MCW to DW, October 11, 1832. *In 1833, Anna moved back*: Penney and Livingston, 36.

7 *They stayed with*: Dorothy Sterling, *Lucretia Mott* (New York: Feminist Press at the City University of New York, 1999), 82–83; Faulkner, *Lucretia Mott's Heresy,* 60.

7 *Three years earlier*: Faulkner, *Lucretia Mott's Heresy,* 61–62; Sterling, 80.

7 *Garrison regarded slaveholding*: Henry Mayer, *All on Fire: William Lloyd Garrison and the Abolition of Slavery* (New York: W. W. Norton, 1998), xvi. At the time, Garrison conceded that the Constitution granted each state the right to make its own decision about slavery. See "American Anti-Slavery Society (AASS), American Abolitionist and Antislavery Activists: Conscience of the Nation," www.americamabolitionists.com/amemrican-anti-slavery-society.html.

8 *Describing him to*: MCW to DW, December 5, 1833. *As an afterthought*: Faulkner, *Lucretia Mott's Heresy,* 64–67; Sterling, 83.

8 *During a discussion*: Faulkner, *Lucretia Mott's Heresy,* 65. *The change was*: Louise Knight, "How Massachusetts Women Became Political: the Grimké Sisters' 1837 Antislavery Petition Campaign," lecture at Radcliffe Institute for Advanced Study, Harvard University, March 10, 2015, www.radcliffe.harvard.edu/video/louise-knight-how-massachusetts-women-became-political.

8 *Martha rapturously told*: December 8, 1833, Penney and Livingston, 41. *prevented from working*: Carol Faulkner email, July 19, 2020. The co-founders of the Philadelphia society included Lucretia's Quaker friend Mary Ann M'Clintock and her African American friends Charlotte Forten (the wife of James Forten, a wealthy Black sailmaker who had served in the Revolutionary War) and Charlotte's daughters Margaretta, Sarah, and Harriet; and the milliner Grace Bustill Douglass and her daughter Sarah Mapps Douglass, a schoolteacher. *Following the lead:* Sally Roesch Wagner, ed., *The Women's Suffrage Movement* (New York: Penguin Books, 2019), 45.

9 *In October 1835*: Mayer, 200–206; Patrick Brown, "The Garrison Mob of 1835, Boston," historicaldigression.com/2016/03/01/the-garrison-mob-of-1835-boston. See Harriet Martineau's account, womhist.alexanderstreet.com/awrm/doc7.htm. They resumed the meeting at the home of Maria Weston Chapman, who later served on executive committees of the Massachusetts Anti-Slavery Society, the New England Anti-Slavery Society, and the American Anti-Slavery Society. She edited the journal *The Non-Resistant* and *The Liberty Bell*, an annual anti-slavery gift book sold at fundraising fairs, and, when Garrison was away, *The Liberator*.

9 *By 1837, from*: Beth A. Salerno, *Sister Societies: Women's Antislavery Organizations in Antebellum America* (DeKalb: Northern Illinois University Press, 2005), Table A; Wagner, 44–45. *That May, in New*: Louise Knight, "The South Carolina Aristocrat Who Became a Feminist Abolitionist," Smithsonian.com, July 24, 2018; Faulkner, *Lucretia Mott's Heresy,* 72–73. *The delegates resolved*: Ann D. Gordon, ed., *African American Women and the Vote, 1837–1965* (Amherst: University of Massachusetts Press, 2018), 3–4.

10 *Lucretia regarded the*: Faulkner, *Lucretia Mott's Heresy,* 73.

11 *"The spinster has thrown"*: Ibid., 72–74. The editor was Col. William Leete Stone, and the paper, *New York Commercial Advertiser*.

11 *The ground floor*: "History of Pennsylvania Hall, Which was Destroyed by a Mob, on the 17th of May, 1838" (Philadelphia: Merrihew and Gunn, 1838), 3; Faulkner, *Lucretia Mott's Heresy,* 77–80.

11 *"I believe I"*: Ibid., 78.

12 *Moving into the*: "History of Pennsylvania Hall," Ibid., 137–56, 168–69. *Lucretia, unfazed by*: The letter was to Edward M. Davis, June 18, 1838, in Beverly Wilson Palmer, ed., *Selected Letters of Lucretia Coffin Mott* (Urbana and Chicago: University of Illinois Press, 2002), 43–44. Sarah Pugh, a founding member of the Philadelphia Female Anti-Slavery Society, held the meeting in her school.

12 *Provoked by disapproval*: Penney and Livingston, 68.

12 *Frances saw nothing*: Patricia C. Johnson, "I Could Not Be Well or Happy at Home . . . When Called to the Councils of My Country: Politics and the Seward Family," *University of Rochester Library Bulletin* XXXI, no. 1 (Autumn 1978), 49.

13 *She was a good*: Osborne, "Recollection of Martha Coffin Wright."

13 *They praised Pope's*: MCW to LM, March 1844. *The New-York Tribune*: Glyndon G. Van Deusen, *William Henry Seward* (New York: Oxford University Press, 1967), 48.

13 *"These ascetics give religion"*: Osborne, "Recollection of Martha Coffin Wright."

14 *The proposed bill:* It was first introduced in 1836 by Judge Thomas Hertel, a member of the state assembly. Two radical reformers—Ernestine Rose, the atheist daughter of a Polish rabbi, and the abolitionist Paulina Wright—were circulating a petition to pass it. See Judith Wellman, *The Road to Seneca Falls: Elizabeth Cady Stanton and the First Woman's Rights Convention* (Urbana and Chicago: University of Illinois Press, 2004), 135–54. *As one legislator*: Ibid., 145.

14 *Frances had approvingly*: *Lecture Delivered Before the Ogdensburgh Lyceum, on the Political Rights of Women*, 1837, Frances Seward's Scrapbook, Seward House Museum Collection; Wellman, *Road to Seneca Falls*, 152.

14 *To her embarrassment*: MCW to LM, December 1841.

14 *When the Wrights*: MCW to LM, May 13, 1846.

15 *One evening, Martha*: MCW to LM, August 24, 1846.

15 *"The only way"*: MCW to LM, March 11, 1844. *they could side*: See William Lloyd Garrison's preface in Frederick Douglass, *Narrative of the Life of Frederick Douglass, An American Slave, Written by Himself* (New York: Antislavery Office, 1845; Penguin Books, 1982), 42.

15 *the underground railroad*: Fergus M. Bordewich, *Bound for Canaan: The Epic Story of the Underground Railroad, America's First Civil Rights Movement* (New York: Amistad, 2005), 4–5.

16 *Governor Seward had*: Stephen J. Valone, "William Henry Seward, the Virginia Controversy, and the Anti-Slavery Movement, 1839–1841," *Afro-Americans in New York Life and History* 31, no. 1 (January 2007); Walter Stahr, *Seward: Lincoln's Indispensable Man* (New York: Simon & Schuster, 2012), 65, 69–71, 81–85; Paul Finkelman, "The Protection of Black Rights in Seward's New York," *Civil War History* 34, no. 3 (1988), 211–34; Jeff Ludwig, Director of Education, Seward House Museum. The second law was used to secure the release of Solomon Northrup, a free man who lived in Saratoga Springs. Northrup wrote in *Twelve Years a Slave* about how in 1841 he was kidnapped in Washington and sold as a slave to a planter in Louisiana.

17 *A large, emotional*: John Stauffer, *The Black Hearts of Men: Radical Abolitionists and the Transformation of Race* (Cambridge, MA: Harvard University Press, 2001), 208. *One Black guest*: Tony Horwitz, *Midnight Rising: John Brown and the Raid That Sparked the Civil War* (New York: Picador, 2011), 32.

17 *Martha loaned him*: Penney and Livingston, 57, MCW to LM, January 18, 1843.

2. A Young Lady of Means (1824–1837)

20 *Accompanied by her*: John M. Taylor, *William Henry Seward: Lincoln's Right Hand* (New York: HarperCollins, 1991), 19.

20 *One poem portrayed*: Kathryn Hughes, "Gender Roles in the 19th Century," *Discovering Literature: Romantics & Victorians*, British Library, May 2014, www.bl.uk/romantics-and-victorians/articles/gender-roles-in-the-19th-century. The poem, written some years later, was mockingly titled "Woman's Rights."

20 *Miller, though taciturn*: Thanks to Jeff Ludwig. *Frances oversaw the*: Thanks to Jennifer Haines.

20 *He was fussy*: Benjamin F. Hall, "Genealogical and Biographical Sketch of the Life of the late Honorable Elijah Miller," 112, William Henry Seward Papers, University of Rochester, River Campus Libraries, Rare Books and Special Collections.

21 *The eldest of*: Ibid., 6–11.

22 *Miller's worshipful biographer*: Ibid., 26. *The board originated*: *Both Sides of the Wall: Auburn and Its Prison*, an exhibit at the Cayuga Museum of History and Art, Auburn, New York.

23 *"I shall always"*: FAS to WHS, June 23, [1829]. *Under pressure from*: See "Emancipation in New York," slavenorth.com/nyemancip.htm, for a brief account of slavery in the state from the Revolutionary War through 1827.

23 *A contemporary recalled*: Mrs. S. Benton Hunt, 1888, Cayuga Museum of History and Art, Auburn, New York. *A friend found*: Emily Howland, "History of Quakers in Cayuga County, ca 1795–1825."

24 *As one of three*: William H. Seward and Frederick W. Seward, *The Autobiography of William H. Seward, from 1801 to 1834, with a Memoir of His Life and Selections from His Letters from 1831 to 1846* (New York: D. Appleton, 1877), 40, 45–47. There is an unproven account of Seward having fathered a child with a slave while he was in Georgia. See Stahr, *Seward*, 14.

24 *Henry moved to*: Stahr, *Seward*, 17–19. *One observer*: David W. Bartlett, *Modern Agitators: or Pen Portraits of Living American Reformers* (Auburn, NY: Miller, Orton & Mulligan, 1865).

24 *Frances and Henry*: Seward and Seward, 55. *Henry assured his father*: Van Deusen, *William Henry Seward*, 8.

25 *Henry regarded the*: Johnson, "I Could Not Be Well," 42.

25 *Returning from a*: Seward and Seward, 55–56.

26 *"I fear, abhor, detest"*: WHS to FAS, April 26, 1847; F. W. Seward, *Seward at Washington as Senator and Secretary of State: A Memoir of His Life, with Selections from His Letters, 1861–1872* (New York: Derby and Miller, 1891), 46; Stahr, *Seward*, 21–22. *"He would prefer"*: FAS to LW, January 15, 1843, https://sewardproject.org/18430115FMS_LMW1.

26 *Childbirth was a*: "Deaths in Childbed from the Eighteenth Century to 1935," pubmed.gov, U.S. National Library of Medicine, National Institutes of Health.

26 *One impeccably credentialed*: Elizabeth Cady Stanton, *Eighty Years and More: Reminiscences 1815–1897* (New York: T. Fisher Unwin, 1898; Northeastern University Press, 1993), 114.

27 *But Jackson was*: Stahr, *Seward*, 21–22, 24; Van Deusen, *William Henry Seward*, 12–13.

27 *"I think you"*: FAS to WHS, June 23, 1829.

27 *Weed, already adept*: Stahr, *Seward,* 27–28. *The trip was a*: Ibid., 32.

28 *Addressing "You dearest"*: FAS to WHS, August 1833; thanks to Jeff Ludwig. *"Do I actually?"*: Stahr, *Seward,* 33.

28 *Henry saw Weed*: Doris Kearns Goodwin, *Team of Rivals: The Political Genius of Abraham Lincoln* (New York: Simon & Schuster, 2005), 71.

29 *A local come-outer*: FAS to WHS, February 25, 1831. *After returning from*: FAS to WHS, February 1, 1831.

29 *Worden sometimes hit*: FAS to WHS, April 17, 1831.

30 *Frances, incensed to*: FAS to WHS, July 9, 1829; February 1, 1831.

30 *"Men have framed"*: FAS to WHS, April 17, 1831.

30 *"Mrs. T. was dressed"*: FAS to LW, February 7, 1832.

31 *One person whose*: Seward and Seward, 166, WHS to FAS, January 12, 1831. *"I believe Henry"*: FAS to LW, March 4, 1832.

31 *Frances wrote during*: FAS to WHS, February 15, 1829, thanks to Jeff Ludwig.

31 *One afternoon, her*: FAS to LW, September 27, 1833.

32 *Still, Frances was*: FAS to LW, December 23, 1833. For accounts of the Seward-Tracy entanglements, see Goodwin, 72–77; Van Deusen, *William Henry Seward,* 32–34; Stahr, *Seward,* 39, 44–45; Taylor, 36–37.

32 *In September 1834*: Goodwin, 74; Stahr, *Seward,* 40–43.

32 *But the upstart*: Stahr, *Seward,* 45. *"What a demon is"*: Goodwin, 75–76.

33 *"I who love you"*: FAS to WHS, February 1832. *Frances left Augustus*: Taylor, 38; Stahr, *Seward,* 46–47.

34 *a few of the tens of thousands*: Edward L. Ayers, *In the Presence of Mine Enemies: The Civil War in the Heart of America, 1859–1863* (New York: W. W. Norton, 2003), 22.

34 My account of the Sewards' journey was taken from Frederick William Seward's *Reminiscences of a War-Time Statesman and Diplomat, 1830–1915* (New York: G. P. Putnam's Sons, 1916), 9–16, and from Frances's journal of the trip, in the Collections of the Seward House Museum.

34 *But in early*: Robert Curtis Ayers, *From Tavern to Temple: St. Peter's Church, Auburn, the First Hundred Years* (Scottsdale, AZ: Cloudbank Creations, 2005), 107–11; Stahr, *Seward,* 49. *Frances remembered that*: FAS to WHS, January 1, 1837.

34 *Concerned that her*: Seward and Seward, 325.

35 *"There is a sort of"*: FAS to Harriet Weed—Thurlow Weed's daughter, who had been helping her take care of Cornelia—September 6, 1837; Goodwin, 80.

35 *Turnout was high*: Stahr, *Seward,* 57. *Frances, pregnant again*: Ibid., 58.

35 *Taking positions that*: Taylor, 45–47. *Frances was his*: Goodwin, xviii.

3. Escape from Maryland (1822–1849)

37 *Almost two centuries*: The scholar was Kate Clifford Larson, author of *Bound for the Promised Land: Harriet Tubman, Portrait of an American Hero* (New York: Ballantine, 2004), See pp. 16–17, 78–79. The three sisters who were sold were Lina, Mariah, Ritty, and Soph.

38 *When Tubman was*: The friend was Emma P. Telford. See her brief account of Tubman's life, "Harriet: The Modern Moses of Heroism and Visions," Cayuga County Museum, Auburn, New York, ca. 1905.

38 *"You are after"*: John W. Blassingame, ed., *Slave Testimony: Two Centuries of Letters,*

Speeches, Interviews, and Autobiographies (Baton Rouge: Louisiana State University Press, 1977), 415. Harriet's brother Henry gave this account. See Larson, 33–35.

39 *Harriet recalled that*: Telford, "Harriet." *At the age of nine*: Sarah Bradford, *Scenes in the Life of Harriet Tubman* (Auburn, NY: W. J. Moses, 1869; London: Forgotten Books, 2012), 12–13.

40 *In a case in*: Douglass, *Narrative*, 68–69. The girl was Douglass's wife's cousin. *Tubman began to*: Ednah Dow Cheney, "Moses," 34.

40 *Harriet's most grievous*: Kate Larson email, July 1, 2109. *Before setting off*: Jean M. Humez, *Harriet Tubman: The Life and the Life Stories* (Madison: University of Wisconsin Press, 2003), 177.

40 *"I had no bed"*: Telford, "Harriet." *"They wouldn't give"*: Statement of Mrs. William Tatlock, Earl Conrad/Harriet Tubman Collection, New York Public Library, Schomburg Center for Research in Black Culture, August 15, 1939. *The trouble in her*: Larson attributes the visions to symptoms of temporal lobe epilepsy, xvi, 3–44, 262–63.

41 *She could cut*: Bradford, *Scenes*, 75.

41 *Harriet's father, Ben*: Thompson Sr. stipulated in his will that Ben Ross should be freed five years after his death; Anthony C. Thompson inherited Ben and freed him in April 1840. See Larson, 70–71, 80, 24 n64.

41 *Thompson Jr. sometimes*: Larson, 63–64, 74. *Such inquiries were*: Stanley Harrold, *Subversives: Antislavery Community in Washington, D.C., 1828–1865* (Baton Rouge: Louisiana State University Press, 2003), 52. Maryland law stipulated that if slaves were sold, it must be by the age of forty-five; otherwise, owners often let them go once they were old and feeble, and posed a burden to the state. Atthow Pattison, Rit's original owner, presented her as a present to his granddaughter, Mary Pattison Brodess, who was Edward Brodess's mother. The wording in the Pattison will was ambiguous, and the lawsuit among the heirs continued long after Harriet and her family had fled. Kate Larson emails, November 17 and 20, 2015; December 22, 2018.

42 *As one said*: Harrold, 52. *Men who drove*: Larson, 56, 65.

42 *Harriet spoke to*: Bradford, *Scenes*, 14–16.

42 *Free people caught*: Douglass, *Narrative*, 123–24. *In one of them*: Bradford, *Scenes*, 16.

43 *On the night of*: Larson, 78. *The Levertons' home was*: www.swarthmore.edu/library/friends/URR_maryland_kelley.htm. *"I started with"*: Bradford, *Scenes*, 21.

43 *Eliza Brodess placed*: Larson, 79.

43 *As she was*: Bradford, *Scenes*, 18.

44 *She took shelter*: Statement of Mrs. William Tatlock; see Humez, 216–17.

44 *"There was such"*: Sarah Bradford, *Harriet Tubman, The Moses of Her People* (New York: G. R. Lockwood, 1886; Dover Publications, 2004), 18.

44 *City life was*: Catherine Clinton, *Harriet Tubman: The Road to Freedom*. (New York: Little, Brown, 2004), 46; Mayer, 173. Also see Gary B. Nash, *Forging Freedom: The Formation of Philadelphia's Black Community, 1720–1840* (Cambridge, MA: Harvard University Press, 1988).

44 *Harriet was directed*: Robert Purvis was married to Harriet Forten, a daughter of Harriet and James Forten. *The Vigilant Committee*: Larson, 114–15.

45 *Robert Purvis described*: Margaret Hope Bacon, "Lucretia Mott: Pioneer for Peace," *Quaker History* 82, no. 2 (Fall 1993), 63.

46 *William Still at first*: William Still, *The Underground Railroad: A Record of Facts, Authentic Narratives, Letters, &c.* (Philadelphia: People's Publishing, 1871), 297.

4. The Freeman Trial (1846)

48 *At about 9:30 p.m.*: This account was drawn from Andrew W. Arpey's *The William Freeman Murder Trial: Insanity, Politics, and Race* (Syracuse, NY: Syracuse University Press, 2003); Benjamin F. Hall, *The Trial of William Freeman, for the Murder of John G. Van Nest, Including the Evidence and the Arguments of Counsel . . .* (Auburn, NY: Derby, Miller, 1848), 22; and David Wright's unpublished memoir in the GFP.

48 *Henry, who had*: Van Deusen, *William Henry Seward,* 81. *He played games*: WHS to FAS, April 22, 1843.

48 *"The occurrence of"*: FAS to WHS, Seward and Seward, 786–77.

49 *A local lawyer*: The lawyer was Judge Miller's friend and biographer, Benjamin Hall, who wrote the definitive book about the case, *The Trial of William Freeman*, 22.

49 *"There is still"*: FAS to WHS, Seward and Seward.

49 *The* Auburn Daily: Arpey, 3–6. *"Fortunately, the law"*: Seward and Seward.

49 *He wrote to*: WHS to TW, May 29, 1846.

50 *"How much I"*: FAS to LW, July 1, 1846.

50 *At Henry's request*: Arpey, 64.

50 *When Seward joked*: Ibid., 60.

51 *Despite Henry's efforts*: *Both Sides of the Wall*, 3–4. Among the innovations at Auburn Prison was the use of electrocution to carry out the death sentence: the first execution by electric chair took place there in 1890.

51 *Henry and David decided*: Seward had tried the insanity defense, unsuccessfully, in a trial some weeks earlier. The white defendant, Henry Wyatt, also had been brutally treated in the prison, and he, too, appeared to be mad. While serving a sentence for burglary and larceny, he had killed another inmate. Seward's defense resulted in a hung jury. In Wyatt's second trial, he was convicted and sentenced to hang. See William Augustus Guy, *Principles of Forensic Medicine* (New York: Harper & Brothers, 1845), 259.

51 *Henry abhorred Van Buren*: Arpey, 31, 57, 100–104. *The patently partisan*: Ibid., 23, 28.

51 *The proceeding to*: Ibid., 63–65.

52 *When someone spoke*: Penney and Livingston, 59.

52 *He spoke for nine*: George E. Baker, *The Works of William Henry Seward, 1801–1872*, vol. 1 (Boston: Houghton, Mifflin, 1884), lxxx; John Austin diary, July 4, 1846; Goodwin, 86.

53 *Henry futilely objected*: Arpey, 66–67; John Austin diary, July 6, 1846.

53 *Henry put his*: Seward and Seward, 815. *Martha pointedly told*: MCW to LM, undated, 1846.

53 *The high drama*: B. F. Hall, *Trial of William Freeman,* 424.

54 *Henry appealed, arguing*: Stahr, *Seward,* 104.

54 *"I pray God"*: FAS to LW, October 3, 1846.

54 *"Poor Bill is gone"*: FAS to WHS, August 21, 1847.

54 *An autopsy on*: Arpey, 124–25. Henry's law partner, Samuel Blatchford, who decades later was appointed to the Supreme Court, assembled the pamphlet. *Weed's* Evening Journal: August 26, 1846; Arpey, 133.

5. Dangerous Women (1848–1849)

55 *she was impatient*: Penney and Livingston, 53; MCW to LCM, April 23, 1846.

56 *"one belonging to"*: Faulkner, *Lucretia Mott's Heresy*, 94.

56 *"I wish you were"*: Vivian Gornick, *The Solitude of Self: Thinking About Elizabeth Cady Stanton* (New York: Farrar, Straus and Giroux, 2005), 20. *A superb student*: E. C. Stanton, 33.

56 *Stanton, then twenty-four*: Elizabeth Cady Stanton, Susan B. Anthony, and Matilda Joslyn Gage, eds., *History of Woman Suffrage, Vol. 1, 1848–1861* (Rochester, NY: Charles Mann, 1889), 422. *Stanton had three*: Tracy A. Thomas, *Elizabeth Cady Stanton and the Feminist Foundations of Family Law* (New York: New York University Press, 2016), 9.

57 *Elizabeth's father gave*: Linda C. Frank, *An Uncommon Union: Henry B. Stanton and the Emancipation of Elizabeth Cady* (Auburn: Upstate NY History, 2016), 157; Scott W. Anderson, *Auburn, N.Y.: The Entrepreneur's Frontier* (Syracuse, NY: Syracuse University Press, 2015), 138. *Children learned to*: E. C. Stanton, 146.

57 *Afflicted with a*: E. C. Stanton, 147; Faulkner, *Lucretia Mott's Heresy*, 138–39. For a discussion of the women who preceded Elizabeth Cady Stanton in pursuing women's rights, see Lisa Tetrault's *The Myth of Seneca Falls: Memory and the Women's Suffrage Movement, 1848–1898* (Chapel Hill: University of North Carolina Press, 2014), 5, 14, passim. *Just a few months*: Wellman, 146–48; E. C. Stanton, 150.

57 *In the fall*: Penney and Livingston, 78–79. The *Gazette* published Martha's essay on September 23, 1846.

58 *One day, describing*: MCW to LCM, February 26, 1852. *Lucretia was entertained*: Penney and Livingston, 208; LM to MCW, September 8, 1855. *Martha wrote, "People"*: January 4, 1858.

58 *Fired up by:* Nancy Isenberg, *Sex and Citizenship in Antebellum America* (Chapel Hill: University of North Carolina Press, 1998), 4; "The First Convention Ever Called to Discuss the Civil and Political Rights of Women," Seneca Falls, New York, July 19, 20, 1848, Library of Congress, www.loc.gov/resource/rbnawsa.n7548/?st=text.

59 *"It was a severe"*: *Narrative*, 151.

59 *Douglass's* Narrative *was*: David W. Blight, *Frederick Douglass: Prophet of Freedom* (New York: Simon & Schuster, 2018), 11–17; Andrew Delbanco, *The War Before the War: Fugitive Slaves and the Struggle for America's Soul from the Revolution to the Civil War* (New York: Penguin Press, 2018), 151–54. *"My feet have been so"*: Douglass, *Narrative*, 72. *Douglass's mother, a*: Ibid., 48.

60 *By the time he*: Blight, *Frederick Douglass*, 191; Andrew Delbanco, *The Abolitionist Imagination* (Cambridge, MA: Harvard University Press, 2012), 8.

60 *Douglass replied to*: Nancy A. Hewitt, *Radical Friends: Amy Kirby Post and Her Activist Worlds* (Chapel Hill: University of North Carolina Press, 2018), 127. The friends were Amy Post, her sister Sarah Hallowell, their niece Mary Hallowell, and their friend Catherine Fish Stebbins.

60 *M'Clintock, a Quaker*: Lori D. Ginzberg, *Elizabeth Cady Stanton: An American Life* (New York: Hill & Wang, 2009), 56; *HWS1*, op. cit., 71; Faulkner, *Lucretia Mott's Heresy*, 138–39.

61 *A Quaker and*: Faulkner, *Lucretia Mott's Heresy*, 140.

61 *At eleven o'clock*: Ginzberg, *Elizabeth Cady Stanton*, 57–58.

62 *In his report*: Blight, *Frederick Douglass,* 196–97.

62 *Lucretia and Martha*: Faulkner, *Elizabeth Cady Stanton,* 141. *"I plead guilty"*: Penney and Livingston, 2.

63 *The new party*: The candidate of the Free Soil Party was Seward's old nemesis, the former president Martin Van Buren.

63 *"the grave of all"*: "Northern Whigs and Democrats," *North Star,* July 7, 1848.

63 *Unable to fully*: MCW to LM, August 21, 1848.

63 *"I can't help loving"*: MCW to LM, October 28, 1848.

64 *"That is Mrs. David"*: Ibid., 110.

6. Frances Goes to Washington (1848–1850)

65 *ridiculed as a:* Fergus M. Bordewich, "Review of 'Arguing About Slavery: The Great Battle in the United States Congress,'" *Smithsonian Magazine,* December 1996.

66 *As she wrote*: FAS to LW, August 1, 1843. *"I used to think"*: Seward and Seward, 672.

66 *"I trust, Mr. Seward"*: WHS to FAS, April 10, 1847, in F. W. Seward, *Seward at Washington,* 44.

66 *Henry, a prominent*: Stahr, *Seward,* 110.

66 *With four generations*: Jeff Ludwig emails, May 12 and 13, 2020.

67 *"Do not on any"*: FAS to WHS, October 11, 1848. *"This is our 24th"*: FAS to WHS, October 21, 1848.

67 *At Tremont Temple*: Stahr, *Seward,* 110. *"Slavery can be"*: George E. Baker, ed., *The Life of William H. Seward with Selections from His Works* (New York: Redfield, 1855), 128–29.

67 *alongside a Democrat*: The Democrat was Daniel S. Dickinson. *"Disinterested benevolence must"*: FAS to LW, February 12, 1849.

68 *sleeping on straw-stuffed*: Van Deusen, *William Henry Seward,* 118; FAS to LW, December 9, 1849. *The Capitol was*: J. D. Dickey, *Empire of Mud: The Secret History of Washington, DC* (Guilford, CT: Lyons Press, 2014), xvi; www.aoc.gov/history-us-capitol-building; "The Washington Canal: Cesspool in the Midst of the Nation's Capital," April 1, 2012, www.blogger.com/profile/15964632266455220663.

68 *Robey's Tavern, the*: Mallhistory.org/explorations/show/mall-slavery; Dickey, 16–17, 77–78. *"A fouler spot scarcely"*: Dickey, 80.

69 *One of four*: FAS to LW, December 14, 1849.

69 *She wrote to Lazette:* FAS to LW, December 21 and 29, 1849.

69 *Frances wasn't sure*: FAS to LW, January 15, 1849. *It was, she*: FAS to LW, December 29, 1849.

70 *If he had*: FAS to LW, February 10, 1850. *"Whatever my own"*: FAS to LW, February 10, 1850.

71 *Frances sat in*: *William Henry Seward,* 120–21.

71 *In the summer*: FAS to WHS, July 29 and 31, 1839. *She had felt*: FAS to LW, Feb 10, 1850.

71 *In the visitors'*: John C. Waugh, *On the Brink of Civil War: The Compromise of 1850 and How It Changed the Course of American History* (Lanham, MD: Rowman & Littlefield, 2003), 77.

72 *Clay took the floor*: F. W Seward, *Seward at Washington,* 118; Robert V. Remini,

Henry Clay: Statesman for the Union (New York: W. W. Norton, 1991), 732. babel.hathitrust.org/cgi/pt?id=uc1.b2825614&view=1up&seq=7.

72 *"He is a charming"*: FAS to LW, February 10, 1850. Their *Henry saw:* Stahr, 131.

72 *Senator Calhoun, who*: "The Positive Good of Slavery," speech before the U.S. Senate, February 6, 1837. The colleague was Virginia senator James Mason, the author of the new Fugitive Slave Act. Calhoun died a few weeks later.

73 *"I wish to speak"*: "The Constitution and the Union," March 7, 1850; Goodwin, 144–45.

73 *Frances thought Webster*: FAS to LW, March 10, 1850.

73 *Henry wasn't given*: Goodwin, 145–46.

74 *"There is a higher"*: William H. Seward, "Freedom in the New Territories," March 11, 1850. Seward was borrowing the phrase from Rufus King, a founder and a senator from New York, from 1813 to 1825. See John Stauffer in Delbanco, *Abolitionist Imagination*, 72: "King stunned both Northern and Southern colleagues by interpreting the Constitution through an abstract reading of the principles of freedom and equality in the Declaration of Independence," and 48, about nineteenth-century believers in the higher-law idea.

74 *The* Richmond Enquirer: Van Deusen, *William Henry Seward*, 124–25. *On the floor*: Remini, 748.

74 *the week after*: FAS to LW, March 21, 1850. *But as people*: Senate.gov., op. cit. *The American and Foreign*: Van Deusen, *William Henry Seward*, 127; Stahr, *Seward*, 125. *"I never shall cease"*: FAS to LW, April 4, 1850.

74 *When Weed weighed*: Stahr, *Seward*, 126–27; WHS to TW, March 31, 1850.

75 *His birthday was*: *William Henry Seward*, 132–33.

75 *"To say that"*: FAS to WHS, July 11, 1850. *Henry was so*: FAS to WHS, July 13, 1850. *"Why, John Jay"*: WHS to FAS, July 15; *William Henry Seward*, 146.

76 *On September 12*: F. W. Seward, *Reminiscences*, 83–84. *"sheet of lightning at midnight"*: Andrew Delbanco, "America's Struggle for Moral Coherence," *The Atlantic*, November 12, 2018.

76 *The transaction was*: FAS to AS, October 14, 1860.

76 *Abolitionist groups and*: Boston's Vigilance Committee freed an arrested fugitive slave, Shadrach Minkins, and got him safely to Canada, but failed with another, Thomas Sims. Members of the committee planned to put a pile of mattresses below the third-floor window of the room where he was held, but authorities heard about the idea, and installed bars on the window. Finally, Sims was escorted to the wharf by hundreds of constables and put on a ship back to Georgia. See Delbanco, *War Before the War*, 5, 280, and Bordewich, *Bound for Canaan*, 324. *She wrote to Augustus*: FAS to AS, October 14, November 13, 1850.

77 *"I wouldn't trust"*: Bradford, *Scenes*, 27.

77 *The auction took*: Larson, 77, 89–90; Betty DeRamus, *Freedom by Any Means: Con Games, Voodoo Schemes, True Love, and Lawsuits on the Underground Railroad* (New York: Atria Books, 2009), 3–4. *As a free man*: Kate Larson email, July 28, 2015.

77 *Nineteen years later*: Martha wrote to Ellen on December 22, 1869, "Harriet Tubman was here last evening. She shewed us a letter from her nephew . . . he is a member of the S. Carolina Legislature!—His letter was well written—How funny it must seem to him"; see Humez, 309.

77 *Harriet soon returned*: Larson, 90.

78 *"the gravest and"*: Delbanco, *War Before the War*, 42.

7. Martha Speaks (1850–1852)

80 *What a pity"*: MCW to LM, February 16, 1850.

80 *A few days*: Penney and Livingston, 92–93, Faulkner, *Lucretia Mott's Heresy*, 40. *She sent five-year-old*: Penney and Livingston, 85. *Willy made a bag*: 99–100.

80 *"His equanimity sometimes"*: MCW to LM, January 29, 1850.

81 *"That catastrophe occurred"*: MCW to LM, January 29, 1850.

81 *May now lived:* The sermon was "The Rights and Condition of Women," November 1845.

81 *The convention attracted*: Wagner, ed., 80.

81 *"Would you have"*: "The Proceedings of the Woman's Rights Convention, held at Worcester, October 23d & 24th, 1850" (Boston: Prentiss & Sawyer, 1851), 53; ECS letter, October 20, 1850, Worcester Women's History Project.

82 *It was sixty-six*: Kate Walbert, "Has Anything Changed for Female Politicians?," *New Yorker*, August 16, 2016. The *North Platte Semi-Weekly Tribune* blamed Rankin for the suicide.

82 *"We want to be something"*: "The Speech That Set the Women's Rights Movement on Fire," New England Historical Society. *"the trampled women"*: "October 24, 1850: First National Woman's Rights Convention Ends in Worcester," www.massmoments.org/moment-details/first-national-womans-rights-convention-ends-in-worcester.htm. *Abigail Kelley Foster*: Christopher Densmore, Carol Faulkner, Nancy Hewitt, and Beverly Wilson Palmer, eds., *Lucretia Mott Speaks: The Essential Speeches and Sermons* (Urbana: University of Illinois Press, 2017), 91 n5.

82 *Garrison wrote that*: *The Liberator*, November 1, 1850; Ellen Carol DuBois, ed., *The Elizabeth Cady Stanton–Susan B. Anthony Reader: Correspondence, Writings, Speeches*, rev. ed. (Boston: Northeastern University Press, 1992), 14. *Greeley's* New York: Penney and Livingston, 98. *The* New York Herald: Faulkner, *Lucretia Mott's Heresy*, 149–51. *"fantastical mongrels, of"*: Sally G. McMillen, *Lucy Stone: An Unapologetic Life* (New York: Oxford University Press), 92. *Phillips and Garrison:* Faulkner, 150; Joelle Million, *Woman's Voice, Woman's Place: Lucy Stone and the Birth of the Woman's Rights Movement* (Westport, CT: Praeger Publishers, 2003), 99–100, 133–36.

83 *Martha wrote to M'Clintock*: Ginzberg, *Elizabeth Cady Stanton*, 75. *Stanton appreciated Martha's*: Penney and Livingston, 208.

83 *"a great moral civil war"*: "More Women's Rights Conventions," National Park Service, www.nps.gov/wori/learn/historyculture/more-womens-rights-conventions.htm.

83 *Martha praised Anthony's*: Penney and Livingston, 101, 109; MCW to LM, March 15, 1855. *Stone, who dodged*: *HWS1*, 541.

84 *As an officer*: Proceedings of the Woman's Rights Convention, held at Syracuse, September 8th, 9th, & 10th, 1852.

84 *Women should show*: Ibid., 539–40. *The audience shouted*: *HWS1*, 539–40. The baby was Margaret Livingston Lawrence, Stanton's first daughter.

84 *A Whig newspaper*: *HWS1*, 542–43. The paper was *The Daily Journal*. *Harriet Taylor Mill*: "Enfranchisement of Women," *Westminster and Foreign Quarterly Review*, July 1851.

85 *"Are we enough?"*: Archibald Henry Grimké, *William Lloyd Garrison, the Abolitionist* (New York: Funk & Wagnalls, 1891), 317.

PART TWO: UPRISINGS (1851–1860)

8. Frances Joins the Railroad (1851–1852)

90 *In May 1851*: "Syracuse and the Underground Railroad," an exhibition of the Special Collections Research Center, Syracuse University Library; Milton C. Sernett, *North Star Country: Upstate New York and the Crusade for African American Freedom* (Syracuse, NY: Syracuse University Press, 2002), 136–40.

90 *"Indignation," he wrote*: Wilbur Henry Siebert, *The Underground Railroad from Slavery to Freedom* (New York: Macmillan, 1898), 109. *"We must trample"*: Bordewich, *Bound for Canaan*, 323.

90 *A fugitive slave*: Bordewich, *Bound for Canaan*, 333–35; Steven Lubet, *Fugitive Justice: Runaways, Rescuers, and Slavery on Trial* (Cambridge, MA: Belknap Press of Harvard University Press, 2010), 87. Smith was holding a political convention of the short-lived Liberty Party.

91 *"I won't obey it!"*: Lubet, 88.

91 *"Let fugitives and"*: Bordewich, *Bound for Canaan*, 337.

91 *By about 8:00 p.m.*: Ibid., 338–39. *They gave Jerry*: Sernett, *North Star Country*, 140.

91 *Over the next*: Ed Sperry, Earl Evelyn, and Franklin H. Chase, *The Jerry Rescue* (Syracuse, NY: Onondaga Historical Association, 1924), 43–44; Samuel J. May, *Some Recollections of Our Anti-Slavery Conflict* (New York: Arno Press and The New York Times, 1968), 373–79; Sernett, *North Star Country*, 141. *The story was covered*: Bordewich, *Bound for Canaan*, 340–41.

91 *May wrote to Henry*: SJM to WHS, September 7, 1853, in Philip S. Foner, *History of Black Americans, vol. 3: From the Compromise of 1850 to the End of the Civil War* (Westport, CT: Greenwood Press, 1983), 45.

92 *Eventually, twenty-six*: Bordewich, *Bound for Canaan*, 339; Sernett, *North Star Country*, 142. *"These are all respected"*: FAS to WHS, October 16, 1851. *Henry returned home:* May, 380. *Henry wrote to*: Van Deusen, *Willian Henry Seward*, 137. *May called the*: May, 381–83.

92 *He died on*: *Seward I*, 172–73.

93 *Two regular guests*: FAS to LW, February 22, 1852.

93 *"Our old home"*: FAS to LW, Christmas 1851.

94 *She wrote to*: FAS to LW, Christmas 1851, December 29, 1851. *"Sometimes I suffer"*: CS to FAS, September 5, 1851–January 1853, Charles Sumner Correspondence, Reel 70, Houghton Library, Harvard University.

95 *Lazette and Martha*: Frances Worden Chesbro, untitled manuscript, 12–13, Seward Collection, Rush Rhees Library, University of Rochester; Judith Wellman, *Uncovering the Freedom Trail in Auburn and Cayuga County, New York* (Historical New York Research Associates, 2008); Peter Wisbey, "In the Emancipation Business: William and Frances Seward's Abolition Activism," February 2004, www.rootsweb.ancestry.com/~nycayuga/ugrr/seward.html.

95 *On cold nights*: Recollection of the Sewards' granddaughter Frances Messenger, thanks to Jennifer Haines, April 4, 2016. *The Sewards' Universalist*: Stahr, *Seward*, 154; John Austin journal, September 13, 1855. *"The 'underground railroad' "*: WHS to FAS, November 18, 1855, in *William Henry Seward*, 258.

96 *Frances and Henry*: Larson, 163–64.

97 *In May 1852*: FAS to WHS, June 2 and 4, 1852. *The school was*: Sernett, *North Star Country*, 68–69. *In July, Frances*: FAS to WHS, July 1, 1852. *"He's very desirous"*: FAS to WHS, June 21, 1852. *"Why can we"*: FAS to WHS, June 4, 1852.

97 *"The land will"*: *Frederick Douglass' Paper*, October 2, 1851, in Blight, *Frederick Douglass*, 242. *"The only way to make"*: "The Fugitive Slave Law," speech to the National Free Soil Convention at Pittsburgh, August 11, 1852, in Philip S. Foner, ed., *The Life and Writings of Frederick Douglass*, Vol. II (NewYork: International Publishers, 1950–75), 207. *"I wish Fred Douglass"*: FAS to WHS, August 13, 1852.

98 *Introducing a bill*: "Freedom National, Slavery Sectional," August 26, 1852.

98 *"It is a noble"*: FAS to CS, September 18, 1852.

98 *Weed called the*: Glyndon G. Van Deusen, *Thurlow Weed: Wizard of the Lobby. (*Boston: Little, Brown, 1947), 192. Scott won only Vermont, Massachusetts, Kentucky, and Tennessee. There were four other parties that year—Free Soil, Union, Whigs, Know Nothings, and Southern Rights. The Free Soilers siphoned off votes from the two main candidates. *Sumner impatiently wrote*: Stahr, *Seward*, 138.

9. Reading *Uncle Tom's Cabin* (1852–1853)

99 *"about as thin and"*: Nancy Koester, *Harriet Beecher Stowe: A Spiritual Life* (Grand Rapids, MI: William B. Eerdmans Publishing, 2014), 152.

100 *Three hundred thousand*: Ibid., 138. *Garrison wrote appreciatively*: John Frick, "Uncle Tom's Cabin on the Antebellum Stage," presentation at a conference at the Harriet Beecher Stowe Center, Hartford, Connecticut, June 2007. *Douglass wrote that*: Blight, *Frederick Douglass*, 247.

100 *Frances recognized one*: Frances later learned that her mother, Hannah Foote Miller, and Harriet Beecher Stowe's mother, Roxana Foote, were first cousins. Both women had died young, and none of the Beecher or Miller children knew of the connection. Henry discovered it when a Senate colleague, Solomon Foot of Vermont, showed him the Foote genealogy in the congressional library, WHS to FAS, December 8, 1857. *"His course in the"*: Letter to Lewis Tappan, 41, in F. W. Seward, *Seward at Washington*, 41.

100 *John Van Zandt lived*: Stahr, *Seward*, 104; Goodwin, 112–13. *Chase called* Uncle: *William Henry Seward*, 40.

101 *As Frances wrote*: FAS to WHS, June 17, 1852.

101 *In Britain, the book*: Koester, 151; Clare Midgley, *Women Against Slavery: The British Campaigns 1780–1870* (London: Routledge, 1995); Evelyn Pugh, "Women and Slavery," https: //www.jstor.org/stable/4248387?. The address was titled, "The Stafford House Address or An Affectionate & Christian Address of Many Thousands of Women of Great Britain & Ireland to their sisters the Women of the United States of America."

101 *The women of Britain*: Susan Zaeske, *Signatures of Citizenship: Petitioning, Antislavery, and Women's Political Identity* (Chapel Hill: University of North Carolina Press, 2003), 43–44; Pugh, "Women and Slavery."

101 *"The Abolitionists &"*: FAS to LW, January 15, 1853.

102 *As if divining*: FAS to LW, January 15, 1853.

102 *"I cannot be idle"*: FAS to WHS, December 1, 1853.

102 *Miner, an evangelical*: Harrold, 174, 177. *Writing to him*: MM to WHS, December 25, 1850; Harrold, 178.

102 *When Miner was*: Harrold, 180–84.

103 *"bringing out & developing"*: Ibid, 191. *"courage and firmness"*: FAS to LW, March 6, 1852.

104 *"There is so much"*: SBA to ECS, 1857; Gornick, 100. *The two formed*: Gornick, 53. *As Henry Stanton*: Elisabeth Griffith, *In Her Own Right: The Life of Elizabeth Cady Stanton* (Oxford: Oxford University Press, 1984), 74.

104 *Martha's common sense*: Faye E. Dudden, *Fighting Chance: The Struggle over Woman Suffrage and Black Suffrage in Reconstruction America* (Oxford: Oxford University Press, 2011), 38. *Given Henry's edict*: E. C. Stanton, 194.

104 *"the law classifies"*: Penney and Livingston, 109. Martha wrote the letter in March 1855, before a Cayuga County women's rights meeting.

105 *"The boasted human"*: Faulkner, *Lucretia Mott's Heresy*, 155. *Lucretia, able to*: See Douglass's description of her address to an 1848 anti-slavery convention, *North Star*, May 19, 1848. *The* New York: September 7, 1853; Hayes Baker-Crothers and Ruth Allison Hudnut, *Problems of Citizenship* (New York: Henry Holt, 1924), 174.

105 *They packed a*: MCW to DW, October 23, 1853; Faulkner, *Lucretia Mott's Heresy*, 156.

105 *"We were made"*: LM to Philadelphia Family, October 17, 1853, in Palmer, ed., 227–28.

106 *Martha replied that*: MCW to DW, October 23, 1853. *"No crying evil"*: *The Liberator*, October 18, 1853. *She said, to*: LM to Philadelphia Family, October 17, 1853, in Palmer, ed., 227–29.

106 *Martha wrote to*: MCW to DW, October 23, 1853.

106 *When he was sixteen*: Penney and Livingston, 84–85. *"I guess he will"*: MCW to DW, November 18, 1853.

107 *He appreciated Martha's*: Penney and Livingston, 222; MCW to DW, December 25, 1853. *Garrison persisted*: Ira V. Brown, " 'Am I Not a Woman and a Sister?' The Anti-Slavery Convention of American Women, 1837–1839," *Pennsylvania History* 50 (1983), 2.

107 *"Am I to be"*: "Debate on the Plenary Inspiration of the Bible, Extract from Martha's letter, dated, Philadelphia, Dec. 4, 1863," *The Liberator*, December 16, 1853. The Presbyterian minister was Rev. W. L. McCalla, and his opponent, Joseph Barker.

107 *"There is neither doll"*: *William Henry Seward*, 213–14. *Frances was in Auburn with*: FAS to WHS, December 1, 1853.

107 *Anna was the eldest*: Jeff Ludwig, email, July 1, 2020. *Frances had met*: FAS to WHS, December 21, 1853. *Fanny, who was*: FS to WHS, Christmas 1853; Trudy Krisher, *Fanny Seward: A Life* (Syracuse, NY: Syracuse University Press, 2015), 41.

108 Uncle Tom's Cabin: Frick, "Uncle Tom's Cabin." *Garrison, after seeing*: " 'Uncle Tom' on the Stage," *The Liberator*, September 9, 1853, 2. *Thirteen-year-old Ellen*: MCW to DW, November 18, 1853.

108 *One South Carolina*: Louisa S. McCord, *Southern Quarterly Review*, January 1853. *"I've heard Uncle Tom's"*: Bradford, *Scenes*, 22.

10. Harriet Tubman's Maryland Crusade (1851–1857)

109 *In anticipation of*: Humez, 183–84. *Shattered, she later*: Cheney, op. cit.; in Humez, 183.

110 *"confidential friends all"*: Larson, 101.

110 The judge in the case, which was heard in New Castle, Delaware, was Supreme Court Justice Roger B. Taney, who had grown up in a slaveholding family in Maryland. (Justices then also sat as trial judges.) *Court records show*: James A. McGowan, *Station Master on the Underground Railroad: The Life and Letters of Thomas Garrett* (Jefferson, NC: McFarland, 2005), 63. *"Judge, thou has"*: Siebert, 110.

111 *"My slave list"*: McGowan, 187. His contacts at the Edinburgh society were Eliza Wigham and her sister Mary Edmundson. *"She does not"*: Ibid., 104.

111 *She credited her*: Larson, 102; Clinton, 91–92.

111 *"If he was weak enough"*: Humez, 235–36.

111 *Arriving in Dorchester*: Larson, 111–12. Larson discovered that the family was not reunited. A few years after Robert's escape, his wife married another man. Robert (later known as John Stewart) arranged to have John Bowley snatch his two sons, John Jr. and Moses, from a farm in Talbot County where they had been indentured around 1867. Robert's daughter, Harriet, stayed with Mary.

111 This scene is drawn from Bradford, *Scenes*, 39, 57, and Larson, 110–13.

112 *One of her routes*: "Freedom: Harriet Tubman Underground Railroad Byway," Driving Tour Guide. Larson, 113, says they might have traveled through Federalsburg. *She hid her passengers*: Julia Isabelle Ives Messenger recollections, 1953, thanks to her granddaughter, Missy Warfield. Julia Ives, born in 1870, grew up in Auburn. *Once, she and six*: Humez, 225. *Frostbite was a*: Larson, 103. *On the trip*: McGowan, 98, 138.

112 *William Still welcomed*: Still, 296.

113 *"The Dover Eight"*: Larson, 137–44; McGowan, 104, 107–14; Robert W. Taylor, *Harriet Tubman: The Heroine in Ebony* (Boston: George H. Ellis, 1901), 9. Before the sheriff could lock up the eight freedom seekers, one of them, Henry Predeaux, grabbed a fireplace shovel and scattered hot coals around the room. As the sheriff shouted to his wife for his pistol, Predeaux smashed the window, and he and his companions jumped into the mud, twelve feet below. Looking back, Predeaux saw the sheriff standing outside in his stocking feet, aiming a gun at him. The gun jammed, and Predeaux escaped over the wall with the others before dawn.

113 *Harriet, concerned about*: Larson, 143–49.

114 *Harriet procured an*: Thomas Garrett to Sarah Bradford, June 1868, in McGowan, 193; Humez, 229.

114 *"These two travelers"*: Still, 396.

114 *When Harriet was*: Larson, 144–49. *Among the freedom seekers*: Nat Amby wrote to William Still from Auburn on June 10, 1858, to ask if he could contact his mother to tell her that he was safe, and to ask her for news of his brothers and sisters. He wanted her to know "that I am well and doing well and state to her that I perform my Relissius dutys and I would like to hear from her and want to know if she is performing her Relissius dutys yet and send me word from all her children I left behind"; see Still, 104.

11. The Race to the Territory (1854)

116 *"Maine, New Hampshire"*: *William Henry Seward*, 216.

116 *Garrison, speaking in*: Mayer, 439–40.

117 *"Some happy spell"*: De Alva Stanwood Alexander, *A Political History of the State of New York, Vol. 2, 1833–1861* (New York: Millibuch, 1969), 158. *The speech was*: Stahr, *Seward*, 142–43. *"May I never"*: LW to WHS, February 21, 1854.

117 *He contrasted the North*: "The Landmark of Freedom," February 21, 1854. *Frances wrote to Sumner*: FAS to CS, February 25, 1854, Charles Sumner Correspondence, 1829–1874, Houghton Library, Harvard University.

117 *At 11:30 p.m. on*: Robert W. Johannsen, *Stephen A. Douglas* (Urbana and Chicago: University of Illinois Press, 1997), 428, 432, 588. *self-government in*: Ibid., 431. *"His arrowy words"*: Ibid., 429. *Sumner and Chase*: Ibid., 438. *Douglas replied, using*: Eric H. Walther, *The Shattering of the Union: America in the 1850s* (Lanham, MD: SR Books, 2004), 41.

118 "*Come on, then*": "Speech of Senator Seward: The Constitution and Compromises," *New York Daily Times*, May 27, 1854. *Pro-slavery extremists*: Mayer, 446.

118 *Frances wrote to*: FAS to CS, June 10, 1854, Charles Sumner Correspondence. *"The Administration organs"*: CS to FAS, ibid., June 17, 1854. *David Wright was*: MCW to LM, August 6, 1854.

119 *"If I sometimes"*: WHS to TP, William Henry Seward, undated letter, 1853.

119 *"<u>You</u>, my dear"*: FD to WHS, April 23, 1853.

119 *Henry won a*: Stahr, *Seward*, 155. *"I am so happy"*: CS to WHS, October 15, 1855, in Stahr, *Seward*, 156.

119 *Newspapers relished the*: "The Meeting of the Douglases—The White Douglas Backed Out," *Chicago Tribune*, October 20, 1854. *Greeley's* Tribune *published*: Blight, *Frederick Douglass*, 260. *"Ebony and ivory are thought"*: William S. McFeely, Frederick Douglass (New York: W. W. Norton, 1991), 188.

120 *"I could travel"*: Johannsen, 451.

120 *In October, when*: MCW to LM, October 11, 1854. *In his speeches*: "The Kansas-Nebraska Bill," October 30, 1854, in P. S. Foner, ed., *Life and Writings* 2, 316–32. The quotations are from Douglass's speech in Chicago.

120 *After Douglass left*: September 29, 1854, in Penney and Livingston, 88.

12. Bleeding Kansas, Bleeding Sumner (1854–1856)

121 *One of the founders*: Letter from Samuel J. Pomeroy to Amos A. Lawrence, September 22, 1854.

122 *They ordered*: Richard Cordley, *A History of Lawrence, Kansas: From the Earliest Settlement to the Close of the Rebellion* (Lawrence, KS: Lawrence Journal Press, 1895), 13, www.kancoll.org/books/cordley_history/.

122 *The hope gave*: David M. Potter, *The Impending Crisis: America Before the Civil War, 1848–1861* (New York: Harper Perennial, 2011), 200. *Martha told an*: MCW to Rev. W. R. G. Mellen, June 6, 1855. *"We will continue"*: *William Henry Seward*, 242.

122 *On election day*: Cordley, Chapter III, 2–3. *The besieged free-staters*: Stahr, *Seward*, 159.

122 *"As a nation"*: Douglass had merged *The North Star* with the *Liberty Paper*, published in Syracuse, in 1851, renaming it *Frederick Douglass' Paper*. This article, cited in Blight, *Frederick Douglass*, 27, appeared in the *FDP* on November 16, 1855.

123 *"It was a noble, mighty"*: WHS to Frances, April 10, 1854. *"I admit that I don't"*: MCW to LM, March 29, 1855.

123 *Frances's approval was*: February 7, 1855; Stahr, *Seward*, 153. *"Will has this"*: LW to WHS, April 29, 1856.

124 *"very dark some"*: FAS to LW, April 26, 1859. *"The incident comes"*: WHS to LW, May 2, 1856.

124 *"He took my"*: WHS to FAS, March 15, 1854. *"Neither my heart nor my"*: Stahr, *Seward*, 160–61.

124 *Sumner memorized his*: Donald, *Charles Sumner*, 281–84.

125 *"This damn fool"*: Ibid., 286. *Members of Congress*: Joanne B. Freeman, *The Field of Blood: Violence in Congress and the Road to Civil War* (New York: Farrar, Straus and Giroux, 2018), 6.

125 *On May 22, Brooks*: Donald, 293–95.

125 *Several senators tried*: Ibid., 247–48.

125 *She wrote home*: FAS to her children, May 22, 1856, Stahr, *Seward*, 161.

126 *"This is the day"*: Paul Williams, *Rebel Guerrillas: Mosby, Quantrill and Anderson* (Jefferson, NC: McFarland, 2018), 9. *They looted stores*: Cordley, Chapter VI.

126 *The previous spring*: On his way to Osawatomie, Brown stopped at the founding convention of the Radical Political Abolitionist Party, led by Douglass and Gerrit Smith. See "Proceedings of the Convention of Radical Political Abolitionists, held at Syracuse, N.Y., June 26th, 27th, and 28th, 1855," West Virginia Department of Arts, Culture and History, www.wvculture.org/history/jbexhibit/radical.html. Smith had started a colony in the Adirondacks on 120,000 acres of land for three thousand African Americans, thus helping them become citizens. Brown cheaply bought 244 acres, where he helped colonists survey and till the land, and lived with his wife and four youngest children. For these events, see David S. Reynolds, *John Brown, Abolitionist: The Man Who Killed Slavery, Sparked the Civil War, and Seeded Civil Rights* (New York: Vintage Books, 2005), 126–27; Horwitz, 41–49; Fergus M. Bordewich, "John Brown's Day of Reckoning," *Smithsonian*, October 2000.

127 *Brown, who denied*: *National Era*, June 12, 1856; Horwitz, 56. *He and the sons*: Reynolds, 198–201.

127 *Martha did not*: Faulkner, *Lucretia Mott's Heresy*, 172. *"I felt very"*: MCW to Charles Pelham [1856], Osborne Family Papers, Syracuse University Libraries, Special Collections Research Center, cited in Penney and Livingston, 149–50.

127 *Brooks's supporters in*: Donald, 301–2, 305.

127 *Now, when a friend*: FAS to LW, May 30, 1856.

128 *Weed, in his*: Van Deusen, *William Henry Seward*, 175–77; Stahr, *Seward*, 163.*"His abandonment seems"*: FAS to WHS, July 20, 1856.

128 *On the Fourth of July*: *Seward I*, 281–82. *"You have served"*: FAS to CS, July 4, 1856. *"Where is our boasted?"*: FAS to WHS, July 4, 1856

13. Frances Sells Harriet a House (1857–1859)

129 *Henry held his*: Excerpt from Mary Grier letter to her mother, January 15, 1857. Mary, a friend of Fanny's and the daughter of a cousin of Henry's, was staying with the Sewards. See sewardproject.org/person-public-fields/390.

130 *Frances sent Aunt Clara*: FAS to Clara, January 19, 1857.

130 *Buchanan knew how*: Jean H. Baker, *James Buchanan*, American Presidents Series (New York: Times Books, 2004), 84. *Abolitionists, Republicans, and*: "Dred Scott," mrlincolnandfreedom.org, Lehrman Institute.

130 *The case had been*: Don Fehrenbacher, *The Dred Scott Case: Its Significance in American Law and Politics* (Oxford: Oxford University Press, 1978), 272, 568; Johannsen, 548–49.

131 *May said that*: SJM to FAS, August 6, 1867. *He found her*: SJM to FAS, August 16, 1857.

131 *One of their*: Henry W. Bellows to Eliza Bellows, Stahr, *Seward*, 362.

131 *"I am sorry the women"*: FAS to LW, March 6, 1852.

132 *"Auburn shuts itself"*: March 15, 1855, in Penney and Livingston, 109.

132 *As expected, she*: FAS to AS, November 12, 1857. *"To think that"*: Gornick, 46.

132 *Stanton described the*: *HWS1*, 463.

132 *He wrote exultantly*: *William Henry Seward*, 330.

133 *They had issued*: Johannsen, 576–81. Douglas was objecting to the Lecompton Constitution, which protected slaveholding in Kansas and excluded free Blacks. In 1855, Congress had rejected the Topeka Constitution, drawn up by the anti-slavery legislature in Topeka. *"I wish I"*: FAS to WHS, December 12, 1857.

133 *Writing about a*: *William Henry Seward, 1846–1861*, 331; WHS to FAS, December 14, 1857.

133 *"In this ill-omened"*: "Freedom in Kansas," March 3, 1858.

134 *President Buchanan was*: Goodwin, 191.

134 *He, too, was:* www.mrlincolnandfreedom.org/pre-civil-war/house-divided-speech.

134 *In five of the thirteen*: Richard C. Rohrs, "Exercising Their Right: African American Voter Turnout in Antebellum Newport, Rhode Island," *New England Quarterly* 84, no. 3 (September 2011), 402–21.

134 *Calling popular sovereignty*: Nichole Etcheson, " 'A living, creeping lie': Abraham Lincoln on Popular Sovereignty," *Journal of the Abraham Lincoln Association* 29, no. 2 (Summer 2008), 1–26.

134 *He impugned Lincoln*: Sean Wilentz, *The Politicians & the Egalitarians: The Hidden History of American Politics* (W. W. Norton, 2016), 224.

134 *He called slavery*: *William Henry Seward*, 351, "The Irrepressible Conflict," Monday, October 25, 1858.

135 *A Republican friend*: Stahr, *Seward*, 176.

135 *Howland wrote in*: EH to FAS, November 26, 1860.

136 *They set out*: Diaries of Fanny Seward, William Henry Seward Papers, Rare Books, Special Collections, and Preservation Department, Microfilm Reel 198, Boxes 134–135, Section IV F, University of Rochester, Rochester, New York, December 25, 29, and 31, 1858; Janet M. Davis, "Animal Protection in the United States," *American Historian*, November 2015, tah.oah.org/.

136 *By noon that day*: FAS to LW, New Year's Day, 1859.

136 *"There are so"*: FAS to LW, early January, 1859.

137 *"She is too noble"*: Van Deusen, 266.

137 *In mid-February*: FAS to LW, February 17, 1859. *Henry wrote in*: WHS to FWS, January 25, in *William Henry Seward*, 334.

138 *She decided that*: Seward scholars have attributed the sale of the property to Henry, but my research indicates that Frances came up with the idea and persuaded Henry to agree.

138 *Harriet was in no*: Larson, 163–64. In a letter on August 15, 1859, from Will Jr. to his father, by August 15, Harriet had paid $225, and promised another $100 by September.

138 *Weed, the ideal*: Stahr, *Seward*, 177; Van Deusen, *Thurlow Weed*, 108; *William Henry Seward*, 371.

139 *He wrote to*: *William Henry Seward*, 371.

139 *Martineau's home, shaggy*: Lynn Steinson, "William Wells Brown, Impressions of Harriet Martineau and the English Lakes, 1851," www.lynnsteinson.com/home/history/william-wells-brown-impressions-of-harriet-martineau-and-the-english-lakes-1851.

139 *Henry found Martineau*: *William Henry Seward*, 371. There are no letters in the Seward collection from Frances to Lazette, or from Frances to Henry, between April 1859 and April 1860. Henry's letters to the family during his trip abroad are excerpted in *William Henry Seward*, 362–436. Cornelia Rogers, the great-granddaughter of Will Seward and his wife, Jenny, gave me a possible explanation for the missing letters: when she was home from college in the mid-1950s, she went to see her grandmother Janet at the Seward house. She was sorting through family possessions, in preparation for turning the private home over to the Emerson Foundation, which now oversees the Seward House Museum. Janet filled a few old wicker laundry baskets with papers she said were "personal." She and Cornelia took the baskets to the cottage Will and Jenny had built on Owasco Lake, made a small bonfire by the water, and threw the correspondence into the flames. At one point, Janet reached down and snatched out a letter, noticing an insignia. Put in the basket by mistake, it was a letter, signed by Lincoln and Seward on July 10, 1861, authorizing Seward to arrange a treaty with Denmark.

14. Martha Leads (1854–1860)

141 *Stanton thought of*: Minutes from the 1874 NWSA meeting in New York City, National Women's Hall of Fame; Ginzberg, *Elizabeth Cady Stanton*, 87; www.womenofthehall.org/inductee/martha-coffin-pelham-wright; HWS2, 545. *The reporter covering*: *Auburn Daily Union*, November 23, 1860.

142 *Martha carried on*: Penney and Livingston, 96–97, 119.

142 *Recently established by*: Robert H. Abzug, *Passionate Liberator: Theodore Dwight Weld & the Dilemma of Reform* (New York: Oxford University Press, 1980), 180–82.

142 *It was coeducational*: Lori D. Ginzberg, *Women and the Work of Benevolence: Morality, Politics, and Class in the Nineteenth-Century United States* (New Haven: Yale University Press, 1990), 105–6. "*The bigoted and narrow-minded*": MCW to DW, October 26, 1854.

143 *Douglass criticized Lucy*: Dudden, 21, 27. See *The Liberator*, December 9, 1853, January 13, 1854, and February 24, 1854, and *Frederick Douglass' Paper*, February 17 and

March 17, 1854. "*Would to God you*": Ginzberg, *Women and the Work of Benevolence*, 84–85.

143 *The highlight of the*: Faulkner, *Lucretia Mott's Heresy*, 123; Ellen Carol DuBois, *Woman Suffrage and Women's Rights* (New York: New York University Press, 1998), 59. *Martha wrote to*: Penney and Livingston, 113. In 1859, David told a group in Auburn that women should be allowed to vote—a comment that elicited only laughter. Ibid., 124.

144 *One man, a doctor*: Penney and Livingston, 112–15.

144 *Rather than feeling*: Ginzberg, *Women and the Work of Benevolence*, 106.

145 *Afterward, Martha expected*: MCW to EW, April 13, 1855, in Harriet Hyman Alonso, *Growing Up Abolitionist: The Story of the Garrison Children* (Amherst: University of Massachusetts Press, 2002), 183–84. For an account of nineteenth-century views of hysteria and neurasthenia, see Jean Strouse, *Alice James: A Biography* (Boston: Houghton Mifflin, 1980), 103–4. *You can never*: MCW to EW, August 27, 1855, in Alonso, 184.

145 *Martha told her*: MCW to EW, January 13, 1856; Alonso, 185.

145 *Ellen enjoyed Anthony's*: EW's journal, September 4, 1860, in Alonso, 190.

145 *In Washington over*: FAS to WHSII, March 3, 18, 1858.

146 *She told Martha*: MCW to LM, September 8, 1855. *She and Henry*: DFS, January 22, 1863, in Krisher, 140.

146 *Fanny didn't tell*: Krisher, 138; DFS, May 7, 1862 and January 22, 1863. *Fanny, sheltered by*: Krisher, 153–54.

147 *In January, she*: Penney and Livingston, 128; HWS1, 691.

147 *Rejected by sixteen*: Eric v.d. Luft, "Celebrating 150 Years of Women in Medicine: The Legacy of Elizabeth Blackwell," State University of New York Upstate Medical University *Alumni Journal*, https://www.hws.edu/about/blackwell/articles/syracuse.aspx.

147 *Like Wollstonecraft, she*: Gornick, 58–59. *Nine years earlier*: Speech of Wendell Phillips, at the Convention Held at Worcester, October 15 and 16, 1851.

148 "*Tyrant law and*": Ann D. Gordon, ed., *Selected Papers of Elizabeth Cady Stanton and Susan B. Anthony, Vol. 1: In the School of Anti-Slavery, 1840–1866* (New Brunswick, NJ: Rutgers University Press, 2001), 428. *Wendell Phillips*: Ibid.

148 "*We have thrown*": Ginzberg, 100. "*This hue & cry*": MCW to SBA, July 17, 1860.

148 "*After all that*": HWS1, 688–89.

15. General Tubman Goes to Boston (1858–1860)

149 *Early in the spring*: Franklin B. Sanborn, "Harriet Tubman," *Commonwealth*, July 17, 1863; Bradford, *Scenes*, 82–83.

150 *Rather than meet*: Larson, 159; Humez, 398; MCW to WLGII, January 10, 1869.

150 "*calmly, so calmly*": Edward J. Renehan, Jr., *The Secret Six: The True Tale of the Men Who Conspired with John Brown* (Columbia: University of South Carolina Press, 1997), 109. *Sanborn ran an*: Horwitz, 61.

150 *Sanborn was awestruck*: Stephen B. Oates, *To Purge This Land with Blood: A Biography of John Brown* (Amherst: University of Massachusetts Press, 1970, 1984), 183–89.

151 *In New York City*: Ibid.,199–200.

151 "*BY FAR the*": Ibid., 225–27, 233–34. The Secret Six were Sanborn; Higginson; Smith; George Luther Stearns, a wealthy linseed oil manufacturer and the chairman of the Massachusetts committee; and Dr. Samuel Gridley Howe, a member of the committee.

151 *As requested, Harriet*: The men were Thomas Elliott; Denard Hughes; Peter Pennington; Joe and William Bailey, whom she'd helped escape; Charles Hall and John Thompson were friends she'd made in Canada. See Larson, 15.
151 *After the meeting*: John Brown to John Brown Jr., April 8, 1858. See Oates, 241–42.
152 *Sanborn, curious to*: Humez, 35, 37. *"she was obliged"*: Humez, 166. *Sanborn again made*: Ibid., 37. *"Mr. Phillips, I"*: Ibid., 35.
152 *"The scene rises"*: Cheney, "Moses"; Humez, 193. *She even turned*: Ibid., 184.
153 *God told her*: Thomas Garrett letter to Sarah Bradford, June 1868, in McGowan, 192.
153 *Higginson, who said*: Oates, 189. *"We learned to speak"*: Thomas Wentworth Higginson, *Cheerful Yesterdays* (Boston: Houghton, Mifflin, 1898), 327–28.
153 *On July 4, 1859*: Humez, 38, 199–200. *Garrison characterized her*: Larson, 171–72.
154 *She had moved*: Ibid., 163. *"Seward has received nothing"*: John Stewart to HT, November 1, 1859, Larson, 177.
154 *On October 16*: Bradford, *Scenes*, 83.
154 *Longfellow wrote in*: Oates, 197, 319; Reynolds, 223. *In a speech*: *The Liberator*, November 11, 1859. *Harriet felt compelled*: MCW to WLGII, January 10, 1869. *"It's clear to me"*: Cheney, "Moses," in Humez, 243. Brown's correspondence implicated Harriet, and on January 17, 1860, a U.S. marshal from Harpers Ferry appeared in Auburn, seeking witnesses for a congressional commission investigating the conspiracy, but she and her family had left town. See Larson, 178.
155 *"Dull and sombre clouds"*: Scott Christianson, *Freeing Charles: The Struggle to Free a Slave on the Eve of the Civil War* (Urbana and Chicago: University of Illinois Press, 2010), 85, 87; Oates, 357.
155 *On the morning*: One of her cousins, John Hooper, a fugitive from Talbot County, Maryland, worked on the underground railroad with his wife. See Larson, 117.
155 *As officers escorted*: *Troy Daily Times*, April 30. *One participant in*: Christianson, 112.
156 *"Drag him to"*: Cheney, "Moses," 37; Humez, 204.
156 *In early July*: July 6, 1860, "Woman's Rights Meeting." *"A FEMALE CONDUCTOR"*: *Baltimore American and Commercial Advertiser*, June 5, 1860; thanks to Christopher Haley, Director of the Study of the Legacy of Slavery in Maryland, Maryland State Archives.
156 *As an older woman*: Samuel Hopkins Adams, *Grandfather Stories* (Syracuse, NY: Syracuse University Press, 1947), 276. Hopkins wrote in dialect. www.google.com/books/edition/Grandfather_Stories/ofhA2miS8YMC?hl=en&gbpv=1&bsq=%22bag%20o%27%20meal%22.

16. The Agitators (1860)

160 *An advertisement in*: *William Henry Seward*, 440; Krisher, 48.
160 *"Oh, God, it is"*: John Austin diary, May 18, 1860; thanks to Kenneth and Audrey Mochel. *Lincoln loyalists from*: "Lincoln and the Election of 1860," Lehrman Institute. *Horace Greeley, a*: Stahr, *Seward*, 194–95; Goodwin, 215–16. *"At the age of"*: FAS to WHS, May 30, 1860.
160 *"It was almost like"*: Gordon, 433. *"I had the"*: Stahr, *Seward*, 194.
160 *He confessed in*: Stahr, *Seward*, 195.
161 *Charles Sumner, one*: Donald, 291. *Nevertheless, on June 4*: Ibid., 353. *Frances wrote, after*: FAS to CS, June 14, 1860, Charles Sumner Correspondence.

161 *Henry promised Frances*: Thanks to Jeff Ludwig. *Fanny wistfully told*: Krisher, 27, DFS, October 14, 1863. *Weed and Charles*: Van Deusen, *Thurlow Weed*, 255–56; Stahr, *Seward*, 195–96. *She was surprised*: FAS to WHS, May 30, 1860. *Henry, though, admitted*: Stahr, *Seward*, 197.

162 *"Church crowded, a"*: Thanks to Jeff Ludwig.

162 *Fanny was awed*: Krisher, 52.

162 *Henry was reinvigorated*: Stahr, *Seward*, 201–7. *Charles Francis Adams*: Charles Francis Adams, *Charles Francis Adams, 1835–1915, An Autobiography* (Boston: Houghton Mifflin, 1916), 64. *In an expansive*: October 2, 1860, *Chicago Tribune*, October 3, 1860.

162 *"Yes, Henry is"*: Goodwin, 270.

163 *"'Mr. Seward must'"*: ECS to FAS, November 14, 1860. *But a few*: Stahr, *Seward*, 208.

163 *"I have faith that"*: WHS to FAS, December 8, 1860, in *William Henry Seward*, 480–81.

164 *"The air is filled"*: Earl Conrad, *The Governor and His Lady: The Story of William Henry Seward and His Wife Frances* (New York: G. P. Putnam's Sons, 1960), 338.

164 *Frances planned a*: Stahr, *Seward*, 215.

164 *"It is inevitable"*: *William Henry Seward*, 487–89.

165 *"I am astonished"*: MCW to Charles Pelham, December 20, 1860.

165 *She had gone*: Larson, 185–86. *At one point*: Clinton, 93.

166 *"We have been"*: MCW to EW, December 30, 1860, in Penney and Livingston, 132. *It was Harriet's*: Larson, 185.

PART THREE: WAR (1861–1864)

17. "No Compromise" (1861)

169 *Henry grandly called:* Kenneth J. Winkle, *Lincoln's Citadel: The Civil War in Washington, D.C.* (New York: W. W. Norton., 2013), 85. *While President-elect*: *William Henry Seward*, 488, 491. *According to the*: Goodwin, 300.

170 *The* Washington Evening Star: Stahr, *Seward*, 223.

170 *"In political affairs"*: January 18, 1861, *William Henry Seward*, 496.

170 *"Compromises based on"*: FAS to WHS, January 19, 1861. *Henry tried to:* WHS to FAS, January 23, 1861, William Henry Seward, 496–97.

171 *For sixteen years*: FAS to WHS, January 19, 1861.

171 *The next morning*: Fanny Seward to her father, January 20, 1861, Frances P.S.

171 *Running into Martha*: MCW to MPM, February 28, 1861. *She wrote from*: LM to MCW, March 3, 1860; Faulkner, *Lucretia Mott's Heresy*, 176.

171 *As the nation*: MCW to EW, June 22, 1863; Penney and Livingston, 160–61. *Anthony resisted the*: Ginzberg, 107–8; Rosalyn Terborg-Penn, *African American Women in the Struggle for the Vote, 1850–1920* (Bloomington and Indianapolis: Indiana University Press, 1998), 22–23; Wendy Hamand Venet, *Neither Ballots Nor Bullets: Women Abolitionists and the Civil War* (Charlottesville: University Press of Virginia, 1991), 29. *Stanton, though, felt*: "Speech to the Anniversary of the American Anti-Slavery Society," May 1860, in DuBois, *Elizabeth Cady Stanton–Susan B. Anthony Reader*, 78–85.

172 *"The mobocrats would"*: Henry B. Stanton to ECS, January 12, 1861, in Gordon, 454.

172 *In Buffalo, where*: www.buffalorising.com. *By 1861, mobs*: *HWS1*, 467. *In Syracuse, protesters*: Recollection of Harriet Smith Mills in Sperry, Evelyn, and Chase, 59.

173 *When she was booed*: Penney and Livingston, 134; Alonso, 191. *Martha, who had*: Penney and Livingston, 133.

173 *It was 14*: MCW to Ellen, February 11, 1861. The mayor was George Hornell Thacher. *The mayor sat*: MCW to EW, February 10, 1961. *One of the*: *The Liberator*, February 15, 1861, fair-use.org/the-liberator/1861/02/15/the-liberator-31-07.pdf.

173 *"I shall always remember"*: MCW to Matilda Joslyn Gage, February 15, 1871. *After the meeting*: *The Liberator*, February 15, 1861, fair-use.org/the-liberator/1861/02/15/the-liberator-31-07.pdf. *"If there is no"*: Blight, 285–86.

174 *While in Albany, Martha*: Larson, 189–92. *Martha supplied the*: Ibid., 191.

174 *Lazette was there*: MCW to EW, February 11, 1861.

174 *Anna wrote to*: Anna Seward to Frances, February 28, 1861. *Henry had asked*: AS to FAS, March 8, 1861.

175 *Wendell Phillips rightly*: "Shall Women Have the Right to Vote?," www.loc.gov/resource/rbnawsa.n8344/?sp=24. *Frances copied a*: *Westminster and Foreign Quarterly Review* 52 (1850), 376–77.

175 *Fanny was amused*: DFS, January 15, 1861.

175 *He replied: "I"*: WHS to FAS, *William Henry Seward*, 505.

176 *"That would be"*: FAS to WHS, February 22, 1861.

176 *Lincoln left Springfield*: "Spies, Lies, and Disguise: Abraham Lincoln and the Baltimore Plot," White House Historical Association.

176 *Shortly after noon*: *William Henry Seward*, 508–11.

176 *Lincoln then raised*: *Philadelphia Inquirer*, February 23, 1861.

177 *As planned, Lincoln*: http://www.perseus.tufts.edu/hopper/text?doc=Perseus%3Atext%3A2001.05.0172%3Achapter%3D6; "Brian Woolly, "Lincoln's Whistle-Stop Trip to Washington," Smithsonianmag.com, February 9, 2011.

177 *"The President-elect"*: *William Henry Seward*, 511.

177 *Lincoln, though, wanted men*: Goodwin, 256, 304, 319; *William Henry Seward*, 521.

177 *The next morning*: Stahr, *Seward*, 239. *"He is very"*: WHS to Frances, February 23, 1861, in *William Henry Seward*, 511–12.

178 *"Although passion has"*: Stahr, *Seward*, 240.

178 *On March 4*: *William Henry Seward*, 516; Johannsen, 842.

178 *"I am sorry. . . ."*: FAS to WHS, March, 9, 1861. *Douglass condemned the*: "The Inaugural Address," *Douglass' Monthly*, April 1861, in P. S. Foner, ed., Vol. 3, 71–80. *To Lucretia, it*: Faulkner, *Lucretia Mott's Heresy*, 177.

178 *"Fort Sumter in"*: WHS to FAS, March 8, 1861; F. W. Seward, *Seward at Washington*, 534.

179 *Seward argued that*: Goodwin, 335–36. *In February 1861*: "Confederate States of America," www.history.com/topics/american-civil-war/confederate-states-of-america.

179 *"I feel condemned"*: FAS to WHS, April 12, 1861.

179 *But it took*: Winkle, 147; Goodwin, 353. *"It is so sad"*: FAS to WHS, April 15, 1861.

180 *Two days later*: Winkle, 145; Harry A. Ezratty, *Baltimore in the Civil War: The Pratt Street Riot and a City Occupied* (Charleston, SC: History Press, 2010), 13, 28, 51–64. *"The true, strong"*: FAS to WHS, April 28, 1861.

180 *Fanny wrote to*: Krisher, 58. *Martha's Willy had*: FAS to Frederick Seward, April 30, 1861. *Jenny's mother begged*: Thanks to Jeff Ludwig.

181 *That spring, Dr.*: Jocelyn Green, "Women's Central Association of Relief During the Civil War," www.jocelyngreen.com; Luft, "Celebrating 150 Years of Women in Medicine." *An old friend*: Tammy Kiter, "Women in Nursing During the Civil War," New-

York Historical Society, March 26, 2016; Mary Elizabeth Massey, *Bonnet Brigades* (New York: Alfred A. Knopf, 1966), 33, 46; Elizabeth Robertson, "The Union's 'Other Army': The Women of the United States Sanitary Commission," https://www.gilderlehrman.org; Judith Giesberg, "Ms. Dix Comes to Washington," *New York Times*, April 27, 2011.

181 *Fanny and a friend*: FAS to Frederick Seward, April 30, 1861; Krisher, 57. *One ladies' group*: Ellen Wright to MCW, June 20, 1861; Massey, 31–32.

181 *Fanny joined thousands*: FS to WHS, April 30, 1861. *That evening, she*: DFS, May 19, 1861.

18. A Nation on Fire (1861–1862)

183 *One national statesman*: Walt Whitman, from *Specimen Days*, in Brooks D. Simpson, Stephen W. Sears, and Aaron Sheehan-Dean, eds., *The Civil War: The First Year Told by Those Who Lived It* (New York: Library of America, 2011), 500. *Postmaster General Blair*: Ibid., 377.

184 *By June, when*: Stahr, *Seward*, 209; Winkle, 156, 158, 165. *Men seeking commissions*: Simpson, Sears, Sheehan-Dean, eds., 377–80. *Soldiers of the*: *William Henry Seward*, 552. *"It begins to be"*: WHS to FAS, April 27, Ibid., 560.

184 *Although Henry complained: Seward I*, 575. *On many evenings*: Stahr, *Seward*, 302. *According to Lincoln's*: Goodwin, 364–65. *"But I have"*: WHS to FAS, June 5, 1861.

184 *"We are on the"*: *William Henry Seward*, 598.

185 *"That is splendid"*: Jim Burgess, "Blood in Bull Run: The Battlefield Today," American Battlefield Trust, Spring 2011.

185 *"What went out"*: *William Henry Seward*, 598–99, July 1861.

185 *Frances, learning of*: FAS to WHS, July 23, 1861. *"One great battle"*: WHS to FAS, July 23, 1861, *William Henry Seward*, 600. *Lincoln turned to*: Goodwin, 403–4.

185 *Sharing the common*: Stahr, *Seward*, 300, 304–5.

186 *"I almost dread seeing"*: FAS to Frederick Seward, June 15, 1861. *The night before*: "Secretary Seward at Home; An Impressive Speech," *Auburn Daily Advertiser*, reprinted in *New York Times*, September 2, 1861.

186 *The Sewards stayed*: FAS to LW, August 1861. *As the train*: DFS, September 1, 1861.

186 *Frances ruefully wrote*: FAS to LW, September 2, 1861.

187 *That evening, Frances*: DFS, September 1, 1861; Goodwin, 386.

187 *Frances woke each*: FAS to LW, August 1861, *William Henry Seward*, 612. *Gradually more voices*: Simpson, Sears, Sheehan-Dean, eds., 383.

188 *In September, she*: FAS to WHS, September 17, 1861.

189 *"The national edifice"*: "Fighting Rebels with Only One Hand," *Douglass' Monthly*, September 1861.

189 *Now he dropped*: Stahr, *Seward*, 320; Goodwin, 400.

189 *"The signs of"*: FAS to LW, December 24, 1861.

190 *"Unpalatable as the"*: FAS to WHS, December 1861.

190 *"I have not"*: FAS to LW, December 11, 1861.

191 *"It is impossible not"*: Taylor, 184–85.

191 *"If any thing were"*: FAS to LW, December 24, 1861.

191 *At the start*: "The Navies of the Civil War," American Battlefield Trust, www.battlefields.org/learn/articles/navies-civil-war. *"The Americans have"*: FAS to LW, January 1, 1862.

19. "God's Ahead of Master Lincoln" (1862)

193 *In peacetime, those*: Benjamin Guterman, "Doing 'Good Brave Work': Harriet Tubman's Testimony at Beaufort, South Carolina," *Quarterly of the National Archives and Records Administration* 32, no. 3 (2000), 156.

194 *Harriet intended to*: MCW to FW, May 28, 1862.

194 *Early in the spring*: See Larson, 196. *Responding to the*: Willie Lee Rose, *Rehearsal for Reconstruction: The Port Royal Experiment* (Athens: University of Georgia Press, 1964), 21–22. Boston's Educational Commission was replicated in New York City, in the Freedmen's Aid Society, and in Philadelphia's Port Royal Relief Society. *Lucretia and the*: Faulkner, *Lucretia Mott's Heresy*, 182. *The first African American:* See Ray Allen Billington, ed., *The Journal of Charlotte L. Forten: A Young Black Woman's Reactions to the White World of the Civil War Era* (New York: W. W. Norton, 1953). *Laura Towne, a white*: Rupert Sargent Holland, *Letters and Diary of Laura M. Towne: Written from the Sea Islands of South Carolina, 1862–1884* (Whitefish, MT: Kessinger Publishing, 2010), xv; see also Akiko Ochiai, "The Port Royal Experiment Revisited: Northern Visions of Reconstruction and the Land Question," *New England Quarterly* (2001), 94–97.

195 *Frances and Lazette*: FAS to LW, February 6, 1862. *Frederick Douglass had*: Clinton, 119.

195 *"kidnapped" her from*: Alice Lukas Brickler to Earl Conrad, July 19, 1939, Earl Conrad/Harriet Tubman Collection, New York Public Library, Schomburg Center for Research in Black Culture. *"She gave the little"*: Ibid., August 14, 1939.

Margaret's origins remained unknown until Kate Larson made a discovery after her biography of Tubman was published. She emailed me on January 2, 2018, to say that Margaret's original name was Margaret Woolford. Born between 1852 and 1854, she had a twin brother named James, a younger sister named Sarah, and a younger brother named Moses. "The Woolfords, Isaac and Mary (Maria), lived a couple of houses away from Ben and Rit in Caroline County. Mary, James, and Sarah died sometime after the 1860 census, leaving Margaret and Moses in the care of Isaac." Perhaps it was then that Harriet "kidnapped" Margaret. "Isaac joined the Union Army in mid-1864 and was killed during the war. Moses was left in the care of a nearby prominent Black family, Harrison Friend and his mother, Gracie." Larson followed up on September 15, 2020: "Finding Margaret's identity has done little to answer the mystery of why Tubman took her."

For published discussions about Margaret's story, see Larson, 197–201; Humez, 348; and Clinton, 117–21.

196 *Discussing with Ednah*: Humez, 249. *"The good Lord"*: May, *Some Recollections*, 406. *"I think we"*: FAS to WHS, March 11, 1862.

196 *When he was*: Van Deusen, 92, 144–45. *"That his heart"*: Johnson, op. cit., 59.

197 *"He will not"*: Van Deusen, 164. *In 1858, at*: Johnson, 59.

197 "*Her patriotism is*: FAS to LW, March 12, 1862.

197 *In January 1862*: FAS to LW, January 1862.

197 *It was the*: Eric Foner, *The Fiery Trial: Abraham Lincoln and American Slavery* (New York: W. W. Norton, 2010), 234.

198 *"I am always for"*: *Seward II*, 237.

198 *Frances wanted Henry*: FAS to WHS, April 21, 1862. *She asked Lazette*: FAS to LW, December 11, 1861.

198 *They made a strange*: Elizabeth Botume, *First Days Amongst the Contrabands* (Boston: C. J. Peters, 1881), 33; Holland, xiii. *"Why, their language"*: Bradford, *Harriet Tubman*, 54.

198 *She also began*: Milton C. Sernett, *Harriet Tubman: Myth, Memory, and History* (Durham, NC: Duke University Press, 2007), 86. *That spring or summer*: Larson, 205.

199 *Rebels controlled the*: Larson, 205–6, 208, 210, 212; Beverly Lowry, *Harriet Tubman: Imagining a Life* (New York: Anchor Books, 2007), 299–300.

199 *In Washington, before*: Edward A. Miller, Jr., *Lincoln's Abolitionist General: The Biography of David Hunter* (Columbia: University of South Carolina Press, 1997), 85, 97–99; E. Foner, *Fiery Trial*, 206; Joseph T. Glatthaar, *Forged in Battle: The Civil War Alliance of Black Soldiers and White Officers* (New York: Free Press, 1990), 7. *Secretary Chase's civilian*: Miller, 100–101; Rose, 145–46; Edward L. Pierce, "The Freedmen at Port Royal," *Atlantic Monthly*, September 1863.

200 *Lincoln revoked Hunter's*: Walter Stahr, *Stanton: Lincoln's War Secretary* (New York: Simon & Schuster, 2017), 202–3; E. Foner, *Fiery Trial*, 207. *That beguiling image*: Bordewich, *Bound for Canaan*, 291–92.

200 *Harriet, noting that*: Humez, 244. *"They may send the"*: Lydia Maria Child, Letter to John Greenleaf Whittier, January 21, 1862, in Carolyn L. Karcher, *The First Woman in the Republic: A Cultural Biography of Lydia Maria Child* (Durham, NC: Duke University Press, 1994), 455. Child, like Martha and other abolitionist writers at the time, transcribed Harriet's words in dialect.

20. Battle Hymns (1862)

201 *Invoking the southern*: Stahr, *Seward*, 338, citing Seward to Charles Francis Adams, February 17 and March 10, 1862.

202 *"I have felt all along"*: FAS to LW, March 12, 1862.

202 *In Auburn, talking*: FAS to WHS, March 11, 1862, August 24, 1862.

202 *Six days later*: Goodwin, 428; "The Peninsula Campaign," American Battlefield Trust; *American Civil War: The Definitive Encyclopedia and Document Collection*.

202 *In the spring of 1862*: *HWS1*, 748.

203 *"Susan B. must"*: DW to MCW, March 27, 1862. *Anthony complained in*: Griffith, 109–10; *HWS1*, 747.

203 *Howe woke up*: Julia Ward Howe, *Reminiscences, 1819–1899* (Boston: Houghton, Mifflin, 1899), 273–75.

204 *The party set off*: Goodwin, 439–41; Stahr, 330. *"At night, the long"*: F. W. Seward, *Seward at Washington*, 89–91. *Henry, one of*: Lincoln Civil War Trust, Peninsula Campaign; "Irvin McDowell," Ohio History Central.

205 *They pulled out*: F. W. Seward, *Seward at Washington*, 91–93.

205 *He wrote that:* Stahr, 330; F. W. Seward, *Seward at Washington*, 93.

205 *McClellan had consistently*: "Seven Days in History," American Battlefield Trust; Robert E. L. Krick, "Peninsula Campaign: Robert E. Lee and the Seven Days," Civil War Trust. *Even southerners were*: "Seven Days in History: A Change in Leadership," Battlefields.org.

206 *"You have done"*: Goodwin, 442–45.

206 *"If it were not"*: WHS to FAS, July 12, 1862, F. W. Seward, *Seward at Washington*, 115–16.

206 *Congress, though, was*: James Oakes, *Freedom National: The Destruction of Slavery in the United States, 1861–1865* (New York: W. W. Norton, 2014), 303; Goodwin, 462.

206 *Five days later*: Oakes, *Freedom National,* 304–5; Goodwin, 464–67.

207 *As he later said*: *Seward II*, 118.

207 *"Proclamations are* paper": WHS to FAS, July 29, 1862. *He asked her to*: Undated fragment from that summer, cited in Goodwin, 471–72.

207 *"Blessed, my dear"*: WHS to FS, August 2, 1862, F. W. Seward, *Seward at Washington,* 120–21.

208 *Lincoln—looking ahead*: AL to HG, August 22, 1862; F. W. Seward, *Seward at Washington*, 117; Sean Wilentz, "Who Lincoln Was," *New Republic*, July 15, 2009.

208 *Martha said she*: MCW to DW, April 5, 1862, in Penney and Livingston, 158. *By the end*: Richard F. Miller, *States at War, Vol. 2: A Reference Guide for New York in the Civil War* (Lebanon, NH: University Press of New England, 2014), 300.

208 *Within a month*: Goodwin, 450, Stahr, 334; Henry Hall, *The History of Auburn* (Auburn, NY: Dennis Bros, 1869), 441. *Regiments, composed of*: Alfred S. Roe, *The Ninth New York Heavy Artillery: A History of Its Organization, Services in the Defense of Washington, Marches, Camps, Battles, and Muster-Out . . . And a Complete Roster of the Regiment* (Worcester, MA: F. S. Blanchard, 1899), 7, 13.

209 *One day, half*: FS to WHS, November 9, 1862.

209 *"As it is obvious"*: FAS to FWS, August 10, 1862.

209 *Soon after Henry*: F. W. Seward, *Seward at Washington*, 126; Goodwin, 473–75.

209 *He refused, saying*: Goodwin, 476, 478–79. *Henry did his*: Ibid., 480.

209 *On September 5*: WHS to FAS, September 4, 1862. *Radical Republicans predicted*: Goodwin, 485–86.

210 *The* Chicago Tribune: Stahr, 354–55.

210 *Will's regiment stayed*: Krisher, 73.

210 *Before dawn on*: Janet W. Seward, *Personal Experiences of the Civil War*: Address prepared for the "Fortnightly," an Auburn women's club, January 20, 1898, William Henry Seward Papers, Rare Books, Special Collections, and Preservation Department, University of Rochester, Rochester, New York, 6–7. *Fort Mansfield was*: Benjamin Franklin Cooling III and Walton H. Owen II, *Mr. Lincoln's Forts: A Guide to the Civil War Defenses of Washington* (Lanham, MD: Scarecrow Press, 2010), 22. *Three months after*: Ibid., 7.

211 *Frances, thinking of*: J. W. Seward, *Personal Experiences of the Civil War.*

211 *On September 17*: Scott Hartwig, Civil War Trust, "The Maryland Campaign of 1862." *He told his*: James M. McPherson, *Tried by War: Abraham Lincoln as Commander in Chief* (New York: Penguin Books, 2008), 130–31.

211 *Frances responded to*: FAS to WHS, September 28, 1862. *Martha wrote to*: Penney and Livingston, 158.

211 *Nonetheless, the Union's*: David Donald, *Lincoln* (New York: Simon & Schuster, 1995), 382; William Miller Owen, "The Battle for Marye's Heights," National Military Park, Virginia, National Park Service; "This Day in History: The Battle of Fredericksburg, December 13, 1862." *"If there is a"*: Michael Burlingame, *The Inner World of Abraham Lincoln* (Urbana: University of Illinois Press, 1994), 105. *That month, the*: David Donald, *Charles Sumner and the Rights of Man* (New York: Alfred A. Knopf, 1970), 87.

211 *He'd come down*: Terry L. Jones, "Brother Against Microbe," *New York Times*, October 26, 2019.

212 *One senator charged*: Goodwin, 488; Stahr, 353. *Senator King and*: Donald, *Charles Sumner and the Rights of Man*, 87–95.

212 *A close adviser*: Stahr, 270, 283; Donald, 20–21. *"I feel more"*: CS to FAS, April 1861, Charles Sumner Correspondence, 1829–1874 (MS 1), Houghton Library, Harvard University.

212 *"They may do as"*: F. W. Seward, *Seward at Washington*, 146–77.

212 *Lincoln saw the*: Donald, *Lincoln*, 403.

213 *Sumner harrumphed about*: Stahr, 358; Goodwin, 491–95.

213 *"He is worthy"*: FAS to ECS, December 24, 1862.

214 *Although the issue*: "The Emancipation Proclamation," National Archives, Online Exhibits. *The only emendation*: Donald, *Lincoln*, 405–6.

21. Harriet's War (1863)

215 *Fanny and her mother*: Krisher, 78–80.

216 *After the president's*: F. W. Seward, *Seward at Washington*, 150–51; Stahr, 362; Goodwin, 499.

216 *Garrison spent the*: Mayer, 546. *Nearby, at Tremont*: Blight, 382–83.

216 *"I had my jubilee"*: Bradford, *Harriet Tubman*, 48–49. *"My people are free!"*: Bradford, Harriet, *The Moses of Her People*, 92–93. Garnet, a militant abolitionist, escaped with his family as a boy, and grew up in New York City. He later returned to New York, where he served at the First Colored Presbyterian Church. From 1842 to 1848, he was pastor of the Liberty Street Presbyterian Church in Troy, and he moved to Washington during the war, where from 1864 to 1866 he was pastor of the Fifteenth Street Presbyterian Church.

217 *A soft-spoken Unitarian*: William A. Dobak, *Freedom by the Sword: The U.S. Colored Troops, 1862–1867* (Washington, D.C.: Center of Military History, United States Army, 2011), 31–34; James M. McPherson, *The Negro's Civil War: How American Blacks Felt and Acted During the War for the Union* (New York: Vintage Books, 1993), 168–69; Miller, 113–14; Rose, 189–91.

217 *Harriet had welcomed*: Sernett, 92. Sernett traces the story about the ducks to Hildegard Hoyt Swift's fictionalized account for children of Tubman's life, *The Railroad to Freedom: A Story of the Civil War*. Swift talked to two of Tubman's nieces, who told her about it. *He was stationed*: Rose, 195.

217 *His tent had*: Billington, ed., 173; Christopher Looby, ed., *The Complete Civil War Journals and Selected Letters of Thomas Wentworth Higginson* (Chicago: University of Chicago Press, 2000), 250–51.

218 *He found one*: Thomas Wentworth Higginson, *Army Life in a Black Regiment and Other Writings* (Mineola, NY: Dover Publications), 16. Higginson recorded the statement in heavy dialect.

218 *Governor Andrew of Massachusetts*: Miller, 173–79. *Douglass's recruits included*: Charles got sick before the deployment of the 54th, and served instead in the 5th Massachusetts Cavalry. *"A black man"*: William C. Davis, *Lincoln's Men: How President Lincoln Became Father to an Army and a Nation* (New York: Touchstone, 1999), 105.

218 *Her scouts helped*: The scouts were Isaac and Samuel Hayward, Mott Blake, Gabriel Cahern, Sandy Sellers, George Chisholm, Solomon Gregory, Peter Burns, Charles Simmons, and Walter D. Plowden. See Larson, 210. *Saxton had initiated*: Dobak,

33–34; Jeff W. Grigg, *The Combahee River Raid: Harriet Tubman and Lowcountry Liberation* (Charleston, SC: History Press, 2014), 64–65.

219 *A marching band*: Rose, 196; Lowry, 310. *One of Higginson's soldiers*: Higginson, *Army Life*, 31.

219 *Dr. William H. Brisbane*: Billington, ed., 273 n32. *Some white officials*: Looby, ed., 77.

219 *On January 7*: Guterman, "Doing 'Good Brave Work,' 157, 163.

220 *In late January*: Rose, 245. *Higginson reported to*: McPherson, *The Negro's Civil War*, 168–69.

220 *Montgomery had fought*: Russell Duncan, ed., *Blue-Eyed Child of Fortune: The Civil War Letters of Colonel Robert Gould Shaw* (Athens: University of Georgia Press, 1992), 346 n7.

220 *The insurgent Montgomery*: Rose, 246–47. *Higginson said of: Higginson, Army Life*, 5, 54. *Montgomery engaged in:* TWH to Louisa Storrow Higginson, June 19, 1863, Looby, ed., 288.

221 *It was "sickly season"*: Grigg, 57–59. *He assigned the*: Ibid., 93; Larson, 210.

222 *"Moses, you'll have"*: Ibid., 41.

222 *At Combahee Ferry*: Grigg, 70–71, 77; July 29, 2019, email; January 28, 2020 email.

223 *William Apthorp*: Grigg, 79; Telford, "Harriet," 19; Humez, 334. *"This was the saddest"*: Grigg, 75.

223 *The boats docked*: Rose, 247; Larson, 214; Grigg, 81.

223 *On June 30*: Humez, 58–61, 299; Larson, 215–19. *"Don't you think?"*: Bradford, *Scenes*, 86.

224 *Harriet's joy about*: Rose, 248.

225 *"vulgar contempt for color"*: John A. Andrew to Francis Shaw, January 30, 1863, in Brooks D. Simpson, ed., *The Civil War: The Third Year Told by Those Who Lived It* (New York: Library of America, 2013), 20–22. *When Mrs. Shaw*: Duncan, ed., 24–25.

225 *Shaw wrote to*: Duncan, ed., 367 n4; Higginson, *Army Life*, 165.

226 *As the steamer*: Robert Shaw to Annie Haggerty Shaw, June 13, 1863, in Duncan, ed., 341–45. *When Shaw objected*: Ibid., 44–45, 48.

226 *As expected, the southern*: Ibid., 44; Dobak, 45–47; Rose, 252–54.

226 *Nurses and doctors*: It is likely that Harriet was on Folly Island during the battle, and that at the time, she met General Alfred Terry. He directed some of the operations against Fort Wagner, and several months later, in February 1864, Harriet was back on the island earning some money by cooking and doing some washing for Terry. See George Garrison to WLGII, February 10, 1864.

226 *On July 11*: George E. Stephen, letter to the editor, *Weekly Anglo-African*, July 21, 1863; Duncan, ed., 48; Dobak, 47–49. *The 54th first*: Luis F. Emilio, *A Brave Black Regiment: The History of the Fifty-Fourth Massachusetts Voluntary Infantry, 1863–1865* (Mount Pleasant, SC: Arcadia Press, 1891, 2017), 65–68.

227 *The men waited under*: Letter from Shaw to his wife, Annie, in Duncan, ed., 385–86.

227 *One division commander*: The commander was Major General Truman Seymour; Glatthaar, 137.

227 *Shaw's advance began*: Duncan, ed., 52; Brian C. Pohanka, "Fort Wagner and the 54th Massachusetts Volunteer Infantry," July 18, 1863, Civil War Trust. *Some could free*: Susie King Taylor, *Reminiscences of My Life in Camp: An African American Woman's Civil War Memoir* (Athens: University of Georgia Press, 2006), 34. *As darkness fell*: Duncan, ed., 52. *Shaw, leading from*: Glatthaar, 139.

228 *"And then we saw"*: Harriet described this scene to Albert Bushnell Hart, who quoted

it in *Slavery and Abolition, 1831–1841, The American Nation: A History* (New York: Harper & Brothers, 1906), 209, cited in Humez, 135. Hart did not identify the location.

228 *Sergeant William Carney*: Glatthaar, 140. *When General Gillmore*: Ibid.

228 *A hundred and fifty*: Gerald Schwartz, ed., *A Woman Doctor's Civil War: Esther Hill Hawks' Diary* (Columbia: University of South Carolina Press, 1984), 50.

228 *The people of*: Ibid., 10, 20, 51.

228 *"I'd go to the hospital"*: Bradford, *Scenes*, 37.

229 *"You say you will"*: AL letter to James C. Conkling, a representative in the Illinois House, read at a rally in Springfield on September 3, 1863.

229 *On July 17*: Duncan, ed. *In coming decades*: Sernett, 92–93; Larson, 367 n102.

22. Willy Wright at Gettysburg (March–July 1863)

231 *"Felt very sad"*: Penney and Livingston, 160, MCW to WPW, March 17, 1863.

232 *"I need it"*: FAS to WHS, June 17, 1863.

232 *"My heart is"*: MCW to WPW, May 14, 1863, Penney and Livingston, 161.

232 *Martha affected a*: MCW to WPW, January 22, 1863; Ibid., April 30, 1863.

233 *On June 25*: William Wright journal, January 20–March 9, 1862, GFP; Andrew Cowan, "Battle Field Near Gettysburg, Pa," July 4, 1863, *Auburn Advertiser and Union*.

233 *On Friday, July 3*: Penney and Livingston, 161–62.

233 *The clouds lifted:* From an unidentified fifty-page handwritten history of the 1st New York Battery, GFP, Series IX, Wright Family Correspondence, Wright, William Pelham, Civil War.

234 *The Union men*: Handwritten history of the 1st New York Battery.

234 *He could feel:* Wartime diary of WPW, quoted in Penney and Livingston, 162. *The exchange of fire*: *Antietam to Appomattox with 118th Penna. Vols., Corn Exchange Regiment* (Philadelphia: J. L. Smith, 1892), 257; thanks to Wayne E. Motts, National Civil War Museum.

234 *A company captain*: Frances A. Donaldson, "This Trial of the Nerves." *Brigadier General Lewis*: American Battlefield Trust.

235 *Willy's captain, Cowan*: Capt. Andrew Cowan, "Repulsing Pickett's Charge—An Eyewitness Account," *Civil War Times* 3, no. 5 (August 1964), 29. *At ten yards*: Penney and Livingston, 163.

235 *A reporter for*: 1st New York Independent Battery, Civil War Newspaper Clippings, New York State Military Museum. *He was mortally*: American Battlefield Trust.

235 *One Auburn man*: JWC, "From Cowan's Battery, Battle Field near Gettysburg, Pa., July 4th, 1863; and Camp at Middletown, Md, July 9, 1863," New York State Military Museum; extract from Dr. Clift's letter to his brother, copied by MCW, July 20, 1863.

236 *On July 6*: MCW to FW, July 8, 1863. *Two days later*: dmna.ny.gov/historic/reghist/civil/artillery/1stIndBat/1stIndBatCWN.htm. *"If I had not"*: MCW to LW, June 25, 1865; Penney and Livingston, 165 n41.

236 *"It was a rough, untidy"*: Wright, "Reminiscences of the War," unpublished manuscript, Part III, 2–3, GFP. *Marianna scrutinized some*: MWM to Anna Hopper, July 10, 1863, GFP.

237 *David and Marianna arrived*: MPM to Anna Hopper, July 20, 1863. *There were only*:

Dr. Jonathan Letterman, medical director of the Army of the Potomac, Gettysburg Report, October 2, 1863.

237 *Directed to the*: David Wright, "Reminiscences of the War," Part III, 5–7, GFP.

237 *She wrote to*: Penney and Livingston, 165.

238 *The soldiers slept*: MPM to Anna Hopper, July 20, 1863.

238 *On one of Marianna's*: MPM to Agnes Harrison, July 1863, GFP.

238 *Marianna's youngest brother*: Penney and Livingston, 165.

238 *In December 1864*: MCW to EW, December 11.

23. A Mighty Army of Women (1863–1864)

240 *Irish factory workers*: Ginzberg, 118. *When the Wrights'*: Penney and Livingston, 166. *Frances thought about*: FAS to WHS, July 18, 1863. *She sent Nicholas*: FAS to Frederick Seward, July 23, 1863.

240 *On the Fourth*: William F. B. Vodrey, "Blood in the Streets: The New York City Draft Riots," Cleveland Civil War Roundtable; FAS to WHS, July 15, 1863.

240 *On the morning*: "How to Escape the Draft," *Harper's Weekly*, August 1, 1863. *The other draft*: Ginzberg, 111. *The Colored Orphan*: "The New York City Draft Riots—1863," *The Civil War in N.Y.C.*, Tenement Museum, City University of New York.

241 *Frances wrote about*: FAS to WHS, July 15 and 18, 1863. *Overlooking France's extreme*: WHS to FAS, July 17 and 21, 1863; F. W. Seward, *Seward at Washington*, 176–77.

241 *During the perilous*: Theodore Stanton and Harriot Stanton Blatch, eds., *Elizabeth Cady Stanton: As Revealed in Her Letters, Diary, and Reminiscences, Vol. 1* (Harper & Brothers, 1927), 197–98; Mayer, 557. *In the summons*: Stanton and Blatch, eds., 198.

241 *Stanton had moved*: Griffith, 113.

242 *Martha took Ellen*: Penney and Livingston, 161. *Stanton proceeded as*: ECS to MCW, August 10, 1862, Elizabeth Cady Stanton Papers, Mabel Smith Douglass Library, Rutgers University Libraries, Special Collections and University Archives. *Stanton subsequently saw*: Ginzberg, *Elizabeth Cady Stanton*, 107.

242 *The Loyal League*: Donald, *Charles Sumner and the Rights of Man*, 125, 136–37, 147–48; SBA to CS, December 13, 1863, and ECS and SBA to CS, February 4, 1864, Sumner MSS. *"Send on the petitions"*: E. C. Stanton, 239.

242 *Stanton employed three*: Ellen Carol DuBois, *Feminism and Suffrage: The Emergence of an Independent Women's Movement in America, 1848–1869* (Ithaca: Cornell University Press, 1978), 53.

243 *Petitioners in New York*: Petition of the Women's Loyal National League for the Abolition of Slavery, January 25, 1864, Petitions and Memorials, Select Committee on Slavery and Freedmen, Records of Early Select Committees (SEN 38A-H20), 38th Congress, Records of the U.S. Senate, Record Group 46, National Archives, Washington, D.C.

243 *In a shameless*: Michael Vorenberg, *Final Freedom: The Civil War, the Abolition of Slavery, and the Thirteenth Amendment* (Cambridge: Cambridge University Press, 2001), 52–53.

243 *On February 9, at*: *HWS1*, 79, 861–76; Donald, 147–48.

243 *Sumner went on*: Donald, 149. *The Senate rejected*: Congressional Globe, Senate, 38th Congress, 1st Session, p. 1488.

243 *"You have quite"*: ECS to FAS, February 15, 1864, in Gordon, ed., 510–11.

244 *"I enclose Mrs"*: FAS to WHS, February 19, 1864.

244 *The new fort*: J. W. Seward, *Personal Experiences*, 12–13.

244 *Jenny was comfortable*: Ibid., 14. For a description of soldiers' and officers' quarters in camp, see "Civil War Cabins," Army Heritage Trail, U.S. Army Heritage and Education Center, ahec.armywarcollege.edu/trail/CivilWarCabins/index.cfm.

245 *Will traveled by*: J. W. Seward, 13–16.

24. Daughters and Sons (1864)

247 *"nice only dolorous"*: Alonso, 178.

247 *In mid-February*: WLGII to MCW and DW, February 14, 1864.

248 *"Please do not"*: EW to MCW and DW, February 17, 1864, in Alonso, 204.

248 *When William learned:* WLG Jr. to MCW, February 21, 1864; Alonso, 204.

248 *In a letter*: EW to WLGII, July 26, 1864, Alonso, 206.

248 *Ellen ceded to William*: Alonso, 283.

249 *After considerable internal*: Ibid., 165.

249 *When the Garrisons'*: Mayer, 520, 551–55. Walter M. Merrill, ed., *The Letters of William Lloyd Garrison: Let the Oppressed Go Free, 1861–1867* (Cambridge, MA: Belknap Press of Harvard University Press, 1979), 167. *Ellen, who had*: Alonso, 163, 209.

249 *"It will all come out"*: MCW to EW, May 15, 1864.

250 *She decorated the*: Alonso, 208–9; Penney and Livingston, 167.

250 *After it was over*: MCW to WLGII, October 2, 1864. *Martha was good*: Osborne, "Recollection of Martha Coffin Wright."

250 *"He's the quietest"*: "The Generals and Admirals: Ulysses S. Grant (1822–1885), Mr. Lincoln's White House," www.mrlincolnswhitehouse.org/residents-visitors/the-generals-and-admirals/generals-admirals-ulysses-s-grant-1822-1885/.

250 *Two months later*: Ulysses S. Grant, "Report of the Operations of the Armies of the United States, 1864–'65," July 22, 1865.

251 *"I cannot yet"*: FAS to WHS Jr., May 20, 1864.

251 *Reinforcing her strength of will*: FAS to AS, May 15, 1864. *"I do not like this"*: FAS to AS, August 4, 1864. *At least Frederick*: FAS to LW, December 1861.

251 *"There was no"*: J. W. Seward, *Personal Experiences of the Civil War*, 18.

251 *At Cold Harbor*: Ron Chernow, *Grant* (New York: Penguin Press, 2017), 403–5. *Several days later*: Krisher, 166.

252 *Still, Grant had*: Chernow, 407.

252 *Will's 9th New York*: Marc Leepson, *Desperate Engagement: How a Little-Known Civil War Battle Saved Washington, D.C., and Changed American History* (New York: Thomas Dunne Books/St. Martin's Press, 2007), 1–2; Ryan T. Quint, *Determined to Stand and Fight: The Battle of Monocacy, July 9, 1864* (El Dorado Hills, CA: Savas Beatie, 2016), introduction by Ted Alexander, xii–xiii. *"my bad old"*: Larry Tagg, *The Generals of Gettysburg: The Leaders of America's Greatest Battle* (Cambridge, MA: Da Capo Press, 1998), 257.

253 *After a night*: Leepson, 80; Quint, 44. *A few hours later*: Leepson, 108. The men who gathered and lit the wheat sheaves were Alfred Nelson Sova, Samuel Mack, and Albert Smith.

253 *Monocacy was a:* Quint, iii; Leepson, 113–14.

253 *On July 10*: AHS to FS, July 10, 1864. *Amid the helter-skelter*: J. W. Seward, *Personal Experiences of the Civil War*, 20; Quint, 80.
254 *"These men died"*: Ibid., xiv.
254 *When Frances heard*: FAS to WHS, July 11, 1864.
255 *A soldier begged*: F. W. Seward, *Seward at Washington*, 234.
255 *The 111th New York*: A. De Lancey Brigham, *Brigham's General Director of Auburn, Weedsport, Port Byron, Union Springs, Aurora, Moravia and Cayuga, and Business Directory of Auburn, 1863 and 1864* (Auburn, NY: Wm. J. Moses' Publishing, 1863), 40–42. *One was Colonel*: "Hugh McNeil," Pennsylvania Civil War 150, pacivilwar150.com/ThroughPeople/Soldiers/HughMcNeil.html.
255 *Howland had left*: Judith Colucci Breault, *The World of Emily Howland: Odyssey of a Humanitarian* (Millbrae, CA: Les Femmes, 1976), 53–56.
255 *In June 1864*: FAS to Anna Seward, June 22, 1864.
256 *Late one night*: FAS to Frederick Seward, July 3, 1864.
256 *That summer, Harriet*: According to Dr. Esther Hill Hawks, Harriet was in Fernandina in May 1864. See Schwartz, ed., 79. *She recalled that*: Telford, "Harriet."
257 *He rushed over* : GG to WLG Jr., February 10, 1864.
257 *Although Harriet tried*: Thanks to Jeff Ludwig. *"Her services to"*: *Commonwealth*, August 12, 1864; Humez, 64.
257 *They had first met*: Blight, 409; McFeeley, 232–34. *A year later*: Blight, 437.
258 *On September 1*: Dennis Frye, "Again Into the Valley of Fire," *Hallowed Ground Magazine*, Fall 2014.
258 *Frances wrote to*: FAS to WHS, November 10, 1864. *"Since my return"*: WHS Jr. to JWS, November 27, 1864, December 30, 1864; Janet W. Seward, Personal Experiences, 21.
259 *Called by a crowd*: Stahr, 413.

PART FOUR: RIGHTS (1864–1875)

25. E Pluribus Unum (1864–1865)

263 *Frances felt blessed*: FAS to LW, December 1861.
264 *Henry was working*: Goodwin, 686–87. *The Senate had*: Vorenberg, 100–102. *"We are like whalers"*: Goodwin, 688, 690. *"The logic and moral"*: Michael Burlingame, *Abraham Lincoln: A Life* (Baltimore: Johns Hopkins University Press, 2008), 750–51.
264 *Sumner's immediate goal*: Donald, *Charles Sumner and the Rights of Man*, 192.
265 *Under pressure from*: Winkle, 396–98.
265 *"What shadows we are"*: FAS to Lazette, December 18, 1864. In October 1866, after Sumner's mother died and left him a bequest, he married Mrs. Hooper. They were tempestuously unhappy. Among other indiscretions, Alice conducted an affair with a Prussian diplomat, and they soon separated. Sumner divorced her on grounds of desertion in May 1873.
265 *For a moment:* Vorenberg, 20. *The* Tribune *declared*: February 1, 1865. *"The greatest measure"*: Goodwin, 689.
266 *There was speculation*: Ronald C. White, Jr., *A. Lincoln: A Biography* (New York: Random House, 2009), 659. *"I congratulate you"*: FAS to WHS, February 3, 1865.
266 *"I felt then that"*: Harold Holzer, *Lincoln as I Knew Him: Gossip, Tributes, and Revela-*

tions from His Best Friends and Worst Enemies (Chapel Hill, NC: Algonquin Books, 1999), 205. *The cast-iron dome*: "The Statue of Freedom," Architect of the Capitol.

266 *Lincoln emerged on*: *Seward II*, 265.

266 *One of his bodyguards*: Smith Stimmel, *Personal Reminiscences of Abraham Lincoln* (Minneapolis, MN: William H. M. Adams, 1928), 70. *At the White House*: Donald, *Lincoln*, 568.

266 *Harriet was in Washington*: The Home for Destitute Colored Women and Children, founded by a woman's association, of which Frances was a nominal member, was mired in scandal: the head teacher, Maria Mann, a niece of the education reformer Horace Mann, had raised enough money from her abolitionist family and friends around Boston to convert the carriage house into a dormitory, and to build a classroom, a dining room, and a laundry. But Mann drove off several matrons. Finally, Lucy Colman, a suffragist ally of Susan B. Anthony from Rochester, was brought in. Colman was shocked by the conditions at the home: hungry children infested with vermin, and empty liquor bottles in the basement. She knew Harriet Tubman through mutual friends in Rochester and asked her to help her restore order. The scandal became a test of wills between two reformers from different camps. Mann went to Congress, which supported the home, accusing Mann of withholding food from the children as a form of punishment; Mann enlisted Secretary of War Stanton to defend her. In the end, Colman was removed.

267 *The night after*: Thanks to Charles Lenhart and Paula T. Whitacre for alerting me to this scene, which is recorded in the diaries of Julia Wilbur, March 5, 1865, Julia Wilbur Papers, Quaker & Special Collections, Haverford College, Haverford, Pennsylvania. *She had last*: Larson, 369 n140.

267 *"'Twas Sojourner Truth"*: Rosa Belle Holt, "A Heroine in Ebony," *Chautauquan*, July 1886, 426.

267 *"They tried to"*: Julia Wilbur diaries.

26. Retribution (1865)

270 *"You are back?"*: Undated letter, F. W. Seward, *Seward at Washington*, 270–72.

270 *Fanny came in*: DFS, April 9, 1865. *As word spread*: "Entering Richmond," Lincoln Institute of the Lehrman Institute.

270 *Lincoln called out*: "Entering Richmond," Mr. Lincoln and Freedom, Lehrman Institute; *Battles and Leaders of the Civil War, Vol. IV* (1888; reprint ed., 1982), 728; "President Lincoln Enters Richmond, 1865," Eyewitness to History, www.eyewitnesstohistory.com (2000).

271 *The hospital was*: National Park Service, Depot Field Hospital, Petersburg National Battlefield. *"He spoke of"*: DFS, April 9, 1865. As the *River Queen* proceeded to Washington, Lincoln read aloud from his favorite play, *Macbeth*, a macabre choice on that day of triumph, twice repeating Macbeth's words to Lady Macbeth:

> *Duncan is in his grave;*
> *After life's fitful fever he sleeps well;*
> *Treason has done his worst: nor steel, nor poison,*
> *Malice domestic, foreign levy, nothing*
> *Can touch him further.*

He remarked "how true a description of the murderer that one was; when, the dark deed achieved, its tortured perpetrator came to envy the sleep of his victim."

271 *Fanny wrote that*: Krisher, 186–87.

271 *In the parlor of*: National Park Service, "Appomattox Court House: Beginning Peace and Reunion"; National Park Service, "The Surrender Meeting." *Grant drafted the*: "Civil War Day by Day," University of North Carolina University Library, blogs.lib.unc.edu/civilwar/index.php/2015/04/09/9-april-1865/.

272 *Buildings were festooned*: Chernow, 519–20. *Fanny noticed that*: DFS, April 13, 1865.

272 *Lincoln was sitting*: F. W. Seward, *Seward at Washington*, 265.

273 *One cabinet member*: Ibid., 274.

273 *Stanton outlined each*: Ibid., 275. *Stanton advised Lincoln against*: Chernow, 523.

273 *At the Club House*: For accounts of the assassination attempt, see DFS, April 14, 1865; F. W. Seward, *Seward at Washington*, 279–80; Krisher, 201–3; Dr. Tullio Verdi, "The Assassination of the Sewards," *Juanita Sentinel*, June 25, 1873; Stahr, 436–37; Goodwin, 737; Donald, *Lincoln*, 598–99.

274 *Later that night*: Krisher, 237. *He described the*: Van Deusen, 414.

275 *"Are you safe?"*: Krisher, 208–9.

275 *The next morning*: DFS, April 14; Donald, 599.

276 *Henry's attacker was*: Van Deusen, 214.

276 *In 1864, Lincoln*: Brenda Wineapple, *The Impeachers: The Trial of Andrew Johnson and the Dream of a Just Nation* (New York: Random House, 2019), xix, xxvii.

276 *Lincoln's funeral service*: "East Room: President Lincoln's Funeral," Lehrman Institute, www.mrlincolnswhitehouse.org/washington/other-government-buildings/east-room-president-lincolns-funeral/. *Major General Weitzel*: Gary W. Gallagher, *The Union War* (Cambridge, MA: Harvard University Press, 2011), 12; Dobak, 421.

276 *In a letter*: WSII to JS, April 21, 1865.

276 *Will located a*: WSII to JS, April 25 and 30, 1865.

277 *"It seems as"*: F. W. Seward, *Seward at Washington*, 286. *Frances said that*: FAS to Mr. Alward, May 11, 1865, ibid., 278–79.

277 *"This is a country"*: Wineapple, xviii, xxiii–iv. *Henry approved of*: F. W. Seward, *Seward at Washington*, 281–85.

278 *She preferred houses*: FAS to Frederick Seward, July 29, 1862.

278 *Picturing her garden*: Stahr, 439.

279 *She told Fanny*: FS to Amanda Schoolcraft, January 26, 1866; Krisher, 227.

279 *Fred called it*: F. W. Seward, *Seward at Washington*, 285. *Fanny, who had*: Stahr, 438. *But she was*: Krisher, 232.

279 *Martha went to see*: MCW to MPM, June 23, 1864. *That day, Lazette*: MCW to her sisters, July 5, 1865. *"Think what a"*: MCW to EWG, April 19, 1865.

279 *"very pale in a plaid"*: MCW to FW, June 29, 1865.

279 *The coffin was*: F. W. Seward, *Seward at Washington*, 285–86. *According to the*: Stahr, 439–40. The Auburn *Advertiser & Union* and the *Times* published their obituaries on June 26, 1865.

280 *Sumner wrote to*: F. W. Seward, *Seward at Washington*, 286–87.

280 *The* Chicago Journal: Ibid., 287–88.

281 *The day before*: MCW to LM, April 1, 1865.

281 *Looking back on*: MCW to LM, July 5, 1865, Penney and Livingston, 172.

27. Civil Disobedience (1865)

283 *Nurses from the*: Humez, 65, 303; Larson, 228.

284 *The Hampton complex*: Mark St. John Erickson, "Civil War Spawns Huge Hampton Hospital," *Daily Press*, August 1, 2012.

284 *The hospital surgeon*: "Soldiers Dying from Hunger and Neglect," *Independent*, July 8, 1865. The executive officer at Hampton Hospital wrote a letter in response, published on July 30. Harriet said that twenty to twenty-five Black men were dying every day—evidently an exaggeration. But the numbers the executive officer cited for June—twenty-six white deaths and seventy "Colored"—reinforced Harriet's argument about the uneven death toll.

284 *In mid-July, when*: Humez, 65.

285 *"They will be"*: F. W. Seward, *Seward at Washington*, 284, 292.

285 *He introduced her*: Larson, 229–31. The pass was issued on July 22.

285 *Back at the hospital*: Clinton, 188.

285 *Lucretia was grieving*: Faulkner, 183–84.

286 *Lucretia liked the*: Anna Davis Hallowell, ed., *James and Lucretia Mott: Life and Letters* (Boston: Houghton, Mifflin, 1884), 407.

286 *Lucretia saw emancipation*: Faulkner, *Lucretia Mott's Heresy*, 177, 186. *When the Civil*: Susan Goodier and Karen Pastorello, *Women Will Vote: Winning Suffrage in New York State* (Ithaca, NY: Three Hill, 2017), 10. *Southern states, with*: "Thirteenth Amendment to the U.S. Constitution: Abolition of Slavery (1865)," ourdocuments.gov; "Black Codes and Jim Crow," sites.google.com/a/email.cpcc.edu/black-codes-and-jim-crow/black-code-and-jim-crow-law-examples; www.digitalhistory.uh.edu/disp_textbook.cfm?smtid=3&psid=3681.

286 *Lucretia was still*: Faulkner, *Lucretia Mott's Heresy*, 191–92. The campaign succeeded. In 1867, the governor signed a law making it a crime to discriminate on the state's trolley cars and trains.

286 *On Harriet's visit*: LM to MCW, October 2, 1865, in Palmer, ed., 363–64. *The Thirteenth Amendment*: The ratification took place without the votes of southern states, which had not yet reentered the Union. As a condition of readmittance into the country, southern states would have to write new constitutions and ratify the amendment.

287 *That put her*: Penney and Livingston, 178. *Stanton and Anthony*: DuBois, *Feminism and Suffrage*, 94.

287 *Hoping to avoid:* Penney and Livingston, 178. *Stanton blamed Phillips*: ECS to Wendell Phillips, January 12, 1866; Gornick, 79. *"I have argued"*: ECS to SBA, August 1, 1865, DuBois, *Feminism and Suffrage*, 60; Mayer, 607.

287 *"Martha, what are you?"*: ECS to MCW, January 6, 1866.

288 *Harriet left Roadside*: Humez, 301. *"Come, hustle out"*: Bradford, *Scenes*, 46.

288 *The conductor hadn't*: MCW to MPM, November 17, 1865.

288 *The pastor introduced*: "Mrs. Harriet Tubman, the Coloured Nurse and Scout—The Bridge Street African M. E. Church Last Evening," *Brooklyn Eagle*, October 23, 1865. *Harriet traveled the*: According to Kate Larson's July 19, 2020, email, one of the other Black women in Auburn to hold a deed of ownership was Harriet Bogart, who worked with her husband, Nicholas, for the Sewards.

28. Wrongs and Rights (1865–1875)

289 *who wouldn't be*: MCW to WLG Jr., October 20, 1874.

290 *In an afterthought*: MCW to WLGII, January 10, 1869.

290 *He had advised*: Larson, 232.

290 *She was responsible*: See ibid., 233, 371 n25, for the family members living with Harriet. The niece, Ann Stewart, was married to Harriet's friend Thomas Elliott, a member of the Dover Eight. *On one occasion*: MCW to EWG, September 6, 1867; MCW to her sisters, July 1, 1868.

291 *"So I always dealt with"*: WHS to FS, July 17 and 18, 1866; Krisher, 231–37.

291 *On October 29*: Larson, 372 n41. *Lazette confessed to:* EH to her mother, October 31, 1866.

291 *Stanton, reminding Wendell Phillips*: Ginzberg, 116–19; Dudden, 70; Tetrault, 1–3; Faulkner, *Lucretia Mott's Heresy,* 187; Carol A. Kolmerten, *The American Life of Ernestine L. Rose* (Syracuse, NY: Syracuse University Press, 1999), 245; *HWS2,* 103ff.

292 *"We press our"*: Proceedings of the Eleventh National Woman's Rights Convention, held at the Church of the Puritans, New York, May 10, 1866.

292 *African American women*: Julie Roy Jeffrey, *The Great Silent Army of Abolitionism: Ordinary Women in the Antislavery Movement* (Chapel Hill: University of North Carolina Press, 1998), 205–7; Ginzberg, 119.

293 *After meeting privately*: Faulkner, *Lucretia Mott's Heresy,* 187–88.

294 *Douglass too joined*: Blight, 488.

294 *Worse, they invited*: Patricia G. Holland, "George Francis Train and the Woman Suffrage Movement, 1867–70," *Books at Iowa* 46 (April 1987), 8–29; Penney and Livingston, 179–80.

294 *Lucy Stone, who*: Griffith, 130. *Garrison called him*: Alonso, 284.

294 *"Mr. Train is"*: ECS to MCW, January 8, 1868, in Stanton and Blatch, eds., 119.

295 *"I am sorry for"*: MCW to ECS, February 20, 1868. *"The Revolution is"*: Faulkner, 189. *Martha, despite her*: MCW to DW, December 12, 1867.

295 *"Harriet, you have"*: Bradford, *Scenes,* 112. *Charles P. Wood*: Manuscript History Concerning the Pension Claims of Harriet Tubman, HR 55A-D1, Papers Accompanying the Claim of Harriet Tubman, Record Group 233, National Archives, Washington, D.C., For Services as Scout, Pay Claim, January 31, 1865. Harriet herself asked for less than the army's standard rate for scouts of $60 a month. Calculating that she had worked from May 25, 1862, to January 31, 1865, and deducting time spent on nursing and the $200 she had been paid at the start of her service, she came up with a total of $766. Larson, 252; Harriet Tubman Collection, Tubman Home Museum, Auburn, New York.

296 *She called the*: Bradford, 1. *"I have wrought"*: FD to HT, August 29, 1868, Bradford, 6–7.

296 *"She was inordinately"*: Sernett, 75.

296 *The Bradford book*: Larson, 248–50.

297 *"Suffrage—What's that?"*: MCW to EWG, December 16, 1868.

297 *When it became*: Ginzberg, 120, 125; Gornick, 81. *She occasionally conceded*: Ellen Carol DuBois and Richard Cándida Smith, eds., *Elizabeth Cady Stanton: Feminist as Thinker* (New York: New York University Press, 2007), 117. *At the same time:* "Manhood Suffrage," *Revolution*, December 24, 1868; see Dudden, 166.

298 *"I tho't Douglass' "*: MCW to DW, May 20, 1869.

298 *Martha joined the*: Goodier and Pastorello, 3.

298 *"In union there"*: MCW to LS, August 22, 1869. Martha wrote a first draft of the letter on the back of a copy of the Women's Loyal League's emancipation petition.

299 *The next month*: Penney and Livingston, 187.

299 *As Anthony said*: Eliza Wright, "Recollection of Martha Coffin Wright" *"I dreaded inexpressibly"*: Penney and Livingston, 213.

299 *"Another scion of the"*: Ibid., 216.

300 *Whenever she was*: MCW to MPW, January 1, 1868, in ibid., 209–10.

300 *"She seemed so"*: EWG to Maria Mott Davis, January 28, 1875, GFP.

300 *"Although you, my"*: David Wright, Reminiscences, GFP.

300 *Anthony wrote to*: SBA to EWG, January 22, 1875, in Penney and Livingston, 213. "Eliza Wright Osborne Dies at Age 83," www.loc.gov/item/rbcmiller002882/.

301 *"It was a great"*: "Frederick Douglass on Woman Suffrage," International Council of Women, Washington, D.C., April 1888.

301 *As Harriet got older*: EWO to HOS, December 16, 1904; EWO to HOS, June 15, 1906; thanks to David Connelly; Osborne Family Papers, Syracuse University Libraries, Special Collections Research Center.

Epilogue

303 *The parlor leads*: Seward retired in 1868, after Ulysses S. Grant was elected. He died on the velvet settee in his library on October 10, 1872, after an afternoon working with Olive Risley on a bestselling book, *William H. Seward's Travels Around the World*. Seward had become devoted to Olive, the daughter of a friend and forty years his junior. In a post-retirement trip, he took her and her sister to Europe and the Middle and Far East. Trailed by innuendo about a romantic relationship, Seward adopted Olive. The book was part travelogue and part political journal, advocating nationalism, modernization, and global cooperation.

304 *Eliza's daughter Helen*: She was married to James Storrow, a wealthy investment banker in Boston. Helen served on the board of the North Bennet Street Industrial School in Boston's North End, which taught vocational skills to immigrants. The school continues today, training students in crafts and trades.

305 *Eliza's sixth guest*: Anthony described this scene on the flyleaf of her copy of the third edition of *Scenes in the Life of Harriet Tubman*, titled *Harriet Tubman: The Moses of Her People*, published in 1901. On January 1, 1903, Anthony wrote about the get-together as "a real love feast of the few that are left, and here came *Harriet Tubman*." The book is in the Library of Congress's Rare Books and Special Collections. *Harriet had survived*: She and Davis ran a small brick-making operation, and adopted an orphan named Gertie, fulfilling Harriet's consuming desire for a daughter. See Larson, 252, 260, 281. Harriet also later adopted her orphaned grandniece, Katy Stewart. See Humez, 348. *Harriet was now*: After acquiring the land at auction, she contacted friends in Syracuse and Boston, and articles soon appeared in the *Chautauquan* and *New England Magazine*. Supporters made donations, and she incorporated the home under the auspices of the AME Zion Church, which she'd helped raise the funds to build. *As the women*: Emily Howland journal, cited in Larson, 386 n75. Anthony died in 1906, fourteen years after the ratification of the 19th Amendment.

305 *Five years later*: "The Moses of Her People: Amazing Life Work of Harriet Tubman.

A Story Stranger Than Fiction. After 80 Years of Devotion She Lives to Lament That She Can Do No More Than Plan," *New York Herald*, September 22, 1907. Drake was a son-in-law of Harriet's biographer Sarah Bradford.

306 *The Harriet Tubman Home*: "Tubman Home Open and Aged Harriet Was Central Figure of Celebration," *Auburn Citizen*, June 24, 1908. Around 1914, the white frame house on the property replaced John Brown Hall as the home for the aged.

306 *Harriet spent her*: Her care was subsidized by Eliza Osborne, Will Seward's wife, Jenny, Emily Howland, and the Empire State Federation of Women's Clubs. See Larson, 288–89.

306 *G. Howard Carter*: "To the Colored Race: Mrs. Seward Was Always a True Friend, Declares This Negro," November 12, 1913; thanks to the New York State Library, Albany, New York.

307 *Auburn citizens raised*: "High Tribute Paid to Harriet Tubman as Memorial Tablet Is Unveiled in Her Honor," *Advertiser-Journal*, Saturday, June 13, 1914. Margaret Stewart had married Henry Lucas, a Civil War veteran. Their children were Alice, Margaret Della, and Allen.

Selected Bibliography

Abzug, Robert H. *Passionate Liberator: Theodore Dwight Weld and the Dilemma of Reform*. New York: Oxford University Press, 1980.

Allen, Danielle. *Our Declaration: A Reading of the Declaration of Independence in Defense of Equality*. New York: Liveright Publishing, 2014.

Alonso, Harriet Hyman. *Growing Up Abolitionist: The Story of the Garrison Children*. Amherst: University of Massachusetts Press, 2002.

Anderson, Scott W. *Auburn, New York: The Entrepreneurs' Frontier*. Syracuse: Syracuse University Press, 2015.

Arpey, Andrew W. *The William Freeman Murder Trial: Insanity, Politics, and Race*. Syracuse, NY: Syracuse University Press, 2003.

Billington, Ray Allen, ed. *The Journal of Charlotte L. Forten: A Young Black Woman's Reactions to the White World of the Civil War Era*. W. W. Norton, 1953.

Blight, David W. *Frederick Douglass' Civil War: Keeping Faith in Jubilee*. Baton Rouge: Louisiana State University Press, 1989.

———. *Frederick Douglass: Prophet of Freedom*. New York: Simon & Schuster, 2018.

———. *Race and Reunion: The Civil War in American Memory*. Cambridge, MA: The Belknap Press of Harvard University Press, 2001.

Bordewich, Fergus M. *Bound for Canaan: The Epic Story of the Underground Railroad, America's First Civil Rights Movement*. New York: Amistad, 2005.

———. *Washington: The Making of the American Capital*. New York: Amistad, 2008.

Bradford, Sarah H. *Scenes in the Life of Harriet Tubman*. Auburn, NY: W. J. Moses, 1869.

———. *Harriet Tubman: The Moses of Her People*. New York: G. R. Lockwood, 1886.

Breault, Judith Colucci. *The World of Emily Howland: Odyssey of a Humanitarian*. Millbrae, CA: Les Femmes, 1976.

Cheney, Ednah Dow. *Reminiscences of Ednah Dow Cheney*. Boston: Lee & Shepard, 1902.

Chernow, Ron. *Grant*. New York: Penguin Press, 2017.

Christianson, Scott. *Freeing Charles: The Struggle to Free a Slave on the Eve of the Civil War*. Urbana and Chicago: University of Illinois Press, 2010.

Clinton, Catherine. *Harriet Tubman: The Road to Freedom*. New York: Little, Brown, 2004.

Conrad, Earl. *The Governor and His Lady: The Story of William Henry Seward and His Wife Frances*. New York: G.P. Putnam's Sons, 1960.

Cott, Nancy F. *The Bonds of Womanhood: "Women's Sphere" in New England, 1780–1835*. New Haven: Yale University Press, 1977.

Dann, Norman K. *Practical Dreamer: Gerrit Smith and the Crusade for Social Reform*. Hamilton, NY: Log Cabin Books, 2009.

Davis, Angela. *Women, Race, and Class.* New York: Vintage Books, 1983.

Delbanco, Andrew. *The Abolitionist Imagination.* Cambridge, MA: Harvard University Press, 2012.

———. *The War Before the War: Fugitive Slaves and the Struggle for America's Soul from the Revolution to the Civil War.* New York: Penguin Press, 2018.

Densmore, Christopher, Carol Faulkner, Nancy Hewitt, and Beverly Wilson Palmer, eds. *Lucretia Mott Speaks: The Essential Speeches and Sermons.* Urbana: University of Illinois Press, 2017.

Denton, Lawrence M. *William Henry Seward and the Secession Crisis: The Effort to Prevent Civil War.* Jefferson, NC: McFarland, 2009.

Dobak, William A. *Freedom by the Sword: The U.S. Colored Troops, 1862–1867.* Washington, D.C.: Center of Military History, United States Army, 2011.

Donald, David. *Charles Sumner and the Coming of the Civil War.* New York: Alfred A. Knopf, 1965.

———. *Charles Sumner and the Rights of Man.* New York: Alfred A. Knopf, 1970.

———. *Lincoln.* New York: Simon & Schuster, 1995.

———. *"We Are Lincoln Men": Abraham Lincoln and His Friends.* New York: Simon & Schuster, 2003.

Douglass, Frederick. *Life and Times of Frederick Douglass, Written by Himself. His Early Life as a Slave, His Escape from Bondage, and His Complete History to the Present Time.* Mineola, NY: Dover Publications, 2003.

———. *My Bondage and My Freedom.* Auburn and Mineola, NY: Miller, Orton & Mulligan, 1855; Dover Publications, 1969.

———. *Narrative of the Life of Frederick Douglass, An American Slave, Written by Himself.* New York: Anti-Slavery Office, 1845; Penguin Books, 1982.

DuBois, Ellen Carol. *The Elizabeth Cady Stanton–Susan B. Anthony Reader: Correspondence, Writings, Speeches,* rev. ed. Boston: Northeastern University Press, 1992.

———. *Feminism and Suffrage: The Emergence of an Independent Women's Movement in America, 1848–1869.* Ithaca: Cornell University Press, 1978.

———. *Woman Suffrage and Women's Rights.* New York: New York University Press, 1998.

Dudden, Faye E. *Fighting Chance: The Struggle Over Woman Suffrage and Black Suffrage in Reconstruction America.* Oxford: Oxford University Press, 2011.

Duncan, Russell, ed. *Blue-Eyed Child of Fortune: The Civil War Letters of Colonel Robert Gould Shaw.* Athens: University of Georgia Press, 1992.

Emilio, Luis F. *A Brave Black Regiment: The History of the Fifty-Fourth Massachusetts Volunteer Infantry, 1863–1865.* Mount Pleasant, SC: Arcadia Press, 1891, 2017.

Faulkner, Carol. *Lucretia Mott's Heresy: Abolition and Women's Rights in Nineteenth-Century America.* Philadelphia: University of Pennsylvania Press, 2011.

———. *Women's Radical Reconstruction: The Freedmen's Aid Movement.* Philadelphia: University of Pennsylvania Press, 2004.

Finkleman, Paul, ed. *His Soul Goes Marching On: Responses to John Brown and the Harpers Ferry Raid.* Charlottesville: University Press of Virginia, 1995.

Foner, Eric. *The Fiery Trial: Abraham Lincoln and American Slavery.* New York: W. W. Norton, 2010.

———. *Gateway to Freedom: The Hidden History of the Underground Railroad.* New York: W. W. Norton, 2015.

———. *Reconstruction: America's Unfinished Revolution, 1863–1877.* New York: Harper & Row, 1988.

———. *The Second Founding: How the Civil War and Reconstruction Remade the Constitution.* New York: W. W. Norton, 2019.

Foner, Philip S., ed. *The Life and Writings of Frederick Douglass*, Vols. I–V, New York: International Publishers, 1950–75.

Frank, Linda C. *An Uncommon Union: Henry B. Stanton and the Emancipation of Elizabeth Cady.* Auburn, NY: Upstate New York History, 2016.

Friedman, Lawrence J. *Gregarious Saints: Self and Community in American Abolitionism, 1830–1870.* Cambridge, Cambridge University Press, 1982.

Ginzberg, Lori D. *Elizabeth Cady Stanton: An American Life.* New York: Hill & Wang, 2009.

———. *Untidy Origins: A Story of Woman's Rights in Antebellum New York.* Chapel Hill: University of North Carolina Press, 2005.

———. *Women and the Work of Benevolence: Morality, Politics, and Class in the Nineteenth-Century United States.* New Haven: Yale University Press, 1990.

Glatthaar, Joseph T. *Forged in Battle: The Civil War Alliance of Black Soldiers and White Officers.* New York: Free Press, 1990.

Goodwin, Doris Kearns. *Team of Rivals: The Political Genius of Abraham Lincoln.* New York: Simon & Schuster, 2005.

Gordon, Ann D., ed. *The Selected Papers of Elizabeth Cady Stanton and Susan B. Anthony, Vol. 1, In the School of Anti-Slavery 1840–1866.* New Brunswick, NJ: Rutgers University Press, 2001.

Gornick, Vivian. *The Solitude of Self: Thinking About Elizabeth Cady Stanton.* New York: Farrar, Straus and Giroux, 2005.

Grigg, Jeff W. *The Combahee River Raid: Harriet Tubman and Lowcountry Liberation.* Charleston, SC: The History Press, 2014.

Gwynne, S. C. *Hymns of the Republic: The Story of the Final Year of the American Civil War.* New York: Scribner, 2019.

Hall, Henry. *The History of Auburn.* Auburn, NY: Dennis Bros, 1869.

Harrold, Stanley. *Subversives: Antislavery Community in Washington, D.C., 1828–1865.* Baton Rouge: Louisiana State University Press, 2003.

Hewitt, Nancy A. *Radical Friend: Amy Kirby Post and Her Activist Worlds.* Chapel Hill: University of North Carolina Press, 2018.

Higginson, Thomas Wentworth. *Army Life in a Black Regiment and Other Writings.* Mineola, NY: Dover Publications.

———. *Cheerful Yesterdays.* Boston: Houghton, Mifflin,1898.

Holland, Rupert Sargent, ed. *Letters and Diary of Laura M. Towne: Written from the Sea Islands of South Carolina, 1862–1884.* Whitefish, MT: Kessinger Publishing, 2010.

Horwitz, Tony. *Midnight Rising: John Brown and the Raid That Sparked the Civil War.* New York: Picador, 2011.

Humez, Jean M. *Harriet Tubman: The Life and the Life Stories.* Madison: University of Wisconsin Press, 2003.

Jeffrey, Julie Roy. *The Great Silent Army of Abolitionism: Ordinary Women in the Antislavery Movement.* Chapel Hill: University of North Carolina Press, 1998.

Johannsen, Robert W. *Stephen A. Douglas.* Urbana and Chicago: University of Illinois Press, 1997.

Jones, Martha S. *Birthright Citizens: A History of Race and Rights in Antebellum America.* Cambridge, England: Cambridge University Press, 2018.

———. *Vanguard: How Black Women Broke Barriers, Won the Vote, and Insisted on Equality for All.* New York: Basic Books, 2020.

Jones-Rogers, Stephanie E. *They Were Her Property: White Women as Slave Owners in the American South.* New Haven: Yale University Press, 2019.

Karcher, Carolyn L. *The First Woman in the Republic: A Cultural Biography of Lydia Maria Child.* Durham, NC: Duke University Press, 1994.

Koester, Nancy. *Harriet Beecher Stowe: A Spiritual Life.* Grand Rapids, MI: William B. Eerdmans Publishing, 2014.

Krisher, Trudy. *Fanny Seward: A Life.* Syracuse, NY: Syracuse University Press, 2015.

Larson, Kate Clifford. *Bound for the Promised Land: Harriet Tubman, Portrait of an American Hero.* New York: Ballantine, 2004.

Lepore, Jill. *These Truths: A History of the United States.* New York: W. W. Norton, 2018.

Loguen, James A. *The Rev. J. W. Loguen, As a Slave and As a Freeman: A Narrative of Real Life.* Syracuse, NY: J. G. K. Truair, 1859.

Looby, Christopher, ed. *The Complete Civil War Journals and Selected Letters of Thomas Wentworth Higginson.* Chicago: University of Chicago Press, 2000.

Lowry, Beverly. *Harriet Tubman: Imagining a Life.* New York: Anchor Books, 2007.

Lubet, Steven. *Fugitive Justice: Runaways, Rescuers, and Slavery on Trial.* Cambridge, MA: Belknap Press of Harvard University Press, 2010.

Massey, Mary Elizabeth. *Bonnet Brigades.* New York: Alfred A. Knopf, 1966.

May, Samuel J. *Some Recollections of Our Anti-Slavery Conflict.* New York: Arno Press and The New York Times, 1968.

Mayer, Henry. *All on Fire: William Lloyd Garrison and the Abolition of Slavery.* New York: W. W. Norton, 1998.

McFeely, William S. *Frederick Douglass.* New York: W. W. Norton, 1991.

McGowan, James A. *Station Master on the Underground Railroad: The Life and Letters of Thomas Garrett.* Jefferson, NC: McFarland, 2005.

McPherson, James M. *The Negro's Civil War: How American Blacks Felt and Acted During the War for the Union.* New York: Vintage Books, 1993.

———. *The War That Forged a Nation: Why the Civil War Still Matters.* Oxford: Oxford University Press, 2015.

Miller, Edward A. Jr. *Lincoln's Abolitionist General: The Biography of David Hunter.* Columbia: University of South Carolina Press, 1997.

Oakes, James. *Freedom National: The Destruction of Slavery in the United States, 1861–1865.* New York: W. W. Norton, 2013.

———. *The Radical and the Republican: Frederick Douglass, Abraham Lincoln, and the Triumph of Antislavery Politics.* New York: W. W. Norton, 2007

———. *The Scorpion's Sting: Antislavery and the Coming of the Civil* War. New York: W. W. Norton, 2014.

Oates, Stephen B. *To Purge This Land with Blood: A Biography of John Brown.* Amherst: University of Massachusetts Press, 1970, 1984.

Painter, Nell Irvin. *Sojourner Truth: A Life, A Symbol.* New York: W. W. Norton, 1996.

Palmer, Beverly Wilson, ed., *Selected Letters of Lucretia Coffin Mott.* Urbana and Chicago: University of Illinois Press, 2002.

Pease, Jane H. and William H. Pease. *They Who Would Be Free: Blacks' Search for Freedom, 1830–1861.* Urbana and Chicago: University of Illinois Press, 1990.

Penney, Sherry H. and James D. Livingston. *A Very Dangerous Woman: Martha Wright and Women's Rights.* Amherst: University of Massachusetts Press, 2004.

Potter, David M. *The Impending Crisis: America Before the Civil War, 1848–1861*. New York: Harper Perennial, 2011.

Quarles, Benjamin. *Black Abolitionists*. New York: Da Capo Press, 1969.

Ratner, Lorman A. and Dwight L. Teeter, Jr. *Fanatics & Fire-Eaters: Newspapers and the Coming of the Civil War.* Urbana and Chicago: University of Illinois Press, 2003.

Remini, Robert V. *Henry Clay: Statesman for the Union*. New York: W. W. Norton, 1991.

Reynolds, David S. *John Brown, Abolitionist: The Man Who Killed Slavery, Sparked the Civil War, and Seeded Civil Rights*. New York: Vintage Books, 2005.

Reynolds, Larry J. *Righteous Violence: Revolution, Slavery, and the American Renaissance*. Athens: University of Georgia Press, 2011.

Rose, Willie Lee. *Rehearsal for Reconstruction: The Port Royal Experiment*. Athens: University of Georgia Press, 1964.

Schwartz, Gerald, ed. *A Woman Doctor's Civil War: Esther Hill Hawks' Diary*. Columbia: University of South Carolina Press, 1989.

Sernett, Milton C. *Harriet Tubman: Myth, Memory, and History*. Durham, NC: Duke University Press, 2007.

———. *North Star Country: Upstate New York and the Crusade for African American Freedom*. Syracuse, NY: Syracuse University Press, 2002.

Seward, Frederick W. *Reminiscences of a War-Time Statesman and Diplomat, 1830–1915*. New York: G. P. Putnam's Sons, 1916.

———. *Seward at Washington, as Senator and Secretary of State, A Memoir of His Life, with Selections from His Letters. 1846–1861*. New York: Derby and Miller, 1891.

Seward, William Henry and Frederick W. Seward. *The Autobiography of William H. Seward, from 1801 to 1834, with a Memoir of His Life and Selections from His Letters from 1831 to 1846*. New York: D. Appleton, 1877.

Siebert, Wilbur Henry. *The Underground Railroad from Slavery to Freedom*. New York: Macmillan, 1898.

Simpson, Brooks D., ed. *The Civil War: The Third Year Told by Those Who Lived It*. New York: Library of America, 2013.

Simpson, Brooks D., Stephen W. Sears, and Aaron Sheehan-Dean, eds. *The Civil War: The First Year Told by Those Who Lived It*. New York: Library of America, 2011.

Sinha, Manisha. *The Slave's Cause: A History of Abolition*. New Haven and London: Yale University Press, 2016.

Stahr, Walter, *Seward: Lincoln's Indispensable Man*. New York: Simon & Schuster, 2012.

Stanton, Elizabeth Cady. *Eighty Years and More: Reminiscences, 1815–1897*. Amherst, NY: Humanity Books, 2002.

Stanton, Elizabeth Cady, Susan B. Anthony, and Matilda Joslyn Gage, eds. *History of Woman Suffrage, Vol. 1, 1848–1861*. Rochester, NY: Charles Mann, 1899.

Stanton, Theodore and Harriet Stanton Blatch, eds., *Elizabeth Cady Stanton: As Revealed in Her Letters, Diary, and Reminiscences*. New York: Harper & Brothers, 1927.

Stauffer, John. *The Black Hearts of Men: Radical Abolitionist and the Transformation of Race*. Cambridge, MA: Harvard University Press, 2001.

Sterling, Dorothy. *Lucretia Mott*. New York: Feminist Press at the City University of New York, 1999.

Still, William. *The Underground Railroad: A Record of Facts, Authentic Narrative, Letters, &c*. Philadelphia: People's Publishing, 1871.

Taylor, John M. *William Henry Seward: Lincoln's Right Hand*. New York: HarperCollins, 1991.

Taylor, Robert W. *Harriet Tubman: The Heroine in Ebony*. Boston: George E. Ellis, 1901.

Taylor, Susie King. *Reminiscences of My Life in Camp: An African American Woman's Civil War Memoir*. Athens: University of Georgia Press, 2006.

Tetrault, Lisa. *The Myth of Seneca Falls: Memory and the Women's Suffrage Movement, 1848–1898*. Chapel Hill: University of North Carolina Press, 2014.

Van Deusen, Glyndon G. *Thurlow Weed: Wizard of the Lobby*. Boston: Little, Brown, 1947.

———. *William Henry Seward*. New York: Oxford University Press, 1967.

Vorenberg, Michael. *Final Freedom: The Civil War, the Abolition of Slavery, and the Thirteenth Amendment*. Cambridge: Cambridge University Press, 2001.

Wagner, Sally Roesch, ed. *The Women's Suffrage Movement*. New York: Penguin Books, 2019.

Weed, Thurlow and Harriet A. Weed, ed. *Autobiography of Thurlow Weed*. Boston: Houghton, Mifflin, 1883.

Wellman, Judith. *Grass Roots Reform in the Burned-Over District of New York: Religion, Abolitionism, and Democracy*. New York: Routledge, 2000.

———. *The Road to Seneca Falls: Elizabeth Cady Stanton and the First Woman's Rights Convention*. Urbana and Chicago: University of Illinois Press, 2004.

Wigham, Eliza. *The Anti-Slavery Cause in America and Its Martyrs*. London: A. W. Bennett, 1863.

Wilentz, Sean. *No Property in Man: Slavery and Antislavery at the Nation's Founding*. Cambridge, MA.: Harvard University Press, 2018.

———. *The Politicians & the Egalitarians: The Hidden History of American Politics*. New York: W. W. Norton, 2016.

Williams, Heather Andrea. *Help Me to Find My People: The African American Search for Family Lost in Slavery*. Chapel Hill: University of North Carolina Press, 2012.

Wineapple, Brenda. *Ecstatic Nation: Confidence, Crisis, and Compromise, 1848–1877*. New York: HarperCollins, 2013.

Winkle, Kenneth J. *Lincoln's Citadel: The Civil War in Washington, D.C.* New York: W. W. Norton, 2013.

Yellin, Jean Fagan. *Women & Sisters: The Antislavery Feminists in American Culture*. New Haven: Yale University Press, 1989.

Image Credits

vi William Henry Seward Papers, Rare Books, Special Collections, and Preservation, River Campus Libraries, University of Rochester
1 Seward House Museum
3 Sophia Smith Collection, Smith College
19 Engraving by John C. Buttre, from a painting by Henry Inman, Seward House Museum
37 *Cambridge Democrat*, Bucktown Village Foundation
47 Artist unknown, painting ca. 1847–50, oil on bedticking, 84 x 107 inches. The Farmers' Museum, Cooperstown, N.Y., Museum Purchase, FO111. 1954. Photograph by Richard Walker.
55 Library of Congress, Prints and Photographs Division
65 Photograph by Captain Montgomery C. Meigs, Architect of the Capitol
79 *Syracuse Daily Journal*, September 13, 1852, Onondaga County Public Libraries
87 Collection of the Smithsonian National Museum of African American History and Culture, Gift of Charles L. Blockson
89 Seward House Museum
99 Smithsonian Libraries
109 Smithsonian Libraries
115 Sketch by J. C. Rice, University of Kansas, Kenneth Spencer Research Library, Lawrence, Kansas, photographs collection
121 New York Public Library
129 Photograph by Benjamin F. Powelson, Collection of Smithsonian National Museum of African American History and Culture, shared with the Library of Congress
141 Sophia Smith Collection, Smith College
149 Daguerreotype attributed to Martin M. Lawrence, Library of Congress, Prints and Photographs Division
159 Sophia Smith Collection, Smith College
167 Lieut. Col. Will Seward, Seward House Museum; *Two Brothers in Arms*, Library of Congress, Prints and Photographs Division, Gladstone Collection of African American Photographs
169 Seward House Museum
183 Metropolitan Museum of Art, the Rubel Collection, Gift of William Rubel, 2001
193 Wood engraving by John G. Darby, National Portrait Gallery, Smithsonian Institution
201 Photograph by Alexander Gardner, Library of Congress, Prints and Photographs Division
215 National Portrait Gallery, Smithsonian Institution

231 Sophia Smith Collection, Smith College
239 Albumen silver print by Napoleon Sarony, National Portrait Gallery, Smithsonian Institution
247 Painting by Keith Rocco for the National Park Service
261 Sophia Smith Collection, Smith College
263 Library of Congress
269 William Henry Seward Papers, Rare Books, Special Collections, and Preservation, River Campus Libraries, University of Rochester
283 Sophia Smith Collection, Smith College
289 Library of Congress, Rare Book and Special Collections Division, National American Woman Suffrage Association Collection
303 Bronze sculpture by Lloyd Lillie, National Park Service, Women's Rights National Historical Park, Seneca Falls

Index

Numbers in italics refer to pages with images.

About the Author

Dorothy Wickenden, the executive editor of *The New Yorker* and the host of its weekly podcast *Politics and More*, is the author of the *New York Times* bestseller *Nothing Daunted: The Unexpected Education of Two Society Girls in the West* and the editor of *The New Republic Reader: Eighty Years of Opinion and Debate*. She lives with her husband in Westchester, New York.

The Agitators

DOROTHY WICKENDEN

This reading group guide for The Agitators *includes an introduction, discussion questions, and ideas for enhancing your book club. The suggested questions are intended to help your reading group find interesting angles and topics for your discussion. We hope that these ideas will enrich your conversation and increase your enjoyment of the book.*

Introduction

Dorothy Wickenden, the *New York Times* bestselling author of *Nothing Daunted*, once again brings historical figures vividly to life in *The Agitators*, a riveting examination of three friends—Harriet Tubman, Frances Seward, and Martha Wright—who collaborate in the quest for abolition and women's rights. Wickenden offers a highly intimate perspective on the classic American stories of abolition, the underground railroad, women's rights activism, and the Civil War.

Topics & Questions for Discussion

1. Discuss the book's epigraph. How does this quote prepare you for the text? In what way does it resonate with current events?

2. The prologue and epilogue bookend the text with vivid descriptions of Fort Hill Cemetery today. What is the value of beginning and ending the book in this way? What effect does this have on your reading experience?

3. The first three chapters establish the very different backgrounds of Martha, Frances, and Harriet and the time in which they lived. What is your sense of their personalities and how they changed over time?

4. In chapter 4, Frances's husband, Henry, decides to defend William Freeman, the twenty-three-year-old Black man who confessed to murdering four members of a white family. This is one of the first uses of the insanity defense, which is based on the belief that a person who is unable to distinguish right from wrong should not be criminally charged because they cannot take moral responsibility for their crime. Henry's father-in-law, a county judge, thought his defense of Freeman would end his political career. Why was Frances so supportive of his choice?

5. In chapter 5, Martha overhears a party guest calling her "a very dangerous woman" because of her social activism and her friendship with Frederick Douglass. Consider what it meant to be a "dangerous woman" in Martha's time and place. Who, or what, is being threatened by Martha's behavior? Is there a modern-day equivalent of the term "dangerous woman"?

6. Discuss these two quotes from chapter 13 and how they have "aged" since:

   "The United States government 'was made by white men for the benefit of white men and their posterity forever.'"
   —Senator Stephen A. Douglas

   "I know, and you know, that a revolution has begun. I know, and all the world knows, that revolutions never go backward."
   —Senator William Henry Seward

7. Each of these women was bold, principled, and intent on changing the world. They express their idealism in different ways. Discuss how each used to try and affect change.

8. At the end of chapter 13, Henry and the British intellectual Harriet Martineau discuss slavery, "the great American question." What might you consider today's "great American question"?

9. Harriet was an extraordinary orator, who, as the author says in chapter 15, knew how to play to "her audiences' enthusiasm for hair-raising first-person accounts of slavery and escape." How do you think Harriet used her storytelling to advance her causes, immediately and into the future?

10. Throughout the book, we see Martha's roles as activist and mother intersect. In chapter 14, "Martha Leads," her daughter Ellen, according to the author, was "overwhelmed by self-doubt" and, "to Martha's dismay," was "more interested in her succession of suitors than in her studies." How does Martha's career as an activist seem to affect her daughter's development? What do you think of Martha's early reservations about becoming a leader and her own doubts about her capabilities? Do you see this conflict present in modern-day mother-daughter relationships?

11. The abolitionist and women's rights movement were aligned through much of the mid-nineteenth century. The movement split in the late 1860s over priorities—some women insisting that the fight for Black male suffrage take precedence over the fight for women's rights, while Elizabeth Cady Stanton and Susan B. Anthony broke away to fight solely for the women's vote. Discuss this interplay and how the conflicts of this period extended to our own.

12. How did the husbands of these women help or hinder them in their goals? What impact did these relationships have on the women in their decision-making?

13. Reflect on the Henry's long anti-slavery career, the battle between Frances and Henry in the early 1860s about immediate emancipation, and the assassination attempt on Henry and two of their sons. Martha blames Henry for Frances's unhappiness and, the author writes, finds him "hungrier for power than for principle." What is your final assessment of Henry and of the difficulties of their marriage?

14. Letters, photos, and portraits appear throughout the book. What do these add to your reading experience?

15. Consider the impact that the actions of the activists in the book may have had directly on your own life. Can you think of an example of how their efforts in the movements benefited you personally?

Enhance Your Book Club

1. Check the National Register of Historic Places for historical sites near you. See what you can learn about your local history!

2. Correspond with your friends through handwritten letters about the book. This way, you might get a sense of what it was like to hold passionate discussions through snail mail as the women in the text did.

3. Brainstorm ways you might contribute to social activism today. Research causes that you are passionate about and take inspiration from Martha, Frances, and Harriet. Is there a local group you can participate in or online resources available in your area?